MONEY IN THE GERMAN-SPEAKING LANDS

SPEKTRUM: Publications of the German Studies Association
Series Editor: David M. Luebke, University of Oregon

Published under the auspices of the German Studies Association, *Spektrum* offers current perspectives on culture, society, and political life in the German-speaking lands of central Europe—Austria, Switzerland, and the Federal Republic—from the late Middle Ages to the present day. Its titles and themes reflect the composition of the GSA and the work of its members within and across the disciplines to which they belong—literary criticism, history, cultural studies, political science, and anthropology.

Volume 1
The Holy Roman Empire, Reconsidered
Edited by Jason Philip Coy, Benjamin Marschke, and David Warren Sabean

Volume 2
Weimar Publics/Weimar Subjects: Rethinking the Political Culture of Germany in the 1920s
Edited by Kathleen Canning, Kerstin Barndt, and Kristin McGuire

Volume 3
Conversion and the Politics of Religion in Early Modern Germany
Edited by David M. Luebke, Jared Poley, Daniel C. Ryan, and David Warren Sabean

Volume 4
Walls, Borders, Boundaries: Spatial and Cultural Practices in Europe
Edited by Marc Silberman, Karen E. Till, and Janet Ward

Volume 5
After The History of Sexuality: German Genealogies with and Beyond Foucault
Edited by Scott Spector, Helmut Puff, and Dagmar Herzog

Volume 6
Becoming East German: Socialist Structures and Sensibilities after Hitler
Edited by Mary Fulbrook and Andrew I. Port

Volume 7
Beyond Alterity: German Encounters with Modern East Asia
Edited by Qinna Shen and Martin Rosenstock

Volume 8
Mixed Matches: Transgressive Unions in Germany from the Reformation to the Enlightenment
Edited by David Luebke and Mary Lindemann

Volume 9
Kinship, Community, and Self: Essays in Honor of David Warren Sabean
Edited by Jason Coy, Benjamin Marschke, Jared Poley, and Claudia Verhoeven

Volume 10
The Emperor's Old Clothes: Constitutional History and the Symbolic Language of the Holy Roman Empire
Barbara Stollberg-Rilinger
Translated by Thomas Dunlap

Volume 11
The Devil's Riches: A Modern History of Greed
Jared Poley

Volume 12
The Total Work of Art: Foundations, Articulations, Inspirations
Edited by David Imhoof, Margaret Eleanor Menninger, and Anthony J. Steinhoff

Volume 13
Migrations in the German Lands, 1500–2000
Edited by Jason Coy, Jared Poley, and Alexander Schunka

Volume 14
Reluctant Skeptic: Siegfried Kracauer and the Crises of Weimar Culture
Harry T. Craver

Volume 15
Ruptures in the Everyday: Views of Modern Germany from the Ground
Andrew Stuart Bergerson and Leonard Schmieding

Volume 16
Archeologies of Confession: Writing the German Reformation 1517–2017
Edited by Carina L. Johnson, David M. Luebke, Marjorie E. Plummer, and Jesse Spohnholz

Volume 17
Money in the German-Speaking Lands
Edited by Mary Lindemann and Jared Poley

Money in the German-Speaking Lands

EDITED BY MARY LINDEMANN AND JARED POLEY

First published in 2017 by
Berghahn Books
www.berghahnbooks.com

© 2017, 2022 Mary Lindemann and Jared Poley
First paperback edition published in 2022

All rights reserved. Except for the quotation of short passages
for the purposes of criticism and review, no part of this book
may be reproduced in any form or by any means, electronic or
mechanical, including photocopying, recording, or any information
storage and retrieval system now known or to be invented,
without written permission of the publisher.

Library of Congress Cataloging-in-Publication Data

Names: Lindemann, Mary, editor. | Poley, Jared, 1970– editor.
Title: Money in the German-speaking lands / edited by Mary Lindemann and Jared Poley.
Description: New York : Berghahn Books, 2017. | Series: Spektrum: publications of the German Studies Association ; volume 17 | Includes bibliographical references and index.
Identifiers: LCCN 2017014884 (print) | LCCN 2017030740 (ebook) | ISBN 9781785335891 (e-book) | ISBN 9781785335884 (hardback : alk. paper)
Subjects: LCSH: Money—Europe, German-speaking—History. | Money—Germany—History. | Europe, German-speaking—History. | Germany—History.
Classification: LCC HG922 (ebook) | LCC HG922 .M665 2017 (print) | DDC 332.4/943—dc23
LC record available at https://lccn.loc.gov/2017014884

British Library Cataloguing in Publication Data

A catalogue record for this book is available from the British Library

ISBN 978-1-78533-588-4 hardback
ISBN 978-1-80073-449-4 paperback
ISBN 978-1-78533-589-1 ebook

https://doi.org/10.3167/9781785335884

~: CONTENTS ~

List of Tables and Figures — vii

Introduction — 1
 Mary Lindemann and Jared Poley

1. Money from the Spirit World: Treasure Spirits, Geldmännchen, Drache — 10
 Johannes Dillinger

2. Perfecting the State: Alchemy and Oeconomy as Academic Forms of Knowledge in Early Modern German-Speaking Lands — 26
 Vera Keller

3. The Money Tree: Living in the Shadow of a Patrician Family in Hamburg — 43
 Almut Spalding

4. Silver Thaler and Ur-Cameralists — 58
 Andre Wakefield

5. "All That Glitters Is Not Gold, But…": German Responses to the Financial Bubbles of 1720 — 74
 Eve Rosenhaft

6. A Conspicuous Lack of Consumption: Money, Luxury, and Fashion in King Frederick William I's Prussia (c. 1713–40) — 96
 Benjamin Marschke

7. "Alles Geld gehet immer auf": Money in an Emerging Consumer and Cash Economy, Göppingen (1735–1860) — 121
 Dennis Frey Jr.

8. Status, Friendship, and Money in Hamburg around 1800: Debit and Credit in the Diaries of Ferdinand Beneke (1774–1848) — 137
 Frank Hatje

9. Luxury and the Nineteenth-Century Württemberg Pietists — 156
 Jan Carsten Schnurr

10. Marx on Money 173
    Jonathan Sperber

11. Modernism, Relativism, and the *Philosophy of Money* 186
    Elizabeth S. Goodstein

12. A Narrative in *Notgeld*: Collecting, Emergency Money, and National Identity in Weimar Germany 203
    Erika L. Briesacher

13. Predatory Speculators, Honest Creditors: Money as Root of Evil or Proof of Virtue in Weimar Germany 219
    Michael L. Hughes

14. Mobilizing Citizens and Their Savings: Germany's Public Savings Banks, 1933–39 234
    Pamela E. Swett

15. "One Would Not Get Far Without Cigarettes": The Cigarette Economy in Occupied Germany, 1945–48 250
    Kraig Larkin

16. When the Deutsch Mark Was in Short Supply: Reconstruction Finance between Currency Reform and "Economic Miracle" 268
    Armin Grünbacher

17. Between Memorialization and Monetary Revaluation: The 1990 Currency Union as a Site of Post-Unification Memory Work 283
    Ursula M. Dalinghaus

Afterword. Simmel's Berlin and Money as Social Consensus 303
    Michael J. Sauter

Index 313

TABLES AND FIGURES

Tables

Table 4.1. Average Annual Silver Production in Central Europe (kg), 1545–1800.   63

Table 7.1. Cash on Hand (*Bargeld*) by 25-Year Periods.   127

Table 7.2. Debt Management by 25-Year Periods.   130

Table 16.1. Share of ERP Loans in Gross Capital Investments in the Federal Republic, 1949–56.   273

Table 16.2. Production Output of Industry and Coal Mining, 1946–51.   274

Figures

Figure 4.1. Das Bergwerksfest im Plauenschen Grund, 1719.   61

Figure 5.1. Map of France's American colonies, engraved by Moritz Bodenehr, from P. J. M. Marperger, *Fortsetzung der Remarquen* [...], n.d., n.p. (Leipzig, 1720?). Ostfriesische Landschaft, Landschaftsbibliothek, Aurich (Q 885 [2,2]), with permission.   81

Figure 5.2. Map of the Louisiana colonies, from G. Zenner, *Historische und geographische Beschreibung des am großen Flusse Mississippi in Nord-America gelegenen herrlichen Landes Louisiana* (Leipzig, 1720). Württembergische Landesbibliothek, Stuttgart (Geogr.oct.743), with permission.   82

Figure 5.3. *Venusiana* cover, *Den verliebten Actien-Handel auf Venusiana* [...] (Dresden, 1720). Universitätsbibliothek, Ludwig-Maximilians-Universität München (W 2 P. germ. 48#44), with permission.   86

Figure 5.4. *Venusiana* text, *Den verliebten Actien-Handel auf Venusiana* [...] (Dresden, 1720). Universitätsbibliothek, Ludwig-Maximilians-Universität München (W 2 P. germ. 48#44), with permission. 87

Figure 5.5. *Venusiana* children, *Den verliebten Actien-Handel auf Venusiana* [...] (Dresden, 1720). Universitätsbibliothek, Ludwig-Maximilians-Universität München (W 2 P. germ. 48#44), with permission. 88

Figure 6.1. "Fridericus Wilhelmus D. G. Princ. Haered. Regni. Prussiae. &c. &c., pre-1713, by Elias Christoph Heiß. Source: British Museum, public domain, http://www.britishmuseum.org/research/collection_online/collection_object_details.aspx?objectId=3362072&partId=1 100

Figure 6.2. "Fridericus Wilhelmus, Rex Borussia," 1713, in *Europäische Fama*. Source: Herzog August Bibliothek, Wolfenbüttel. 100

Figure 6.3. Frederick William I, 1729, by Antoine Pesne. Source: Bildarchiv Preußischer Kulturbesitz, Art Resource. 101

Figure 6.4. Tabakskollegium, c. 1736, by Georg Lisiewski. Source: Bildarchiv Preußischer Kulturbesitz, Art Resource. 102

Figure 6.5. August II of Saxony-Poland and Frederick William I, c. 1733, by Louis de Silvestre. Source: Bildarchiv Preußicher Kulturbesitz, Art Resource. 103

Figure 6.6. King George II of Great Britain, c. 1716, by Sir Godfrey Kneller. Source: Wikipedia Commons, public domain, https://commons.wikimedia.org/wiki/File:King_George_II_by_Sir_Godfrey_Kneller,_Bt.jpg 104

Figure 6.7. Schloß Wusterhausen, photograph. Source: Wikipedia Commons, public domain, https://commons.wikimedia.org/wiki/File:Koenigs_Wusterhausen_Schloss.jpg 106

Figure 6.8. Jagdschloß Stern, photograph by author. 106

Figure 6.9. Berlin Cityscape, c. 1730, by Friedrich Bernhard Werner. Source: Wikipedia Commons, public domain, https://commons.wikimedia.org/wiki/File:Berlin_Map_1730_Werner.jpg 107

Figure 6.10. "Häuserbau im Süden der Berliner Friedrichstadt," c. 1735, by Dismar Degen. Source: Stiftung Preußische Schlößer und Gärten Berlin-Brandenburg (SPSG), photograph by Gerhard Murza. 108

Figure 6.11. Plan von der Königl. Residentz Stadt Berlin, 1737, by Abraham Guibert Dusableau. Source: Wikipedia Commons, public domain, https://commons.wikimedia.org/wiki/File:Berlin_Dusableau_1737.jpg   109

Figure 7.1. Debt management (Loans minus Debts) of all cases.   131

Figure 12.1. 25 Pfennig note (10 February 1920). This note detailing the Schleswig Plebescite emphasized the border state of Schleswig-Holstein and its unique German-Danish populations. Courtesy of The Permanent Collection, the University Museum, Southern Illinois University Edwardsville.   206

Figure 12.2. One Mark note, 12–24 August 1921, *Kultur- und Sportwoche*, Hamburg. This series promoting Hamburg's festival included references to "black-white-red" and body culture in the Weimar Republic. Courtesy of The Permanent Collection, the University Museum, Southern Illinois University Edwardsville.   211

Introduction

MARY LINDEMANN AND JARED POLEY

The European Commission, the European Central Bank, and the International Monetary Fund agreed in May 2010 to provide a package of EUR 110 billion meant to provide financial assistance to Greece. More than EUR 22 billion of those came from Germany. This so-called first bailout (a second bailout package followed in 2012 and a third, worth EUR 86 billion, in August 2015), which was meant to confront the Greek government-debt crisis brought on by the housing bubble and the global recession, revealed the economic and political fault lines of the European Union and the eurozone. The bailout was represented in the German popular-right press as a catastrophe. *Bild* bluntly counseled in its headline of 27 October 2010: "Sell your islands, you bankrupt Greeks . . . and the Acropolis too!" ["Verkauft doch eure Inseln, ihr Pleite-Griechen . . . und die Akropolis gleich mit!"].[1] German Chancellor Angela Merkel took a different line, indicating the importance of financial stability to the continued political dream of Europe. "The euro is our common fate," Merkel argued in December 2010, "and Europe is our common future."[2] Those ideals would be tested repeatedly over the next five years, in the debates about whether a third bailout package should be extended to Greece. Merkel promoted the value of a unified Europe, but as she explained in a speech to the Bundestag, while the euro may have indeed created a European *Schicksalsgemeinschaft*—a community of fate—it nonetheless demanded a political vision of Europe that was also founded as a *Rechts- und Verantwortungsgemeinschaft*, a community of law and responsibility.[3] Money, these developments made clear, was the foundation and the lubricant of the New Europe.

These developments also make clear that Europeanization, in its current form, is organized and enacted through German money, and in that sense they form part of a longer historical trajectory of attempts to forge political unification with the tools of economic integration. *Money in the German-Speaking Lands*, therefore, follows this trajectory from the late Renaissance until the close of the twentieth century. While a good number of contributions emphasize the connection between economics and politics in German history, it also explores the cultural and symbolic aspects of money. The two paths are not parallel but intersect repeatedly in interesting and informative ways.

The first theme can be exemplified by Napoleon's continental system, which employed a common currency, weights, and measures in the so-called inner empire.[4] While the system was both unevenly effective and annoying to those polities most directly affected by the blockade of British shipping, it did produce a vision of a political union enforced through economic means. The continental system also perhaps offered a model—albeit a flawed one—of the instrumental use of money to achieve political aims. If in the late nineteenth century, war was just politics taken to the next level, it should be remembered that economics had long filled a similar role. In this regard, the assemblers of the *Zollverein* (customs union) of 1834 sought to forge the political unification of member German states through an economic integration. Money, in other words, was at the logical center of early nineteenth-century models of political unification. This logic was then implemented wholesale after the political unification of 1871, when use of the gold-backed *mark* was institutionalized between 1873 and 1876 in place of the *Vereinsthaler, Gulden,* Bremen *thaler,* Hamburg mark, and French franc that had been issued by the various states subject to unification in January 1871. Both the Zollverein and the mark, it is important to note, were politically inclusive as well as exclusive. Habsburg Austria, for example, was not invited to participate as an element of the Bismarckian plan to forge a "small Germany" centered on Prussia. The fragile political union, crafted in steps and as a response to martial violence between 1854 and 1871, was cemented by the new national currency. And then, as now, money lubricated the wheels of the New Europe.

While no chapter in this collection focuses on the euro, its specter haunts its pages. The euro represents no state or nation but is a supra-regional, supranational entity that is also ephemeral. The historically dramatic appearance of the euro suggests memories of things that never existed and bridges never built. The emotional attachment to it is weak or even hostile despite its obvious economic advantages. Despite its imperfections, the euro, like the mark before it, represents the centrality of money to the landscape of political cohesion and integration. Yet money is more than some instrument used to implement a political vision. Its fungibility, symbolic importance, and connections to morality indicate the ways that money is as much about culture and ideas as it is about the quotidian anxieties of bankers and civil servants. Money is an instrument—it has a meditative quality or functions as the terrain upon which object relations are worked out—but it is also a psychological force field through which the very human problems of creating wealth and assigning value, determining the relationships between production and consumption, and implementing ideological terror are forged.

In considering money as forming a "psychological force field," these essays also address the symbolic and cultural aspects of money. As an instrument of value, exchange, and ideology, money—as the bankers say—never sleeps.

It has "velocity," represents "potential," and marks both the value of objects and of people. The words used to describe it—streams, fluids, pools, flows, currencies, and conversion—trace not only the history of mechanical nature, physics, and religion, but also indicate how the tidal flows of exchange have marked the historical qualities of humanity itself, both shaping and reflecting culture. Money seems to touch, at one time or another, on all aspects of the human experience. This book applies that insight to the ways that money has formed a central element of German history and culture.

Given the vast variety of topics that are apprehended by the topic of money in Germany, astute readers can easily discern the gaps in the volume. There should be more work included on gender and money, on money in literature, on inflation (both on the Kipper und Wipper inflation of the seventeenth and on the hyperinflation after World War I with its political, social, and psychological effects), adulteration, speculation, the political intrigues of the euro. Likewise missing here are discussions of the price revolution of the sixteenth century, the enterprises of the great south German entrepreneurs such as the Fuggers and the Welsers, the development of international and global networks beginning in the medieval period with the Hanse and proceeding through imperial networks to post-colonialism and the "new" globalism of the late twentieth and early twenty-first centuries. All these events were of enormous economic importance, but all bore equally great symbolic, psychological, and cultural meanings.

Certainly, this volume is not per se an economic history; indeed, although many of the contributions handle economic themes with considerable economic sophistication. Instead *Money in the German-Speaking Lands* addresses the ways money has "worked" in Germany over the course of several centuries; it provides therefore neither an economic survey or an extended business history, but rather a *Wirkungsgeschichte* arranged around seven central themes and seven critical problems in the history of money-at-work. One theme centers on how Germans have confronted periods of economic transition or decline, considering especially the ways that the process of a collapse in value required creative solutions on the part of Germans. The essays in the volume also tackle in direct ways the political nature of money in German-speaking Europe in essays that span the chronological framework of the volume and that allow us to see how money has done political work in different historical periods. Other essays examine the ways that money entered into larger European and global transitions, considering for instance how Germans used money to understand better the transitions to capitalist exchange, to a consumerist society, to the economic levers of debit, credit, and banking systems. A fourth theme of the volume addresses the cultural and intellectual matrix created by money, looking, for example, at the connections that were drawn between money and morality, or between money and correct behavior, or how religious ideals transformed people's relationships with the finances. The role that money played in German understandings of the natural world—whether that understanding was magical and esoteric in its orientation, scientific and rational, or some combination of the two—forms a fifth theme. Several chapters then probe the intersection of memory and money, our sixth theme. Appearing in nearly each contribution is some larger perspective on the problem of how money was used in symbolic or socially productive ways. Together, the essays illustrate the thematic cohesion of the volume, and also suggest both change and continuity—how some aspects of money are, at some times and places, more important than others; how certain aspects fade, others replace them, or they reappear in different forms or persist over long periods of time.

The volume's chronological ambit stretches back to the Renaissance. This chronology moves across the early modern/modern divide and thus allows us to see how Germans in different historical contexts approached the financial. We see persistence and change across centuries, allowing us greater insight into how Germans experienced the large economic transitions affecting Europe and the world since the fifteenth century. The volume's focus on the experiences of Germans remains a significant strength. By looking at money in Germany, we note the special significance of money to the German experience, and we also see in fresh ways the contributions of Germans to our modern economic system (and its critique). Imagine a sixteenth-century world without Jakob Fugger's wealth, or a nineteenth-century one without Marx and Engels, or a twentieth century lacking Simmel, Weber, and Freud, and the impact of Germans and their money (or their ideas about money) on global structures is thrown into sharp relief.

The volume contains five chronologically oriented sections. The contributions from Johannes Dillinger and Vera Keller invite readers to consider early modern material. In different ways, Dillinger and Keller probe the existence of old ideas about magic and nature, connecting those thought styles to financial attitudes about wealth, its origins, and ways to measure its symbolic and real value. Dillinger reminds us that this economic *Weltanschauung* was "part and parcel of a basic economic concept that avoided competition and respected community values," an orientation that persisted throughout the early modern period (and later as well). The subsequent five chapters focus on the critical period in the eighteenth century, when consumerism, cameralism, and capitalism created a new range of possible economic answers to long-standing questions about trans- and international commerce, state and personal finance, and the novel logic of boom and bust. Almut Spalding, for instance, in examining the networks maintained by the prominent Reimarus family in Hamburg, emphasizes the ways in which money formed a "social currency" used to knit together and sustain social relationships, while also tracing an important historical shift from vertical to horizontal obligations.

Andre Wakefield focuses on the symbolic quality of money in its "concrete" form by following the rise of the "silver thaler." He argues that silver and silver ore "spawned technologies, cultures, and sciences." Increasingly in the eighteenth century, however, money in its most tangible form—as coin—yielded in significance to money as an imaginary good. Bills of exchange, stocks, and money of account, representing the shift from "hard" to "soft" money, raised important issues of trust as the first great financial "bubbles" burst. Unlike Britain, France, and, if to a lesser extent, the Dutch Republic, the German-speaking lands suffered no major material losses from the bubble disasters. Yet as Eve Rosenhaft demonstrates, "their imaginations were mobilized" and their consternation found its greatest expression in literature (especially satire) and art (especially caricature). Benjamin Marschke takes up the fraught topic of luxury and probes the changing valuation of conspicuous consumption among the rulers of eighteenth-century Prussia, in particular that of the man once generally referred to as the "Potsdam Führer," King Frederick William I. His famous (or notorious) rejection of formality and his equally famous parsimony were forged in the crucible of this crisis. His peculiar form of "display" implicitly attacked the "spectacular consumption" of other rulers. The essay by Dennis Frey Jr. on "Alles Geld gehet immer auf" moves the discussion of monetarization from the stratosphere of court life down to a more terrestrial plane: artisans in southwestern Germany. Here, he traces the ways in which even artisans in a smallish town became deeply involved in broader economic (and thus also cultural) networks: regional, "national," European, and even global. Money allowed artisans to participate in a consumerist world. Frey shows that although artisans had ever more cash on hand, including even U.S. dollars, money was still "really about credit."

Chapters focusing on the nineteenth century carry us deeper into the far more monetarized world that Frey's artisans had just entered. Yet even here, money was never "just money," and the essays in this section develop themes associated with the social (status and friendship), the religious (pietist approaches to money), and the political (Marx). Each essay reveals aspects of continuity and change, offering a parallax view of historical development in the period. Like Spalding and Frey, Frank Hatje uses personal recordings, in this case the diary of the prominent Hamburg civil servant, Ferdinand Beneke, to illustrate the evolution of increasingly sophisticated ways of dealing with money and managing debts and credit even among those who were not, primarily, "money men." In detailing the spread of this new monetary expertise, Hatje also provides an excellent example of how Beneke and those around him used "cultural capital to generate social capital" while simultaneously employing "social capital to generate economic capital." Hatje's initial observation that "money can be perceived from a variety of perspectives" is further explored in the essay by Jan Carsten Schnurr. Although many scholars accept that, by the nineteenth century, the "luxury debate" had been more or less settled and "pleasure came into its own," Schnurr demonstrates that not everyone found the accommodation with luxury desirable; the "young Pietists," for instance, continued to view it with skepticism and sometimes even aversion. What may first seem an atavistic holdover from an earlier mentality, Schnurr shows to be closely linked to a contemporary political and social crisis—the events of 1848—as well as to the major social problem of the day, pauperism. The year 1848, of course, also marked the appearance of Karl Marx on the big stage of European thought and politics. In his essay, Jonathan Sperber argues that Marx's "investigations into the nature of money stood at the very beginning of his interest in economics" and also shaped his conception of what a communist future would look like. Much of Marx's research focused on discovering the elusive nature of money. Sperber's magisterial Marx biography, as its title indicates, situates Marx firmly within the context of the nineteenth century. Yet his interest in the "velocity of the circulation of money [Geldumlauf]," lays bare the eighteenth-century roots of his thought found in the work of the Hamburg political economist, Johann Georg Büsch.

The arguments presented in that section are developed further in the chapters dedicated to money in Germany in the first half of the twentieth century. Elizabeth S. Goodstein considers the important theoretical contributions Georg Simmel advanced in his 1900 *Philosophy of Money*. Simmel's evaluation of money was expansive in the extreme; he linked "economic events" to "the ultimate values and means of everything human." As the "synecdoche of synecdoches," money demonstrated how "human symbolic practice . . . operates." But what if money, as a way of understanding culture, should vanish? Or lose its value entirely? This is the conundrum upon which Erika L. Briesacher reflects in analyzing the "emergency money" (*Notgeld*) of the Weimar Republic. Curiously, as money's meaning as "money" virtually disappeared, it gained new cultural and symbolic values, expressed in a rage for collecting it and displaying it in an almost philatelic manner. Each collector, in how he or she arranged a collection, created his or her own narrative of what Germany meant. The hyperinflation of the 1920s, as Michael L. Hughes observes, revived in curious ways the much older debate of the moral implications attached to money. Here, instead of a moral debate turning on luxury and conspicuous consumption, we find a moral debate turning on speculation, as creditors were branded as speculators or even criminals. Money and virtue are apparently inextricably linked and certainly not only in the early modern world or in religious terms, as the Pietists framed the issues. Pamela E. Swett shows how the Nazis transformed the idea of savings as a "fundamentally German virtue" to accommodate consumerism, albeit public rather than private consumption, under the motto of "first save, then buy." Her essay, along with that of Almut Spalding, is also one of the few in this collection to address the issue of gender explicitly. Communal savings banks, of which women were important clients, were effectively used by the Nazis to mobilize private funds to serve the party's and the state's agendas. The lack of money, or the substitution of other things *for* money, likewise forms a central theme in Kraig Larkin's treatment of the cigarette economy as monetary "substitution." Larkin uses the seemingly trivial or demeaning practice of *Kippensammlung* (butt-collection), to analyze the contingent nature of money; having access to tobacco products (rather than cash) determined economic power in the immediate postwar German world. The revival of a "real" currency system forms the topic of the subsequent essay, by Armin Grünbacher, on the 1948 currency reform. Few Western scholars have seen the "economic miracle" of the 1950s in anything but a positive light. Here, however, Grünbacher reveals aspects of the short-term negative social effects currency reform had on many members of the West German population. The seemingly inevitable triumph of the deutsche mark was by no means so certain and by no means so thoroughly beneficial as is often believed. The final essay in the collection, by the anthropologist Ursula M. Dalinghaus, discusses a subsequent currency "reform": the 1990 currency union of East and West Germany following reunification. She collected a series of interviews in Leipzig and uses the narratives on the experience of the union as a way to understand the "lived experience" and the memory of the transformation of the East. Instead of uniting the two sides of Germany, the currency union "created and conserved a sense of disproportionate experiences of transformation." She thus highlights the critical importance of money for generating, or regenerating, a nation. Thus, at the very end of our collection, she returns us to a discussion of how the symbolic, cultural, social, and political aspects of money proved so critical in the German-speaking world, whether in the cities and towns of the early modern world, the theoretical investigations of thinkers like Marx and Simmel, the bent backs of those who picked up the valuable "butts," or in the conflicted memories of Leipzigers reflecting on *die Wende*. R. H. Tawney hated the stuff, but money—in all its many forms—remains at the heart of Western consciousness. The now somewhat checkered history of the euro illustrates once again that we cannot ignore the multifarious, even magical, powers that money exerts over us all.

Mary Lindemann is Professor and Chair, Department of History, University of Miami, Coral Gables, Florida and current President of the German Studies Association (2017–18). She is the author of many articles and five books in the history of early modern northern Europe: *The Merchant Republics: Amsterdam, Antwerp, and Hamburg, 1648–1790* (Cambridge University Press, 2015); *Liaisons dangereuses: Sex, Law, and Diplomacy in the Age of Frederick the Great* (Johns Hopkins University Press, 2006); *Medicine and Society in Early Modern*

Europe (Cambridge University Press, 1999; 2nd ed. 2010, with translations into Portuguese, Spanish, and Turkish); *Health and Healing in Early Modern Germany* (Johns Hopkins University Press, 1996); and *Patriots and Paupers: Hamburg, 1712–1830* (Oxford University Press, 1990). She has coedited a volume in the SPEKTRUM series with David Luebke, *Mixed Matches: Transgressive Unions in Early Modern Germany* (Berghahn Books, 2014).

Jared Poley is Professor of History at Georgia State University. He is the author of *Decolonization in Germany: Weimar Narratives of Colonial Loss and Foreign Occupation* (2005) and *The Devil's Riches: A Modern History of Greed* (2016), and coeditor of *Conversion and the Politics of Religion in Early Modern Germany* (2012), *Kinship, Community and Self: Essays in Honor of David Warren Sabean* (2014), and *Migrations in the German Lands, 1500–2000* (2016).

Notes

1. "Verkauft doch eure Inseln, ihr Pleite-Griechen . . . und die Akropolis gleich mit!," *Bild*, 27 October 2010, http://www.bild.de/politik/wirtschaft/griechenland-krise/regierung-athen-sparen-verkauft-inseln-pleite-akropolis-11692338.bild.html.
2. Stephen Castle and Judy Dempsey, "In Maintaining Support for the Euro, Who Speaks for Europe?," *The New York Times*, 15 December 2010, http://www.nytimes.com/2010/12/16/business/global/16union.html.
3. Angela Merkel, "Rede von Bundeskanzlerin Merkel Zum Thema Griechenland" (Bundestag, Berlin, 17 July 2015), http://www.bundesregierung.de/Content/DE/Rede/2015/07/2015-07-20-merkel-bt-griechenland.html.
4. Katherine B. Aaslestad and Johan Joor, eds, *Revisiting Napoleon's Continental System: Local, Regional and European Experiences* (New York, 2014).

Bibliography

Aaslestad, Katherine B., and Johan Joor, eds. *Revisiting Napoleon's Continental System: Local, Regional and European Experiences*. New York, 2014.
Büsch, Johann Georg. *Abhandlung von dem Geldumlauf in anhaltender Rücksicht auf die Staatswirthschaft und Handlung*. Hamburg, 1800.
Castle, Stephen, and Judy Dempsey. "In Maintaining Support for the Euro, Who Speaks for Europe?" *The New York Times*, 15 December 2010. http://www.nytimes.com/2010/12/16/business/global/16union.html.
De Vries, Jan. *The Industrious Revolution: Consumer Behavior and the Household Economy, 1650 to the Present*. Cambridge, 2008.
Merkel, Angela. "Rede von Bundeskanzlerin Merkel: Zum Thema Griechenland." Presented at the Bundestag, Berlin, 17 July 2015. http://www.bundesregierung.de/Content/DE/Rede/2015/07/2015-07-20-merkel-bt-griechenland.html.

Porter, Roy. "Introduction." In *Pleasure in the Eighteenth Century,* edited by Roy Porter and Marie Mulvey Roberts. New York, 1997.

Sperber, Jonathan. *Karl Marx: A Nineteenth-Century Life.* New York, 2013.

"Verkauft Doch Eure Inseln, Ihr Pleite-Griechen . . . und Die Akropolis Gleich Mit!" *Bild,* 27 October 2010. http://www.bild.de/politik/wirtschaft/griechenland-krise/regierung-athen-sparen-verkauft-inseln-pleite-akropolis-11692338.bild.html.

CHAPTER ONE

Money from the Spirit World
Treasure Spirits, Geldmännchen, Drache

JOHANNES DILLINGER

This chapter analyzes early modern German magical beliefs and practices that were oriented around the idea that one might receive money from spirits. We concentrate on three kinds of spirits: spirits thought to guard or to bring treasure; *Geldmännchen* (money manikin) spirits supposedly capable of magically creating money; and *Drache* (dragon) spirits that allegedly brought one money and salable goods. This study is the first one to discuss at length, and in English, Geldmännchen and Drache, economically motivated attempts on the part of early modern Germans to deal with spirits and the place of such magical practices in the social context. This chapter argues that spirit belief interpreted various patterns of economic behavior and thereby justified or condemned them. Because magic was unlawful, we will investigate carefully how financial magic was sanctioned. This text draws on several sources: trial records, demonological and scientific treatises from Germany, Scandinavia, and the Baltic area dating from the sixteenth to the eighteenth centuries.

Treasure Spirits

As I have dealt with treasure beliefs at length elsewhere, a short survey will suffice here.[1] Early modern treasure hunting was magical, neither historical nor archaeological in character. Treasures were often said to have been watched over by ghosts. The idea of a wraith guarding a treasure belonged to a whole set of beliefs about the spirits of the dead doing penance or trying to fulfill certain tasks. Ghosts had to walk until a task they had left unfulfilled in their lifetimes was completed or until some guilt was expiated. The treasure's owner clearly had unfinished business. He had hoarded money without putting it to some proper use. Thus, the former owner of a treasure had to return as a ghost. The discovery of the treasure was in the ghost's own interest as it formed a precondition for its redemption. The treasure hunters indirectly helped the ghost to leave the visible world. Thus, for many, treasure hunting was a godly deed and a Christian duty.[2]

The cult of saints also played an important role in treasure hunting. There were innumerable versions of the so-called St. Christopher prayer, an often lengthy litany-like spell that implored Christ and the saints, especially the popular holy giant St. Christopher, to help the treasure hunters. St. Christopher was asked to protect the treasure hunters from any harm, to keep evil spirits away, and to lead the treasure seekers safely to their goal.[3] Saints were also said to be able to bring treasures. Praying the St. Christopher prayer allowed believers to address the saint directly and to ask him to grant or to give a treasure or a certain sum of money. The treasure seeker in return had to give a large part of that money to the poor.[4]

Even though learned demonologists were never much interested in the idea, demons were supposed to be able to help treasure hunters. Demons did not "own" treasures, but they knew where to find them. Some treasure hunters did try to conjure demons. The conjurers either wanted to keep these supernatural beings from hindering the treasure hunt or asked them to assist the treasure seekers actively.[5] A handwritten book of spells confiscated in Rodach in 1729 mentioned one demon that helped to find treasure and another that gave treasures; a third demon in the book carried treasures away. Importantly, the book gave magical formulas to deal with all of them.[6] A Hessian magical manuscript of the late seventeenth century listed a number of demons who spoke directly to the reader, offering their services: "Aziel a spirit of hidden treasures and goods which I [Aziel] hid as I liked and which I reveal and give to anyone I please."[7]

It is one of the most remarkable results of the historical research into treasure hunting that treasure seekers were as a rule not regarded as witches, even if they had attempted to deal with demons. Apart from very few exceptions, magical treasure hunting was punished very leniently. Most culprits were condemned to a fine, short spells in prison, or a couple of weeks forced labor for superstition or non-malevolent magic.[8]

Geldmännlein and Geldmännchen

There is no real English equivalent for the German words *Geldmännlein* or *Geldmännchen*. The word translates literally as "little money man" or "money manikin." "Money figurine" might be a better description of what the term actually meant. A Geldmännchen was a magical item, usually some kind of doll, which was said to house a spirit. This spirit produced money magically. It was enough to keep the Geldmännchen in the money chest, since the spirit ensured that money would multiply miraculously. The term *Heckethaler* (exuberantly growing thaler [thaler = a monetary unit]) was an equivalent of Geldmännchen that emphasized this point. Even though Geldmännchen as money producing objects should have been priceless, they were bought and sold. The Geldmännchen was magical merchandise. The Geldmännchen were also identified with the mandrake (German: *Alraune*). Roots that had been carved and clothed to give them the appearance of dolls were presented as Geldmännchen. Sometimes elements of the well-known mandrake legend illustrated Geldmännchen stories. The alraune myth, for instance, claimed that a Geldmännchen was made out of a root that grew from the urine or semen discharged by a thief when he was hanged.[9] However, the mandrake supposedly had a number of magical and medical properties not attributed to the Geldmännchen.[10]

In 1673, Grimmelshausen published a book-length warning against Geldmännchen which he considered tricks of the devil. The author readily suggested a parallel between owners of Geldmännchen and milk witches. A milk witch or magical milk thief used magic to transfer milk from the neighbor's cows to her own, thus using magic for economic gain. Grimmelshausen insisted that the money the Geldmännchen allegedly produced was really brought by the devil. Thus, it was wrong to assume that the ghost of the hanged thief from whose semen the Geldmännchen had grown and whose spirit lived on in the root was responsible for procuring the money.[11] This idea was perhaps an embellishment of Grimmelshausen's, as no trial that I have seen mentions it. Most sources imply that the Geldmännchen made money rather than bringing it. In one case that took place in Lutheran Württemberg in 1716, a magician clearly maintained that the Geldmännchen would "create money [*Geld machen*]."[12]

Sometimes, Geldmännchen were made from animal parts. In 1711, people from Göppingen in Württemberg bought a large beetle wrapped in colorful rags as a Geldmännchen for the very considerable sum of fifty florins.[13] An insect used as a Geldmännchen was part of a fraud case in Württemberg in 1716. Other scams included using a pig's stomach as a Geldmännchen, a ploy that promptly failed because the potential buyer noted that it "was no spirit, as it was lifeless."[14] In Protestant Hohenlohe, in 1727, a Geldmännchen had been made from black wax with white stones for eyes; it was about four inches long, wrapped in cotton, and placed in a small box. This particular Geldmännchen supposedly created one ducat a day. This Geldmännchen was sold for thirty florin, thirty kreuzer; had it worked it would have been quite a bargain.[15]

Many people who tried to obtain a Geldmännchen felt rather nervous because the business smacked of witchcraft. A cunning man from Hohenlohe, when asked if he could get a Geldmännchen, answered brusquely that one would have to go to hell to get one. In the same case, a person who pretended to be a Catholic priest likened the Geldmännchen to a bottle imp; he claimed he could "seal one of the twelve chief devils . . . into a chalice, then it would have to bring him money enough."[16] People who complained that their Geldmännchen did not work were advised by the seller that they should "pray and work efficiently [and] that would not do any harm to their bodies and to their souls." He thus implied that owning a real Geldmännchen could be a danger to both body and soul.[17] A Württemberg trial from 1695 called a supposed owner of a Geldmännchen a "devil's man [*Teufelsmann*]," but not a witch. The trial records hinted that the Geldmännchen's owner could only avoid damnation if he sold his Geldmännchen before his death.[18] In another Württemberg case from 1716, a man accused of fraud claimed to own a Geldmännchen. According to the trial record, the culprit explained that he wanted to sell the Geldmännchen in order "to rid himself of the spirit because he had already had it for twenty-two years and the knacker's cart was already waiting in front of his door—meaning that he was already an old man. If he should die before he got rid of the spirit he would have to go to hell together with it."[19] The idea of selling one's sin together with a Geldmännchen to someone else was totally incompatible with demonology.

Essentially two types of Geldmännchen narratives appear in trial records. The first type was about a person who had tried to get a Geldmännchen. This person was accused of magic and superstition but might try himself to get those who had sold him a Geldmännchen punished as frauds. The second type involved someone rumored to possess a Geldmännchen. This person usually considered these rumors slanderous and brought charges. It is impossible to decide which narrative was older because they coexisted and intermingled.

A few examples demonstrate the social implications and legal consequences of being reputed to own a Geldmännchen. In 1650, Michael Pusper, the administrator of the hospital of the Catholic Swabian town of Rottenburg, suggested to the vintner Johann Widmeyer to "teach him something that would allow him to work less."[20] Pusper explained that he knew how to make a Geldmännchen. During Pusper's trial, it was suggested that Pusper was a homosexual—he had claimed that he needed Widmeyer's sperm for magical rituals—and this accusation made his situation even worse. Under prolonged torture, Pusper confessed that he was fully guilty of witchcraft.

With the exception of Pusper's rather special case, the Geldmännchen trials that we know of did not simply identify the Geldmännchen magic with witchcraft. In fact, the punishments meted out were comparatively mild; both buyers and sellers involved in a Württemberg case from 1695 were sentenced to prison terms lasting only four days and two weeks.[21] In the same territory, a person who admitted trying to purchase a Geldmännchen was let off with a simple warning in 1716.[22] In the same year and in the same territory, several people actively involved in complicated fraudulent dealings involving Geldmännchen were all sentenced to forced labor of two to four weeks.[23] In 1746, a person from Württemberg who had tried to procure a Geldmännchen was sent to the fortress at Ludwigsburg at the duke's discretion, not so much because he had tried to dabble in magic but because he was known as a violent drunkard.[24] In 1758, the bailiff (*Schultheiß*) of Sulzbach in the Limburg territory lost his position and had to pay thirty florins when the government learned that he tried (in vain) to obtain a Geldmännchen.[25]

The source material shows that all the people who allegedly had a Geldmännchen or tried to get one were men. These men fall into two categories: expert magicians and social climbers who seemed to have come into money recently. Soldiers had a reputation for using magic and were thought to be able to provide Geldmännchen.[26] The Limburg bailiff wanted to buy a Geldmännchen from a person who pretended to be an army surgeon but who really was a knacker's apprentice.[27] The Geldmännchen sold in Göppingen in 1711 came from a herdsman; another occupation often said to be healers with magical knowledge.[28] In a case from Forchtenheim in the Hohenlohe region from 1727, the seller of the Geldmännchen was a poor weaver who made some additional money as a cunning man who used magical means to cure livestock. He claimed to have received the Geldmännchen from a hangman; executioners were thought to be able to draw on magic due to their connection with the dead.[29]

Even though Pusper came from a humble background, he had managed to become the master of the hospital—one of the most lucrative positions in the town but also one that the burghers of Rottenburg regarded as the center of an entirely corrupt administration. Pusper maintained that people spread rumors about his knowledge of Geldmännchen simply because they envied his economic success.[30] A quarrel between young men that led to a criminal investigation in Langenburg in Hohenlohe in 1725 sheds additional light on the social meaning of Geldmännchen beliefs.[31] Hans Trommenschmidt's son told the son of Peter Hepp that he was "always so bigheaded, your father just has a Geldmännchen and thus money enough . . . that is why they [the Hepps] claim everywhere to be so great . . . [Hepp senior] had a Geldmännchen . . . which is a damnable sin." Peter Hepp complained to the authorities because having a Geldmännchen was "as bad as witchcraft itself and if it were true I would have the living devil in the house." However, during the official investigation, the teacher Zobel, Hepp's next-door neighbor, explained that Hepp "had been robbed about two years ago and yet he had lent money to others directly afterwards, he [Zobel] could not know where [Hepp] got it [the money], but people were talking a lot about that. . . . Hepp was . . . at times a really bad neighbor." It is useful to quote the characterizations of Hepp in full as they offer us a glimpse at the kind of behavior that triggered Geldmännchen suspicions. Hepp "had made himself notorious, because he is an unruly character [*unruhiger Kopf*] in the taverns and everywhere else, he leaves nobody alone whoever it may be . . . he laughs at everybody because of his money and he agitates [*agiere*] the people in strange ways. . . . He had said . . . that compared to him, this or that man was a nobody." Hepp explained his wealth in other ways: he had borrowed money from a noblewoman, worked ceaselessly, and lived austerely. The court acknowledged that Hepp "did not go anywhere else but worked efficiently in his business." The court punished Trommenschmidt's son for slander but stressed that "the accusation concerning the Geldmännchen [is] at this time yet unproven." Hepp seems to have been an arrogant nonconformist who enjoyed competing with his neighbors. Likewise, in a case from Protestant Saxony in 1657, the defendant countered allegations that a Geldmännchen had made him rich by insisting that he had only modest needs and lived extremely frugally.[32] Clearly, certain economic behaviors could bring forth a charge of magical gain.

Persons who tried to obtain a Geldmännchen often faced serious economic hardship. They were the opposite of the social climbers rumored to *own* such objects. The stonecutter Riz from Franconian Protestant Marbach tried to buy a Geldmännchen in 1716. He had married comparatively young and had then forced his father out of the family business but was unable to pay his father for his share. Common gossip held that Riz was simply no good as a householder.[33] Thirty years later, a Hans Ezzler from the Protestant Swabian town of Fellbach sought to get a Geldmännchen. He was a former soldier who worked as a wheelwright and tried to make additional money as a tavern keeper. However, he failed in both his professions as he drank and wandered about "instead of working." When his wife, whose money he spent freely, became ill, the family was finally completely ruined. Ezzler beat his wife and planned to rejoin the army leaving his family in the lurch.[34] For Riz and Ezzler alike, owning a Geldmännchen offered a way out of a desperate situation.

In sum, four things characterized Geldmännchen magic. First, it was unclear where the money actually came from; supposedly, the Geldmännchen could create money out of thin air. In social terms, people said to have a Geldmännchen were considered social and economic upstarts. Although these upstarts attributed their economic success to hard work, fellow villagers saw it differently; the Geldmännchen was responsible. People who tried to get one were often in a desperate economic situation. Geldmännchen magic was punished very leniently. In some respects, the Drache was the complete opposite of that.

Drache

The Drache or Drak was not the monstrous dragon of medieval epics yet its ability to fly and its affinity to fire might have suggested transferring the name of the medieval monster to this rather peculiar spirit. Flying into the house through a window or down the chimney, the Drache brought its master or mistress money as well as goods like grain, milk, or butter. As the seventeenth-century lawyer Melchior Goldast wrote: "The common man usually says that people who become rich swiftly and without any problems have a Drache . . . that helps them win honor and riches."[35] Evidently, the Drache helped to explain why some householders did so much better than their neighbors. In return, the Drache expected a reward, usually food. If the owner of this most useful spirit failed to reward it, it could burn down the house thanks to its fiery nature. Where did the goods the Drache brought come from? The Drache was not supposed to possess a hidden treasure. Rather, it stole the money and all the other goods it brought from somebody else. In a way, the Drache embodied transfer magic: it took goods magically from their original owner and gave them to the person with whom it was in league. Some early modern German peasants used counter-magic to keep the Drache from stealing from them.[36]

The Drache appeared in a variety of forms, as a snake, a cat, or a man.[37] People claimed to have observed Drachen flying in the night sky. In 1652, a Saxon source described the Drache as having the head of a stag or a cow, its front thick as a vat but its rear thin and fiery.[38] In a 1699 witch trial from the Rhön region, we find an extraordinary detailed description of the Drache. The spirit had "a black pointy head. It was the size of a large man, the upper half as black as coal and tar, but fiery downwards."[39] Other witch trials simply said that the Drache had a rather thick head and long fiery tail that looked like a pole but threw sparks.[40] The very sighting of a Drache was suspicious; even if involuntary, it constituted contact with the devil. A herdsman from Protestant Coburg in northern Bavaria who was often out in the open at night and who was therefore considered likely to have seen a flying Drache explained in 1611 that he had never seen it because he always said his prayers, especially on Walpurgis Night.[41]

Spirits like the Drache were well-known in eastern Europe.[42] In 1636, the theologian Paul Einhorn wrote about flying, fiery spirits in the Baltic region "today still owned by many" that steal "grain and goods" for their masters. Einhorn believed in these "evil and horrible idols of wealth" and condemned their cult as demon worship. Given the close resemblance between the Drache and spirits from Slavic folklore and the fact that the Drache seems not to have appeared in sources from any of the German principalities west of contemporary Thuringia, we might assume that the Drache belief originated in eastern Europe. One of the earliest commentators, Dionysius Fabricius, in his history of Livonia from 1620, connected the Drache with the Baltic belief in the magical power of snakes kept as pets.⁴³

A small academic debate about dragons occurred in eastern Germany and Scandinavia in the second half of the seventeenth century.⁴⁴ It was probably sparked by reports about recent sightings of dragons or perhaps by new scientific publications that commented on the belief in dragons.⁴⁵ At least from the middle of the seventeenth century onward, scientists identified the flying Drache directly with meteorites or suggested that they might be burning bubbles of sulfuric gas in the air.⁴⁶ Some authors were very familiar with the Drache in folklore. They even explained why the Drache seemed to fly down chimneys: the hot, fat, and sooty air from the chimney attracted the equally hot and fat concentration of gas of which the Drache was composed. Villages that burned too much wood were more likely to see the Drache than others; the Drache was apparently a smog phenomenon.⁴⁷ In a text on fire and lightning published in Danzig (Gdansk) in 1650, one academic explained that the Drache was a meteorological problem. However, he also gave all the details of popular Drache lore linked to demonological explanations.⁴⁸

The Bible presented the devil as a dragon. Thus, it was easy to see all beings called Drache (dragons) as demons and to integrate the belief in the Drache into the popular demonology that shaped German witch hunts. In the context of witch beliefs, all spirits could be denounced as demons. In addition, the Drache's thievery made a negative interpretation of contact with this spirit likely. In the words of a 1670 witch trial from the Franconian Rodach region: "The Drache had come flying often and at various times into her father's house and thus the general suspicion had been voiced that the culprit could not be free of witchcraft."⁴⁹ When a woman from Saxon Fichtenberg identified the term Drache with "milk devil and grain devil" in 1652, she stressed its diabolic nature.⁵⁰ The Drache appears in a number of witch trials from Saxony, Thuringia, and northern Bavaria between the early sixteenth and the late seventeenth century.⁵¹

Witnesses in witch trials repeatedly insisted that they had seen the Drache fly into a defendant's house. Claus Füßlein from Thuringia was accused of witchcraft in 1615 because his neighbors had seen a Drache slip down his chimney.⁵² The accusation of witchcraft brought against Margaretha Hönin from Coburg in 1580 rested among other things on rumors about *Drachenschießen* (dragon shooting) seen in front of her house. The law faculty of the University of Jena wrote an expert opinion that not only accepted the Drache story but also decided that the evidence justified the use of torture.⁵³ In the 1611 trial against the Coburg widow Ecksteinin, alleged contact with the Drache played an important role: the Drache was said to go "like a friend to and from" her house, indeed to come to her "every day in the evening."⁵⁴

In 1686, Claus Rottmann from the district of Coburg escaped a witch trial mainly because his neighbors had seen the Drache flying toward his house but hesitated to confirm that it had flown into his house.[55]

In some cases, the Drache was directly identified with a *Buhlteufel* or incubus, a demon who allegedly visited a witch regularly to have sex with her. In a witch trial that took place in 1536 in Brücken in Saxony, the defendant confessed that her demonic lover changed at will between having the appearance of a handsome young man and a Drache monster. "She fed it butter and cheese which the Drache itself had . . . brought . . . and when it wanted to fly away again, it laid a handful of money on the table." This was the earliest Saxon witch trial that mentioned witches having sex with demons. A Saxon woman who claimed to be clairvoyant, and thus able to identify witches, claimed in 1652 that she had seen a Drache in the sky having sex with a number of women from her neighborhood.[56]

In the Coburg district in the seventeenth century, many trials combined the accusation of having a Drache with the accusation of being a milk witch.[57] Within the logic of witch belief, it was rather likely that a milk witch also had a Drache or indeed that the Drache brought the milk. Persons who seemed to prosper while most others faced economic loss or simply people who apparently had more money or more goods than their household could possibly produce fell prey to witchcraft accusations. The best-known example was Margaretha Ramhold, mentioned in Johann Matthäus Meyfart's 1635 book on witch trials. Ramhold came from a family of modest artisans yet, over time, had become rather affluent, selling beer and milk even though they only owned one cow. In time, the Ramholds began lending money to other people at interest. This sudden wealth stimulated rumors of witchcraft that quickly focused on the mistress of the household. The Protestant superintendent was informed that a Drache lived in Ramholds' house. Margareta Ramhold was executed in 1628.[58] In a 1670 trial, a suspect from Bad Rodach was said to have always more cheese than her neighbors, leading to her being suspected as a milk witch and of having a Drache.[59]

The 1580 trial against Hönin from Coburg also mentioned that she was known to have a Drache. This allegation was directly linked to the rumor that Hönin made considerably more butter than was possible from the milk her cows gave. When asked where she got all the milk, Hönin merely laughed. In addition to that, Hönin's economic behavior seemed inconsistent: she was rather well-off; she employed a number of servants and owned a vineyard. Nevertheless, she complained persistently about her poverty. When she had guests, she took the meat and the bread from the table and to her room before they had finished the meal. This behavior clearly suggested that she was irrationally and antisocially preoccupied with her wealth and obsessed with the fear of losing it.[60] Other cases demonstrate similar social dynamics.

The record of the trial against Ecksteinin combined charges of magic and allegations of antisocial economic behavior in such an intricate way that is impossible to separate one from the other. The suspect's family was rather prosperous. They had been able to move into a new and presumably better house. The person who lived in their former home had fallen ill and was thought to be bewitched. The fact that Ecksteinin had denied a small loan to a relative even though she might have been able to afford it became evidence in the witch trial. Her husband had quarreled violently with the neighbors about various plots of land. He had tried to sell eggs at exaggerated prices deemed fraudulent or usurious. He and his wife were rumored to have stolen grain from their neighbors' fields under cover of a thick fog they had magically created. Both were thought notorious milk witches.[61] Four years later, Petronella Liebermännin from Coburg was accused of having a Drache; she was known as a ruthless and usurious creditor and was rumored to bewitch negligent debtors. A cow she had sold quickly stopped giving milk, thus suggesting that not only had she fraudulently sought economic gain but also might be a milk witch.[62]

A small town near Eisenach, in the Protestant territory of Saxony-Eisenach, was thrown into shock when, in the winter of 1672–73, a strange fire was seen repeatedly in the house of one Hans Adam Gemeiths. Witnesses declared that shortly before this light appeared a "lump of fire" had flown through the air in the direction of Gemeiths's house. Even the earliest reports about that case mention as a matter of course that Gemeiths was suspiciously wealthy. Although he had gone from door-to-door begging for bread only a few years ago, Hans Gemeiths had purchased a number of fields recently and was even able to lend others money on interest—the grand total amounting to the very respectable sum of 100 florins. As Gemeiths made his living knitting socks, it was difficult to see where his money came from. The villagers remembered that Gemeiths's godfather had been a counterfeiter. However, the whole investigation rested on the assumption that a link existed between Gemeiths's mysterious wealth and the strange fire, both of which were interpreted as proof of a Drache at work.[63]

Comparison and Interpretation

The treasure seekers dealing with demons and saints in an unorthodox way, the owners of Geldmännchen, and those said to have a Drache, each tried to obtain money with the help of the spirit world. All of them were at least thought to have dealt with demons. Although treasure and Geldmännchen magicians were treated very leniently by the authorities, people rumored to harbor a Drache were burned as witches. This difference seems even more remarkable if we consider that the treasure hunters indeed tried to conjure demons and that the people interested in Geldmännchen wanted them even though they were regarded as demonic. The belief in the Drache had no such basis in real magical behavior. The true difference between the treasure and the Geldmännchen on one hand, and the Drache on the other, seems to be that they stood for different economic outlooks and styles of behavior. People who conjured demons in order to find treasure and people who sought to obtain Geldmännlein wanted to get rich, but they did not take anything away from anybody else. Indeed, they seemed to have found ways of improving their economic situation that avoided competition. The money they hoped to get came purely from the spirit world. It did not take anything away from the pool of goods and money available to society as a whole.[64] The treasure narratives were about people who sought money or wished to become rich. Most Geldmännchen narratives were people who wanted to get rich by obtaining a Geldmännchen. Only some, evidently the more aggressive and dangerous rumors, were about social climbers who allegedly owed their economic success to a Geldmännchen. Here, the Geldmännchen stories explained the acquisition of sudden wealth. The Drache narratives did the same. Alleged owners of Geldmännchen and Drache witches seem to have been essentially the same social type—parvenus—people who had experienced significant economic success only recently. Damaging rumors about Geldmännchen and Drache indirectly condemned the "selfish," one might say proto-capitalist, behavior of these people. Why, then, were the alleged owners of Geldmännchen not accused of witchcraft while the Drache magicians were? Gender is not the answer. Even though all Geldmännchen owners known so far were male, not all Drache witches were female. Confession did not seem to matter either. Recent witchcraft research has shown that confession did not play a large role in witch hunts.[65] Catholics and Protestants were among the treasure hunters and Geldmännchen magicians. We find most Drache narratives in the mostly Protestant eastern part of Germany—in contemporary Thuringia, Saxony, and northern Bavaria. However, this narrative does not appear in ultra-Protestant northern Germany or in Lutheran Württemberg. Thus, it might be better to attribute the prevalence of the Drache in Germany's eastern principalities to the influence of the neighboring Slavic regions where the Drache was well known. The answer to the question why only Drache magicians were condemned as witches lies in the content of the narratives themselves: it was unclear where the money of the Geldmännchen came from. Transfer magic did not play a role in the Geldmännchen narratives. The Drache narratives were all about magical transfers. The Drache stole from others. Whoever got rich with its aid did so at the direct expense of others. Thus, the Drache, like the milk witch, stood for economically aggressive magic and magical thievery.

When courts and communities punished magic, they indirectly sanctioned economic behaviors. The severity of the punishment depended on two factors. The perceived aggressiveness of economic strategies used by defendants was one. Economic actions that avoided competition, like treasure hunting or buying Geldmännchen, were treated mildly, even when they implied contact with demons. Overtly competitive behavior—like that of alleged Drache witches or owners of Geldmännchen—was regarded as "selfishness" and "greed" and provoked severe sanctions. Secondly, magical imagination itself played a role. A narrative that implied theft, like the Drache belief, made the magician seem more aggressive. A narrative like the Geldmännlein belief left the question where the magical riches came from unanswered and thus allowed for a more lenient treatment of the accused.

In conclusion, we might say that the treasure, the Geldmännchen, and the Drache were all ciphers that stood for the community's interpretation of different economic concepts. Treasures and Geldmännchen were part and parcel of a basic economic concept that avoided competition and respected community values. The Drache was different: it stood for a seemingly egoistic fixation on individual profit at the expense of everybody else. Thus, only Drache magic was condemned as witchcraft; the almost proto-capitalist and anticommunal economic orientation it represented was thus sanctioned most harshly.

Johannes Dillinger is Professor of Early Modern History at Oxford Brooks University. He holds a doctorate from Trier University and has published widely on topics related to folk belief. His publications include *Kinder im Hexenprozess* (2013), *Magical Treasure Hunting in Europe and North America* (2011), and *Evil People: A Comparative Study of Witch Hunts in Swabian Austria and the Electorate of Trier* (2009).

Notes

1. Johannes Dillinger, *Magical Treasure Hunting in Europe and North America* (Basingstoke, 2012).
2. Kathryn Edwards, *Leonarde's Ghost: Popular Piety and "the Appearance of a Spirit" in 1628* (Kirksville, MO, 2008); Owen Davies, *The Haunted: A Social History of Ghosts* (Basingstoke, 2007); Dillinger, *Magical*, 72–79.
3. Hessisches Hauptstaatsarchiv Wiesbaden (hereafter: HHStAW) 144a/36 Bd. I and II; Dillinger, *Magical*, 85–90.
4. Ibid., 87–90.
5. Manfred Tschaikner, *Schatzgräberei in Vorarlberg und Liechtenstein* (Bludenz, 2006), 53, 60; Dillinger, *Magical*, 61–66, 90–91.
6. Staatsarchiv Coburg (hereafter StAC), LAF 8147.
7. HHStAW, 144a/36 Bd. I.
8. Dillinger, *Magical*, 114–46.

9. Ibid., 107–8; Israel Fromschmidt, *Simplicissimi Galgen-Männlin* (Nuremberg, 1674); Carl Friedrich Gerstlacher, *Handbuch der teutschen Reichsgesetze, Eilften Theils erste Abtheilung* (Stuttgart, 1793), 2389–90.
10. Cornelius van Eck and Andreas Holtzbom, *Disputatio medica inauguralis de mandragora* (Utrecht, 1704); Jacob Thomasius, *Disputatio philologica de mandragora von der Alraun-Wurzel* (Halle, 1739).
11. Fromschmidt, *Simplicissimi*, 6, 10–11, 24, 29–30, 53–57.
12. Hauptsstaatsarchiv Stuttgart (hereafter HStASt), A 209 Bü 625.
13. HStASt, A 209 Bü 961.
14. HStASt, A 209 Bü 625.
15. Hohenlohe-Zentralarchiv Neuenstein (hereafter HoZAN), We 20, Schubl. 10, Fasz. 74.
16. Ibid.
17. Ibid.
18. HStASt, A 206 Bü 3195.
19. HStASt, A 206 Bü 625.
20. Johannes Dillinger, Thomas Fritz, and Wolfgang Mährle, *Zum Feuer verdammt: Hexenverfolgungen in der Grafschaft Hohenberg, der Reichsstadt Reutlingen und der Fürstpropstei Ellwangen* (Stuttgart, 1998), 1–161, here 130–33.
21. HStASt, A 206 Bü 3195.
22. HStASt, A 209 Bü 625.
23. Ibid.
24. HStASt, A 209 Bü 835.
25. Staatsarchiv Wertheim (hereafter StAW), 7 Rep 180N Nr. 16.
26. E.g. HStASt, A 209 Bü 835, A 209 Bü 625.
27. StAW, 7 Rep 180N Nr. 16.
28. HStASt, A 209 Bü 961.
29. HoZAN, We 20, Schubl. 10, Fasz. 74.
30. Dillinger, et. al., *Zum Feuer verdammt*, 130–33.
31. HoZAN, La 35 Bü 1770.
32. StAC, LAF 12577.
33. HStASt, A 209 Bü 625.
34. HStASt, A 209 Bü 835.
35. Melchior Goldast von Haiminsfeld, *Rechtliches Bedenken von Confiscation der Zauberer und Hexen-Güter* (Bremen, 1661), 70; Johann Georg Schmidt, *Die gestriegelte Rocken-Philosophie*, 2 vols (Chemnitz, 1718–22; reprinted Leipzig, 1988), 1: 26–27, 177–80.
36. Haiminsfeld, *Rechtliches*, 70; Schmidt, *Rocken-Philosophie*, 1: 15–16, 26–27, 177–80, 460–63; Ernst Keller, *Das Grab des Aberglaubens* (2nd ed., Stuttgart, 1785), 146–48; Reinhold Knopf, *Der feurige Hausdrache* (PhD thesis, Bonn, 1943); Dagmar Linhart, *Hausgeister in Franken* (Dettelbach, 1995), 213–67; Yvonne Luven, *Der Kult der Hausschlange* (Cologne, 2001).
37. Dillinger, *Magical*, 71–72.
38. Manfred Wilde, *Die Zauberei- und Hexenprozesse in Kursachsen* (Cologne, 2003), 204.
39. Thüringisches Hauptstaatsarchiv Weimar (hereafter ThHStAW), EA, Rechtspflege 1563.
40. E.g. Egbert Friedrich, *Hexenjagd im Raum Rodach und die Hexenprozessordnung von Herzog Johann Casimir* (Rodach, 1985), 56–58.

41. StAC, LAF 12542.
42. Luven, *Kult*, 86, 148–53.
43. Ibid., 145–56.
44. Olaus Borrichius, *Dissertation philologica de lucta Frothonis I cum dracone thesauro incubante* (Copenhagen, 1686); Esaias Fleischer and Nikolaus Svenonius, *De dracone dissertation philosophica* (Copenhagen, 1686), unpaginated; Georg Kaspar Kirchmaier, *Disputationes zoologicae de basilisco, unicornu, phoenice, behemoth et leviathan, dracone* . . . (Wittenberg, 1661; reprinted Jena, 1736), 80; Peter Lagerlööf and Daniel Norlind, *Dissertatio de draconibus* (Uppsala, 1683; reprinted Uppsala, 1685), 1.
45. Jakob Mylius and Benjamin Praetorius, *Diatribe physica de dracone volante et igne fatuo* (Leipzig, 1653), unpaginated; Kirchmaier, *Disputationes*, 79, 89–91; Georg Kaspar Kirchmaier and Johann Daniel, *De draconibus volantibus* (Wittenberg, 1675), unpaginated; Lagerlööf and Norlind, *Dissertatio*, 11–12, 19, 22, 27, 39–40.
46. Ibid., 19–22.
47. Johannes Francus and Kaspar Pomeranus, *Exercitationum physicarum nona de meteoris* (Frankfurt, 1624), unpaginated; Mylius and Praetorius, *Diatribe*; Kaspar Hammius, "De igne lambente, dracone volante et natura fulminis," in *Theoria meteorological*, ed. Daniel Lagus (Gdansk, 1650), unpaginated; Schmidt, *Rocken-Philosophie*, 1: 462.
48. Hammius, "Igne."
49. Friedrich, *Hexenjagd*, 95.
50. Wilde, *Zauberei*, 204.
51. Schmidt, *Rocken-Philosophie*, 1: 15. An alternative concept of the dragon may be found in Manfred Tschaikner, *Hexenverfolgungen im Toggenburg* (Wattwil, 2010), 73–75. I would like to thank Manfred Tschaikner for alerting me to this interesting case.
52. Kreisarchiv Hildburghausen, 338/6784.
53. StAC, LAF 12534, 12535.
54. StAC, LAF 12542.
55. StAC, LAF 12591/II; see also Friedrich, *Hexenjagd*, 57.
56. Wilde, *Zauberei*, 113–14, 204, 267; see also StAC, LAF 12549; Friedrich, *Hexenjagd*, 94.
57. Examples in StAC, LAF 12449, 12542, 12546, 12549.
58. Rainer Hambrecht, "Margaretha Ramhold (ca. 1570–1628)," in *"Seien Sie doch vernünftig!" Frauen der Coburger Geschichte*, ed. Gaby Franger (Coburg, 2008), 56–72; Rainer Hambrecht, "Johann Matthäus Meyfahrt (1590–1642) sein Traktat gegen die Hexenprozesse und der Fall Margaretha Ramhold," in *Thüringische Forschungen*, ed. Michael Gockel and Volker Wahl (Weimar, 1993), 157–79.
59. Friedrich, *Hexenjagd*, 94–95.
60. StAC, LAF 12535.
61. StAC, LAF 12542.
62. StAC, LAF 12546.
63. ThHStAW, EA, Rechtspflege, Nr. 1563.
64. Dillinger, *Magical*, 190–203.
65. Johannes Dillinger and Jürgen Schmidt, eds., *Hexenprozess und Staatsbildung—Witch-Trials and State-Building* (Bielefeld, 2008).

Bibliography

Borrichius, Olaus. *Dissertation philologica de lucta Frothonis I cum dracone thesauro incubante.* Copenhagen, 1686.

Davies, Owen. *The Haunted: A Social History of Ghosts.* Basingstoke, 2007.

Dillinger, Johannes. *Magical Treasure Hunting in Europe and North America.* Basingstoke, 2012.

Dillinger, Johannes, Thomas Fritz, and Wolfgang Mährle. "Zum Feuer verdammt: Hexenverfolgungen in der Grafschaft Hohenberg, der Reichsstadt Reutlingen und der Fürstpropstei Ellwangen. Stuttgart, 1998.

Dillinger, Johannes, and Jürgen Schmidt, eds. *Hexenprozess und Staatsbildung— Witch-Trials and State-Building.* Bielefeld, 2008.

Eck, Cornelius van, and Andreas Holtzbom. *Disputatio medica inauguralis de mandragora.* Utrecht, 1704.

Edwards, Kathryn. *Leonarde's Ghost: Popular Piety and "the Appearance of a Spirit" in 1628.* Kirksville, MO, 2008.

Fleischer, Esaias, and Nikolaus Svenonius: *De dracone dissertation philosophica.* Copenhagen, 1686.

Francus, Johannes, and Kaspar Pomeranus. *Exercitationum physicarum nona de meteoris.* Frankfurt, 1624.

Friedrich, Egbert. *Hexenjagd im Raum Rodach und die Hexenprozessordnung von Herzog Johann Casimir.* Rodach, 1985.

Fromschmidt, Israel (Hans Jakob Christoffel von Grimmelshausen). *Simplicissimi Galgen-Männlin.* Nuremberg, 1674.

Gerstlacher, Carl Friedrich. *Handbuch der teutschen Reichsgesetze, Eilften Theils erste Abtheilung.* Stuttgart, 1793.

Haiminsfeld, Melchior Goldast von. *Rechtliches Bedenken von Confiscation der Zauberer und Hexen-Güter.* Bremen, 1661.

Hambrecht, Rainer. "Johann Matthäus Meyfahrt (1590–1642) sein Traktat gegen die Hexenprozesse und der Fall Margaretha Ramhold." In *Thüringische Forschungen,* edited by Michael Gockel and Volker Wahl, 157–69. Weimar, 1993.

———. "Margaretha Ramhold (ca. 1570–1628)." In *"Seien Sie doch vernünftig!" Frauen der Coburger Geschichte,* edited by Gaby Franger, 56–72. Coburg, 2008.

Hammius, Kaspar. "De igne lambente, dracone volante et natura fulminis." In *Theoria meteorological,* edited by Daniel Lagus. Gdansk, 1650.

Keller, Ernst. *Das Grab des Aberglaubens.* 2nd ed. Stuttgart, 1785.

Kirchmaier, Georg Kaspar. *Disputationes zoologicae de basilisco, unicornu, phoenice, behemoth et leviathan, dracone.* Wittenberg, 1661; reprinted Jena, 1736.

Kirchmaier, Georg Kaspar, and Johann Daniel. *De draconibus volantibus.* Wittenberg, 1675.

Knopf, Reinhold. "Der feurige Hausdrache." PhD diss., University of Bonn, 1943.

Lagerlööf, Peter, and Daniel Norlind. *Dissertatio de draconibus.* Uppsala, 1683; reprinted Uppsala, 1685.

Linhart, Dagmar. *Hausgeister in Franken.* Dettelbach, 1995.

Luven, Yvonne. *Der Kult der Hausschlange.* Cologne, 2001.
Mylius, Jakob, and Benjamin Praetorius. *Diatribe physica de dracone volante et igne fatuo.* Leipzig, 1653.
Schmidt, Johann Georg. *Die gestriegelte Rocken-Philosophie,* 2 vols. Chemnitz, 1718–22; reprinted Leipzig, 1988.
Thomasius, Jacob. *Disputatio philologica de mandragora von der Alraun-Wurzel.* Halle, 1739.
Tschaikner, Manfred. *Hexenverfolgungen im Toggenburg.* Wattwil, 2010.
———. *Schatzgräberei in Vorarlberg und Liechtenstein.* Bludenz, 2006.
Wilde, Manfred. *Die Zauberei- und Hexenprozesse in Kursachsen.* Cologne, 2003.

CHAPTER TWO

Perfecting the State
Alchemy and Oeconomy as Academic Forms of Knowledge in Early Modern German-Speaking Lands

VERA KELLER

Lucriferous and Luciferous Arts

The ability of a form of knowledge to enter the academy can serve as a barometer for its wider social acceptability. Both alchemy and *oeconomia* suffered from the premodern denigration of the lucriferous, or money-making arts. Aspiring to what they saw as higher epistemic goals, alchemists succeeded in entering the university curriculum first. The prior respectability of perfective, that is, alchemical, theories, applied to the state by writers on the treasury, offered a scientific basis for the study of circulation and value on a large scale.

Alchemy flourished in the German-speaking lands in the sixteenth and seventeenth centuries. The new academic discipline of oeconomia likewise grew from roots in the German-speaking lands, where the first professorships of oeconomia were established in the early eighteenth century. Many transitional *oeconomic* thinkers, such as Johann Joachim Becher (1635–82) and Wilhelm von Schroeder (1640–88), were themselves alchemists and drew upon perfective matter theories in order to develop their understanding of the body politic and how to improve it. These two heavily German-accented forms of knowledge were related and indeed coproduced in ways that changed markedly over time.

Money-making served as a barrier to a discipline's entry in the premodern academy. Profit-oriented knowledge belonged to the lower lucriferous (money-bearing) arts rather than the liberal, luciferous (light-bearing) ones worthy of trust, sustained study, and academic authority. Alchemists defended themselves against the charge that they were mere "goldmakers."[1] Academic alchemists claimed that their discipline rose above the lucriferous trades or "mechanical arts." Unlike mechanical craftsmen, they argued, who merely imitated natural structures, alchemists deployed laboratory means (such as "spagyria" or separation of matter through acids or fire) to uncover the structures of matter. They then intervened in those structures in order to improve upon or "perfect" natural powers.[2]

Alchemists succeeded in overcoming the barrier of their lucriferous identity in order to become an academic discipline beginning in 1609, over a century before oeconomia did.[3] Academic dissertations on commerce and other lucriferous forms of knowledge were few and far between until the second half of the seventeenth century.[4] Oeconomia did not receive its first chairs until 1727 (Halle), 1729 (Frankfurt an der Oder), and 1730 (Rinteln).[5]

Many early oeconomic thinkers drew on the perfective attitudes of alchemy to describe their own form of knowledge. They too, they argued, uncovered the makeup of the political body and the processes that allowed it to survive, grow, and flourish. They then suggested stratagems for intervening and improving upon those processes. Proponents of oeconomia thus borrowed theoretical underpinnings from the formally constituted philosophical and academic discipline of alchemy. The notion of "perfecting" the body politic through the development and administration of profitable industries helped to lend epistemic authority to a science of wealth production. Paul Slack has recently argued that improvement, which has no cognate in other vernaculars, was a distinctively English early modern category.[6] However, German oeconomia offered particularly powerful claims to an ability to better natural materials for the benefit of the commonweal.[7]

Writing about the history of both alchemy/chemistry and oeconomia/economics involves important issues of categorization that reflect the changing contours of these two related forms of knowledge.[8] An older history of science identified a theoretical divide, often located within the work of Lavoisier (1743–94), between alchemy and chemistry proper, as we call the study and manipulation of matter and its interactions today. Increasingly, historians of science see a much less definitive boundary shaped not by a shift in episteme or theories, but by changing practices and *personae* (themselves largely formed by the concurrent changes undergone by oeconomia).[9]

Like alchemy, oeconomia (literally "the rule of the household" in Latinized Greek), was an older, indeed, an ancient genre. When Renaissance authors attempted to recover all aspects of ancient life, they included ancient views concerning household management and diet.[10] Such resuscitations contributed to the so-called *Hausväterliteratur* (aimed in fact at both men and women), the guides to household management that flourished in German between 1600 and 1750.[11] This literature offered practical guidance in managing a household, estate, or other resources, including everything from agriculture to cookery and practical alchemical processes such as distillation and the domestic production of medicaments.[12] While few academic dissertations appeared on either reason of state or commerce in the first half of the seventeenth century, jurists, political counselors, and treasury employees published works on these topics.[13] Following the conclusion of the Thirty Years War, dissertations on both the reason of state and commerce proliferated, perhaps sparked by rebuilding efforts of the many small principalities in the region and their attendant universities.[14]

The new state-oriented science of wealth production known as oeconomia from the mid seventeenth century did not reject, but rather embraced this older meaning of household management. It did so in part by considering the princely state itself as a large house.[15] It also considered the ways individuals and their interactions built up the matter of the body politic. With this new perspective, the practical alchemical processes long discussed in domestic literature were now reoriented to benefit the state as a whole. While the *Hausväterliteratur* had generally addressed the agrarian household, market-oriented oeconomic theorists stressed art's perfective ability to improve upon natural resources.[16] The latter, therefore, promoted urbanization, population increase, industry, and trade, and directed the study of matter toward those ends.

Historians of economic rationality, however, see little sense in connecting programs of political improvement to forms of knowledge later considered irrational, such as alchemy. Accounts of the relationship between the history of science and economics have often appeared, but they have tended to concentrate on forms of knowledge currently considered scientifically palatable, such as mechanics or mathematics.[17] The recent resurrection of alchemy in the history of science and the steadily increasing recognition of its importance in many walks of life, practices, and forms of knowledge, problematizes this historiographic orientation. Several historians have begun to explore the relationship between alchemy and oeconomic thought, particularly in the wake of Pamela Smith's groundbreaking *Business of Alchemy*.[18]

Early Seventeenth-Century Writers on Perfective Oeconomia

Whether alchemy ought to be allowed or not was a frequently debated political question. It touched upon not only the health of the population being treated with chemical medicaments (and their spiritual well-being in the case of black magic), but also upon the princely treasury, which could expend very considerable sums on alchemical projects. Jakob Bornitz (ca. 1560–1625), an advocate for the Habsburg imperial treasury, was a strong advocate of alchemy. He made the alchemically inspired "mastery of nature," which encouraged Rudolf II in Prague to patronize new industries, into an explicit political theory.[19]

Bornitz is responsible both for the first discussion of reason of state in German-speaking lands, as well as for a thorough theorizing of the body politic based on alchemical views of natural bodies. In particular, in his last and greatest work, *On a Sufficiency of Things* (1625), he stressed that money and circulated goods operated as a "second blood," circulating through society. This formulation preceded William Harvey's formulation of the circulation of the blood and was based on widespread alchemical views linking circulation and distillation to the purification of the blood within the human body.[20] According to Bornitz, the ways in which this circulation nourished all members of a society united them not only metaphorically, but actually, into a body. The spirits in their blood derived immediately from the nourishing goods produced by society. Such spirits were continually circulated; they departed the blood as the individual continued to exert himself and were replaced as the individual continued to nourish himself from the circulation of goods. It is through the effects of the replenishment of the "second blood," that is, goods, that human blood is generated, and individuals can live, first as a natural body and then as a civil body ("ex quo homo vivat, primùm naturaliter, et postea civiliter"). One who is not sustained as a natural body cannot fulfill his civil functions within common society.[21] The comparison between money and blood was a very old one.[22] For Bornitz however, this was not merely an analogy, but an actual relationship connecting the living spirits in individual bodies and the body politic as a whole.

The innovative ideas Bornitz developed based on this model included not only the political elevation of profit and profit-oriented professions, but also positive valuations of luxury consumption. Bornitz suggested many bureaucratic institutions and practices that the prince might employ in nurturing processes of circulation and transmutation.[23] Rather than extending the political borders of the state, such policies would amplify the internal strength of the body politic by increasing riches, manufactures, and population.[24] So doing would also amplify the contents of the princely treasury, an idea Bornitz had previously treated in earlier works entitled *On Coins* and *On the Princely Treasury*.[25]

Many political writers who discussed the princely treasury in the early seventeenth century approvingly cited Bornitz's views concerning the prince's ability to perfect nature through the patronage of the arts.[26] Nevertheless, such authors sometimes remained more cautious concerning the patronage of alchemy itself. Hermann Lather (1583–1640), a jurist from Husum, cited Bornitz's work *On Rewards*. Lather recommended the patronage of arts in general, which keep the people busy and free from thoughts of revolt, and which could also improve the matter of nature through art.[27] He even recommended the seemingly useless arts of the *Kunstkammer*, which offered displays of human ingenuity.[28] He proved more circumspect than Bornitz, however, on the question of alchemy, citing Tacitus, "the expectation of wealth is among the causes of public poverty."[29] He also cited Besold's views, that private persons should not be allowed to pursue this art, lest they be misled, "driven by the desire for lucre."[30] Lather urged caution, and advised princes to seek out philosophically inclined alchemists, rather than those driven by need or greed. Despite the many cautionary tales of deceived princes, he ended on a positive note; the legitimate use of alchemy offered many wonderful arts that promised much comfort to human life, such as glass production.[31]

Unlike Bornitz and Lather, Christopher Besold (1577–1638) was an academic, and one whose political publications integrated ideas concerning the marketplace, industry, and the princely treasury. He often followed the ideas of Bornitz and Lather, as in an academic dissertation over which he presided at Tübingen, *On the Treasury*, in 1614, which he also issued as an independent work in 1615 and in many revised editions thereafter.[32] He cited Bornitz frequently, beginning with his opening definition of the *res publica* or princely state as a civil body in which money served as the sinews for accomplishing anything.[33] Both Bornitz and Lather showed how the state could attract coin from other lands by welcoming foreign craftsmen and cultivating their industry.[34] Besold argued against Bornitz's view, however, that alchemy could prove fruitful for public finances.[35] He also advised against private individuals pursuing alchemy for gain. Besold was not opposed to alchemy per se; without it, "the secrets of nature are sought in vain." Yet those who sought to profit often lost more than they won.[36]

Rebuilding the Body Politic: Postwar Writings on Oeconomia

Another early seventeenth-century lawyer whose works would prove important to academic treatments of wealth in German-speaking lands was Francis Bacon. Bacon's influence can be observed in the works of Johann Balthasar Schupp (1610–61), a professor of rhetoric at Marburg. Better known today as a satiric stylist and pedagogue, Schupp steadily promoted the academic study of wealth.[37] The title of his anonymously published *On the Art of Becoming Wealthy* (*de arte ditescendi*; 1648) mimicked a perfectly acceptable theme of rhetoric, "de arte dicendi." There he described the dystopian condition of Germany's war-torn lands, and the necessity for learning from Francis Bacon's ideal society as described in his utopian *New Atlantis*. Indeed, the work is largely a tissue of citations from Bacon, voiced by various representative social types. For example, according to some Thuringian farmers, "Money is like muck, not good except it be spread," a direct quotation from Bacon's *Essays*.[38]

Schupp argued that academies in "Germania" should hire "Professors of Oeconomic prudence" who would not merely examine juridical opinions, but who would investigate oeconomic arts (*artes Oeconomicas*) like those practiced by Prince Ernst of Schaumburg.³⁹ Ernst had founded a forward-thinking university, the Ernestina at Rinteln, where Ernst's physician, the alchemist Peter Finxius (1573–1624), was rector.⁴⁰

In a later work, *Salomo*, Schupp portrayed an older and wiser figure, Antenor, who advised a young character, Philanderson, in political lessons learned from the life of Solomon. Antenor argued that King Solomon, the ideal ruler, had been an alchemist. Antenor so admired *chymia*, that without it, he did not think anyone deserved the title of natural philosopher (*physicus*). The Aristotelianism of the schools was mere pedantry. One needed to be a good natural philosopher to be a good politician, since humans were modeled upon the macrocosm.⁴¹ However, although he admitted that some contemporaries knew true alchemy, many were mere goldmakers and deceivers. Like Lather, Schupp offered many cautionary tales of alchemical deception, concluding with a pun, "I consider those people clever, who give themselves to alchemy [*Alkühmisterey*], and make gold out of cow muck [*Kühmist*]. 'For money is like muck, no good unless it be spread.'"⁴²

Such calls for the training and appointment of academic professors of oeconomia would continue. Following the conclusion of the Thirty Years War, rebuilding dukes such as Ernst the Pious, Duke of Saxe-Gotha and Saxe-Altenburg would patronize oeconomia. Ernst founded, for example, a vernacular school in 1660 praised by early writers on oeconomia, such as Christoph Heinrich Amthor and Johann Hermann Fürstenau, for offering an innovatively utilitarian curriculum, including "mathematics, ethics, politics, oeconomics, physics, history, genealogy, law, medicine, and speaking and writing in German."⁴³ However, at Jena, the university Ernst patronized, although many members of the faculty pursued oeconomic themes in private, these did not appear in the curriculum. By contrast, alchemy had long been taught at Jena, by figures such as Zacharias Brendel the Younger, Werner Rolfink, and Georg Wolfgang Wedel.⁴⁴ In 1673, Erhard Weigel (1625–99), professor of mathematics, promoted oeconomia among other practical disciplines furthering "peace and utility."⁴⁵

The seminal oeconomic figures of the latter half of the seventeenth century, such as Veit Ludwig von Seckendorff, Wilhelm von Schroeder, and Johann Joachim Becher, benefited from the informal treatment of oeconomic themes offered by figures such as Weigel and from the patronage of postwar state-building heads of state. Both von Seckendorff and von Schroeder were products of the court at Gotha. Schroeder was a student of Weigel, who was also a friend of Becher's and a correspondent of Seckendorff.⁴⁶

Important transitional figures such as Becher, Seckendorff, and Schroeder held courtly but not academic positions. These positions were often multivalent; for example, both Becher and Schroeder were also alchemists. In their writings and activities at court, they continued to draw longstanding relationships between the studies of natural bodies and the role of oeconomia in the body politic.[47] The case of the interrelationship between oeconomia and alchemy in Becher's case has been excellently explored by Pamela Smith. Wilhelm von Schroeder, who succeeded Becher as councilor of commerce in Vienna in 1677, offers another example.

Before publishing the *Princely Treasury* (1686), which would assure his place in the annals of the history of economic thought, von Schroeder had published a straightforward alchemical work, *Instruction in Goldmaking*, in 1684. These two works were reprinted together regularly through the mid eighteenth century.[48] Furthermore, throughout the *Princely Treasury*, von Schroeder drew on alchemical metaphors, processes, and authorities to support his views.[49] For instance, he quoted the classic Emerald Tablet of Hermes, "Through this the marvels of the work of one thing are procured and perfected," in support of the idea that the key source of wonderful effects in the polity was one thing: money.[50]

Alchemy in the Oeconomic Enlightenment

Johann Hermann Fürstenau (1688–1756) occupied one of the first chairs of oeconomia at the Ernestina at Rinteln in 1730 (thus fulfilling Schupp's dream that professors of oeconomia would teach the arts promoted by Ernst). Fürstenau's very first publication upon occupying this new chair indicates how centrally he integrated oeconomia with natural study, and *chymia* in particular. In 1731, he supervised a dissertation on twelve *desiderata oeconomica* desired for this new discipline. These were having professors of oeconomia, new works about oeconomia (in particular those "underpinned by mathematical and natural philosophical principles"),[51] study of princely oeconomia and the patronage of manufactures, safe global transport of goods, more Utopian accounts of oeconomia in the style of Thomas More, invention of agricultural machinery, multiplication of crops (as Christian Wolff had discovered in his experiments on wheat fertility), fertilization of fields as explored by Johann Joachim Becher (who claimed to possess a new vegetable mercury, or the "Gas" of van Helmont) or through the experimental mixtures of nitrous and alkaline salts discussed in the physico-medical journals, propagation of trees, new and curious foods such as the American potato (which Becher reported could be grown successfully in Austria), study of astronomic effects upon oeconomic affairs, investigation of animal diseases, and finally, profits from improving mining, vineyards, breweries, and the like.[52] Fürstenau distanced his new discipline from popular works of household management through recourse to more sophisticated and professionalized forms of natural knowledge.

Like the other new chairs of oeconomia, Fürstenau also published a comprehensive handbook of oeconomia to rival the *Hausväterliteratur*.⁵³ He began with a history of the discipline. Fürstenau included alchemy among previous works pertaining to oeconomia. In this chronology, the medieval period fared surprising well, due to the flourishing of alchemy and other arts such as glass and paper production. He praised such medieval alchemists as Geber, Albertus Magnus, Roger Bacon, Raymund Lull, Arnold de Villa Nova, Johannes de Rupescissa, Hollandus, and Basilius Valentinus.⁵⁴ Beginning in the sixteenth century, philosophy as a whole appeared clothed in better Latin, but not truly changed until the seventeenth century. Because "everything has its appropriate time," however, oeconomia in particular had to wait to flourish until the eighteenth.⁵⁵ In the beginning of the seventeenth century, Bacon enlightened all of philosophy with a new way of philosophizing, "called experimental."⁵⁶

Among other oeconomic writers of the seventeenth century, Fürstenau included Lather, Becher, von Seckendorff, and Schupp, "whose writings are full everywhere with oeconomic truths, examples, rules, and observations (*oeconomischen Wahrheiten, Exempeln, Regeln, und Anmerckungen*)," and he praised in particular Schupp's dissertation on becoming rich.⁵⁷ Finally in the eighteenth-century, real professors of oeconomia appeared, something Fürstenau noted had been desired by many seventeenth-century authors, including von Seckendorff.⁵⁸ Fürstenau attempted to include older literature within his history of oeconomia, even retroactively identifying medieval alchemical works as part of his discipline. He clearly delineated, however, the arrival of oeconomia as a true discipline in the eighteenth century.

Outside the walls of academe, the lawyer Gottfried August Hoffmann (1700–75) also sought to establish oeconomia as a scientific discipline in his *Prudentia oeconomica*, appearing in five volumes between 1731 and 1755. Fürstenau would criticize Hoffmann's presumption for claiming to establish oeconomia as a science when new academic chairs of oeconomia were already publishing their own systematic accounts of the discipline (although Hoffmann was to be praised for his lively style).⁵⁹ The manner in which Hoffmann related natural knowledge to oeconomia would differ signally from that of Fürstenau.

Margrit Fiederer situates Hoffmann's work at a moment of transformation in the meaning of the term oeconomia, from a primarily agrarian sense of household management, to cleverness and skill in acquiring, as well as preserving, wealth. Hoffmann addressed his work not only to those who already possessed goods to manage, but to those who had none but wished to acquire them.⁶⁰ He divided his first, theoretical volume (1731) into oeconomic prudence for an individual and for a state, exploring general topics such as the nature of worth. In the second volume (1732), he turned to particular topics, including a manual on "physical-oeconomic tasks" and a guide to bookkeeping and contracts. A third volume (1742) expanded further upon household recipes, processes, and arts. The fourth (1749) explored how private oeconomia related to physics, chymia, and mathematics. The fifth and final volume (1755) explored a wide range of agricultural topics with an appendix on manufacturing.

Hoffmann aimed his work at a broad audience and thus sought cost effective means for uniting the study of nature and oeconomia. Unlike Fürstenau's desiderated application of the experimental study of gases to oeconomia, Hoffmann argued that "an experiment with an air pump is not to be despised, but an experiment with a cow is even more artful and moreover more useful." What he called "oeconomic experiments" had the advantage, he claimed, of being immediately useful and profitable, while also serving natural philosophical debate (*physikalisches Raisonnement*). Sophisticated experiments cost money and only served the latter. Oeconomic experiments also enjoyed the advantage of universality, since they could be performed by hundreds, whereas one often had to trust a single man's report for the more expensive experiments.[61] Hoffmann attacked those "who wish to perform and understand rare experiments in natural philosophy [Physic], and not vulgar ones. For while not all of oeconomia, and not even all of commerce, belongs to natural philosophy, yet a part of it belongs to a part of natural philosophy."[62] That overlap, argued Hoffmann, defined forms of knowledge that ought to be immediately useful, profitable, and available to all.

Hoffmann continued to spread profitable knowledge to the common man by publishing in the journal, the *Oeconomische Nachrichten*, of Peter Freiherr von Hohenthal (1725–94), to whom he would also dedicate the 1755 volume of his *Prudentia oeconomica*. Appearing from 1749–62 in 180 numbers (with a further 60 appearing as the *Neue Oeconomische Nachrichten* of 1763–73), the *Oeconomische Nachrichten* has been called "one of the two main German-language journals of the Economic Enlightenment."[63] Between 1752 and 1760, Hoffmann published nineteen essays in the journal, including the prize-winning *Chymie zum Gebrauch des Haus-Land-und Stadtwirthes, des Kunstlers, Manufacturiers, Fabricantens und Hand-werkers*, which took up the entire 1757 issue (number 109) and was also published separately. There, he defined *Chymie* as the science (*Wissenschaft*) through which natural bodies might be made more suitable for human use through a natural transformation. He sharply distinguished *Chymie* from mechanics, mathematics, and all forms of manipulation that did not transform the nature of things. Although *Chymie* was "a very large part" of the natural sciences, it did not encompass all of it.[64]

While alchemy (and thus a large part of the natural sciences in general) and oeconomia overlapped significantly for Hoffmann, he did not draw on matter theory to provide the theoretical basis for his oeconomic generalizations, as had several seventeenth-century precursors. He did not seek to borrow epistemic status from the natural sciences for oeconomia, but rather argued that financial concerns should shape experimental science. Nor did he seek to cloak his new discipline in an academic mantle. The profit-oriented nature of his oeconomia required no defense; the lucriferous arts' battle for moral and epistemic status had already been won.

Conclusion

Before the eighteenth century, the science of wealth was excluded from formal education in Europe. It was not a classical liberal art, and it offended both social and scholarly sensibilities. Over the course of the seventeenth century, however, such attitudes changed in the German-speaking lands, and this transformation bore profound repercussions for the study of wealth. First, alchemy, and then oeconomia entered the academy, transforming each other in the process.

Exploring the interrelationship of alchemy and oeconomy casts new historiographical light on the history of economic thought more generally. Modern historians of science are reluctant to judge science practices in the past by measuring them against today's "scientific knowledge." By contrast, continuing close relationships between economics and the history of economic thought encourage historians of these subjects to question the efficacy of past ideas.[65] Cameralist sciences might not be considered effective today and may not even have been considered effective by many in the past (as was also the case for alchemy). Nevertheless, their larger role in transforming the status of lucriferous knowledge invites more attention from historians of science, of economic and political thought, and intellectual and cultural historians.

Vera Keller is Associate Professor of History at the University of Oregon. A historian of science and an early modern Europeanist, Keller is interested in the emergence of experimental science. Her first book, *Knowledge and the Public Interest, 1575–1725* (2015), explored the coproduction of science and politics by analyzing how new discussions concerning the public interest shaped scientific and political practice. She is currently completing a monograph on the alchemist, philosopher, and inventor, Cornelis Drebbel (1572–1633).

Notes

1. Tara Nummedal, *Alchemy and Authority in the Holy Roman Empire* (Chicago, 2007).
2. For an introduction, Bruce Moran, *Distilling Knowledge: Alchemy, Chemistry and the Scientific Revolution* (Cambridge, MA, 2005).

3. Bruce Moran, *Chemical Pharmacy Enters the University: Johannes Hartmann and the Didactic Care of Chymiatria in the Early Seventeenth Century* (Madison, WI, 1991); and Allen Debus, "Chemistry and the Universities in the 17th century," *Mededelingen van de Koninklijke Academe voor Wetenschappen, Letteren, en Schone Kunsten van Belgie* 48 (1986): 13–33.
4. Joseph Freedman, "Evolving Attitudes towards Commerce in Academic Philosophical Writings during the Seventeenth Century," unpublished talk presented at the Baroque Conference of the Herzog August Bibliothek, Wolfenbüttel, 22–24 August 2012 on "'Eigennutz' und 'gute Ordnung,' Ökonomisierungen der Welt im 17. Jahrhundert."
5. Keith Tribe, *Governing Economy: The Reformation of German Economic Discourse 1750–1840* (Cambridge, 1988); and Lars Magnusson, "Economics and the Public Interest: The Emergence of Economics as an Academic Subject during the 18th Century," *The Scandinavian Journal of Economics* 94 (1992): 249–57.
6. Paul Slack, *The Invention of Improvement: Information and Material Progress in Seventeenth-Century England* (Oxford, 2015).
7. Marcus Popplow, "Die Ökonomische Aufklärung als Innovationskultur des 18. Jahrhunderts zur optimierten Nutzung natürlicher Ressourcen," in *Landschaften agrarisch-ökonomischen Wissens: Strategien innovativer Ressourcennutzung in Zeitschriften und Sozietäten des 18. Jahrhunderts*, ed. Marcus Popplow (Münster, 2010), 2–48.
8. In this article, I have elected to deploy either the term used in the sources cited, or else, alchemy and oeconomia. All translations are my own.
9. William Newman and Lawrence Principe, "Alchemy vs. Chemistry: The Etymological Origins of a Historiographic Mistake," *Early Science and Medicine* 3 (1998): 32–65.
10. G. E. Fussell, "The Classical Tradition in West European Farming: The Sixteenth Century," *Economic History Review* 22, no. 3 (1969): 538–51.
11. Ibid., 547.
12. Claus Priesner, "'Der zu vielen Wissenschaften anweisende curiöse Künstler': Alchemie, Volksmagie und Volksmedizin in barocken Hausbüchern," *Sudhoffs Archiv* 95, no. 2 (2011): 170–208.
13. J. C. Glaser, "Anfänge der ökonomisch-politischenWissenschaften in Deutschland," *Zeitschrift für die gesamte Staatswissenschaft/Journal of Institutional and Theoretical Economics* 10, no. 3/4 (1854): 682–96.
14. See Johann Heinrich Scheurl, *Exercitatio Academica de divitiis* (Helmstedt, 1649); and Johann Paul Felwinger, *Ars Chrematistike, hoc est; Explicatio politica rationis ditescendi* (Frankfurt, 1652). Dissertations on the reason of state began to become common in the 1650s. Merio Scattola, "La discussion sur la souveraineté et la naissance de la science politique dans les universités allemandes du XVIIe siècle," in *Penser la souveraineté à l'époque moderne et contemporaine*, ed. G. M. Cazzaniga and Y. C. Zarka (Paris, 2001), 1: 159–79.
15. The *Hausväterliteratur* informed Otto Brunner's account of the "Ganzes Haus" as well as Volker Bauer's *Hofökonomie*. Otto Brunner, "Das 'Ganze Haus' und die alteuropäische 'Ökonomik,'" in *Neue Wege der Verfassungs- und Sozialgeschichte*, ed. Otto Brunner (Göttingen, 1980), 103–27. Volker Bauer, *Hofökonomie: Der Diskurs über den Fürstenhof in Zeremonialwissenschaft, Haus- väterliteratur und Kameralismus* (Vienna, 1997). For criticism of Brunner, see Claudia Opitz, "Neue Wege der

Sozialgeschichte? Ein kritischer Blick auf Otto Brunners Konzept des 'Ganzen Hauses,'" *Geschichte und Gesellschaft* 20, no. 1 (1994): 88–98.
16. Hans Derks, "Über die Faszination des Ganzen Hauses," *Geschichte und Gesellschaft* 22, no. 2 (1996): 221–42.
17. Richard Hadden, *On the Shoulders of Merchants: Exchange and the Mathematical Conception of Nature in Early Modern Europe* (Albany, NY, 1994); and Deborah Redman, *The Rise of Political Economy as a Science: Methodology and the Classical Economists* (Cambridge, MA, 1997).
18. Pamela Smith, *The Business of Alchemy: Science and Culture in the Holy Roman Empire* (Princeton, NJ, 1994); Margaret Schabas, "Adam Smith's Debts to Nature," in *Oeconomies in the Age of Newton*, ed. M. Schabas and N. de Marchi (Durham, NC, 2003), 262–81; Ted McCormick, "Alchemy in the Political Arithmetic of Sir William Petty (1623–1687)," *Studies in History and Philosophy of Science* 37, no. 2 (2006): 290–307; Carl Wennerlind, *Casualties of Credit* (Cambridge, 2011); Vera Keller, *Knowledge and the Public Interest, 1575–1725* (Cambridge, 2015).
19. Thomas DaCosta Kaufmann, *The Mastery of Nature: Aspects of Art, Science, and Humanism in the Renaissance* (Princeton, NJ, 1993).
20. Sergius Kodera, "The Art of the Distillation of 'Spirits' as a Technological Model for Human Physiology: The Cases of Marsilio Ficino, Joseph Duchesne and Francis Bacon," in *Blood, Sweat and Tears: The Changing Concepts of Physiology from Antiquity into Early Modern Europe*, ed. M. Horstmanshoff, H. King, and C. Zittel (Leiden, 2012), 139–70.
21. Jakob Bornitz, *Tractatus Politicus de Rerum Sufficientia in Rep. & Civitate procuranda* (Frankfurt, 1625), 227–28.
22. Jerah Johnson, "The Money=Blood Metaphor, 1300–1800," *The Journal of Finance* 21, no. 1 (1966): 119–22.
23. Michael Stolleis, *Pecunia Nervus Rerum: Zur Staatsfinanzierung in der frühen Neuzeit* (Frankfurt, 1983), 131; Winfried Schulze, *Vom Gemeinnutz zum Eigennutz: Über den Normenwandel in der ständischen Gesellschaft der Frühen Neuzeit* (Munich, 1987), 25; Michel Senellart, "La critique allemande de la raison d'état machiavélienne dans la première moitié du XVIIe siècle: Jacob Bornitz," *Corpus: revue de philosophie* 31 (1997): 175–87; Justus Nipperdey, "Ansätze zur Ökonomisierung in der Politiktheorie des frühen 17. Jahrhunderts," in *Departure for Modern Europe: A Handbook of Early Modern Philosophy (1400–1700)*, ed. H. Busche (Hamburg, 2011), 105–16.
24. On internal amplification, Justus Nipperdey, *Die Erfindung der Bevölkerungspolitik: Staat, politische Theorie und Population in der Frühen Neuzeit* (Göttingen, 2012), 212–21.
25. Jakob Bornitz, *De nummis* (Hanau, 1608) and Jakob Bornitz, *Aerarium* (Frankfurt, 1612). For more on Bornitz's views, see Keller, *Knowledge and the Public Interest*, 95–126.
26. Ibid., 96.
27. Hermann Lather, *De Censu* (Frankfurt, 1618).
28. Ibid., 990, 997.
29. Ibid., 670. "Et divitiarum exspectatio, inter causas paupertatis publicae erat."
30. Ibid., 668–69.
31. Ibid., 678.
32. Christoph Besold, *De Aerario Publico, Curaque Sustentationis Et Valetudinis Subditorum* (n.p., 1614).

33. Christoph Besold, *de Aerario Publico Discursus* (Tübingen, 1615), 1.
34. Christoph Besold, *de Aerario Publico Discursus* (Strasbourg, 1626), 92.
35. Besold, *de Aerario Publico Discursus* (1615), 38.
36. Ibid., 39.
37. Hildegarde E. Wichert, *Johann Balthasar Schupp and the Baroque Satire in Germany* (New York, 1952).
38. Johann Balthasar Schupp, *De arte ditescendi* (Marburg, 1648), 41. "Nummus instar fimi, non fructificat, nisi per agrum dispergatur." Francis Bacon, *Essayes or Counsels, Civill and Morall* (London, 1625), 85.
39. Schupp, *De arte ditescendi*, 16–17.
40. Gerhard Schormann, *Academia Ernestina: Die schaumburgische Universität zu Rinteln an der Weser (1610/21–1810)* (Marburg, 1982); Howard Hotson, *Commonplace Learning: Ramism and Its German Ramifications, 1543–1630* (New York, 2007), 35.
41. Johann Balthasar Schupp, *Salomo, oder Regenten-Spiegel* (1658), [Diir-Diiir].
42. Ibid., [Dviv].
43. Anastasius Sincerus [Christoph Heinrich Amthor], *Project der Oeconomic in Form einer Wissenschaft* (Frankfurt, 1716), 56–57; Johann Hermann Fürstenau, *Gründliche Anleitung zu der Haushaltungs-Kunst* (Lemgo, 1736), 72.
44. Debus, "Chemistry and the Universities," 13–33.
45. Erhard Weigel, *Die Fried- und Nutzbringende Kunst-Weißheit* (Jena, 1673).
46. On Weigel and Becher, see Smith, *Business*, 89–90. On Weigel and Seckendorff, see Georg Wagner, *Erhard Weigel, ein Erzieher aus dem XVII. Jahrhundert* (Leipzig, 1903), 145–46.
47. On Becher, Smith, *Business*.
48. The two were reprinted together in 1704–5, 1713, 1721, 1727, 1737, and 1752.
49. For more examples, see Vera Keller, "'A Political *Fiat Lux*': Wilhelm von Schroeder (1640–1688) and the Co-production of Chymical and Political Order," in *"Eigennutz" und "gute Ordnung": Ökonomisierungen der Welt im 17. Jahrhundert*, ed. S. Richter and G. Garner (Wolfenbüttel, 2016), 353–78.
50. Wilhelm von Schroeder, *Nothwendiger Unterricht Vom Goldmachen* (Leipzig, 1684), 12–13. "In tabula smaragdina Hermetis stehet/ suo quidem sensu ibi acceptum, ad perpetranda miracula rei unius. Pater ejus est Sol, Mater autem Luna. Mit Gold und Silber können wir Wunder thun."
51. Johann Hermann Fürstenau, *Desiderata Oeconomica* (Rinteln, 1731), 5, "Oeconomiam principiis physicis & mathematicis suffultam."
52. For more on Fürstenau and *desiderata*, see Keller, *Knowledge and the Public Interest*, 314.
53. Johann Hermann Fürstenau, *Gründliche Anleitung zu der Haushaltungs-Kunst* (Lemgo, 1736).
54. Ibid., 49–50.
55. Ibid., 53.
56. Ibid., 57.
57. Ibid., 64.
58. Ibid., 72.
59. Ibid., 73–74.
60. Margrit Fiederer, *Geld und Besitz im bürgerlichen Trauerspiel* (Würzburg, 2002), 220; Gottfried August Hoffmann, *Klugheit Hauszuhalten oder Prudentia Oeconomica vulgaris in formam artis redacta* (Dresden, 1731).

61. Hoffmann, *Hauszuhalten* (1732), 8.
62. Ibid., 7. Christian Ernst Künhold would likewise defend useful experiments against curious ones in his *Oeconomia experimentalis* (Erfurt, 1735).
63. Holger Böning, "The Scholar and the Commonweal: Christian Wolff, Albrecht von Haller and the Economic Enlightenment," in *Scholars in Action: The Practice of Knowledge and the Figure of the Savant in the Eighteenth Century*, ed. Andre Holenstein, Hubert Steinke, and Martin Stuber (Leiden, 2013), 773–98, 778.
64. Gottfried August Hoffmann, *Chymie zum Gebrauch des Haus-Land-und Stadtwirthes, des Kunstlers, Manufacturiers, Fabricantens und Hand-werkers* (Leipzig, 1757), 2–3.
65. Herrade Igersheim and Charlotte Le Chapelain, "A New Methodology for the History of Economic Thought," *Historical Social Research/Historische Sozialforschung* 31, no. 3 (2006): 245–52; Igersheim and Le Chapelain argue for connecting the history of economic thought and "current economic theory" still more. For another view, Francesco Boldizzoni, *The Poverty of Clio: Resurrecting Economic History* (Princeton, NJ, 2012).

Bibliography

Amthor, Christoph Heinrich. *Project der Oeconomic in Form einer Wissenschaft.* Frankfurt, 1716.
Bacon, Francis. *Essayes or Counsels, Civill and Morall.* London, 1625.
Bauer, Volker. *Hofökonomie: Der Diskurs über den Fürstenhof in Zeremonialwissenschaft, Haus- väterliteratur und Kameralismus.* Vienna, 1997.
Besold, Christoph. *De Aerario Publico, Curaque Sustentationis Et Valetudinis Subditorum.* n.p., 1614.
———. *de Aerario Publico Discursus.* Strasbourg, 1626.
———. *de Aerario Publico Discursus.* Tübingen, 1615.
Boldizzoni, Francesco. *The Poverty of Clio: Resurrecting Economic History.* Princeton, 2012.
Böning, Holger. "The Scholar and the Commonweal: Christian Wolff, Albrecht von Haller and the Economic Enlightenment." In *Scholars in Action: The Practice of Knowledge and the Figure of the Savant in the Eighteenth Century*, edited by Andre Holenstein, Hubert Steinke, and Martin Stuber, 773–98. Leiden, 2013.
Bornitz, Jakob. *Aerarium.* Frankfurt, 1612.
———. *De nummis.* Hanau, 1608.
———. *Tractatus Politicus de Rerum Sufficientia in Rep. & Civitate procuranda.* Frankfurt, 1625.
Brunner, Otto. "Das 'Ganze Haus' und die alteuropäische 'Ökonomik.'" In *Neue Wege der Verfassungs- und Sozialgeschichte*, edited by Otto Brunner, 103–27. Göttingen, 1980.
Debus, Allen. "Chemistry and the Universities in the 17th century." *Mededelingen van de Koninklijke Academe voor Wetenschappen, Letteren, en Schone Kunsten van Belgie* 48 (1986): 13–33.
Derks, Hans. "Über die Faszination des 'Ganzen Hauses.'" *Geschichte und Gesellschaft* 22, no. 2 (1996): 221–42.

Felwinger, Johann Paul. *Ars Chrematistike, hoc est; Explicatio politica rationis ditescendi*. Frankfurt, 1652.

Fiederer, Margrit. *Geld und Besitz im bürgerlichen Trauerspiel*. Würzburg, 2002.

Freedman, Joseph. "Evolving Attitudes towards Commerce in Academic Philosophical Writings during the Seventeenth Century." Unpublished talk presented at the Baroque Conference of the Herzog August Bibliothek, Wolfenbüttel, 22–24 August 2012 on "'Eigennutz' und 'gute Ordnung,' Ökonomisierungen der Welt im 17. Jahrhundert."

Fürstenau, Johann Hermann. *Desiderata Oeconomica*. Rinteln, 1731.

———. *Gründliche Anleitung zu der Haushaltungs-Kunst*. Lemgo, 1736.

Fussell, G. E. "The Classical Tradition in West European Farming: The Sixteenth Century." *Economic History Review* 22, no. 3 (1969): 538–51.

Glaser, J. C. "Anfänge der ökonomisch-politischen Wissenschaften in Deutschland." *Zeitschrift für die gesamte Staatswissenschaft/Journal of Institutional and Theoretical Economics* 10, no. 3/4 (1854): 682–96.

Hadden, Richard. *On the Shoulders of Merchants: Exchange and the Mathematical Conception of Nature in Early Modern Europe*. Albany, NY, 1994.

Hannaway, Owen. *The Chemists and the Word: The Didactic Origins of Chemistry*. Baltimore, MD, 1975.

Hoffmann, Gottfried August. *Chymie zum Gebrauch des Haus-Land-und Stadtwirthes, des Kunstlers, Manufacturiers, Fabricantens und Hand-werkers*. Leipzig, 1757.

———. *Klugheit Hauszuhalten oder Prudentia Oeconomica vulgaris in formam artis redacta*. Dresden, 1731–55.

Hotson, Howard. *Commonplace Learning: Ramism and Its German Ramifications, 1543–1630*. New York, 2007.

Igersheim, Herrade, and Charlotte Le Chapelain. "A New Methodology for the History of Economic Thought." *Historical Social Research / Historische Sozialforschung* 31, no. 3 (2006): 245–52.

Johnson, Jerah. "The Money=Blood Metaphor, 1300–1800." *The Journal of Finance* 21, no. 1 (1966): 119–22.

Kaufmann, Thomas DaCosta. *The Mastery of Nature: Aspects of Art, Science, and Humanism in the Renaissance*. Princeton, NJ, 1993.

Keller, Vera. "'A Political *Fiat Lux*': Wilhelm von Schroeder (1640–1688) and the Coproduction of Chymical and Political Order." In *"Eigennutz" und "gute Ordnung": Ökonomisierungen der Welt im 17. Jahrhundert*, edited by S. Richter and G. Garner. 353–78. Wolfenbüttel, 2016.

———. *Knowledge and the Public Interest, 1575–1725*. Cambridge, 2015.

Kodera, Sergius. "The Art of the Distillation of 'Spirits' as a Technological Model for Human Physiology: The Cases of Marsilio Ficino, Joseph Duchesne and Francis Bacon." In *Blood, Sweat and Tears: The Changing Concepts of Physiology from Antiquity into Early Modern Europe*, edited by M. Horstmanshoff, H. King, and C. Zittel. 139–70. Leiden, 2012.

Künhold, Christian Ernst. *Oeconomia experimentalis*. Erfurt, 1735.

Lather, Hermann. *De Censu*. Frankfurt, 1618.

Magnusson, Lars. "Economics and the Public Interest: The Emergence of Economics as an Academic Subject during the 18th Century." *The Scandinavian Journal of Economics* 94 (1992): 249–57.

McCormick, Ted. "Alchemy in the Political Arithmetic of Sir William Petty (1623–1687)." *Studies in History and Philosophy of Science* 37, no. 2 (2006): 290–307.

Moran, Bruce. *Chemical Pharmacy Enters the University: Johannes Hartmann and the Didactic Care of Chymiatria in the Early Seventeenth Century*. Madison, WI, 1991.

———. *Distilling Knowledge: Alchemy, Chemistry and the Scientific Revolution*. Cambridge, MA, 2005.

Newman, William, and Lawrence Principe. "Alchemy vs. Chemistry: The Etymological Origins of a Historiographic Mistake." *Early Science and Medicine* 3 (1998): 32–65.

Nipperdey, Justus. "Ansätze zur Ökonomisierung in der Politiktheorie des frühen 17. Jahrhunderts." In *Departure for Modern Europe: A Handbook of Early Modern Philosophy (1400–1700)*, edited by H. Busche, 105–16. Hamburg, 2011.

———. *Die Erfindung der Bevölkerungspolitik: Staat, politische Theorie und Population in der Frühen Neuzeit*. Göttingen, 2012.

Nummedal, Tara. *Alchemy and Authority in the Holy Roman Empire*. Chicago, 2007.

Opitz, Claudia. "Neue Wege der Sozialgeschichte? Ein kritischer Blick auf Otto Brunners Konzept des 'Ganzen Hauses.'" *Geschichte und Gesellschaft* 20, no. 1 (1994): 88–98.

Popplow, Marcus. "Die Ökonomische Aufklärung als Innovationskultur des 18. Jahrhunderts zur optimitierten Nutzung natürlicher Ressourcen." In *Landschaften agrarisch-ökonomischen Wissens: Strategien innovativer Ressourcennutzung in Zeitschriften und Sozietäten des 18. Jahrhunderts*, edited by M. Popplow, 2–48. Münster, 2010.

Priesner, Claus. "'Der zu vielen Wissenschaften anweisende curiöse Künstler': Alchemie, Volksmagie und Volksmedizin in barocken Hausbüchern." *Sudhoffs Archiv* 95, no. 2 (2011): 170–208.

Redman, Deborah. *The Rise of Political Economy as a Science: Methodology and the Classical Economists*. Cambridge, MA, 1997.

Scattola, Merio. "La discussion sur la souveraineté et la naissance de la science politique dans les universités allemandes du XVIIe siècle." In *Penser la souveraineté à l'époque moderne et contemporaine*, edited by G. M. Cazzaniga and Y. C. Zarka, 159–79. Paris, 2001.

Schabas, Margaret. "Adam Smith's Debts to Nature." In *Oeconomies in the Age of Newton*, edited by M. Schabas and N. de Marchi. 262–81. Durham, NC, 2003.

Scheurl, Johann Heinrich. *Exercitatio Academica de divitiis*. Helmstedt, 1649.

Schormann, Gerhard. *Academia Ernestina: Die schaumburgische Universität zu Rinteln an der Weser (1610/21–1810)*. Marburg, 1982.

Schroeder, Wilhelm von. *Nothwendiger Unterricht Vom Goldmachen*. Leipzig, 1684.

Schulze, Winfried. *Vom Gemeinnutz zum Eigennutz: Über den Normenwandel in der ständischen Gesellschaft der Frühen Neuzeit*. Munich, 1987.

Schupp, Johann Balthasar. *De arte ditescendi*. Marburg, 1648.

Schupp, Johann Balthasar. *Salomo, Oder Regenten-Spiegel*. n.p., 1658.
Senellart, Michel. "La critique allemande de la raison d'état machiavélienne dans la première moitié du XVIIe siècle: Jacob Bornitz." *Corpus: revue de philosophie* 31 (1997): 175–87.
Slack, Paul. *The Invention of Improvement: Information and Material Progress in Seventeenth-Century England*. Oxford, 2015.
Smith, Pamela. *The Business of Alchemy: Science and Culture in the Holy Roman Empire*. Princeton, NJ, 1994.
Stolleis, Michael. *Pecunia Nervus Rerum: Zur Staatsfinanzierung in der frühen Neuzeit*. Frankfurt, 1983.
Tribe, Keith. *Governing Economy: The Reformation of German Economic Discourse 1750–1840*. Cambridge, 1988.
Wagner, Georg. *Erhard Weigel, ein Erzieher aus dem XVII. Jahrhundert*. Leipzig, 1903.
Weigel, Erhard. *Die Fried- und Nutzbringende Kunst-Weißheit*. Jena, 1673.
Wennerlind, Carl. *Casualties of Credit*. Cambridge, 2011.
Wichert, Hildegarde E. *Johann Balthasar Schupp and the Baroque Satire in Germany*. New York, 1952.

CHAPTER THREE

The Money Tree
Living in the Shadow of a Patrician Family in Hamburg

ALMUT SPALDING

This paper explores the implications of patrician wealth in eighteenth-century Hamburg. The family in question is that of Hermann Samuel Reimarus (1694–1768) and his wife, Johanna Friderica née Fabricius (1707–83). Their family united two often divergent economic realities: that of the educated elite whose high public regard typically stood in stark contrast to very modest economic circumstances and that of the well-to-do merchant world. As partial heir to the estate of Hermann Wetken (ca. 1627–1712), one of Hamburg's richest merchants and philanthropists around 1700, the Reimaruses could maintain a lifestyle that Hermann Samuel's professorial salary alone would never have supported.[1] At the same time, however, a host of other people also relied on the Reimaruses for their own survival. Monetary exchanges with these individuals over many years corroborate, unsurprisingly, that lack of money created dependency, but also show how access to money created social and moral obligations.

As kinship studies have shown, the manner in which money and property pass from one generation to the next depends on kinship patterns, that is, on how people are related to each other and who counts as family.[2] During the eighteenth century, kinship patterns all across Europe shifted, affecting how different populations could access economic resources. Precisely this period is the object of investigation here, as this transformation in social relations can be seen in the financial transactions of the Reimarus family.

Before about 1700, an apprentice or journeyman without resources could establish himself with relative ease in a new town, partly on his own merit or by marrying into already economically and socially established networks. This pattern can also be observed in the Reimarus family. Hermann Samuel

Reimarus's father, Nicolaus Reimarus (1663–1724), came to Hamburg initially as a tutor in the household of Hamburg's future mayor, Johann Diederich Schaffshausen (1643–97). After landing a teaching post at the city's Latin school, the *Johanneum*, Nicolaus in 1691 married his former employer's first cousin, Johanna Wetken (1664–1712).[3] This marriage made the immigrant Nicolaus Reimarus part of one of the richest and most influential families of Hamburg.[4] Indeed, this was the source of the Hamburg Reimaruses' relative wealth which, in turn, would become visible in the financial transactions of later generations—the ones examined here.

Such relationships, common before 1700, provided people of modest means access to significant resources. In the course of the eighteenth century, however, social strata became increasingly fixed.[5] By the nineteenth century, marrying across social ranks was virtually unthinkable. Families with money intermarried with other families of means, assuring that wealth stayed within the family.[6] By the same token, people with meager resources would marry people who also did not have much. Their chances of ever rising out of the social and economic situation of their birth dwindled; for them, family ties meant less, rather than more, access to financial resources.

While this shift in kinship paradigms occurred, relationships common during an earlier era and those anticipating nineteenth-century family patterns existed side by side. This study demonstrates how these two different patterns also found expression in monetary terms. During the eighteenth century, people with few financial resources openly relied on well-to-do relatives or acquaintances for support. A century later, the sense of rights and obligations that came with resources would have changed.[7] By then, the same people whom the Reimaruses supported financially might not have asked for help, nor might a wealthy family have felt responsible for supporting anyone beyond the closest relatives. This study examines how money moved from a family who controlled major resources to individuals who did not, pointing to kinship or quasi-kinship relations representative of both earlier and later eras. The image of the proverbial money tree is apt; the story of the Reimarus family shows how a flourishing tree attracted into its shade a variety of people eager to collect ripe fruit for themselves.

Account Books: Sources for Historical Social Networks

Just how wide a range of persons depended on and benefited from the financial support of their prosperous Reimarus acquaintances is documented in four volumes of account books covering fifty-two consecutive years.[8] The first entries date from 1728 when Hermann Samuel Reimarus became professor at Hamburg's *Akademisches Gymnasium*. For the rest of his life, he meticulously kept track of income and expenses. After his death, his daughter, Elise (1735–1805), seamlessly continued the record through 1780, when the last surviving ledger ends.

Though keeping accounts was common in a city of merchants, the particular dual bookkeeping system that Hermann Samuel Reimarus utilized was still new in northern Germany.[9] This method, dubbed "Italian" bookkeeping (*alla veneziana*), juxtaposed income and expenses on the same open page, and allowed for a quick grasp of the net financial balance or profit margin.[10] Reimarus recorded thus on the left side of each double page his assets and any income he received (*debet*), and facing, on the right side, any expenses he incurred and payments he made (*credit*). The labeling of assets as *debet* and of expenses as *credit* appears confusing, but this was standard practice.[11] If expenses were intended as advances, or if income represented the repayment of a loan, the Reimaruses explicitly recorded it. Transaction figures for loans and repayments match reliably, and when a debtor fell short, the Reimaruses noted the loss.

In an era when even sizeable businesses often did not realize their profit margin, using this rather sophisticated accounting system for a family's private affairs was rather unusual. Furthermore, the diligence with which the Reimaruses kept their accounts over decades makes these records unusual. No other comparable published records, nor unpublished documents known to this author, come close to the extent and completeness of the Reimarus ledgers.[12] Thanks to their particularly rich details, therefore, these account books provide rare insights into the family's monetary transactions over the course of half a century.

Money is the thread that allows us to reconstruct and render visible the many different persons who depended on the Reimaruses, near and far. While these people were all vulnerable in economic terms, their *social* rank differed greatly. The following case studies represent two groups of people whom the Reimaruses supported financially: one of a social rank *similar* to the Reimaruses, and another of distinctly *lower* social rank. The needs of these people and their use of monetary assistance consequently differed, but each case illustrates how those who requested and received money from the Reimaruses advanced their particular aims.

Those of a social rank resembling the Reimaruses sought monetary support especially to maintain a lifestyle that they deemed appropriate to their status. Their expectations and behaviors anticipated the horizontal kinship paradigm of a later era, where families of similar rank intermarried and circulated resources among themselves. Those of distinctly lower social rank than the Reimaruses usually sought support to move up on the social ladder. Their expectations and behaviors reflect the vertical kinship paradigm of an earlier era, when someone with close enough ties to wealthier acquaintances could rightfully expect monetary support, even if those ties were based on service rather than family relations.

Beneficiaries of Similar Social Rank

Those of similar social rank whom the Reimaruses supported financially were overwhelmingly clergy in various locations across north Germany.[13] Clergy families possessed significant symbolic capital, based on education, but their economic station was typically much lower.[14] Men among this group sought monetary support, for example, to finance university studies, although sometimes also to provide basic necessities. Women asked for financial assistance typically after losing a male provider.

The most poignant example for this kind of financial support is the family of a third cousin to Hermann Samuel Reimarus, the pastor Samuel Reimarus (1668–1751) in Siek, a hamlet in Danish Holstein northeast of Hamburg.[15] Money matters shaped relations between these two families for two generations as the Hamburg Reimaruses disbursed funds that assisted at least seven individuals of their less prosperous relations for forty years.

Formerly a troop chaplain who "lost everything" during the Great Northern War, Samuel Reimarus assumed his pastorate in Siek in 1722, at age fifty-five.[16] When Hermann Samuel Reimarus in 1728 recorded his first expenses related to this family, his cousin was in his early sixties, with a very young family from his third marriage.[17] These relatives—pastor Reimarus and his three children—expected, requested, and received money from Hermann Samuel Reimarus over decades.

Samuel Reimarus must have entrusted his Hamburg cousin funds to invest, presumably his pension from his troop chaplaincy.[18] Interest payments from these funds, which Hermann Samuel Reimarus dispersed, then served pastor Samuel Reimarus as a cushion when extraordinary events caused financial stress for him personally or delayed his regular salary for months. For example, in February 1746, pastor Reimarus reported a death in his household, prompting cousin Hermann Samuel to send sixty-four marks for burial expenses.[19] Later that same year, pastor Reimarus requested more money due to debts resulting from a devastating storm.[20] Hermann Samuel Reimarus again immediately dispatched sixty marks. This time, however, he noted that the money represented funds normally disbursed the following year.[21] Thus, while using his own funds to tide over his cousin during hard times, Hermann Samuel Reimarus nevertheless kept track of the advance.

Other payments on behalf of this family concerned Samuel Reimarus's son, Johann Christian (b. ca. 1730, d. 1770). Beginning in 1745, he attended Hamburg's *Johanneum*, with his uncle Hermann Samuel covering tuition, room, and board.²² Clearly the family expected Johann Christian eventually to pursue a university education, although his lack of interest and progress raised concern.²³ In the spring of 1748, while officially enrolled at the *Johanneum*, Johann Christian somehow ended up in the garrison of Rendsburg, 100 kilometers north of Hamburg. His family turned to Hermann Samuel Reimarus for the ransom fee of twenty thaler.²⁴ Actually, uncle Hermann Samuel paid more than the requested sum, over seventy marks, to get Johann Christian "released from soldiers in Rendsburg."²⁵ With this sum, one could have heated a house for an entire winter, or employed a maid for eight years.²⁶ The family of pastor Reimarus apparently took this help for granted; no hint suggests that anyone treated it as a loan.

Two years later, in the spring of 1750, Johann Christian Reimarus matriculated at the university in Jena. Over the next four years, his financial support depended entirely on his uncle. Initially, his father would have been responsible for his upkeep in Jena. But now over eighty years old and with poor vision, Samuel Reimarus could not handle his own finances, and his daughters, Maria Sophia (d. 1766) and Margaretha Dorothea (d. 1759), systematically resisted sending any portion of their future inheritance to their younger brother.²⁷ Hence, it was again Hermann Samuel on whom Johann Christian relied for cash. As a student in Jena, he received from his uncle some 1,200 marks in total, about 300 marks per year.²⁸ While pastor Samuel Reimarus was alive, Hermann Samuel kept track of the dispersed funds as payments of earned interest; later, he recorded the payments as payout from the estate.²⁹

After their father's death in 1751, the sisters pressured Johann Christian to break off his studies in Jena. Unmarried and apparently unable or unwilling to support themselves, concerned about their inheritance, and facing a move from the parsonage where they had lived for free with their father, they became angry at their brother for disregarding their wishes.³⁰ All the while, they themselves received regular payments from Hermann Samuel Reimarus, although indeed individually less than their brother.

During Johann Christian's university years, Hermann Samuel Reimarus forwarded to his two sisters jointly about the same amount as to their brother. Individually, each sister thus received half of her brother's support.³¹ This differential treatment cannot be called misogyny, given how Hermann Samuel advocated for women's inheritance elsewhere.³² Presumably he calculated the assets needed for paying the two sisters a pension from Samuel Reimarus's estate for the rest of their lives, whereas Johann Christian with a university degree would be on his own. Indeed, Johann Christian received his last payment from his uncle at the end of his studies in 1754, enough to pay most of his debts in Jena and return home.³³

The two sisters, on the other hand, continued to receive regular payments from Hermann Samuel Reimarus until the end of their lives, between two and nine installments per year. The amount ranged anywhere from 100 marks in 1755 for both sisters together,[34] to 449 marks in 1759 to the surviving sister, Maria Sophia.[35] The latter for several years received payments for rent and end-of-life care.[36] In 1761, her uncle dispersed to her nearly 260 marks, roughly what his manservant earned in six-and-a-half years of employment, or 17 percent of his own annual salary at the time.[37] By the time Maria Sophia died in 1765, her estate totaled over 1,005 marks, almost as much as her brother had received in the course of four years at the university.[38]

One could argue that, as manager of Samuel Reimarus's funds and estate, Hermann Samuel did not generally spend his own money; that it was not really *his* financial support that Samuel Reimarus and his children sought, because the money was theirs in the first place. But who legally owned the funds mattered less than who controlled access to them—and that was Hermann Samuel. He took his legal guardianship of Maria Sophia and Margaretha Dorothea Reimarus very seriously,[39] managing their funds in their best interest even when they rendered this task difficult.[40]

After Maria Sophia's death in 1766, the sole heir to her estate was her brother, now living in Courland along the Baltic coast. The Hamburg Reimaruses had not heard from him in more than twelve years.[41] Locating Johann Christian Reimarus through an advertisement in a St. Petersburg newspaper and receiving the legal documentation for him to claim his inheritance took more than a year.[42] Negotiations on how to transport the money safely to Courland were still ongoing when Hermann Samuel Reimarus died and the next generation of Hamburg Reimaruses took over. After settling old debts in Jena,[43] Johann Christian's remaining inheritance was finally en route to him in July 1770, only to arrive back in Hamburg by October because he himself had died.[44]

It took another six years to locate three distant cousins, Johann Christian Reimarus's closest living relatives, for the final distribution of the inheritance.[45] At last, in the spring of 1777, a merchant Johann Jacob Witte took the money to the male cousin in Berlin, who then forwarded the appropriate amount to his two sisters.[46] The latter, both widows of pastors in Pomerania, were particularly grateful for this unexpected financial windfall.[47]

This case stands for numerous other instances where persons of similar social rank received financial support from the Reimaruses. The overwhelming majority of these cases were relatives, but the Reimaruses also supported others, including an intellectual fugitive,[48] by employing them as tutors. For those individuals, such income meant surviving without relying on public charity.

Beneficiaries of Lower Social Rank

Persons of distinctly *lower* social rank also benefited from the Reimaruses' financial resources. Frequently, this support involved the baptismal sponsorship of a newborn. Such uneven but close ties formed quasi-kin relationships, carrying symbolic and monetary weight that allowed lower-class immigrants to Hamburg to advance in a still fluid early modern urban society.

Between 1728 and 1776, with very few exceptions, the Reimaruses sponsored at least one newborn's baptism annually, and up to eight in a single year.[49] For baptismal sponsorships across social ranks, the highest concentration falls between 1756 and 1772. For the Reimaruses, this period represented mostly stability, economically and otherwise, excepting the two years following Hermann Samuel's death in 1768. Of the fifty-four baptismal sponsorships during these sixteen years for which the Reimaruses noted monetary gifts, two-thirds crossed social ranks, almost always pertaining to children of former domestic employees or their siblings.

These baptismal sponsorships show distinctively gendered patterns. Hermann Samuel recorded sixty-two baptismal gifts during his lifetime, of which he left eleven unidentified. Based on the size of the monetary gift, it is safe to say that the latter recipients belonged to lower social classes. His daughter, Elise, however, identified every single recipient of the twenty-one baptismal gifts she recorded between 1768 and 1780. This suggests that for Hermann Samuel, the gifts' monetary value was relatively more important than the relationships it represented, whereas for Elise, the recorded gift represented a relationship as much as money. Furthermore, the key players in these uneven, quasi-kin relationships were overwhelmingly female. Even if Hermann Samuel recorded the baptismal gift, the godparent was most often his wife or a daughter, and the baby's link to the Reimarus household almost always a woman. The following examples show variations of baptismal sponsorships across social ranks.

Adelheid "Antje" Ficken was employed by the Reimaruses as a maid.[50] During the decade of her employment, the Reimaruses gave and loaned money to Antje's sister and brother-in-law, and Elise became godparent for their baby.[51] Antje married a former Reimarus employee, Georg Fichelmann, once a tailor in Schwerin; their firstborn also had Elise Reimarus as a godparent.[52] The monetary gift for this occasion, twelve marks, was typical for the Reimaruses' baptismal gifts to recipients of lower social rank. This was equivalent to six months of Antje's salary.[53] At least as much worth as the monetary gift was the social capital of the godparent relationship. Georg Fichelmann eventually became a brewer and Hamburg citizen with property and legal rights, moving quite a few rungs up the social ladder compared with the young tailor who first set sight on the city.[54]

Another example of quasi-kin relations through baptism is that of the Reimaruses and the extended family of three tailors—Ernsting, Mester, and Willmer. Elisabeth Anna Ernsting (d. 1768), wife of Gerhard Jacob Ernsting (d. 1759), had known the Reimaruses since her employment in the Fabriciuses' home; they were Hermann Samuel's in-laws. She later served as the Reimaruses' washerwoman, sharing key family events, and during crises, proved to be one of the most trusted caregivers, for which she was separately remunerated.[55] Above all, the Ernstings kept the Reimaruses supplied with clothing for decades.[56]

Two Ernsting daughters then married tailors who would continue to do business with the Reimaruses, Johann Nicolaus Mester (d. 1774)[57] and Johann Carl Willmer (1717–95).[58] Of the children born to these two couples, five newborns would have Reimarus family members among their baptismal sponsors. The quasi-kin relations between these families and the Reimaruses now stretched across three generations. The gifts presented at these baptisms ranged from eleven to seventeen marks each.[59] A single gift could represent as much as four years' worth of linens for a manservant, and definitely more than the average seamstress's bill that the Reimaruses paid about twice a year.[60] Baptismal sponsorship thus represented a substantial amount of real cash. It also indicated symbolic ties and provided assurance of a long-term steady income.

The above examples illustrate how employers and employees remained separated by social rank. But their shared life experiences—births, deaths, life-threatening illnesses—brought them together like kin. Baptismal sponsorship formally validated these long-term relations.

All families of lower social rank who sought the Reimaruses as baptismal sponsors were immigrants to Hamburg. For them, families like the Reimaruses could play an important role as substitute kin. Economically secure and firmly integrated into Hamburg's civic fabric, the Reimaruses provided material resources and symbolic capital on which vulnerable newcomers could fall back while adjusting to city life. For women, these quasi-kin relationships were particularly important because they had no access to professional structures, such as guilds, that facilitated the transition to city life. Because of their key roles in *creating* baptismal sponsor relationships, women probably played a much more significant role than is generally recognized in solidifying their families' position in early modern cities.

The material support and symbolic capital of baptismal sponsorship could play a critical role especially for women who became pregnant outside marriage.[61] One example is Elise Reimarus's baptismal sponsorship of a newborn in September 1753. In the account books, Hermann Samuel identifies the mother only as the gardener for "H. Dr. M." The monetary gift at the baby's baptism, ten marks, was typical for a gift to someone of lower rank.

Unusual is the additional recorded gift of one-and-a-half marks, explicitly for the witnesses of the baptism at St. Peter's church, which is notably missing from church records.[62] All circumstances suggest that the child's mother was unmarried, and that Dr. Johann Wilhelm Momma (1695–1757), whose garden the Reimaruses visited frequently, was the baby's father. Presumably the gardener was "Momma's Lisbeth" for whom Hermann Samuel several years later recorded another gift, twelve marks for her wedding one year after Momma's death.[63] The symbolic and material kinship ties that the Reimaruses created with this woman—Elise as a godparent and Hermann Samuel as provider of money—provided support at an especially vulnerable time.

In another variation of this scenario, it was again Elise who assumed the baptismal sponsorship for a child conceived outside marriage. In this case, a tutor and student at the *Akademisches Gymnasium*, Johann David Heinrich Goedecke, had impregnated the daughter of the family where he boarded.[64] Goedecke was expelled from school,[65] the couple married, and the baby was born several days later. As baptismal gift, Elise recorded a *ducat*, a coin worth seven-and-a-half marks.[66] In terms of monetary worth, this was one of the most modest baptismal gifts recorded for all Reimarus baptismal sponsorships—comparable with gifts for families of a carpenter, butcher, or maid—far below what one would expect within academic circles. But the special *gold* coin rendered this gift more distinctive, more fitting for the educated elite. This difference shows again how baptismal gifts functioned as a gauge of social status. The case also demonstrates that Elise Reimarus was not afraid to assume baptismal sponsorship for children born in unorthodox circumstances. The gift of the *ducat* signaled the ambivalent social status of the young family, but also their chances of improving their state.

Most of the families of low social status for whom the Reimaruses served as godparents continued to benefit economically from this relationship long after the birth of those children, through gifts, loans, and trade. The Reimaruses never intermarried with this group. Nonetheless, their sense of obligation toward the economically weak remained strong. For instance, Elise's last will and testament also includes a former maid as an heir.[67] For the Reimaruses, uneven, quasi-kinship ties, usually more common before 1700, were still very much a reality.

Conclusion

This essay examined how one eighteenth-century family who had money related to people who wished they did; and how people of modest means gained access to money through their relationship with this family. The Reimaruses' monetary transactions with people of lesser means reveal a multiplicity of kinship and quasi-kinship relations. Most people of *similar* social rank whom the Reimaruses supported financially were also relatives, even if distantly removed. Money the Reimaruses gave to those people anticipated the horizontal kinship patterns of the future. For the many people of *lower* social rank whom the Reimaruses supported, baptismal sponsorships played an important role. They created quasi-kin relations with long-term social and monetary implications. The sheer number of such relationships documented in the Reimarus account books suggests how important these ties remained in eighteenth-century Hamburg for people of lower ranks to gain access to monetary resources and economic advancement. Before 1800, a flourishing money tree signaled an invitation for people of diverse backgrounds to step into its shade and collect fruit for themselves.

Almut Spalding is Professor of Modern Languages at Illinois College. She is, with Paul Spalding, editor of the multi-volume *Account Books of the Reimarus Family of Hamburg*, and author of *Elise Reimarus (1735–1805), The Muse of Hamburg: A Woman of the German Enlightenment* (2005).

Notes

1. Without descendants, Hermann Wetken willed major gifts to five existing charitable institutions and a new paupers' school, the future *Wetkensche Armenschule*. Nicolaus Reimarus, ed., *Das Geschlecht-Register der Vier Reimarorum* (Lüneburg, 1720), handwritten notes on table VII: 10–11, Staatsarchiv Hamburg (hereafter StAHbg), Bestand 622-1/86 Reimarus, Signatur G. Hereafter this document will be referred to as *Geschlecht-Register*.
2. On kinship and property, see David Warren Sabean and Simon Teuscher, "Kinship in Europe: A New Approach to Long-Term Development," in *Kinship in Europe: Approaches to Long-Term Development (1300–1900)*, ed. David Warren Sabean, Simon Teuscher, and Jon Mathieu (New York, 2007), esp. 2–3, 24.
3. Nicolaus Reimarus, *Lexikon der hamburgischen Schriftsteller bis zur Gegenwart*, vol. 6, ed. Hans Schröder (Hamburg, 1873), entry no. 3131, 205–6.
4. Johanna Wetken's father, Dieterich Wetken (1624–80), mayor Johann Diederich Schaffshausen's mother, Elisabeth Schaffshausen (1621–92), and the wealthy merchant Hermann Wetken were siblings. *Geschlecht-Register*, handwritten notes on table VII: 10–11 and 16–17.
5. Christopher H. Johnson and David Warren Sabean, "From Siblingship to Siblinghood: Kinship and the Shaping of European Society (1300–1900)," in *Sibling Relations and the Transformations of European Kinship, 1300–1900*, ed. Christopher H. Johnson and David Warren Sabean (New York, 2011), 2, 9.
6. David Warren Sabean, "From Clan to Kindred: Kinship and the Circulation of Property in Premodern and Modern Europe," in *Heredity Produced: At the Crossroads of Biology, Politics, and Culture, 1500–1870*, ed. Staffan Müller-Wille and Hans-Jörg Rheinberger (Cambridge, 2007), 18.

7. Hans Medick and David Warren Sabean, "Interest and Emotion in Family and Kinship Studies: A Critique of Social History and Anthropology," in *Interest and Emotion: Essays on the Study of Family and Kinship*, ed. Hans Medick and David Warren Sabean (Cambridge, 1984), 13–14, 20.
8. For a critical edition of these four account books, see Almut Spalding and Paul S. Spalding, *The Account Books of the Reimarus Family of Hamburg, 1728–1780: Turf and Tailors, Books and Beer*, 2 vols. (Leiden, 2015). Subsequent references to original ledger entries relate to this edition, listed as *The Account Books*.
9. Mathematicians who taught Italian bookkeeping around 1800 received explicit recognition for it, for example, Johann Reimer (1731–1803) and Daniel Richter (d. 1805). Hans Schröder, *Lexikon der hamburgischen Schriftsteller bis zur Gegenwart*, vol. 6 (Hamburg, 1873), entries no. 3137 and 3193, respectively.
10. Marie-Louise Pelus-Kaplan, "Zu einer Geschichte der Buchhaltung im hansischen Bereich: die Handelsbücher der Lübecker Kaufleute vom Anfang des 16. bis zum Ende des 17. Jahrhunderts," *Zeitschrift des Vereins für Lübeckische Geschichte und Altertumskunde* 74 (1994): 32.
11. Ibid., 38.
12. Contemporary published account books include *Voltaire's Household Accounts, 1760–1778*, ed. Theodore Besterman (New York, 1968); *Jefferson's Memorandum Books . . . 1767–1826*, ed. James Bear and Lucia Stanton (Princeton, NJ, 1997); *Lübeck 1787–1808: Die Haushaltungsbücher des Kaufmanns Jacob Behrens des Älteren*, ed. Björn Kommer (Lübeck, 1989); for a Lübeck merchant's wife's account book covering the years 1758–65, see Otto Wiehmann, "Aus dem Tagebuch der Christina Elisabeth Lang (1718–1775)," *Zeitschrift des Vereins für Lübeckische Geschichte und Altertumskunde* 81 (2001): 369–76.
13. Almut Spalding and Paul Spalding, "Living in the Enlightenment: The Reimarus Household Accounts of 1728–1780," in *Between Philology and Radical Enlightenment: Hermann Samuel Reimarus (1694–1768)*, ed. Martin Mulsow (Leiden, 2011), esp. 206–13.
14. On symbolic capital, see Paul S. Adler and Seok-Woo Kwon, "Social Capital: Prospects for a New Concept," *The Academy of Management Review* 27, no. 1 (2002): 17; and Pierre Bourdieu, "Social Space and Symbolic Power," *Sociological Theory* 7, no. 1 (1989): 17, 20–21.
15. The extended Reimarus family included four individuals by that name living simultaneously, all easily confused. For their relationships, see *The Account Books*, vol. 1, chart 3, 76–77.
16. *Geschlecht-Register*, handwritten note on table V.
17. *The Account Books*, entry for 6 July 1728, 1: 88. For Protestant clergy, employment as parish pastor required marrying. See Priscilla A. Hayden-Roy, *"Sparta et Martha": Pfarramt und Heirat in der Lebensplanung Hölderlins und in seinem Umfeld* (Ostfildern, 2011).
18. *The Account Books*, entries for 26 September 1744, 1: 165; 5 May 1745, 1: 175; 13 August 1746, 1: 192.
19. Samuel Reimarus to Hermann Samuel Reimarus, 14 Feb. 1746, StAHbg, Bestand 622-1/86 Reimarus, A23, vol. 2, Unterakte Samuel Reimarus und Kinder. The woman who died ("meine Frieben") was perhaps a maid, definitely not his wife Maria (d. 1748) or a daughter. *The Account Books*, entry for 15 February 1746, 1: 187.

20. Samuel Reimarus to Hermann Samuel Reimarus, 12 August 1746, StAHbg, see note 19.
21. *The Account Books*, entry for 13 August 1746, 1: 192.
22. Werner Puttfarken, ed., *Album Johannei, Teil 2: Schülerverzeichnis 1732–1802* (Hamburg, 1933), 181. Johann Christian Reimarus was officially enrolled 1745–49. *The Account Books*, entries for 20 October 1745, 1: 167; August–September 1745, 1: 180; and November 1745, 1: 182.
23. Samuel Reimarus to Hermann Samuel Reimarus, 23 January 1745 and 14 February 1746, StAHbg, see note 19.
24. Margaretha Dorothea Reimarus to Hermann Samuel Reimarus, 25 April 1748, StAHbg, see note 19.
25. *The Account Books*, entry for 22 April 1748, 1: 216. Twenty thaler were equivalent to seventy marks.
26. For the 1747 heating season, Reimarus recorded seventy-one marks total (*The Account Books*, entries for 6 and 20 July 1747, 1: 205). The maid Antje Stapelfeld, in the Reimaruses' employ 1740–48, was hired for eight marks per year (*The Account Books*, 1: 241).
27. Johann Christian Reimarus to Hermann Samuel Reimarus, 29 Aug. 1751, Staats- und Universitätsbibliothek Hamburg (hereafter SUBHbg), NRS:Br.:R32.
28. This figure is based on ledger entries that name Johann Christian Reimarus explicitly or implicitly as a recipient of funds; and on Johann Christian Reimarus's letters during the same period to Hermann Samuel Reimarus. *The Account Books*, entries for 11 March 1750, 1: 253; 2 February 1751, 1: 266; 21 September 1751, 1: 275; December 1751, 1: 281; December 1752, 1: 300; 2 April 1753, 1: 306; December 1753, 1: 319; and 15 December 1754, 1: 335. Johann Christian Reimarus to Hermann Samuel Reimarus, 13 March 1751; 29 August 1751; 25 October 1751; 26 March 1752; 10 May 1752; 17 October 1752; 4 February 1753; 26 March 1753; 7 May 1753; 7 September 1753; 1 March 1754; n.d. [summer 1754]; 12 December 1754; and to his sisters, 26 March 1752; all SUBHbg, NRS:Br.:R31–43, R46–47.
29. *The Account Books*, entry for 2 February 1751, 1: 266; December 1751, 1: 281; December 1752, 1: 300.
30. Johann Christian Reimarus to Hermann Samuel Reimarus: 29 August 1751; 17 October 1752; 7 September 1753. SUBHbg, NRS:Br.:R32, 37, 41.
31. These calculations are based on entries of payments to the sisters: *The Account Books*, December 1751, 1: 281; 6 March 1752, 1: 285; 18 May 1752, 1: 289; December 1752, 1: 300; 29 February 1753, 1: 304; 25 May 1753, 1: 308; 8 October 1752, 1: 315; December 1753, 1: 319.
32. Hermann Samuel Reimarus assisted his cousin, Catharina Elisabeth Bötticher née Wetken (b. 1695), to attain her share of an inheritance that Hamburg courts had assigned solely to her brothers. Johann Georg Bötticher to Hermann Samuel Reimarus, 19 February 1743, SUBHbg, NRS:Br.:B17.
33. The last entry in the account book where Johann Christian Reimarus appears implicitly as recipient of an inheritance payment, together with his sisters, dates from December 1754. *The Account Books*, entry for December 1754, 1: 335.
34. *The Account Books*, entries for 11 September 1755, 1: 345; and 20 November 1755, 1: 348.
35. *The Account Books*, entry for December 1759, 1: 405.

36. *The Account Books*, entries for 20 September 1760, 1: 415; 6 November 1762, 1: 445; 5 May 1755, 1: 427; February 1766, 1: 482; March 1766, 1: 483.
37. Payments to Maria Sophia Reimarus in 1761: *The Account Books*, entries for 4 February 1761, 1: 422; 14 April 1761, 1: 426; 5 June 1761, 1: 427; 18 July 1761, 1: 429; 11 September 1761, 1: 431; and 3 November 1761, 1: 433. The wages for Hinrich Kammerer, employed January 1748–May 1754, amounted to 228 marks, plus linens and shoes: *The Account Books*, 1: 390. Hermann Samuel Reimarus's salary in 1761, paid in quarterly installments, amounted to 1,609 marks. *The Account Books*, entries for 17 March 1761, 1: 423; 20 June 1761, 1: 427; 28 September 1761, 1: 430; 22 December 1761, 1: 433.
38. *The Account Books*, entry for 30 June 1766, 1: 486. The amount of 1,005 marks, 1 shilling, 6 pennies was the sum declared to the *Zehnpfennigamt*, the Hamburg office where inheritances from noncitizens had to be declared and taxed.
39. Legal guardianship contract, 30 July 1759, SUBHbg, NRS, Sign. I b 9, 2 (R).
40. Johann Christian Reimarus to Hermann Samuel Reimarus, 4 March 1767, SUBHbg, NRS:Br.:R44.
41. Having learned of his sister Margaretha Dorothea's death in 1761, Johann Christian Reimarus entrusted a sailor from Lübeck with a letter to the Reimaruses, but it never arrived. Johann Christian Reimarus to Hermann Samuel Reimarus, 4 March 1767, SUBHbg, NRS:Br.:R44.
42. Johann Christian Reimarus to Hermann Samuel Reimarus, 25 April 1767, SUBHbg, NRS:Br.:R45. The text of the St. Petersburg newspaper advertisement, and the draft of Hermann Samuel Reimarus's response to Johann Christian Reimarus, dated 28 July 1767, also survive in SUBHbg, NL H.S.Reimarus, IVR27.
43. Johann Christian Reimarus to Hermann Samuel Reimarus, 4 March 1767, SUBHbg, NRS:Br.:R44.
44. *The Account Books*, entries for expenses in July 1770 and on 21 April 1777; and income on 1 October 1770, 1: 535, 536, 624, respectively. For Johann Christian Reimarus's biography, see *The Account Books*, 2: 1177–79.
45. Heirs were children of pastor Samuel Reimarus's younger brother Nicolaus Reimarus (b. 20 October 1680): Anna Christina Schultz (1712–after 1776) and Eleonora Elisabeth Grünenthal (ca. 1718–after 1776), and Balthasar Friedrich Reimarus (1720–95), war counselor and privy archivist in Berlin. For their relation to the Hamburg Reimaruses, see *The Account Books*, chart 3, 1: 78; 2: 1178, n1186.
46. Balthasar Friedrich Reimarus to Johann Albert Hinrich Reimarus, 3 July and 9 November 1776, and 19 April 1777: SUBHbg, NRS:Br.:R1–3.
47. Eleonora Elisabeth Reimarin, widow of Grünenthaler, to Johann Albert Hinrich Reimarus, 11 November 1776: SUBHbg, NRS:Br.:R24.
48. Paul S. Spalding, *Seize the Book, Jail the Author: Johann Lorenz Schmidt and Censorship in Eighteenth-Century Germany* (Purdue, IN, 1996); Almut Spalding and Paul Spalding, "Der rätselhafte Tutor bei Hermann Samuel Reimarus: Begegnung zweier radikaler Aufklärer in Hamburg," *Zeitschrift des Vereins für Hamburgische Geschichte* 7 (2001): 49–64.
49. For a listing of all godparent instances recorded with a gift, see *The Account Books*, entry "Gevatterschaft," 2: 942–43.
50. *The Account Books*, 2: 913.
51. *The Account Books*, entries for 29 April 1766, 1: 570; 3 May 1766, 1: 484; August 1767, 1: 150; December 1767, 1: 502.

52. StAHbg, Hochzeitenbücher der Wedde, Bestand 332–1, Wedde, I 29, 39:55. *The Account Books*, entry for 7 June 1772, 1: 560.
53. Adelheid Ficken's pay for eighteen months during 1764–66 was thirty-six marks. *The Account Books*, 1: 570.
54. For more details on Georg Fichelman, see *The Account Books*, 2: 913.
55. For instance, *The Account Books*, entries for November 1743, 1: 157 (Hermann Samuel's illness); December 1746, 1: 197 (illness and death of son Johann Joachim Reimarus, 1741–46).
56. On Elisabeth Anna and Gerhard Jacob Ernsting, see *The Account Books*, 2: 894–95.
57. On Anna Dorothea and Johann Nicolaus Mester, see *The Account Books*, 2: 1082–83.
58. On Johann Carl Willmer, see *The Account Books*, 2: 1339–40.
59. Mester babies with Reimarus godparents: *The Account Books*, entries for 2 June 1756, 1: 356; 9 November 1761, 1: 433; and 5 February 1765, 1: 469. Willmer babies with Reimarus godparents: *The Account Books*, entries for 11 June 1749, 1: 232; and 12 July 1756, 1: 357.
60. In March and April 1762, two seamstresses—unrelated to the Ernsting-Mester-Willmer families—earned seven and four marks respectively for making mourning clothes. *The Account Books*, entries for 15 March and 3 April, 1: 437.
61. Concerning social and symbolic capital, see Bourdieu, "Social Space and Symbolic Power," 14–25; and Adler and Kwon, "Social Capital," 17–40.
62. *The Account Books*, entry for 30 September 1753, 1: 315.
63. *The Account Books*, entry for 10 March 1758, 1: 378. The marriage must have taken place outside Hamburg; no such marriage appears among Hamburg wedding records.
64. For more on Goedecke, see *The Account Books*, 2: 950.
65. No. 2821, in C. H. Sillem, *Die Matrikel des Akademischen Gymnasiums in Hamburg 1613–1883* (Hamburg, 1891), 138.
66. *The Account Books*, entry for October 1771, 1: 551.
67. Elise Reimarus, "Last Will and Testament," in Almut Spalding, *Elise Reimarus, the Muse of Hamburg: A Woman of the German Enlightenment* (Würzburg, 2005), Appendix VIII, no. 2, 517.

Bibliography

Adler, Paul S., and Seok-Woo Kwon. "Social Capital: Prospects for a New Concept." *The Academy of Management Review* 27, no. 1 (2002): 17–40.

Bourdieu, Pierre. "Social Space and Symbolic Power." *Sociological Theory* 7, no. 1 (1989): 14–25.

Hayden-Roy, Priscilla A. *"Sparta et Martha": Pfarramt und Heirat in der Lebensplanung Hölderlins und in seinem Umfeld*. Ostfildern, 2011.

Die Haushaltungsbücher des Kaufmanns Jacob Behrens des Älteren. Edited by Björn Kommer. Lübeck, 1989.

Jefferson's Memorandum Books . . . 1767–1826, edited by James Bear and Lucia Stanton. Princeton, NJ, 1997.

Johnson, Christopher H., and David Warren Sabean. "From Siblingship to Siblinghood: Kinship and the Shaping of European Society (1300–1900)." In *Sibling

Relations and the Transformations of European Kinship, 1300–1900, edited by Christopher H. Johnson and David Warren Sabean, 1–28. New York, 2011.

Medick, Hans, and David Warren Sabean. "Interest and Emotion in Family and Kinship Studies: A Critique of Social History and Anthropology." In *Interest and Emotion: Essays on the Study of Family and Kinship*, edited by Hans Medick and David Warren Sabean, 9–27. Cambridge, 1984.

Moderow, Hans. *Die Evangelischen Geistlichen Pommerns von der Reformation bis zur Gegenwart. Part I: Regierungsbezirk Stettin.* Stettin, 1903.

Pelus-Kaplan, Marie-Louise. "Zu einer Geschichte der Buchhaltung im hansischen Bereich: Die Handelsbücher der Lübecker Kaufleute vom Anfang des 16. bis zum Ende des 17. Jahrhunderts." *Zeitschrift des Vereins für Lübeckische Geschichte und Altertumskunde* 74 (1994): 38.

Puttfarken, Werner, ed. *Album Johannei. Teil 2: Schülerverzeichnis 1732–1802.* Hamburg, 1933;

Reimarus, Nicolaus, ed. *Das Geschlecht-Register der Vier Reimarorum.* Lüneburg, 1720.

Sabean, David Warren. "From Clan to Kindred: Kinship and the Circulation of Property in Premodern and Modern Europe." In *Heredity Produced: At the Crossroads of Biology, Politics, and Culture, 1500–1870*, edited by Staffan Müller-Wille and Hans-Jörg Rheinberger, 37–59. Cambridge, 2007.

Sabean, David Warren, and Simon Teuscher. "Kinship in Europe: A New Approach to Long-Term Development." In *Kinship in Europe: Approaches to Long-Term Development (1300–1900)*, edited by David Warren Sabean, Simon Teuscher, and Jon Mathieu, 1–32. New York, 2007.

Schröder, Hans, ed. *Lexikon der hamburgischen Schriftsteller bis zur Gegenwart*, 8 vols. Hamburg, 1851–83. https://schroeder.sub.uni-hamburg.de/

Sillem, C. H. *Die Matrikel des Akademischen Gymnasiums in Hamburg 1613–1883.* Hamburg, 1891.

Spalding, Almut. *Elise Reimarus, the Muse of Hamburg: A Woman of the German Enlightenment.* Würzburg, 2005.

Spalding, Almut, and Paul Spalding. *The Account Books of the Reimarus Family of Hamburg, 1728–1780: Turf and Tailors, Books and Beer*, 2 vols. Leiden, 2015.

———. "Der rätselhafte Tutor bei Hermann Samuel Reimarus: Begegnung zweier radikaler Aufklärer in Hamburg." *Zeitschrift des Vereins für Hamburgische Geschichte* 7 (2001): 49–64.

———. "Living in the Enlightenment: The Reimarus Household Accounts of 1728–1780." In *Between Philology and Radical Enlightenment: Hermann Samuel Reimarus (1694–1768)*, edited by Martin Mulsow, 201–29. Leiden, 2011.

Spalding, Paul S. *Seize the Book, Jail the Author: Johann Lorenz Schmidt and Censorship in Eighteenth-Century Germany.* Purdue, IN, 1996.

Voltaire's Household Accounts, 1760–1778, edited by Theodore Besterman. New York, 1968.

CHAPTER FOUR

Silver Thaler and Ur-Cameralists

ANDRE WAKEFIELD

> Money (*Geld*): coined metal, insofar as it is
> the measure of things in trade and commerce.
> —Johann Georg Krünitz, *Oekonomishe Encyklopädie, oder
> allgemeines System der Staats-, Stadt-, Haus- und Landwirthschaft*

Adam Smith caricatured mercantilists in his *Wealth of Nations*. "A rich country, in the same manner as a rich man," he argued, "is supposed to be a country abounding in money; and to heap up gold and silver in any country is supposed to be the readiest way to enrich it." Genghis Khan's Tatars, Smith quipped, asked whether there were many sheep and cattle in France, because they wanted to know whether it was worth conquering. They believed that wealth consisted in goats, sheep, and oxen; mercantilists and Spaniards, on the contrary, held that gold and silver were the foundation of all wealth. "Of the two, the Tartar notion, perhaps, was the nearest to the truth."[1] Smith was having a little fun, sticking it to the French, to the Spanish, and to bloviating merchants. But today, over two centuries later, his Scottish barbs have taken on the odor of liberal economic triumphalism, and his humor goes lost on those who want to defend the French, Spanish, and others from neoliberalism.

According to Smith, mercantilists equated silver and gold with wealth. Exhibit A in their case was Thomas Mun's *England's Treasure by Forraign Trade* (1664), which had urged the government to attend to balance of trade as a means of keeping gold and silver from leaving the kingdom. Mun's arguments, although Smith considered them sophistical, had been effective, convincing parliaments, princes, nobles, and country gentlemen that markets had to be protected and industries nurtured. Moreover, Mun and his compatriots had successfully initiated a whole line of faulty thinking. "The wealth of a kingdom," Smith explained in his lectures, "has by almost all authors after Mun been considered as consisting in the gold and silver in it."[2]

But the mercantilists, it turns out, were not such simpletons about money. As Antoin Murphy put it, "Smith's stereotyping of Mun as favouring some bizarre fetishistic hoarding propensity was both inappropriate and disappointing for a writer of his calibre."[3] Equally biting, in its own way, was Mark Blaug's account:

> Once upon a time everyone believed that national prosperity depended upon the accumulation of gold bullion resulting from a favourable balance of payments. A man called Adam Smith denied this and later another man called David Ricardo actually proved that free trade and leaving the balance of payments to take care of itself produced the best of all possible worlds. Thereafter, every schoolboy could expose the fallacies of "mercantilism."[4]

Over fifty years of relentless scholarship has demolished the fallacy that mercantilists were silver fetishists.[5] But it is not as if the ghost of Adam Smith has been exorcised. Far from it. Consider George Stigler's 1983 Nobel lecture, in which he began by outlining what he called "Prescientific Economics: Mercantilism." Ironically, given that he cited none of the historical literature after 1935, Stigler emphasized that mercantilism was prescientific because it did not exhibit cumulative progress over time, or a sense of its own change over time.[6] Stigler notwithstanding, historians of political economy have made some progress. We know now that these authors were more nuanced and more attuned to the real economic challenges of their times than Smith and his followers in the classical school of economics suggested. Scholars of mercantilism responded to these stereotyped critiques by citing chapter and verse from the writings of mercantilist authors.[7] Based on these careful studies, it now seems more than evident that English mercantilists were not silver fetishists.

But there is another problem. Just as there is a long history of labeling mercantilists as simple bullionists, so, too, is there a tradition of treating German cameralism as a subset of mercantilism: "Cameralism—the science of state administration—developed in a sense as a logical extension of Mercantilism"; "Cameralism is the specific version of mercantilism, taught and practiced in the German principalities (*Kleinstaaten*) in the 17th and 18th centuries"; "Cameralists, named after the German royal treasure chamber, the *Kammer*, propounded an extreme form of mercantilism."[8] I have argued elsewhere that this is a mistake, but the long tradition of approaching cameralists as German mercantilists will not go away just because I complain about it; moreover, it is a tradition that has left its marks deep in the fabric of historiography on cameralism.[9] One of the distinguishing features of German cameralism, as opposed to mercantilism, involves its relationship to money—in particular, money as silver coin. We need not demean it as silver fetishism, but cameralism as a doctrine, I argue, was built on its relationship to the silver thaler that circulated through the German lands from 1500 into the nineteenth century.

Dresden, 1719

Prince Friedrich August, the heir apparent to Saxony's throne, was marrying Maria Josepha, the daughter of the Holy Roman emperor; the wedding festivities needed to match, in their splendor, the magnitude of the occasion.[10] And so the Festival of Saturn, the central event in a month-long extravaganza of celebrations in Dresden, had to be perfect. By the light of torches, 1,600 miners and smelters, all in uniform, marched into the *Plauenshen Grund*, the base of a narrow valley outside of Dresden, with shadows dancing on the surrounding cliffs. To the amazement of the spectators, the marching miners and smelters ferried great machines and furnaces with them; one of these, the Great Furnace (*Hohe Ofen*), was not only very large (about seven feet high), but actually *in use* during the parade. Descriptions of the machine read: "A smelting machine, the smelting furnace, to be operated by twelve smelters, among which the first smelter, with a fork, and one hauler, with a poker, went along, adding water and coals, and carrying off the slags; the smelting was actually done during the parade march, and afterward, directly in front of the high lords, pierced and poured out."[11]

The chief mining office (*Obergbergamt*) and the smelters were initially against the plan to include large furnaces in the parade. It seemed too dangerous. The furnace had to be fired up two hours before the event, and if the winds were unfavorable, the lords and ladies would be subjected to smoke and "smelting smell." But the king and his court insisted on it. The mining parade had to be right.[12] August's insistence on *displaying* the operations involved in the production of money, of Saxony's very own coin, revealed the remarkable and uniquely Saxon attitude to silver. Silver coin was not something that you simply hoarded or collected or traded; it was something that you made. The Festival of Saturn carefully displayed the many aspects of labor involved in silver production. Metallurgical knowledge and labor, in all of their manifold divisions, were laid bare.

During the reign of August the Strong, Saxony produced about 4.5 tons of silver each year. The elector got about 27 percent of that yield for himself and his treasury. Seven percent came from the "tenth part."[13] Twenty percent of the elector's yield came from the smelting and assaying operations, which included a sprawling array of smelting huts, assayers, stamping works, and minting operations responsible for preparing the ores that had been extracted from underground. The yields from the mining tithe and the smelting operations were crucial for August II, because he needed huge sums of money—personal money—to pursue his ambitions to be King of Poland. He used that silver from the Saxon mines to bribe and cajole the Polish nobility, so that they would support his candidacy. The entire affair cost August millions of thaler.

Figure 4.1. Das Bergwerksfest im Plauenschen Grund, 1719.

The Saxon estates were generally opposed to August's Polish adventure, largely because his election would involve his conversion to Catholicism. Within this constellation of dynastic scheming, negotiations with the estates, and confessional politics, mining and smelting operations took on special importance. By producing bullion for the treasury, the miners and smelters of the Ore Mountains at the same time produced a measure of independence for their sovereign.[14] Every thaler of Freiberg silver that they extracted and refined meant one thaler less of dependence for the elector, one thaler less that he had to squeeze out of his fractious estates. Moreover, the wealth produced by Saxony's mines—silver, tin, cobalt, copper, iron, and amethyst—helped generate the luxury and splendor for which Saxony was so famous.[15] Today, the glistening treasures of the Green Vault (*Grünes Gewölbe*) in Dresden survive as the legacy of Saxony's mineral politics.

German Silver

If we are talking about money in early modern Germany, then we are talking about silver. At least, that is true for any time after 1486. Earlier than that, it would have been gold. But there was not much gold to be had in the

German lands, so coin shortages had become severe by the last decades of the fifteenth century. In Tirol, where there was native silver in the mountains, they substituted silver for gold—and that is how the first sanctioned silver coin, the *Tiroler Guldiner*, got its name. Tirol was only the beginning. The idea soon spread to silver-rich Saxony, where the coin ordinance of 1500, and the Saxon silver industry it stimulated, laid the groundwork for the thaler, *the* central European coin for the next 271 years and the etymological parent of the dollar.[16]

My focus here will be on the "silver states" of the Holy Roman Empire, the territories that mined, refined, and coined their own silver for use as thaler. These thaler circulated throughout the empire and beyond. Because the German silver states produced coin, and profited from it, their interests differed from other territories in the empire. Most obviously, it was to their advantage to keep the value of silver high, and to avoid an influx of too much foreign coin. In this, their financial interests often diametrically opposed those of other German territories.

There were not many German silver states. Almost all of the silver produced after 1648 came from one of three places: (1) the mines of the Harz Mountains (controlled by Braunschweig-Wolfenbüttel and Electoral Hanover), (2) the mines of the Ore Mountains (Electoral Saxony), (3) and the mines of Habsburg Austria, especially those of "lower Hungary," near Schemnitz (Banská Štiavnica). In these silver-producing centers, mining intensified even as the arrival of Spanish galleons flooded Europe with countless tons of American gold and silver.[17] By the late fourteenth century, the more easily accessible silver veins (that is, those near the surface) had been largely exhausted, and Europe experienced a severe shortage of bullion. By the end of the fifteenth century, as technical improvements allowed mining at greater depth, rich new silver veins were discovered in the same mines that had been abandoned during the twelfth and thirteenth centuries. Ironically, as the mines around Freiberg, Clausthal/Zellerfeld, and Schemnitz began producing unprecedented quantities of silver, the Spanish discovered the Bolivian mines around Potosí, which yielded silver in previously unimagined quantities and helped trigger the dramatic inflation of the sixteenth century.[18] Silver now plummeted to less than half its former value.[19] The inflation, and the concomitant drop in the value of precious metals, caused many smaller mines to be abandoned; domestic production suffered. By the beginning of the Thirty Years War, central Europe's mines were already in sharp decline. By the end of the war, when twenty years of depredation had caused most mines to be abandoned, silver production dropped to its lowest point. It would be another 150 years before the mines again yielded as much silver as they had in the mid sixteenth century.

Because of such economic pressures and social dislocations, the early modern period witnessed a progressive centralization and concentration of

Table 4.1. Average Annual Silver Production in Central Europe (kg), 1545–1800[20]

Years	Electoral Saxony	Hanover/ Braunschweig-Wolfenbüttel	Austrian Habsburg Lands*	Other	Total
1545–60	13,150	3,400	30,000	3,300	49,850
1561–80	9,000	3,500	23,500	2,500	38,500
1581–1600	7,550	4,500	17,000	2,250	31,300
1601–20	5,100	3,550	11,000	1,750	21,400
1621–40	3,100	1,900	8,000	1,000	14,100
1641–60	2,600	2,800	8,000	1,100	14,500
1661–80	2,950	2,900	10,000	1,150	17,000
1681–1700	3,800	5,850	10,000	1,750	21,400
1701–20	4,800	8,050	10,000	2,500	25,350
1721–40	6,500	15,200	12,500	3,500	37,700
1741–60	6,800	10,850	24,000	3,500	45,150
1761–80	7,200	7,900	24,000	3,000	42,100
1781–1800	12,100	7,800	26,000	4,000	49,900

* Includes mining regions in Austria, Bohemia, Hungary, Tirol, and Transylvania.

central Europe's mines, since only larger, concentrated operations could withstand the dramatic drop in the value of silver occasioned by Spanish imports from the Americas. A few great mining districts had come to dominate central European silver production by the later sixteenth and seventeenth centuries. In the Ore Mountains, for example, where rich silver veins had been discovered in the twelfth century, Freiberg became the administrative center of the Saxon mining apparatus.[21] In the Upper Harz Mountains, where the Guelfs and their descendants in Hanover and Braunschweig-Wolfenbüttel exploited an area of rich silver deposits, the towns of Zellerfeld and Clausthal developed into the administrative center of mining.[22] Finally, to the east, in the Carpathians, the legendary silver and gold deposits of lower Hungary helped make Schemnitz the administrative and scientific heart of silver mining in the lands of the Austrian Habsburgs.

Although the by-products of silver production, lead and zinc, gained in significance during the eighteenth century, and although tin, copper, and iron also became more important during this period, silver mining remained paramount.[23] Moreover, centuries of construction and state administration directed specifically at silver extraction shaped the character of all other ore mining well into the nineteenth century.

Financially, the large silver mines of the Harz, the Ore Mountains, and the Carpathians were unusual in the amount of capital expenditure they demanded. Successful mining ventures entailed substantial investment to fund the construction of large water-pumping operations, water tunnels, artificial ponds, extensive smelting works, and other mining infrastructure. Accordingly, states frequently attempted to woo groups of foreign investors—the Dutch were favorites—to provide capital.[24] Another peculiarity of the mines stemmed from the high value of silver ore, which encouraged theft and corruption. The loss of large quantities of silver through corrupt foremen, black market smelters, dishonest contribution collectors, and fraudulent assayers was a chronic and generally acknowledged problem for fiscal officials, who responded by promulgating a dense web of ordinances and administrative structures designed to generate a climate of intensive policing and oversight.[25] This same goal promoted the gradual concentration, consolidation, and centralization of mining operations throughout the German lands.[26] By the late seventeenth century, as territorial rulers strove to consolidate power and financial resources, the mining districts around Freiberg, Clausthal/Zellerfeld, and Schemnitz had become concentrated centers of wealth, natural scientific knowledge, big technology, and intensive policing.

Cameralist mining administration was based on a long-established mineral privilege (*Bergregal*). In the Germanies, the mineral privilege had several sovereign prerogatives associated with it: (1) collecting a part (the "tenth part") of metal yield; (2) administering justice in and around the mines; (3) appointing mining officials; and (4) establishing good order and discipline.[27] Mining officials, the agents of the territorial ruler, were charged with protecting and exploiting his mineral privilege.

In territories with silver ore, the period between the sixteenth and eighteenth centuries witnessed the progressive development of the mining state, a peculiar juridical, political, epistemological, and administrative space in the mining regions of central Europe.[28] In territories heavily dependent on metal ores, the mining state was truly a state within a state. Miners held special privileges from the ruler, forming a class of subjects free from prosecution by the civil courts. Like soldiers or university professors, miners had a claim to special juridical rights. But in return for their special rights and privileges, miners submitted not only to the harsh conditions of their work but also to the complete direction and control of the state's mining officials. In the *Bergstaat*, the territorial ruler and his officials ruled absolutely.

The growth and development of the mining state had great impact on the literature of German cameralism. The most important cameralist authors, those who wrote textbooks for generations of students—Johann Joachim Becher, Johann von Justi, and Joseph von Sonnenfels among them—lived and worked in the German silver states. Moreover, many of them (including Becher and Justi) worked directly in mining and metallurgy. Georg Engelhard von Löhneyß, who wrote about both well-policed mines and good governance, served as chief mining official in Braunschweig-Wolfenbüttel during the early seventeenth century.[29] His 1617 *Report on Mining* became one of the most important early modern texts on German mines and mining, and his *Art of Court, State, and Governance* of 1622 interspersed images and descriptions of mining technology and administration with descriptions of good police. Johann Joachim Becher, whose 1668 *Political Discourse* became a classic cameralist text, was an accomplished alchemist famous for his apparent transmutation of lead into silver at Leopold I's court in 1675. Becher's *Underground Philosophy (Physica Subterranea)*, published one year after his *Discourse*, was, in his own words, a "natural history" of metals.[30] Wilhelm Freyherr von Schröder, another famous seventeenth-century cameralist, succeeded Becher as director of the Manufactures House in Vienna. He, too, experimented with metallurgical chemistry, published on "making gold," and, at the end of his life, was appointed cameral court councilor for the Kingdom of Hungary, probably because of the rich silver and gold deposits in Hungary and *Siebenbürgen* (today's Romania).[31] Veit Ludwig von Seckendorff, dubbed the "Adam Smith of cameralism" by Albion Small early in the twentieth century, served as a privy court and cameral councilor for Ernst of Gotha, where he gained a reputation for skillful financial administration.[32] Seckendorff's 1656 *The German Principality (Teutscher Fürsten Stat)*, probably the most important cameralist text of the seventeenth century, accorded special consideration to mining as a source of income, treating it as the first and most important of the many special privileges and regalia territorial rulers possessed.[33] Philipp Wilhelm von Hörnigk, whose 1684 *Austria above Everything, If Only It Wants to Be (Oesterreich über alles, Wann es nur will)* became a mainstay of cameralist literature, stressed the importance of mining as a source of territorial independence and security.[34]

In the eighteenth century, the bond between cameralists and the mines persisted. Johann von Justi, who served as Imperial Finance and Mining Councilor in Maria Theresa's Austria during the early 1750s, provides the most striking case. While in the service of the empress, Justi was dispatched on inspection tours of mining districts in the Habsburg hereditary lands. Justi retained the title of mining councilor upon his arrival in Göttingen in 1755, and in 1766 he entered Prussian service as chief mining official under Frederick the Great.[35] Other cameralists, like Daniel Gottfried Schreber and Georg Heinrich Zincke, devoted substantial sections of their economic-cameralist journals to mines and mining, and Schreber himself would be recruited, though unsuccessfully, as a Prussian mining official.[36]

The close connection between cameralism and the mines was more than fortuitous. The early modern silver mines were central Europe's great cameralist incubators; treasury and mining officials were the Ur-cameralists. Territorial rulers had special regalian rights that gave them control over metals and other minerals discovered in their lands and, as a rule, their treasury officials oversaw the administration of the mines. Fiscal administrators, who were responsible for the collection, distribution, and increase of the ruler's revenue, thus had an interest in mining as a real and potential source of princely income especially in areas blessed with silver and other metals: Electoral Saxony, Upper Silesia, Hanover, Austria, and Hungary. Moreover, many cameralists came to regard natural sciences like mineralogical chemistry or geognosy as cameral sciences; that is, as knowledge that could maintain and increase mining revenues.[37] Since the ruler's mineral privilege was the most lucrative of regalia in many German territories, it should come as little surprise that many well-known cameralists served as mining and smelting officials.

Justi's half-brother, Christoph Traugott Delius, wrote *the* textbook for aspiring mining officials in Maria Theresa's Austria. "Mining-cameral-science (*Berg-Kammeralwissenschaft*)," he explained there, "is the knowledge, in lands blessed with ore-bearing rock, of how one makes mining prosper, and keeps it prosperous, through wise principles and ordinances, and for the benefit of the state."[38] Regalia, as Delius explained, were the "rights of the highest sovereign authority" over objects which, due to their very nature, belonged to the "general wealth of the state" rather than to private individuals. "Minerals belong to the regalia, and it follows that the ruler has the sole right to construct mines, and to mint gold and silver for general circulation ... and also to mine base metals for the good of the land."[39] Property owners, the local lords of the manor or estate owners, thus had few rights over metals found on their own lands. Territorial rulers, as holders of the mineral privilege, leased their monopoly rights over metals and minerals to certain investor groups. In return, they received payment in the form of established tithes and duties.[40] Like the hereditary domain lands, the mineral privilege was property, and it entitled territorial rulers to collect rent on all silver, gold, copper, tin, cobalt, aluminum, and other metals discovered within their borders.[41]

"All civilized lands," argued Delius, placed the mines directly under the "highest authority and direction of the sovereign." Delius's own rulers, the Austrian Habsburgs, had promulgated laws and issued mining ordinances to declare and publicize the mineral privilege. In the Kingdom of Hungary, for example, home to some of the richest mining districts in all of Europe, Maria Theresa could lay claim to all mines and minerals based on an ordinance issued in the sixteenth century under the Holy Roman Emperor Maximilian II. Maximilian, who retained possession of Royal Hungary in return for a substantial annual tribute to the Ottoman Sultan, had confirmed and established his mineral privilege with a few simple words: "all mines and minerals in the Kingdom of Hungary ... are our sovereign possession."[42]

The logic of the mineral privilege implied a related principle of sovereign oversight and direction. This principle, which came to be known as the "Principle of Direction" (*Direktionsprinzip*), had a dramatic impact on the development of central Europe's mines and mining administration. Simply put, the Principle of Direction was the state's right of direction and supervision over all ore mining and smelting within its borders. The Principle of Direction became a driving force behind the gradual development of the mining state.[43] Rulers who hoped to collect full rent for the use of their mineral possessions, and to increase that rent, had to know precisely the amount of silver, gold, and other metals extracted from the mines in their lands. Moreover, they had to monitor, and encourage, all mining in their territories. The dictates of the Principle of Direction entailed the cultivation of skilled and trustworthy mining officials— the rulers by proxy of the mining state—to represent the territorial ruler. They were the Ur-cameralists of the German lands.

Conclusion

Bullion, as it turns out, was not at the center of English mercantilist political economy, even though Adam Smith and his disciples would have us believe it. But silver *was* at the very core of German cameralism. Not in any simple way, however. German cameralists, no more than English mercantilists, equated value or wealth with heaps of gold and silver. Nevertheless, the German silver states of early modern Europe had an extremely close relationship with their silver; it spawned technologies, cultures, and sciences. And, of most relevance for our purposes, it was at the heart of cameralism, too. If we are to understand cameralism—as a literature and as an early modern administrative culture— then it is time to stop subsuming it under the broader category of mercantilism.

Nor was the discourse of cameralism, as some would have it, only written in the treatises and academic textbooks of the German lands. It was also inscribed in the thousands of mines and adits, or drainage tunnels, which littered the German silver states. Many of these shafts and tunnels, largely the product of simple pick and hammer work, are still there today. If you go underground in the Harz or Ore Mountains, you can still see long stretches of chiseled tunnel walls and ceilings shimmering in the glow of your headlamp.[44] There one finds the telltale etchings of the diggers, and the *Gedingezeichen* of the foremen. These distinctive symbols, carved into the rock at regular intervals, marked the progress of the diggers.[45] And slow progress it was. Each inch of hard rock would have taken one man a full day to chisel away. The vestiges of that world, which now lie largely hidden underground, represent a staggering investment of human labor. To take just one example, the famous *19-Lachter-Stollen*, an adit that stretched almost twelve miles underground, took 139 years to build.[46] It was all done to drain water, so that the miners could go deeper. It was all done for the silver thaler.

Andre Wakefield is Professor of History at Pitzer College. He is the author of *The Disordered Police State: German Cameralism as Science and Practice* (2009) as well as a translation (with Claudine Cohen) of G. W. Leibniz's *Protogaea* (2008).

Notes

1. Adam Smith, *An Inquiry into the Nature and Causes of the Wealth of Nations*, 2 vols., ed. R. H. Campbell, A. S. Skinner, and W. B. Todd (Oxford, 1976), 1: 429–30.
2. Adam Smith, *Lectures on Jurisprudence*, eds. R. L. Meek, D. D. Raphael, and P. G. Stein (Oxford, 1978).
3. Antoin E. Murphy, "Introduction," in *Monetary Theory: 1601–1758*, 6 vols., ed. Antoin E. Murphy (London, 1997), 1: 1–54, here 15.
4. Mark Blaug, "Economic Theory and Economic History in Great Britain, 1650–1776," *Past & Present* 28 (1964): 111–16.
5. The list goes on and on, but important early contributions include: J. D. Gould, "The Trade Crisis of the Early 1620s and English Economic Thought," *Journal of Economic History* 15 (1955): 121–33; Barry Supple, "Currency and Commerce in the Early Seventeenth Century," *Economic History Review* 10 (1957): 239–55; and R. W. K. Hinton, "The Mercantile System in the Time of Thomas Mun," *Journal of Economic History* 7 (1955): 277–90. See also Lars Magnusson, *Mercantilism: The Shaping of an Economic Language* (London, 1994).
6. George J. Stigler, "Nobel Lecture: The Process and Progress of Economics," *Journal of Political Economy* 91, no. 4 (1983): 529–45.
7. See Andrea Finkelstein, *Harmony and the Balance: An Intellectual History of Seventeenth-Century English Economic Thought* (Ann Arbor, MI, 2000).
8. Mark Perlman and Charles R. McCann Jr., *The Pillars of Economic Understanding: Ideas and Traditions* (Ann Arbor, MI, 1998), 127; Horst Claus Recktenwald, "Cameralism," in *The New Palgrave: A Dictionary of Economics*, ed. John Newell, Murray Milgate, Peter Newman, and Robert H. I. Palgrave (London, 1987), 1: 313–14; Murray N. Rothbard, *Economic Thought before Adam Smith* (Auburn, AL, 1995), 492.
9. Andre Wakefield, "Cameralism: A German Alternative to Mercantilism," in *Mercantilism Reimagined: Political Economy in Early Modern Britain and Its Empire*, ed. Philip J. Stern and Carl Wennerlind (Oxford, 2013), 134–50.
10. On the celebrations in Dresden, see Cornelia Jöchner, "Dresden, 1719: Planetenfeste, kulturelles Gedächtnis und die Öffnung der Stadt," *Marburger Jahrbuch für Kunstwissenschaft* 24 (1997): 249–70; H. Winckelmann, "Das Saturnfest und der Berghäuerzug 1719," *Der Anschnitt* 10 (1958): 3–10.
11. Eberhard Neubert, "Ein sächsischer Bergaufzug im Jahre 1719," in *Die historische Bergparade anläßlich des Saturnusfestes im Jahre 1719*, ed. Eberhard Wächtler und Eberhard Neubert (Leipzig, 1982), 13–18.
12. Neubert, "Ein sächsischer Bergaufzug," 17; Ingrid S. Weber, *Planetenfeste Augusts des Starken zur Hochzeit des Kurprinzen 1719* (Munich, 1985), 75–81.
13. On the *Bergzehnt*, see Adolf Laube, *Studien über den erzgebirgischen Silberbergbau von 1470 bis 1546* (Berlin, 1974).
14. Fritz Kaphan, "Kurfürst und kursächsische Stände im 17. und beginnenden 18. Jahrhundert," *Neues Archiv für sächsische Geschichte* 43 (1922): 67–79.

15. Eberhard Wächtler, "Kursachsen zu Beginn des 18. Jahrhunderts," in *Die historische Bergparade anläßlich des Saturnusfestes im Jahre 1719*, ed. Eberhard Wächtler and Eberhard Neubert (Leipzig, 1982), 8–12.
16. Herbert Rittmann, *Deutsche Geldgeschichte 1484–1914* (Munich, 1975); Tristan Weber, *Die sächsische Münzprägung von 1500 bis 1571: Eine quantitative Studie* (Regenstauf, 2010).
17. S. M. H. Bozorgnia, *The Role of Precious Metals in European Economic Development* (Westport, CT, 1988), 164–65. Most European silver mining outside of the Holy Roman Empire and Austrian Habsburg lands took place in Scandinavia. Silver mining in England, France, and Spain remained negligible. See Adolf Soetbeer, *Edelmetall-Produktion und Wertverhältniss zwischen Gold und Silber seit der Entdeckung Amerika's bis zur Gegenwart* (Gotha, 1879) for a general overview. Also, John U. Nef, "Silver Production in Central Europe, 1450–1618," *Journal of Political Economy* 49 (1941): 575–91.
18. Soetbeer, *Edelmetall-Produktion*, 70–71; Bozorgnia, *Precious Metals*, 168–70.
19. Bozorgnia, *Precious Metals*, 169; John U. Nef, "Mining and Metallurgy in Medieval Civilization," in *The Cambridge Economic History of Europe*, vol. 2: *Trade and Industry in the Middle Ages*, ed. M. M. Postan and E. E. Rich (Cambridge, 1952), 429–92.
20. Soetbeer, *Edelmetall-Produktion*. For detailed commentary on and criticism of Soetbeer's estimates, see Nef, "Silver Production in Central Europe." Individual studies provide more reliable figures for individual regions. Christoph Bartels recent study of mining in the upper Harz, for example, includes extensive estimates of annual silver production. See Christoph Bartels, *Vom frühneuzeitlichen Montangewerbe zur Bergbauindustrie: Erzbergbau im Oberharz, 1635–1866* (Bochum, 1992).
21. Hans Baumgärtel, "Bergbau und Absolutismus: Der sächsische Bergbau in der zweiten Hälfte des 18. Jahrhunderts und Massnahmen zu seiner Verbesserung nach dem Siebenjährigen Kriege," *Freiberger Forschungshefte* D44 (1963): 26–33.
22. Bartels, *Vom frühneuzeitlichen Montangewerbe zur Bergbauindustrie*, 46–86.
23. Baumgärtel, "Bergbau und Absolutismus," 10.
24. Saxony was, in this respect, distinct from administration in the Harz Mountains, where the private *Gewerken* played a smaller role than in Saxony. See Bartels, *Vom frühneuzeitlichen Montangewerbe zur Bergbauindustrie*, 476; Hans Joachim Kraschewski, "Zur Arbeitsverfassung des Goslarer Bergbaus am Rammelsberg im 15. und 16. Jahrhundert," in *Bergbau und Arbeitsrecht: Die Arbeitsverfassung im Europäischen Bergbau des Mittelalters und der frühen Neuzeit*, ed. Karl Heinz Ludwig and Peter Sika (Vienna, 1989), 275–304.
25. See, for example, Johann Christian Lünig, ed., *Codex Augusteus oder Neuvermehrtes Corpus Juris Saxonici* (Leipzig, 1724), 377–488.
26. There were also significant technological and economic reasons for the concentration of mining operations. See Otfried Wagenbreth and Eberhard Wächtler, eds., *Der Freiberger Bergbau: Technische Denkmale und Geschichte* (Leipzig, 1985).
27. Veit Ludwig von Seckendorff, *Teutscher Fürsten Stat* (Frankfurt, 1665; reprinted Glashütten, 1976), 1: 394–96.
28. On Saxony, see Baumgärtel, "Bergbau und Absolutismus," 25–51; Wolfhard Weber, *Innovationen im Frühindustriellen deutschen Bergbau und Hüttenwesen—Friedrich Anton von Heynitz* (Göttingen, 1976), 132–33, 137–41. On how the parade dress of miners and officials reflected the structure of, and changes in, mining administration, see Karl-Ewald Fritzsch and Friedrich Sieber, *Bergmännische Trachten des 18.*

Jahrhunderts im Erzgebirge und im Mansfeldischen (Berlin, 1957). On the Harz, see Bartels, *Vom frühneuzeitlichen Montangewerbe zur Bergbauindustrie*; Hans Joachim Kraschewski, "Das Direktionsprinzip im Harzrevier des 17. Jahrhunderts und seine wirtschaftspolitische Bedeutung," in *Vom Bergbau- zum Industrierevier*, ed. Ekkehard Westermann (Stuttgart, 1995). On the Austrian lands, see Karl-Heinz Ludwig, "Der Bergbau zur Zeit des Absolutismus," in *Paracelsus (1493–1541): Keines andern Knecht*, ed. Heinz Dopsch (Salzburg, 1993).

29. *Allgemeine deutsche Biographie (ADB)* 19: 133–35.
30. See Pamela Smith, *The Business of Alchemy: Science and Culture in the Holy Roman Empire* (Princeton, NJ, 1994).
31. *ADB* 32: 530–33; Wilhelm Roscher, *Geschichte der National-Oekonomik in Deutschland* (Munich, 1874), 294.
32. Albion Small, *The Cameralists: The Pioneers of German Social Polity* (Chicago, 1909), 285; *ADB* 33: 519–24.
33. Seckendorff, *Teutscher Fürsten Stat*, 1: 394–415.
34. Philipp Wilhelm von Hörnigk, *Oesterreich über alles, Wann es nur will* (Vienna, 1684); *ADB* 13: 157–58; Roscher, *Geschichte der National-Oekonomik in Deutschland*, 290; Small, *The Cameralists*, 130–31.
35. Andre Wakefield, *The Disordered Police State: German Cameralism as Science and Practice* (Chicago, 2009), 49–110.
36. See, for example, Daniel Gottfried Schreber, *Neue Sammlung verschiedener in die Cameralwissenschaften einschlagender Abhandlungen und Urkunden, auch andrer Nachrichten* (Bützow, 1762–65); also Georg Heinrich Zincke, *Cameralisten-Bibliothek* (Leipzig, 1751–52).
37. Eighteenth-century proposals and plans for cameralist faculties and academies, for example, consistently included mineralogy and metallurgical chemistry (i.e. the mining sciences) as auxiliary sciences for aspiring cameralists, even in regions, like Baden, not especially known for their mineral wealth. See Wakefield, *The Disordered Police State*.
38. Christoph T. Delius, *Anleitung zu der Bergbaukunst nach ihrer Theorie und Ausübung, nebst einer Abhandlung von den Grundsätzen der Berg-Kammeralwissenschaft* (Vienna, 1773), "Abhandlung," 3. (The "Abhandlung" on mining-cameral-science appears at the end of Delius's textbook and has its own pagination.)
39. Ibid., 14–15.
40. In Saxony, as elsewhere, the most important of these levies was the *Zehnt*, which, according to tradition, bound the *Gewerken* to pledge a tenth of all ore as tribute to the ruler. Though the *Zehnt* hovered around 10 percent of total silver yield for centuries, it generally amounted to less than that since one had to make concessions to the *Gewerken* for maintaining the "contribution mines" (*Zubußgruben*); i.e. for maintaining unprofitable mines and infrastructure. *Quatembergeld*, originally instituted as a fund for paying mining officials, was a small constant tax of four to six groschen per mine per season. *Schlagschatz*, formally a fee paid to defray the cost of minting coins, derived from the minting privilege of the sovereign. In actuality, however, income from the minting privilege far outstripped the costs of minting. The *Schlagschatz*, while very high in the fifteenth century, gradually sank after that. By 1763, it was only eight groschen per mark of silver (320 g = 1 mark of silver), or about 2 percent of income. Baumgärtel, "Bergbau und Absolutismus," 31–33.

41. The most important exception was coal, which was exempted from princely monopoly rights by the 1743 *Steinkohlenmandat*, a decree granting local property owners rights over the coal deposits on their lands.
42. Delius, *Anleitung zu der Bergbaukunst*, "Abhandlung," 15.
43. See Johann Köhler, "Die Keime des Kapitalismus im sächsischen Silberbergbau (1168 bis zum 1550)," *Freiberger Forschungshefte* D13 (1955): 106–7; Baumgärtel, "Bergbau und Absolutismus," 25–26.
44. See Andre Wakefield, "The Hardrock Mines of Early Modern Germany," *Earth Sciences History* 31, no. 2 (2012): 326–31.
45. On the symbols used by *Steiger* in the Harz mines, see Wolfgang Lampe, "Stuffenzeichen im Harzer Bergbau," *Ausbeute: Mitteilungsblatt der Arbeitsgemeinschaft Harzer Montangeschichte* 3 (2008): 26–30.
46. Wilfried Ließmann, *Historischer Bergbau im Harz: Kurzführer*, 3rd ed. (Heidelberg, 2010), 67–75.

Bibliography

Bartels, Christoph. *Vom frühneuzeitlichen Montangewerbe zur Bergbauindustrie: Erzbergbau im Oberharz, 1635–1866*. Bochum, 1992.

Baumgärtel, Hans. "Bergbau und Absolutismus: Der sächsische Bergbau in der zweiten Hälfte des 18. Jahrhunderts und Massnahmen zu seiner Verbesserung nach dem Siebenjährigen Kriege." *Freiberger Forschungshefte* D44 (1963): 26–33.

Blaug, Mark. "Economic Theory and Economic History in Great Britain, 1650–1776." *Past & Present* 28 (1964): 111–16.

Bozorgnia, S. M. H. *The Role of Precious Metals in European Economic Development*. Westport, CT, 1988.

Delius, Christoph T. *Anleitung zu der Bergbaukunst nach ihrer Theorie und Ausübung, nebst einer Abhandlung von den Grundsätzen der Berg-Kammeralwissenschaft*. Vienna, 1773.

Finkelstein, Andrea. *Harmony and the Balance: An Intellectual History of Seventeenth-Century English Economic Thought*. Ann Arbor, MI, 2000.

Fritzsch, Karl-Ewald, and Friedrich Sieber. *Bergmännische Trachten des 18. Jahrhunderts im Erzgebirge und im Mansfeldischen*. Berlin, 1957.

Gould, J. D. "The Trade Crisis of the Early 1620s and English Economic Thought." *Journal of Economic History* 15 (1955): 121–33.

Hinton, R. W. K. "The Mercantile System in the Time of Thomas Mun." *Journal of Economic History* 7 (1955): 277–90.

Hörnigk, Philipp Wilhelm von. *Oesterreich über alles, Wann es nur will*. Vienna, 1684.

Jöchner, Cornelia. "Dresden, 1719: Planetenfeste, kulturelles Gedächtnis und die Öffnung der Stadt." *Marburger Jahrbuch für Kunstwissenschaft* 24 (1997): 249–70.

Kaphan, Fritz. "Kurfürst und kursächsische Stände im 17. und beginnenden 18. Jahrhundert." *Neues Archiv für sächsische Geschichte* 43 (1922): 67–79.

Köhler, Johann. "Die Keime des Kapitalismus im sächsischen Silberbergbau (1168 bis zum 1550)." *Freiberger Forschungshefte* D13 (1955): 106–7.

Kraschewski, Hans Joachim. "Das Direktionsprinzip im Harzrevier des 17. Jahrhunderts und seine wirtschaftspolitische Bedeutung." In *Vom Bergbau- zum Industrierevier*, edited by Ekkehard Westermann, 125–50. Stuttgart, 1995.

———. "Zur Arbeitsverfassung des Goslarer Bergbaus am Rammelsberg im 15. und 16. Jahrhundert." In *Bergbau und Arbeitsrecht: Die Arbeitsverfassung im Europäischen Bergbau des Mittelalters und der frühen Neuzeit*, edited by Karl Heinz Ludwig and Peter Sika, 275–305. Vienna, 1989.

Krünitz, Johann Georg. *Oekonomishe Encyklopädie, oder allgemeines System der Staats-, Stadt-, Haus- und Landwirthschaft*, vol. 17. Berlin, 1779.

Lampe, Wolfgang. "Stuffenzeichen im Harzer Bergbau." *Ausbeute: Mitteilungsblatt der Arbeitsgemeinschaft Harzer Montangeschichte* 3 (2008): 26–30.

Laube, Adolf. *Studien über den erzgebirgischen Silberbergbau von 1470 bis 1546*. Berlin, 1974.

Ließmann, Wilfried. *Historischer Bergbau im Harz: Kurzführer*, 3rd ed. Heidelberg, 2010.

Ludwig, Karl-Heinz. "Der Bergbau zur Zeit des Absolutismus." In *Paracelsus (1493–1541): Keines andern Knecht*, edited by Heinz Dopsch, 311–17. Salzburg, 1993.

Lünig, Johann, Christian, ed. *Codex Augusteus oder Neuvermehrtes Corpus Juris Saxonici*. Leipzig, 1724.

Magnusson, Lars. *Mercantilism: The Shaping of an Economic Language*. London, 1994.

Murphy, Antoin E. "Introduction." In *Monetary Theory: 1601–1758*, 6 vols, edited by Antoin E. Murphy.1: 1–54. London, 1997.

Nef, John U. "Silver Production in Central Europe, 1450–1618." *Journal of Political Economy* 49 (1941): 575–91.

Neubert, Eberhard. "Ein sächsischer Bergaufzug im Jahre 1719." In *Die historische Bergparade anläßlich des Saturnusfestes im Jahre 1719*, edited by Eberhard Wächtler and Eberhard Neubert, 13–19. Leipzig, 1982.

Perlman, Mark, and Charles R. McCann Jr. *The Pillars of Economic Understanding: Ideas and Traditions*. Ann Arbor, MI, 1998.

Recktenwald, Horst Claus. "Cameralism." In *The New Palgrave: A Dictionary of Economics*, edited by John Newell, Murray Milgate, Peter Newman, and Robert H. I. Palgrave, 1: 313–14. London, 1987.

Rittmann, Herbert. *Deutsche Geldgeschichte 1484–1914*. Munich, 1975.

Roscher, Wilhelm. *Geschichte der National-Oekonomik in Deutschland*. Munich, 1874.

Rothbard, Murray N. *Economic Thought before Adam Smith*. Auburn, AL, 1995.

Schreber, Daniel Gottfried. *Neue Sammlung verschiedener in die Cameralwissenschaften einschlagender Abhandlungen und Urkunden, auch andrer Nachrichten*. Bützow, 1762–65.

Seckendorff, Veit Ludwig von. *Teutscher Fürsten Stat*. Frankfurt, 1665; reprinted Glashütten, 1976.

Small, Albion. *The Cameralists: The Pioneers of German Social Polity*. Chicago, 1909.

Smith, Adam. *An Inquiry into the Nature and Causes of the Wealth of Nations*, 2 vols, edited by R. H. Campbell, A. S. Skinner, and W. B. Todd. Oxford, 1976.

———. *Lectures on Jurisprudence*, edited by R. L. Meek, D. D. Raphael, and P. G. Stein. Oxford, 1978.

Smith, Pamela. *The Business of Alchemy: Science and Culture in the Holy Roman Empire*. Princeton, NJ, 1994.

Soetbeer, Adolf. *Edelmetall-Produktion und Wertverhältniss zwischen Gold und Silber seit der Entdeckung Amerika's bis zur Gegenwart*. Gotha, 1879.

Stigler, George J. "Nobel Lecture: The Process and Progress of Economics." *Journal of Political Economy* 91, no. 4 (1983): 529–45.

Supple, Barry. "Currency and Commerce in the Early Seventeenth Century." *Economic History Review* 10 (1957): 239–55.

Wächtler, Eberhard. "Kursachsen zu Beginn des 18. Jahrhunderts." In *Die historische Bergparade anläßlich des Saturnusfestes im Jahre 1719*, edited by Eberhard Wächtler and Eberhard Neubert, 1–12. Leipzig, 1982.

Wagenbreth, Otfried, and Eberhard Wächtler, eds. *Der Freiberger Bergbau: Technische Denkmale und Geschichte*. Leipzig, 1985.

Wakefield, Andre. *The Disordered Police State: German Cameralism as Science and Practice*. Chicago, 2009.

———. "The Hardrock Mines of Early Modern Germany." *Earth Sciences History* 31, no. 2 (2012): 326–31.

———. "Cameralism: A German Alternative to Mercantilism." In *Mercantilism Reimagined: Political Economy in Early Modern Britain and Its Empire*, edited by Philip J. Stern and Carl Wennerlind, 134–50. Oxford, 2013.

Weber, Ingrid S. *Planetenfeste Augusts des Starken zur Hochzeit des Kurprinzen 1719*. Munich, 1985.

Weber, Tristan. *Die sächsische Münzprägung von 1500 bis 1571: Eine quantitative Studie*. Regenstauf, 2010.

Weber, Wolfhard. *Innovationen im Frühindustriellen deutschen Bergbau und Hüttenwesen—Friedrich Anton von Heynitz*. Göttingen, 1976.

Winckelmann, H. "Das Saturnfest und der Berghäuerzug 1719." *Der Anschnitt* 10 (1958): 3–10.

Zincke, Georg Heinrich. *Cameralisten-Bibliothek*. Leipzig, 1751–52.

CHAPTER FIVE

"All That Glitters Is Not Gold, But..."
German Responses to the Financial Bubbles of 1720

EVE ROSENHAFT

The everyday economy of early modern Germans, as of most Europeans of the period, was shaped by practices designed to compensate for limitations on the supply of metal coinage. The many forms of borrowing and lending that flourished in preindustrial Europe can be understood in this light, whether, like purchasing on credit, pawning goods, and neighbor-to-neighbor lending, they contributed to the subsistence of peasants and city dwellers or, like letters of credit and bills of exchange, they kept the wheels of a merchant economy turning.[1] In the opening lines of a pamphlet published in Leipzig in 1720, Paul Jacob Marperger remarked on the shortage of coin that his readers were suffering at the time, observing that if Homer were to arrive with the Nine Muses in tow and offer to recite his epics, the first thing people would ask was whether they had brought any hard cash with them. Marperger went on to list the ways in which people with some money had learned to increase their wealth by looking to the future rather than relying on what they might have in their pockets. He cited investment practices that included insurances, bottomry, buying "futures" in agricultural produce, the purchase of shares in domestic monopolies, and—particularly meaningful for his Saxon readership—buying and selling shares in mines (known as *Kuxe*).[2]

Marperger was reminding his readers of familiar practices in order to introduce something that was a novelty to most Germans: the business of buying and selling stock (*Actien*) in overseas trading companies. More particularly, he was trying to explain to them what was going on in Paris. The years 1718–22 were those of the Mississippi Bubble, based in Paris, and the South Sea Bubble, with its focus in London. Both originated in the efforts of governments to deal with heavy indebtedness following the War of the Spanish Succession by deploying joint-stock trading companies to capitalize the debt. In Paris, the Scot John Law, adviser to the French Regent, used the occasion to launch a radical modernization project; he established a national bank and sought to fund it through stock issues against the French India Company's project for the settlement and exploitation of colonial territories in America. Both the Mississippi and the South Sea schemes led to waves of speculative trading in company shares that ended in spectacular failure.[3] A plethora of textual and visual images of the locations of the respective stock markets, Exchange Alley in London and rue Quincampoix in Paris, established the vision of a new epoch in financial culture, characterized by the participation of ever-wider sectors of the population. And the two bubbles had repercussions all over Europe. For most literate Germans, the events of those years constituted their introduction to the world of stock trading, and this chapter explores the ways in which information and imaginative visions of that world circulated among them, focusing on responses to the Mississippi scheme.

In opening his pamphlet with observations on the familiar problem of how to make a little cash go a long way, Marperger put his finger on a central promise of the two schemes. In the French case, the establishment of a paper-money regime was at the center of Law's project, and in the crisis involved a policy of forcibly exchanging coin for paper. Key to the internal dynamics of both the bubbles, and to the discourses of disillusionment that emerged when they burst, was the notion of "paper credit"—a phrase that signaled a wider shift in which the nature of money was implicated as part of a threatened destabilizing of measures of value. What changed hands in a stock transaction was at most a piece of paper, and often not even that, because under normal circumstances, the transfer of shares was simply an accounting procedure. Beyond this, "paper" signified a move away from concrete and tangible relationships in economic transactions. The paper documents that recorded traditional credit relations generally registered investments in material objects or direct transactions among individuals known to each other, and often incurred obligations on the part of the creditor or investor as well as the debtor; the link with materiality was transparent, and trust was placed (credit resided) in real people who could in principle be called on to fulfill their obligations.[4] The legitimacy of paper money depended on trust in a state or a system—indeed, in the paper itself—while the wealth generated through the trade in company stock bore little relation to any underlying material value.

Unlike the French and English, Germans very largely played the role of intrigued but disinterested observers in this development. The traces left by the events in German print culture indicate, however, that their imaginations were mobilized. Moreover, while in the wake of the crash "Mississippi" became a watchword for folly and gullibility in financial affairs, for most of 1719 and 1720, German reportage and comment took a positive or at any rate neutral approach to Law's experiment, reflecting equally a popular interest in colorful anecdotes and the insight that some educated publicists had into the politico-economic logic of Law's system. More imaginative forms of representation show Germans engaging with central problems of the crisis and the power of "paper," including questions of the personal and the impersonal, firsthand knowledge, trust, and the shifting meanings of credit. But what dominates German Mississippi texts (even when they discussed paper) is a set of reflections on the relationships between "here" and "there," the local and the global. A key feature of German pamphlet and periodical accounts is the way in which they combined a project of teaching the public about the nature of stock trading with encouragements to reflect specifically on Germans' position in a globalizing world: what Germans were observing in London and Paris was the first crisis of a system that linked the global market in goods to an increasingly integrated Atlantic financial market, and 1720 posed the question of how, if at all, they might partake of its promise as well as of its risks.

There is some evidence for direct financial involvement of Germans in the bubbles of 1720, but also that it was limited to particular circles. A press report of mid 1720 speaks of Hamburg investors purchasing South Sea stock through "good friends" in London,[5] and in other respects, Hamburg features as a key site of cultural transfer in financial practices. The great bubbles found a little echo there in a brief episode of the summer of 1720, when a group of merchants began to sell stock in a new insurance company; the anxious city fathers of Hamburg brought the project to an end within six weeks.[6] Of the twenty-nine individuals on record as holding South Sea stock who were based in the German lands, most had family connections that linked them to international commercial and information networks, including the dynastic networks that connected the royal courts of Britain, France, and the German principalities.[7]

Contemporary publications, however, indicate that the wider German public was at least curious about what was going on. By 1720, the German lands were well served by numerous news sheets and intelligencers, some appearing more than once a week. Produced in more than thirty cities, these carried local, supra-regional, and international news and were distributed well beyond their places of publication through the imperial postal system. Readers in Hamburg, who had at least four intelligencers to choose from as well as a dedicated financial press carrying details of exchange rates and stock prices, were no doubt among the first to get the news from abroad.[8] But newspapers all over the country carried bulletins about events in Paris; during 1720 the Halle *Weekly Account* (*Wöchentliche Relation*), brought news of Law and his scheme in all but seven weeks of the year. Other periodicals reported less swiftly but often in greater detail. Chief among these was Leipzig's *European Fama* (*Europäische Fama*). It reported from all over the world in irregular issues (eight were published in 1719, twelve in 1720, and nine in 1721), each of which focused on one or two key regions or major diplomatic or military events. It devoted seven reports to the Mississippi scheme, beginning with a long account in the autumn of 1719 and ending in mid 1721 with a kind of obituary. By early 1721, when reports on Mississippi were being paired with accounts of the South Sea Bubble in the *Fama*'s pages, its tone was distinctly negative: "For the most part Germany has observed the sufferings of its neighbors from afar, but now it is more to be hoped than to be expected that it will remain unaffected by the disorder that reigns abroad." Still, the *Fama*'s first report on Law's scheme was positive: it opened by observing how Paris was crowded with foreigners seeking to make a fortune and went on to detail the apparently unending supply of cash in circulation as well as the plan to put the unemployed to work, commenting: "This is what the cleverness of a thoughtful Regent can achieve!"[9]

A third periodical genre that covered the Paris events was the "Supplements" to Johann Hübner's *Historical, Genealogical and Geographic Questions* (*Historische, Genealogische und Geographische Fragen*). The *Questions* was an encyclopedic serial covering the history of the world; the "Supplements" appeared in the form of annual reviews of events, with the volume for the years 1716–19 published in 1726 and for 1720–23 published in 1728. Hübner thus took advantage of hindsight to begin his reporting on Law's system in the 1718 volume, but like the *Fama*, Hübner's "Supplements" succeed in maintaining the "newsy" feel of information which by the time of publication was no longer news.[10]

In addition to these periodicals, there survives a corpus of books and pamphlets that carried information about Law's system to German readers. The French translation of Law's *Money and Trade Considered*, published in the Hague in 1720, was in circulation in Germany (the one extant copy to which we can attach an original owner belonged to the Huguenot governess of Frederick the Great and his sisters), and it appeared in a German translation that autumn.[11] The publication history of these works is itself an index of the level of public interest in the theme "Mississippi": a *Historical and Geographical Description of the Splendid Land Louisiana Lying along the Great Mississippi River in North America* (*Historische und geographische Beschreibung des am großen Flusses Mississipi in Nord-America gelegenen herrlichen Landes Louisiana*; hereafter *HGB*), by the jobbing scholar and journalist Gottfried Zenner, was first offered for sale in January 1720; in the course of that year it went through three editions. The third edition was still being offered for sale in the autumn of 1721, and survives in at least three variants.[12] The anonymous *Curious Observations on the State of France* (*Curieuse Anmerckungen über den Staat von Franckreich*) first came on the market in the spring of 1720 and was still selling in September 1721. Christian Gottfried Hoffmann's *Present Condition of the Finances in France* (*Gegenwärtiger Zustand derer Finantzen in Frankreich*) went on sale as an independent item in September 1720 and remained on the market for at least a year; it was also available as a supplement to the *European Fama*.[13] A further publication of 1720 was the anonymous

Reflections on Mr Law's New System of Finance (*Reflexions über Mr Laws neues Systema der Financen*).¹⁴ Finally, among the most ubiquitous works of 1720 is Paul Jacob Marperger's eight-page pamphlet cited in the introduction. Entitled *Brief Remarks on the World-Renowned Mississippi Stock-Trading in Paris* (*Kurtze Remarques über den jetziger Zeit weltberuffenen Misisippischen Actien-Handel in Paris*), this work exists in at least five variants, of which two are dated Leipzig 1720; it is quite possible that the first draft was produced as early as the end of 1719. Marperger followed this with a ten-page continuation. The "feedback effect" of rapidly circulating news media can be seen in the revisions to *HGB*, which may be the result of interventions by Marperger himself; among other revisions, both the second and third editions incorporate verbatim the last two pages of the *Brief Remarks*.¹⁵

More generally, German Mississippi texts display a hybrid and syncretic character that is in many ways typical of late baroque informational and encyclopedic literature. They incorporate extracts from one another and from other printed and oral reports, often reproducing the same details, tales, or tropes; a letter home from a colonist depicting the satisfactions of life in Louisiana, actually a piece of propaganda by the French India Company, was frequently reprinted. Characteristic of the period, too, is the fact that Mississippi texts often place side-by-side material from different sources, of different kinds and with contradictory messages, sometimes explicitly inviting the reader to note the contrast and sometimes entirely without comment.¹⁶

Hybridity and intertextuality crossing national and linguistic boundaries were also features of the wider field of printed works on Law's system, however, and German Mississippi texts participated in an international circulation of information, argument, and imagery. French, German, English, and Dutch accounts often served as intertexts for one another. There were genuinely bilingual offerings, and there were texts that purported to be more foreign than they actually were. Sometimes the exotic attribution was manifestly playful, as when the pamphlet *Curious Observations* was given the imprint "Mississippi State Printing House." *Reflections on Mr Laws' New System* is allegedly translated from the French, but it concludes with a "letter" from a Dutch writer promoting the Dutch General Assurance Company that was one of the by-products of the boom. There were genuine translations: A Dutch version of *HGB*, attributed to Marperger, was published in 1721 as the appendix to a translation of Law's *Money and Trade Considered*.¹⁷ Popular verses circulating in Paris found their way into German texts in original French versions: each of the editions of *HGB* closes with the text of the song "Le Mississippi"—and in one of the editions of his *Brief Remarks*, Marperger made a point of criticizing that version as "very corrupt and distorted" and providing his own rendition.¹⁸ The Paris correspondent of the *European Fama* quoted five other songs. The rise and fall of the Mississippi scheme was a pan-European event in the realm of the popular imagination as well as in the world of finance. It gave ordinary readers the chance to air their national stereotypes, but also a new chance to reflect on the wider world and their place in it.

German publicists nevertheless recognized that their own readers had particular interests and particular needs. In *Curious Observations*, a dedication addressed to Law declares "All Europe is watching you," and proceeds to enumerate the responses of different nations to his scheme: "Germany admires the boldness of your undertakings but still cannot get used to them, and so it shouts for *Fama* and *Mercurius* to deliver the news in detail. Some whose names could recently be read on the Leipzig exchange are even hurrying to Paris."[19] Germans know where to look for information, the author tells us (*Fama* and *Mercurius* may be generic terms for circulating rumor and news, but they were also newspaper titles). A note of disapproval sounds in this text of spring 1720; it would be universal by the autumn, when Mississippi stock prices were in free-fall. In the form of a close discursive association between the term *Actie* and illegitimate speculation or profiteering, this tone persisted in German lexica well into the nineteenth century, and may be attributable to the outcome of the crisis itself.[20] In 1720, however, it was generally agreed that Germans needed to have the whole business explained to them. The Halle *Weekly Account* was relatively sober and circumstantial in reporting the rise and fall of stock prices, the politics that lay behind them, and their more colorful social consequences. Its first accounts offered no critique of Law's system. Early in 1720, it addressed the perceived ignorance of its readers:

> Since the unprecedented events associated with the current trade in stock [*Actien-Handel*] in France are causing so much excitement in most of Europe, and many people don't have a clear understanding of the business, we wanted to explain in brief what we have been able to learn and understand, until such time as we are able to provide more detailed and accurate information. There are actually two important things here: First, to show what is meant by the word stock and what stock is really like. And second, what the reason is for the extraordinary rise in stock prices in France.[21]

Among the pamphleteers, it was Marperger who took the most consistently matter-of-fact approach, offering readers a thoughtful account of the motivation for the scheme and the workings of the stock market. Marperger was a well-known and highly prolific author of instructional works on economic and commercial subjects. He is in many respects a liminal figure. Described by his own contemporaries as a *Polyhistor*, a term applied to the relatively indiscriminate compilers of the seventeenth century, he was also acknowledged in his own time as a contributor to the *Kameralwissenschaften*.[22] In fact, in the course of a career that took him to France, Austria, and Denmark, he not only became an admirer and translator of French commercial policy and literature, but also associated with and learned from the leading Austrian cameralists of the first generation. In 1712, he was appointed by the elector of Saxony to establish a Commercial Commission tasked with carrying out a general economic reform, but like many a cameralist before and since, he found his ambitions systematically frustrated. It seems likely that the *Brief Remarks* was one of a series of monthly pamphlets that he was self-publishing at the time in order to keep solvent while awaiting unpaid salary. What principally distinguished Marperger from the "canonical cameralists" was a supra-territorial breadth of vision in which a deliberate address to a middle-class readership combined with a project of commercial enlightenment aimed at lifting the whole of *Teutschland* (his term) out of its backwardness.[23]

Accordingly, Marperger's 1720 writings are distinguished by a detailed understanding of the nature of the stock market as well as of the logic of Law's scheme. He is the only author who acknowledges that the price of stock in the Company is not related to the value of the land in Louisiana, and he is careful to distinguish among three types of market participants: those who invest for the sake of interest or dividend income, speculators, and the agents of the bank acting to drive up prices. He also provides a step-by-step account of how stock is bought and sold, using the Dutch East India Company as a model.

But the *Brief Remarks* are also evidence of a wider cosmopolitanization of the German imagination—or at any rate an explicit negotiation between provincialism and cosmopolitanism—that can be observed in the Mississippi crisis. Marperger's view of the Mississippi scheme was generally positive. In the *Continuation* that followed the publication of *Brief Remarks* (which among other things gives detailed critical attention to Law's paper money policies), he berates Germans for their provincialism:

> All that glitters is not gold, but not all Columbian projects are a waste of time, although many people who are not at home outside their four walls cannot understand this. From that point of view I have good grounds for my opinion that in some countries particularly well endowed by nature this kind of *Actien-Handel* ... may redound to the good of a prince and his subjects.... So every such land has its own Mississippi in itself and need not seek it many hundred miles over the sea, still less seek to achieve it through means that give the public cause for dispute.[24]

The idea that "every land has its own Mississippi in itself" is a call to Germans to put their own house in order, and may appear to be an explicit dismissal of colonial projects. Yet this dismissal is undermined by the way in which Marperger draws his readers' attention, at the very end of the text, to the materiality and geography of France's American colonies. He urges them to consider this map.

Figure 5.1. Map of France's American colonies, engraved by Moritz Bodenehr, from P. J. M. Marperger *Fortsetzung der Remarquen* [...], n.d., n.p. (Leipzig, 1720?). Ostfriesische Landschaft, Landschaftsbibliothek, Aurich (Q 885 [2,2]), with permission.

The use of the map, produced by the Dresden engraver Moritz Bodenehr, links Marperger's brief and sober treatise to a wider literature that makes an even stronger appeal to the imagination. Many Mississippi texts have a substantial element of travelogue, offering a more or less detailed account of the Louisiana territory itself; Louis Hennepin's classic description of 1683 was frequently invoked.[25] The first report in the *European Fama* of 1719, cited above, also includes an account of the Louisiana colony, incorporating the ubiquitous colonist's letter home.[26] All versions of *HGB* quote extensively from Hennepin, and they also invite readers to picture Louisiana's natural wealth by including a map (Figure 5.2).

At the very least, these treatises operated by linking the excitement of finance, including the prospect of getting rich quick, with visions of global adventure and the exotic. Closer examination reveals something more. A key feature of *HGB* is that it situates 1720 in the histories both of speculation and of colonization. Zenner compares the South Sea and Mississippi Bubbles to the Dutch Tulip Mania (as does Marperger in his *Continuation*). But he inserts this into a detailed historical account, based on cited sources, of all the colonial enterprises undertaken by Europeans since the sixteenth century, including failed German settlements and joint-stock-trading projects, and their financial consequences.[27]

Figure 5.2. Map of the Louisiana colonies, from G. Zenner, *Historische und geographische Beschreibung des am großen Flusse Mississippi in Nord-America gelegenen herrlichen Landes Louisiana* (Leipzig, 1720). Württembergische Landesbibliothek, Stuttgart (Geogr.oct.743), with permission.

Zenner's text in particular sheds some new light on the history of the German colonial imagination. Germany only acquired a colonial empire in the 1880s, and our vision of the eighteenth-century scene was long dominated by Susanne Zantop's proposition that Germans' understanding of empire was limited to a set of "colonial fantasies," in which disappointment at being left behind in European expansion was compensated for by narratives that *imagine* Germans in the tropics as enlightened paternalists.[28] In the scholarship on German cameralism, the term "ersatz imperialism" has more recently been introduced to characterize and explain its focus on promoting territorial development, at best importing the exotic (e.g. plants) rather than trying to follow it across the seas. The "Cameralist lands," argues Sophus Reinert, were "caught between globalization and exceedingly local constraints," their rulers having learned from actual failures to challenge the hegemony of the Atlantic powers.[29]

The German Mississippi texts may best be situated in this latter context, as evidence of an active conversation about the possibilities of empire, grounded in local knowledge about past overseas projects and proceeding within a wider international discussion. Some of their readers would have had firsthand knowledge, for example, of the Brandenburg African Company, which operated between West Africa and the Caribbean from 1682 to 1711.[30] From this point of view, the Mississippi pamphlet literature provides a textual bridge between economic improvers like Marperger—whose vision could comprehend "Columbian projects" both at home and abroad—and a substantial number of Germans who really were looking beyond their four walls. Among the latter, alongside the relatively few who moved in international circles and had firsthand experience of the financial operations associated with trading companies, we need to picture a much larger group who participated in the colonial and trading enterprises of the English, French, and Dutch (as sailors, soldiers, colonists, plantation managers, engineers, doctors, or scientists), or who travelled in their own right as Pietist and Jesuit missionaries. The reading public was also part of the conversation.

The texts that reached those readers included not only the works of jobbing scholars like Marperger and Zenner, whose survival in libraries testifies to the interest they continued to have for Germany's educated elites well beyond 1720. Once the bubble had burst, Germans also wrote and read satires of the kind that were appearing in France, Britain, and the Netherlands. A pamphlet of 1721, *The Despairing Bankrupt*, has a characteristically bilingual title: *Le Banquerotteur en desespoir* [sic]; *das ist: der verzweifflende Banquerottirer*. It contains all the tropes of disillusionment and folly that are familiar from the pan-European visual and textual corpus on the events of 1720. Published in Leipzig, it carries the colophon "After the Hamburg copy," which was probably a dig at Hamburg businessmen's involvement in the bubble rather than evidence of provenance.[31] In the autumn of 1720, a version of Pieter Langendijk's popular Dutch comedy *Quincampoix*, translated and adapted for German readers, appeared on the book market.³²

A similarly imaginative but quite different text was published in Dresden in the spring of 1720. It is a three-page wedding poem, of the kind that was commonly produced in printed versions among the middle and upper classes in Germany from the sixteenth to the nineteenth century.³³ As such, it constitutes a kind of conversation among friends, and in that sense, it brings us as close as possible to seeing the role that the Mississippi scheme played in the everyday imaginary of Germans. A tribute to "the loving trade in Venusiana stock" (*den verliebten Actien-Handel auf Venusiana*), it celebrates the wedding of the Dresden court jeweler, Carl Heinrich Schrötel, and Johanna Elisabeth, daughter of the bell-founder Michael Weinhold. The engraver, and very likely the author of the text, was Moritz Bodenehr. He was certainly acquainted with the couple, because he was court engraver in Dresden. He was also, of course, the creator of Marperger's map of Louisiana. The text takes the form of a rebus, and it opens and closes with pictures of hoop skirts, both of which can be lifted up; under the first of these is the loving couple.

The text begins by describing the various forms and costumes that Amor, or Cupid, adopts as he spreads love around the world, and then moves to a discussion of his financial circumstances:³⁴

Heut ist er bettelarm doch morgen wieder reich,	Today he's as poor as a beggar, tomorrow rich again,
Und diß sein Reichthum wird fast itzo täglich größer,	And this his wealth is growing greater every day,
Weil Amor einen Fund durch Actien erdacht.	Because he's building up a fund by selling stock.
Verspricht der kluge Laws in Frankreich gulden Schlößer,	In France the clever Laws is promising golden palaces,
Vielleicht hat dieser schon es vielmahl höher bracht.	But Cupid has already made much more.
Louisiana zeigt zwar nur durch Perspective	To be sure, Louisiana only shows us through the telescope
Viel Morgen Lands und giebt vor Actien Papier.	Many acres of land, and it gives us paper for our stock.
Gesezt, daß endlich auch die reichste Flott einlieffe	Even if the richly laden ships actually arrive,
Venusiana geht doch Mississippi für.	Venusiana is better than Louisiana.
Hier kann mit schmäzgen man viel Actien erkauffen.	Here you can buy plenty of stock with kisses.
Ein neuer Fischbein Rock muß gar der Pharus sein,	A new petticoat must be the lighthouse.
Und dieser zieht das Volck, wie der Magnet mit hauffen,	And it draws the people like a magnet,

Doch einer lauffet nur in Amors Hafen ein.	But only one man can dock in Amor's harbor.
Warum weil er versteht was Actien bedeuten,	Why? Because he knows what stock is all about,
Drum giebt er anfangs gleich wohl tausend schmäzgen an,	And so he starts by offering a thousand kisses,
Wenn er die Morgen Lands nuhr noch bey Frühlings-Zeiten Bestellen und die Saat in Acker bringen kann.	So that when spring comes he can plow the acres and spread his seed.
Euch ist geehrtes Paar der Actien Kauff gelungen.	You, honored couple, have had success on the stock market.
Der Himmel gebe nun pro Cent ein altes Schock,	May heaven grant you an old Schock's worth per Cent,[35]
So leben in zehn Jahr zehn Mädchen und zehn Jungen.	Then in ten years you'll have ten girls and ten boys.
Seht diese Algebra steckt unterm Reiffen Rock.	Look—this algebra is waiting under the hoop skirt.

Lifting up the second skirt reveals the twenty children who represent 20 percent interest on the Venusiana stock—a trope that recalls the fact that successive issues of Mississippi stock were known as *mères, filles,* and *petites filles* (mothers, daughters, and granddaughters).

The first of many striking features of the text is the way it invokes the theme that all German Mississippi texts have in common: the question of who knows what about stock trading. Here, we are told emphatically that the bridegroom knows what stock is all about. This may refer to a real situation. The wedding took place in April 1720, when the price of Mississippi stock was near its height and relatively stable. The bridegroom Carl Heinrich Schrötel was a well-to-do goldsmith with connections to aristocratic circles, and thus fits the profile of a Mississippi *actionnaire*. Accordingly, the statement that the couple had succeeded in their stock purchases might have been the literal truth.

At the same time, the elaborate play of metaphors—its effect intensified by the pictures that make up the rebus—invokes a number of themes that recur in the international discourse around the 1720 bubbles. Here, the themes of materiality/immateriality and distance/closeness cluster around the adjacent figures of the telescope and the bundle of paper. The text lends itself to two kinds of readings. Superficially, the emphasis is on the uncertainty of the promise held out by Mississippi: even if the richly laden ships promised by Law actually did come in (and of course they never did), Venusiana is to be preferred to Louisiana. After all, we know Louisiana only at second hand "*durch Perspective*," as seen through telescopes. The placement of the picture of the telescope in the rebus reminds us that in metaphorical terms, the telescope

Figure 5.3. *Venusiana* cover, *Den verliebten Actien-Handel auf Venusiana* […] (Dresden, 1720). Universitätsbibliothek, Ludwig-Maximilians-Universität München (W 2 P. germ. 48#44), with permission.

Figure 5.4. *Venusiana* text, *Den verliebten Actien-Handel auf Venusiana* […] (Dresden, 1720). Universitätsbibliothek, Ludwig-Maximilians-Universität München (W 2 P. germ. 48#44), with permission.

Figure 5.5. *Venusiana* children, *Den verliebten Actien-Handel auf Venusiana* [...] (Dresden, 1720). Universitätsbibliothek, Ludwig-Maximilians-Universität München (W 2 P. germ. 48#44), with permission.

can also stand for the mass of published descriptions of Louisiana (to which, as we have seen, Bodenehr also made his contribution). The bundle of paper that appears immediately below the telescope invokes the ubiquity of those pamphlets and the way they function as "paper telescopes" delivering second-hand images. What is explicitly stated about the paper, though, is that Venusiana is better than Louisiana because, unlike the bride, Louisiana can be held and enjoyed only in the form of a piece of paper: "Louisiana gives us [not even merchandise, but] paper for our stock."

If we read this text in terms of a contradiction between paper and authentic material or moral values, we can see it as a comment on the problem of "paper credit" outlined in the introduction. In the English context, it has been argued that the South Sea Bubble made the contrast between "paper credit" and trust based on personal knowledge an urgent moral and epistemological problem. One consequence was the emergence of the modern novel, which deployed the medium of paper to generate the impression of authenticity (and to provoke emotions experienced as authentic), and at whose center there was always a quest to determine the true character of an individual.[36] In France, too, scholars have claimed epochal cultural significance for the events of 1720. The accelerated circulation of news, propaganda, and argument has been credited with kick-starting a print-based public sphere, while the beginnings of a long-term impact on the national economic imagination have been traced in the literary work of key authors of the 1730s and 1740s: Prévost, Montesquieu, and Melon.[37]

That the events of 1720 were assessed in terms of the challenge they posed to notions of individual and public credit even in the German lands is suggested in *The Despairing Bankrupt*. It ends with the arrival of the news of the impending funeral of "the world-famous Business Credit [*weltberühmten Commercien-Credit*]" following a period of intense fever: "Details of the arrangements will be communicated . . . as soon as they can be translated into German."[38] The very tone of this comment reminds us that the Germans' role in this drama was mainly that of interested and amused observers. If 1720 was a watershed in German-speaking Europe, it was not the kind of broad cultural crisis that is proposed for the bubble capitals.

Rather, the way in which "paper" is deployed in the Dresden wedding poem invokes the accessibility of other kinds of knowledge and the possibilities, once again, of compassing a wider material world. It is tempting to offer a more optimistic reading of Venusiana stock trading, composed as it was at a time when the market in Mississippi stock was at its peak and challenges to political order were a problem for foreigners. Beyond the familiar contradiction between appearance and reality, we can see here a more complex and ambivalent reflection on distance and closeness, the local and the global. To be sure, the telescope signals distance, but it is also a technology that allows us to overcome the effect of distance. We take up the telescope when we want to see a landscape—the many acres—that is far distant. In the moment of looking through the lens, however, we are brought closer to the object of our observation; we are simultaneously here and there.[39]

Similarly, we can read the "Venusianian" reflection on paper stock as a celebration of possibilities rather than a dismissal of immaterial promises. The paper *billet* then becomes a ticket for an imaginary journey to Louisiana especially if people imagined, as Zenner among others encouraged them to do, that in buying Mississippi stock, they were acquiring a piece of the colony. Or to put it another way, even if the stock is *only* paper, the buyer has Louisiana *in* that paper.

The excitement of the bubble years did raise enthusiasm and optimism about the possibilities of world trade and inspire a number of new enterprises in the German-speaking lands, as the episode of the Hamburg insurance company attests. Other initiatives included "bubble companies" of various kinds, authentic projects and chimeras, sometimes the work of adventurers from the British Isles whose intentions were meaner and whose expertise was more limited than those of John Law.[40] One of the most ambitious ventures was the project undertaken by the Holy Roman Emperor Charles VI in 1722 to develop Ostend as a port and establish a joint-stock company for the China trade in more or less open competition with the Dutch and English East India Companies. This scheme was based on a clear and not unrealistic vision of reviving the fortunes of the inland cities and river ports of the empire that were declining as seagoing commerce expanded.[41] In that sense, it was of a piece with the spirit of Law's political economy and with the global imaginings of Zenner and Marperger. The suspension of operations by the Austrian East India Company under pressure from Britain in 1727 may be said to have brought the Germans' Mississippi to a close and to have sealed as a memory of failure and folly what had begun in the spirit of experiment.

Eve Rosenhaft is Professor of German Historical Studies at the University of Liverpool (UK). She studied at McGill University and the University of Cambridge, and has held fellowships in Britain, Germany, and the United States. She has published widely on aspects of German social history since the eighteenth century, including labor, gender, urban culture, and issues of race and ethnicity. Her most recent publications include *Black Germany: The Making and Unmaking of a Diaspora Community 1884–1960* (Cambridge, 2013, with Robbie Aitken). The present chapter is one in a series of publications on the theme of gender, finance, and middle-class culture, and marks the beginning of a project on how Germans learned to invest in the eighteenth century.

Notes

1. On credit practices in early modern Europe, see Jürgen Schlumbohm, ed., *Soziale Praxis des Kredits: 16.–20. Jahrhundert* (Hanover, 2007); G. B. Clemens, ed., *Schuldenlast und Schuldenwert. Kreditnetzwerke in der europäischen Geschichte 1300–1900* (Trier, 2009).
2. [Paul Jacob Marperger], *Kurtze Remarques über den jetziger Zeit weltberuffenen Missisippischen Actien-Handel zu Paris* ... (Leipzig, 1720), [1]. On the place of mining in the economy of Electoral Saxony, see Chapter 4 in this volume. On *Kuxe*, see Johann Georg Krünitz, *Oeconomische Encyclopädie, oder allgemeines System der Land- Haus- und Staats-Wirthschaft*, 242 vols (Berlin, 1773), 57: 639–80. On credit, investment, and speculation in merchant cities, see Mary Lindemann, *The Merchant Republics: Amsterdam, Antwerp, and Hamburg, 1648–1790* (Cambridge, 2015), 224–55.
3. For the most recent research on the bubbles, see Helen J. Paul, *The South Sea Bubble* (New York, 2011); Antoin E. Murphy, *John Law: Economic Theorist and Policy Maker* (Oxford, 1997); Hans-Joachim Voth, "Blowing Early Bubbles: Rational Exuberance in the South Sea and Mississippi Bubbles," in *The Great Mirror of Folly: Finance, Culture and the Crash of 1720*, ed. W. N. Goetzmann, C. Labio, K. G. Rouwenhorst, and T. G. Young (New Haven, CT, 2013), 89–105.
4. For the awareness that even relatively familiar instruments like bills of exchange could be fraudulent, see Lindemann, *The Merchant Republics*, 224–31.
5. *Schlesischer Nouvellen-Courier* (Breslau), 1 July 1720.

6. Friedrich Plaß, *Geschichte der Assecuranz und der hanseatischen Seeversicherungs-Börsen* (Hamburg, 1902), 123–38; Lindemann, *The Merchant Republics*, 262.
7. See Eve Rosenhaft, "Women and Financial Knowledge in Eighteenth-Century Germany," in *Women and Their Money: Essays on Women and Finance 1700–1950*, ed. A. Laurence, J. Maltby, and J. Rutterford (New York, 2008), 59–72.
8. Holger Böning and Emmy Moepps, *Deutsche Presse: Biobibliographische Handbücher zur Geschichte der deutschsprachigen periodischen Presse von den Anfängen bis 1815, 1/1 Hamburg* (Stuttgart, 1996).
9. *Die Europäische Fama*, 227. Teil 1719: 601–77 (quote 601–3), 241. Teil 1721: 3 (quote), 247. Teil 1721: 531–63 (final report).
10. *Supplement... zu Hn. Johann Hübners Historischen, Genealogischen und Geographischen Fragen, Dritter Tomus über die Jahre 1716, 1717, 1718, 1719* (Leipzig, 1726), 76–77.
11. John Law, *Herrn Laws Controlleur general der Financen in Franckreich Gedancken vom Waaren- und Geldhandel* (Leipzig, 1720). On the provenance of the copy in the Herzog-August Library in Wolfenbüttel, see Christoph Boveland, "Auf den Spuren der verborgenen Bibliothek von Mlle de Montbail," *Wolfenbütteler Notizen zur Buchgeschichte* 35, no. 1 (2010): 71–80.
12. The second and third editions are entitled: *Ausführliche historische und geographische Beschreibung*; all editions are dated 1720. They were published anonymously; for Gottfried Zenner's authorship and career see his entry in *Allgemeine Deutsche Biographie*.
13. [Christian Gottfried Hoffmann], *Gegenwärtiger Zustand derer Finantzen in Frankreich* (Leipzig, 1720). Published anonymously; on Hoffmann and his authorship, see the entry in G. W. Goetten, *Das jetztlebende gelehrte Europa*, 2nd ed., 4 vols (Braunschweig, 1735; Zelle, 1737), 1: 324–34; 3: 762–64.
14. Anonymous, *Reflexions über Mr Laws neues Systema der Financen* (Leipzig, 1720).
15. [Marperger], *Kurtze Remarques*; [Paul Jacob Marperger], *Fortsetzung der Remarquen...*, n.p., n.d.
16. On the late Baroque literary and journalistic context, see Gerhild Scholz Williams, *Ways of Knowing in Early Modern Germany* (Aldershot, 2006); Daniel Bellingradt, *Flugpublizistik und Öffentlichkeit um 1700* (Stuttgart, 2011).
17. Anonymous, *Aanmerkingen over den koophandel en het geldt: Als meede: historische en geographische beschryving van Louisiana* (Amsterdam, 1721).
18. Marperger's version is in the copy of *Kurtze Remarques* with the imprint "Cum Censura, Leipzig 1720," held by the Library of the Ratsgymnasium in Bielfeld, 27–30. In the third edition of *HGB*, a German translation of the song was added. For the text of the song, see Emil Raunié, *Chansonnier historique du XVIIIe Siècle*, 10 vols (Paris, 1880), 3: 132–36.
19. Anonymous, *Curieuse Anmerckungen über den Staat von Franckreich* (Leipzig, 1720) [4–5].
20. For example, Johann Heinrich Zedler, *Vollständiges Großes Universal-Lexicon aller Wissenschaften und Künste*, 64 vols (Halle, 1732), 1: 393–94; Krünitz, *Oeconomische Encyclopädie*, 1: 391.
21. *Wöchentliche Relation* (Halle), 13 January 1720: 7.
22. Georg Heinrich Zincke, "Anmerckungen von des Hn. Hof. Rath Marpergers seel. Leben und Schrifften," *Leipziger Sammlungen und Allerhand zum Land- und Stadt-Wirthschafftlichen Policey-, Finanz- und Cammer-Wesen dienlichen Nachrichten...* (1745), 2: 429–40.

23. Hannelore Lehmann, "Paul Jacob Marperger (1656 bis 1730), ein vergessener Ökonom der deutschen Frühaufklärung," *Jahrbuch für Wirtschaftsgeschichte* 4 (1971): 125–57. On cameralism and its discontents, see Chapter 4 in this volume and the literature cited there.
24. [Marperger], *Fortsetzung* [5].
25. Louis Hennepin, *Description de la Louisiane, nouvellement découverte au Sud-Ouest de la Nouvelle France* (Paris, 1683).
26. *Die Europäische Fama*, 227; from 1720, 676. Visual satires on the Mississippi and South Sea schemes deliberately subverted the association between exotic geographies and the promise of riches: Darius A. Spieth, "The French Context of *Het groote tafereel der dwasheid*: John Law, Rococo Culture, and the Riches of the World," in *The Great Mirror of Folly*, 219–34.
27. [Gottfried Zenner], *Historische und geographische Beschreibung des am großen Flusses Mississipi in Nord-America gelegenen herrlichen Landes Louisiana*, 1st ed. (Leipzig, 1720), 70–74.
28. Susanne Zantop, *Colonial Fantasies: Conquest, Family and Nation in Precolonial Germany, 1770–1870* (Durham, NC, 1997).
29. Sophus Reinert, *Translating Empire: Emulation and the Origins of Political Economy* (Cambridge, MA, 2011), 238–45, quote on 238.
30. Sven Klosa, *Die Brandenburgische-Africanische Compagnie in Emden* (Frankfurt, 2011).
31. Anonymous, *Le Banquerotteur en desespoir; das ist: der verzweifflende Banquerottirer* (Leipzig, 1721).
32. Peter Langendyck [sic], *Quincampoix oder der Wind-Handel der neuen Actionisten . . .* (Hamburg, 1720). On the Dutch original, see Inger Leemans, "Verse Weavers and Paper Traders: Financial Speculation in Dutch Theater," in *The Great Mirror of Folly*, 175–90.
33. [Moritz Bodenehr], *Den verliebten Actien-Handel auf Venusiana wollte bey der Schrötel-Weinholdischen Ehe-Verbindung 1720 am 9ten April unter einem Fischbein-Rock der charmanten Welt vor Augen stellen der unter diesem Nahmen bekannte Redebohn* [Dresden, 1720]. See Barbara Krafft, "Der verliebte Actien-Handel auf Venusiana, oder Wie liest man ein Dresdner Rebus von 1720?" in *Arbeitskreis Bild Druck Papier: Tagungsband Dresden 2005*, ed. Christa Pieske, Konrad Vanja, Detlef Lorenz, and Sigrid Nagy (Münster, 2006), 53–72.
34. Krafft, "Der verliebte Actien-Handel," provides a solution to the rebus.
35. In the currency of Electoral Saxony, an old Schock was worth 20 shill*ings*.
36. Catherine Ingrassia, *Authorship, Commerce and Gender in Eighteenth-Century England* (Cambridge, 1998); Deidre Lynch, *The Economy of Character: Novels, Market Culture, and the Business of Inner Meaning* (Chicago, 1998).
37. Julia V. Douthwaite, "How Bad Economic Memories Are Made: John Law's System in *Les lettres persanes, Manon Lescaut*, and 'The Great Mirror of Folly,'" *L'Esprit créateur* 55, no. 3 (2015): 43–58; Yves Citton, "Les comptes merveilleux de la finance. Confiance et fiction chez Jean-François Melon," *Féeries* (2005): 125–60; Orain, Arnaud and Laurent Thézé. "Publicité, contre-publicité et représentations économiques du système de Law: Le motif alchimique dans les poésies et chansons de la Régence." In *"Gagnons sans savoir comment!" Représentations du système de Law du XVIIIe à nos jours*, ed. Florence Magnot-Ogilvy (Rennes, 2017) 129–48.
38. Anonymous, *Le Banquerotteur en desespoir* [24].

39. For evidence that contemporaries understood the uses of the telescope in this sense, see Florian Welle, *Der irdische Blick durch das Fernrohr* (Würzburg, 2009), 83–99; Constantijn Huygens, "In Telescopium," http://www.let.leidenuniv.nl/Dutch/Huygens/HUYG32.html, accessed 8 December 2013; Karl Richter, "Teleskop und Mikroskop in Brockes *Irdischem Vergnügen in Gott*," in *Prägnanter Moment: Studien zur deutschen Literatur der Aufklärung und Klassik,* ed. Karl Richter (Würzburg, 2000), 3–18.
40. On the pan-European wave of "bubble companies," see most recently Stefano Condorelli, *The 1719–20 Stock Euphoria: A Pan-European Perspective* (Working Paper, University of Bern, 2015), https://mpra.ub.uni-muenchen.de/68652/, accessed 25 July 2016.
41. Georges-Henri Dumont, *L'Épopée de la compagnie d'Ostende* (Brussels, 2000).

Bibliography

Anonymous. *Aanmerkingen over den koophandel en het geldt: Als meede: historische en geographische beschryving van Louisiana.* Amsterdam, 1721.

———. *Le Banquerotteur en desespoir; das ist: Der verzweifflende Banquerottirer.* Leipzig, 1721.

———. *Curieuse Anmerckungen über den Staat von Franckreich.* Leipzig, 1720.

———. *A Discovery of a Large, Rich and Plentiful Country in the North America Extending above 4000 Leagues.* London, 1720.

———. *Reflexions über Mr Laws neues Systema der Financen.* Leipzig, 1720.

Bellingradt, Daniel. *Flugpublizistik und Öffentlichkeit um 1700.* Stuttgart, 2011.

[Bodenehr, Moritz.] *Den verliebten Actien-Handel auf Venusiana wollte bey der Schrötel-Weinholdischen Ehe-Verbindung 1720 am 9ten April unter einem Fischbein-Rock der charmanten Welt vor Augen stellen der unter diesem Nahmen bekannte Redebohn.* Dresden, 1720.

Böning, Holger, and Emmy Moepps. *Deutsche Presse: Biobibliographische Handbücher zur Geschichte der deutschsprachigen periodischen Presse von den Anfängen bis 1815, 1/1 Hamburg.* Stuttgart, 1996.

Boveland, Christoph. "Auf den Spuren der verborgenen Bibliothek von Mlle de Montbail." *Wolfenbütteler Notizen zur Buchgeschichte* 35, no. 1 (2010): 71–80.

Citton, Yves. "Les comptes merveilleux de la finance: Confiance et fiction chez Jean-François Melon." *Féeries* (2005): 125–60.

Clemens, Gabriele B., ed. *Schuldenlast und Schuldenwert: Kreditnetzwerke in der europäischen Geschichte 1300–1900.* Trier, 2009.

Condorelli, Stefano. *The 1719–20 Stock Euphoria: A Pan-European Perspective* (Working Paper). University of Bern, 2015. https://mpra.ub.uni-muenchen.de/68652/. Accessed 25 July 2016.

Douthwaite, Julia V. "How Bad Economic Memories Are Made: John Law's System in *Les lettres persanes, Manon Lescaut,* and 'The Great Mirror of Folly.'" *L'Esprit créateur* 55, no. 3 (2015): 43–58.

Dumont, Georges-Henri. *L'Épopée de la compagnie d'Ostende.* Brussels, 2000.

Goetten, G. W. *Das jetztlebende gelehrte Europa*, 2nd ed., 4 vols. Braunschweig, 1735; Zelle, 1737.
Hennepin, Louis. *Description de la Louisiane, nouvellement découverte au Sud-Ouest de la Nouvelle France*. Paris, 1683.
[Hoffmann, Christian Gottfried]. *Gegenwärtiger Zustand derer Finantzen in Frankreich*. Leipzig, 1720.
Huygens, Constantijn. "In Telescopium." http://www.let.leidenuniv.nl/Dutch/Huygens/HUYG32.html. Accessed 8 December 2013.
Ingrassia, Catherine. *Authorship, Commerce and Gender in Eighteenth-Century England*. Cambridge, 1998.
Klosa, Sven. *Die Brandenburgische-Africanische Compagnie in Emden*. Frankfurt, 2011.
Krafft, Barbara. "Der verliebte Actien-Handel auf Venusiana, oder Wie liest man ein Dresdner Rebus von 1720?" In *Arbeitskreis Bild Druck Papier: Tagungsband Dresden 2005*, edited by Christa Pieske, Konrad Vanja, Detlef Lorenz, and Sigrid Nagy, 53–72. Münster, 2006.
Krünitz, Johann Georg. *Oeconomische Encyclopädie, oder allgemeines System der Land- Haus- und Staats-Wirthschaft*, 242 vols. Berlin, 1773.
Langendyck, Peter. *Quincampoix oder der Wind-Handel der neuen Actionisten*. Hamburg, 1720.
Law, John. *Herrn Laws Controlleur general der Financen in Franckreich Gedancken vom Waaren- und Geldhandel*. Leipzig, 1720.
Leemans, Inger. "Verse Weavers and Paper Traders: Financial Speculation in Dutch Theater." In *The Great Mirror of Folly: Finance, Culture and the Crash of 1720*, edited by W. N. Goetzmann, C. Labio, K. G. Rouwenhorst, and T. G. Young, 175–90. New Haven, CT, 2013.
Lehmann, Hannelore. "Paul Jacob Marperger (1656 bis 1730), ein vergessener Ökonom der deutschen Frühaufklärung." *Jahrbuch für Wirtschaftsgeschichte* 4 (1971): 125–57.
Lindemann, Mary. *The Merchant Republics: Amsterdam, Antwerp, and Hamburg, 1648–1790*. Cambridge, 2015.
Lynch, Deidre. *The Economy of Character: Novels, Market Culture, and the Business of Inner Meaning*. Chicago, 1998.
[Marperger, Paul Jacob]. *Fortsetzung der Remarquen . . .* n.p., n.d.
——. *Kurtze Remarques über den jetziger Zeit weltberuffenen Missisippischen Actien-Handel zu Paris*. Leipzig, 1720.
Murphy, Antoin E. *John Law: Economic Theorist and Policy Maker*. Oxford, 1997.
Orain, Arnaud, and Laurent Thézé. "Publicité, contre-publicité et représentations économiques du système de Law: Le motif alchimique dans les poésies et chansons de la Régence." In *"Gagnons sans savoir comment!" Représentations du système de Law du XVIIIe à nos jours*, Florence Magnot-Ogilvy ed. 129–48. Rennes, 2017.
Paul, Helen J. *The South Sea Bubble*. New York, 2011.
Plaß, Friedrich. *Geschichte der Assecuranz und der hanseatischen Seeversicherungs-Börsen*. Hamburg, 1902.
Raunié, Emil. *Chansonnier historique du XVIIIe Siècle*, 10 vols. Paris, 1880.

Reinert, Sophus. *Translating Empire: Emulation and the Origins of Political Economy.* Cambridge, MA, 2011.

Richter, Karl. "Teleskop und Mikroskop in Brockes *Irdischem Vergnügen in Gott.*" In *Prägnanter Moment: Studien zur deutschen Literatur der Aufklärung und Klassik,* edited by Karl Richter, 3–18. Würzburg, 2000.

Rosenhaft, Eve. "Women and Financial Knowledge in Eighteenth-Century Germany." In *Women and Their Money: Essays on Women and Finance 1700–1950,* edited by A. Laurence, J. Maltby, and J. Rutterford, 59–72. New York, 2008.

Schlumbohm, Jürgen, ed. *Soziale Praxis des Kredits: 16.–20. Jahrhundert.* Hanover, 2007.

Spieth, Darius A. "The French Context of *Het groote tafereel der dwasheid:* John Law, Rococo Culture, and the Riches of the World." In *The Great Mirror of Folly: Finance, Culture and the Crash of 1720,* edited by W. N. Goetzmann, C. Labio, K. G. Rouwenhorst, and T. G. Young, 219–34. New Haven, CT, 2013.

Voth, Hans-Joachim. "Blowing Early Bubbles: Rational Exuberance in the South Sea and Mississippi Bubbles." In *The Great Mirror of Folly: Finance, Culture and the Crash of 1720,* edited by W. N. Goetzmann, C. Labio, K. G. Rouwenhorst, and T. G. Young, 89–105. New Haven, CT, 2013.

Welle, Florian. *Der irdische Blick durch das Fernrohr.* Würzburg, 2009.

Williams, Gerhild Scholz. *Ways of Knowing in Early Modern Germany.* Aldershot, 2006.

Zantop, Susanne. *Colonial Fantasies: Conquest, Family and Nation in Precolonial Germany, 1770–1870.* Durham, NC, 1997.

Zedler, Johann Heinrich. *Vollständiges Großes Universal-Lexicon aller Wissenschaften und Künste,* 64 vols. Halle/Leipzig, 1732.

[Zenner, Gottfried]. *Historische und geographische Beschreibung des am großen Flusses Mississipi in Nord-America gelegenen herrlichen Landes Louisiana.* Leipzig, 1720.

Zincke, Georg Heinrich. "Anmerckungen von des Hn. Hof. Rath Marpergers seel. Leben und Schrifften." *Leipziger Sammlungen und Allerhand zum Land- und Stadt-Wirthschafftlichen Policey-, Finanz- und Cammer-Wesen dienlichen Nachrichten ... Anderer Band* (1745): 429–40.

CHAPTER SIX

A Conspicuous Lack of Consumption
Money, Luxury, and Fashion in King Frederick William I's Prussia (c. 1713–40)

BENJAMIN MARSCHKE

The Luxury Debates and the Crisis of Baroque Representation[1]

Money, luxury, and conspicuous consumption were problematic in early eighteenth-century Germany and the Atlantic world. Historians agree that this was the age of the "consumer revolution," and contemporaries, too, were aware of the magnitude of the changes involved, and they engaged in a vociferous series of "luxury debates."[2] By the early eighteenth century, conspicuous consumption was in crisis. Ostentatious spending had been regarded as a sign of grandeur and *gloire*.[3] Criticisms of "luxury" had been socially conservative: the problem typically recognized was that unworthy people were buying and flaunting luxury goods and "representing" themselves above their social station. The result of this had been the constant pursuit of the latest fashions and an inflation of "spectacular consumption" as the elites sought to keep pace with each other and keep ahead of parvenus.[4]

The age of Louis XIV had been the apogee of baroque conspicuous consumption, but spectacular consumption then collapsed in the early eighteenth century. Its demise was not because ostentatious display was no longer affordable; rather it was no longer effective. There were simply too many "people of distinction" competing for esteem through ostentatious display.[5] Moreover, competitive consumption and opulent fashions had reached the point of absurdity.[6]

At the same time, the early eighteenth century experienced a "crisis of representation" as the baroque unity of appearance and reality broke down,[7] and representation was exposed as "unreal, flimsy, and insubstantial."[8] Post-baroque society saw baroque illusions as illusions and instead craved authenticity.[9] Superficiality, superfluity, and artificiality were widely condemned, and genuineness, simplicity, and naturalness were idealized.[10] Conspicuous consumption, then, was rejected as falsity.[11]

It was no coincidence that this crisis of baroque representation in the early eighteenth century came at the same time as a crisis or failure of masculinity.[12] Baroque opulence in general, and ostentatious clothing and hairstyles in particular, were seen as superficial and frivolous: i.e. womanly. Fashion became synonymous with the feminine and effeminate. Vanity, pomp, and luxury were thought to enervate and effeminize men.[13] Men were to be self-disciplined in the pursuit of luxury and disinterested in the world of fashion.[14] An excess of luxury was linked to sexual incontinence—a man who sought pleasure in luxury with too much passion or too indiscreetly was presumed to seek sexual gratification in the same way.[15] Those who took too much interest in their own appearance were "fops," "macaronis," or *petit maîtres*."[16] So, consumerism was largely reassigned to women, who were understood to be uniquely suited to be consumers because of their natural lack of discipline, their frivolity, and their superficiality.[17]

Perhaps most significant of all, opulence was not the same thing as good taste, and baroque splendor was increasingly seen as simply bad taste.[18] In the early eighteenth century, the emphasis was increasingly placed on displaying one's taste rather than one's wealth, and ostentatious displays were seen as tasteless or vulgar.[19] Worst of all, overwrought fashions were seen as ridiculous, and publicly mocked.[20]

Rather than straining to "keep up with the Joneses," elites increasingly opted out of the competition in the early eighteenth century, even if it was difficult, perhaps even impossible, "to break out of the vicious cycle of escalating competitive consumption."[21] Nonetheless, what resulted was a fundamental change in men's taste and fashion in the early eighteenth century. In keeping with the idea that "simplicity may be the best way of making oneself conspicuous,"[22] men embraced plainness and adopted a "stark, almost Spartan style."[23] A "plain and uniform costume" became an aristocratic masculine ideal representing an "elite understatement," and a "noble simplicity."[24]

King Frederick William I of Prussia

King Frederick William I of Prussia (1713–40) was a ruler who did "break out of the vicious cycle" and reject contemporary norms of ostentatious consumption. Unlike some of the smaller courts in the empire, whose austerity was rooted in financial necessity,[25] the Prussian royal court could have (and had previously) easily afforded a more conventional baroque ruling style.[26] Yet Frederick William was not the only ruler or even the first one to reject baroque cultural norms and embrace understatement as a ruling style. Charles XII of Sweden (1697–1718) and Peter I of Russia (1696–1725), both of whose reigns preceded and overlapped with that of Frederick William, had already done so.[27] Some of Frederick William's own reform-minded high nobles, too, seem to have influenced his ruling style and tight-fisted handling of money.[28] Of course, Frederick William's conspicuous lack of consumption was also noted by contemporaries, and he in turn became a kind of a model.[29]

Frederick William sometimes seems self-contradictory to historians because his ruling style changed dramatically over the course of his reign.[30] If lumped together synchronically and compared anachronistically, the king's different self-representations in different phases of his reign appear erratic or enigmatic. The historical context, however, allows us to understand how the king and his ruling style changed over time.

In late 1710, Frederick William and his "crown prince's party" forced out the favorite ministers of his father, Elector/King Frederick III/I (1688–1713), and effectively seized power.[31] Frederick William and his favorites immediately began reining in the court's budget. When Frederick William took the throne in 1713, he unleashed a budget-cutting "iconoclasm."[32] Famously, he quickly did away with baroque court ceremony and many of the palaces, servants, and luxury items accumulated by Frederick III/I.

This iconoclasm has been interpreted by historians as a sign that Frederick William was uninterested in representing himself or his reign, but this is wrong. Instead, we should understand Frederick William's rejection of baroque court norms not as a lack of monarchical self-representation, but as a radically new form of it. Frederick William's intention was less to save money and more to take over the government with a theatric *Donnerschlack* that would unnerve the members of the court and demonstrate and reinforce his own authority.[33]

After the iconoclasm, however, the court budget quickly rebounded.[34] Frederick William had cut the court payroll by almost two thirds, but the payroll quickly increased again to the level it had been under his father and predecessor.[35] Salaries totaled 157,647 Reichsthaler in the 1711–12 court budget. In the 1713–14 budget, this figure dropped to 54,086 thaler, but by 1715–16 salaries totaled 80,779 thaler—an increase of almost 50 percent. In 1723–24, salaries totaled 104,097 thaler, which was scarcely less than the 105,694 thaler for salaries budgeted by Frederick I in 1702–3.

Likewise, although much has been made of the "militarization" of the Prussian court under Frederick William, this process took years.[36] Frederick William's favorite military officers only began to receive special allowances in the 1720–21 court budget, and only in the 1721–22 budget was the category *Generals und andere vornehme Officirer* added to the existing category of special allowances for prominent courtiers (*Vornehme Bediente*). Not until the 1722–23 budget were military officers as a whole paid as much as the *Vornehme Bediente* as a whole, and not until the 1723–24 budget were the military officers listed before the *Vornehme Bediente*.[37] The allowances paid to military officers then skyrocketed over the course of the 1720s. In the 1720–21 court budget, two officers were paid a total of 2,500 Reichsthaler. In the 1723–24 budget, twenty-two officers were paid a total of 22,900 thaler; in 1726–27, twenty-six officers received 32,815 thaler—half again as much as all the *Vornehme Bediente* together. Thus, in 1726–27, a full third of court salaries (totaling 98,500 thaler) and almost one fifth of the entire court budget (173,800 thaler) were diverted to allowances for military officers.[38]

Food, Clothing, and Shelter

Frederick William is infamous for having slashed the food budget of the Prussian royal court.[39] Except for salaries, the court's greatest expense was food and drink, and this was where a great deal of money could be saved. Frederick William thus dismissed the court confectioner in 1713 and repeatedly issued admonitions to the kitchen staff about wasting food and money.

In 1702–3, the court spent 65,526 Reichsthaler on the kitchen, 45,348 thaler on the cellar, 9,672 thaler on the confectionary, plus 5,788 for grain (126,334 thaler, total). In 1706–7, the numbers were respectively 104,443, 47,794, 15,990, and 5,457 thaler (a total of 173,684 thaler). In 1711–12, under the crown prince and his party, the budget was 85,000 thaler for the kitchen, 44,000 thaler for the cellar (including 10,000 thaler for wine), 6,000 thaler for the confectionary, plus 5,000 thaler for flour (140,000 thaler in all). In 1713–14, these figures plummeted to 30,000 thaler for the kitchen, 10,000 thaler for the cellar, and 3,000 thaler for the confectionary (43,000); they remained at this level for the rest of Frederick William's reign.[40] However, Frederick William's conspicuous cost-cutting—serving simple dishes on earthenware, rather than serving "effeminizing delicacies" on womanly porcelain—also had symbolic meaning as a rejection of opulent display and luxury.[41]

Frederick William's clothing and hair also sent a message. As crown prince and early in his reign, Frederick had still worn a typical ostentatiously long and tall baroque ceremonial wig, not unlike that of Louis XIV.[42] He was pictured this way in portraits (Figure 6.1) and on coins into the late 1710s.[43] However, Frederick William also began appearing wearing his own hair (Figure 6.2).[44]

This was a conspicuous step toward austerity, and it seems to have happened at about the same time that Frederick William beginning to wear a simple army officer's uniform. Perhaps it was no coincidence that Frederick William stopped wearing a large wig just as the fashion became widespread, in the

Figure 6.1. (left) "Fridericus Wilhelmus D. G. Princ. Haered. Regni. Prussiae. &c. &c., pre-1713, by Elias Christoph Heiß. Source: British Museum, public domain, http://www.britishmuseum.org/research/collection_online/collection_object_details.aspx?objectId=3362072&partId=1

Figure 6.2. "Fridericus Wilhelmus, Rex Borussia," 1713, in *Europäische Fama*. Source: Herzog August Bibliothek, Wolfenbüttel.

1710s and 1720s; once wearing a wig was no longer a mark of distinction, to do so was pointless.[45] Finally, later in his reign, as smaller, more convenient, natural-looking, and less expensive wigs became widespread even among common people, Frederick William also began wearing a basic "round" wig, with a pony tail (Figure 6.3).[46]

These changes did not happen by accident; Frederick William and his favorites at court were quite aware of fashion, and they recognized how they wore their hair and how they dressed as something that set them off from outsiders. If we look at a picture of Frederick William's *Tabakskollegium*, then this is more apparent (Figure 6.4, c. 1736). The king, in the armchair in the foreground, and everybody else are outfitted similarly. Everyone has his hair done the same, or is wearing basically the same style wig. The king and half the others are wearing their blue military uniforms; the remainder of the guests are dressed relatively austerely.

Figure 6.3. Frederick William I, 1729, by Antoine Pesne. Source: Bildarchiv Preußischer Kulturbesitz, Art Resource.

Figure 6.4. Tabakskollegium, c. 1736, by Georg Lisiewski. Source: Bildarchiv Preußischer Kulturbesitz, Art Resource.

The *Tabakskollegium* was a rather informal and private affair, so we might expect the king and his companions to have been dressed informally. However, it was obviously *not* the case in Frederick William's Prussia that elites "appeared on the street in costumes [that] . . . dominated the street."[47] For example, when August Hermann Francke visited Berlin in 1725, he passed by the king on the street without recognizing him.[48]

We might be tempted to think that Frederick William routinely attired himself rather unpretentiously when among his subjects and underlings, but we should realize that the king was dressed with exceptional informality even at formal occasions. For example, in 1729 Frederick William (and crown prince Frederick) wore their everyday military uniforms to his daughter's wedding, as her new in-laws noted.[49] The commemorative paintings done to record the reciprocal visits to Dresden and Berlin by Frederick William and August "the Strong" of Saxony-Poland, in 1728–29, also reveal the Prussian king's relative informality (Figure 6.5) August is wearing a gold-laced red jacket with big cuffs, a long gold vest, and a tall, baroque wig; Frederick William is wearing his officer's uniform and either his own hair or a simple wig. Presumably the court painter portrayed the rulers as was desired, and this contrast was the result.[50] Yet before August the Strong visited Berlin, a lengthy discussion had ensued about how to receive the Saxon-Polish king and about the potential for making a negative impression if the Prussian court's cost-cutting should

Figure 6.5. August II of Saxony-Poland and Frederick William I, c. 1733, by Louis de Silvestre. Source: Bildarchiv Preußicher Kulturbesitz, Art Resource.

become too apparent.⁵¹ In this context, we should understand Frederick William's austerity not as the result of indifference, but by design.

This awareness of the differences in fashion could also be quite biting, or even deliberately insulting. While the Great Northern War against Sweden was winding down, Sweden's ally France stymied Frederick William at the negotiations. In retaliation, Frederick William insulted the French ambassador and his entourage by parodying how they dressed.⁵² Furthermore, Prussia and Great Britain almost went to war in 1729 when it came out that Frederick William had repeatedly mocked his brother-in-law, King George II, as a *petit-maître* (Figure 6.6).⁵³

Frederick William and his court poked fun at the hairstyles and clothing of not only their foreign enemies, but also local parvenus, such as the presumptuous president of the Berlin Royal Society of Sciences (and court fool), Paul Jacob von Gundling.⁵⁴ Among the many reasons for Gundling's unpopularity at court was his fondness for ostentatious clothes and wigs. Among the many humiliations that Gundling suffered were the exaggerated cut of the clothes and the gargantuan wig that he was forced to wear.

Not only foreign enemies or unpopular courtiers were in danger of being mocked by the king and his favorites for their overly fashionable attire, rather this was a general phenomenon at the Prussian court.⁵⁵ Frederick William's rejection of *unnöthige Kleider-Pracht* was reported in the *Europäische Fama* with ambivalence, perhaps even praise; describing what the Prussian

Figure 6.6. King George II of Great Britain, c. 1716, by Sir Godfrey Kneller. Source: Wikipedia Commons, public domain, https://commons.wikimedia.org/wiki/File:King_George_II_by_Sir_Godfrey_Kneller,_Bt.jpg

king had abolished as "unnecessary" implies approval.[56] It was certainly no longer the case that "the gaudy brilliance of courtiers underlined the splendor of the monarch."[57] On the contrary, Johann Michael von Loen's description of Frederick William's court in 1718 makes the point that greatness did not depend on a ruler appearing in "äusserlichen Pomp" and accompanied by a "langen Schweiff bundfärbigter, mit Gold und Silber beschlagenen Creaturen."[58]

Clearly by the 1710s, at least in some quarters, "superficial pomp" and a "long entourage" of gaudy courtiers were not seen as legitimizing splendor, but as empty vanity. Indeed, Loen and the *Europäische Fama* both referred approvingly to Frederick William's dismissal of *unnöthige Bediente und Müßiggänger*.[59] In the eighteenth century, domestic servants were typically employed more as props than as workers, and superfluous, well-dressed servants were recognized as ostentatious display.[60] It makes sense, then, that the *Fama* approved of Frederick William's dismissal of "unnecessary servants and idlers."

In addition to the conspicuous lack of consumption in food and clothing at court, Frederick William also pursued a conspicuously austere architectural program. Although he kept the major palaces, and even finished ongoing construction projects, Frederick William liquidated most of the other royal palaces as part of his iconoclasm, either by leasing them out or auctioning them off.[61]

Frederick William also did away with the baroque garden at the palace in Berlin—he famously had it flattened into a parade ground, so that he could drill his troops there. Less well known is that Frederick William converted the baroque garden in Oranienbaum into a simple orchard.[62] In this rejection of baroque gardens, too, Frederick William fit into the culture of the day, which increasingly regarded baroque gardens as passé or even distasteful.[63] As criticisms of such opulence spilled over into sexualized political criticism, it was even claimed that the "circumcising" and "raping" of nature in baroque gardens betokened despotism.[64]

However, it would be wrong to think that Frederick William did not create representative architecture.[65] Rather than building or furnishing baroque palaces, Frederick William preferred to hold court at smaller palaces, which better resembled bourgeois homes than royal residences.[66] The modest "palace" at Wusterhausen, which had been his residence as crown prince, remained his favorite retreat for his entire reign (Figure 6.7). During his reign, he built only the extremely small and unpretentious "Jagdschloß Stern" outside Potsdam (Figure 6.8), which resembled one of the houses in the new *Holländisches Viertel* in Potsdam (see below).

Instead of palaces, Frederick William built churches.[67] After the Petri-Kirche in Berlin burned in 1730, Frederick William planned and began to reconstruct it with a steeple that would have been the tallest in Europe. The

Figure 6.7. Schloß Wusterhausen, photograph. Source: Wikipedia Commons, public domain.

Figure 6.8. Jagdschloß Stern, photograph by the author.

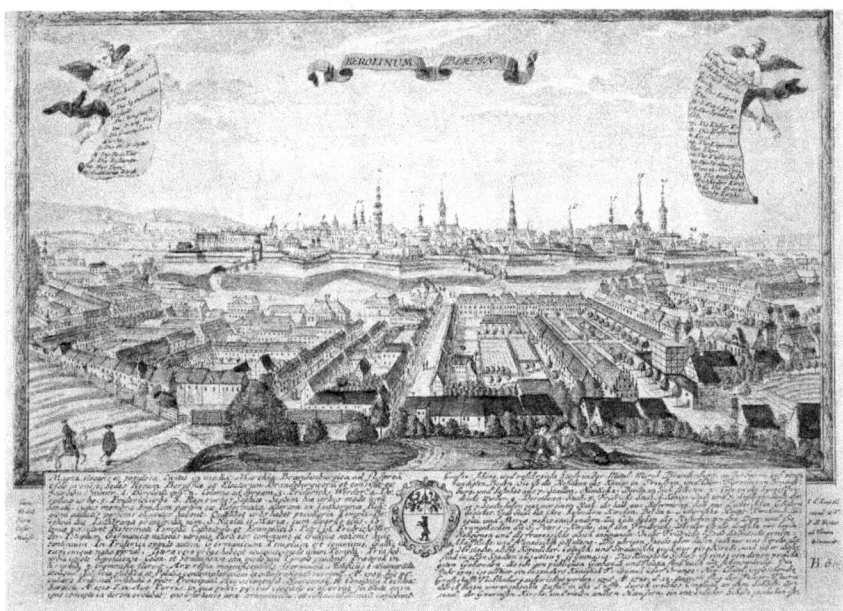

Figure 6.9. Berlin Cityscape, c. 1730, by Friedrich Bernhard Werner. Source: Wikipedia Commons, public domain, https://commons.wikimedia.org/wiki/File:Berlin_Map_1730_Werner.jpg

steeple collapsed during construction and the project was abandoned, but Frederick William clearly did not lack architectural ambition. Frederick William retained the foremost architects of the day for these projects and successfully erected tall and expensive baroque towers atop churches in Berlin and Potsdam, which were probably the most conventionally majestic architecture that he built.[68] These towers, typically topped by his "FWR" monogram in the form of a weathervane, were re-represented in celebratory illustrations of the Prussian capital and residence cities. Contemporary periodicals and commemorative literature from the Prussian court reported on the construction and dedication of these churches and enthusiastically pointed out how much taller, more beautiful, and more fashionable they were than those in Paris or Vienna.[69] Judging from the maps of Berlin produced at the end of Frederick William's reign, the capital city was dominated by the churches he built (Figure 6.9).

Also more visible—and far more expensive—than Frederick William's palaces were the new suburbs of Berlin and Potsdam.[70] Although long delays and huge cost overruns marked these projects,[71] their explicit rejection of baroque architecture made them edifices to the Prussian monarchy's efficiency and frugality. These expansions were not designed to accommodate new residents—

Figure 6.10. "Häuserbau im Süden der Berliner Friedrichstadt," c. 1735, by Dismar Degen. Source: Stiftung Preußische Schlößer und Gärten Berlin-Brandenburg (SPSG), photograph by Gerhard Murza.

one reason for delays was the difficulty in finding people to build homes in the new suburbs—but to create more *Zierde und Ansehen*.[72] As part of his program to beautify Berlin, Frederick William encouraged elites to construct representative homes by granting subsidies in cash and building materials.[73] Furthermore, he ordered royal officials and the urban elites to build homes, and when these people were lacking, he distributed noble titles and promotions to potential home builders.[74] The costs of these projects spiraled out of control, so much so that toward the end of Frederick William's reign, the cost of building materials and building subsidies far outstripped the budget of the entire royal court. In 1735–36, for example, the costs of "Bau Gelder" and "Bau-Materialien" more than doubled from the previous year to 343,814 Reichsthaler—that year's the entire court budget was 183,515 thaler.[75]

The orderly, symmetrical, and uniform homes and the straight and wide streets of the new "Dutch Quarter" in Potsdam or the new Friedrichstadt in Berlin were indeed impressive.[76] New boulevards were lined with linden trees, suitable for "*hübsche Leuthe*" to promenade, which was encouraged by Frederick William toward the end of his reign.[77] Court painters produced aerial views of the construction and "fictive architecture" of these new suburbs

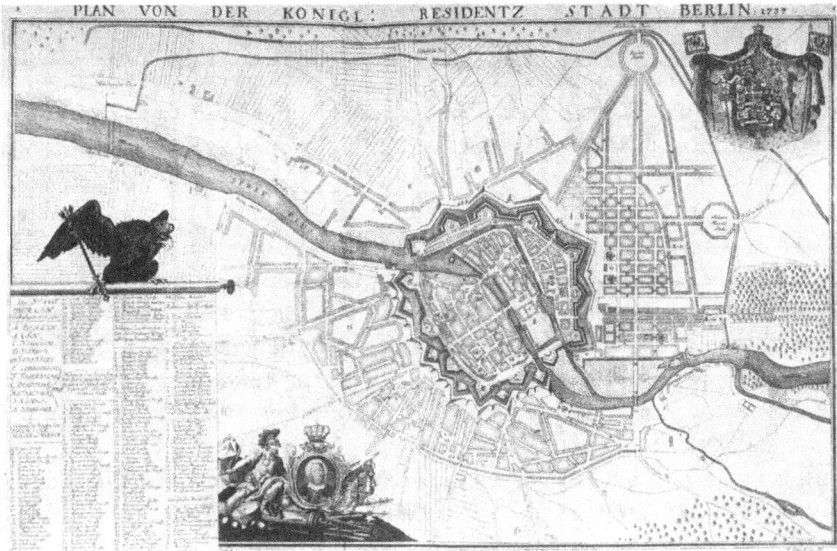

Figure 6.11. Plan von der Königl. Residentz Stadt Berlin, 1737, by Abraham Guibert Dusableau. Source: Wikipedia Commons, public domain, https://commons.wikimedia.org/wiki/File:Berlin_Dusableau_1737.jpg

to "re-represent" this representative architecture (Figure 6.10). Furthermore, the expansion of these cities were portrayed in new maps (Figure 6.11).

The contemporary public seems to have approved of Frederick William's "breaking out" of the "vicious cycle of escalating competitive consumption." For his part, Frederick William not only did nothing to hide his cost-cutting measures, but wanted them to be known, and regaled in the reports about them.[78]

Conclusions

Frederick William was not unfashionable. It might be overreaching to say that Frederick William was a trendsetter, or even that he moved at the cutting edge of fashion, but he certainly was not out of touch with contemporary fashions. Indeed, Frederick William and his favorites at the Prussian court clearly possessed a very clear sense of taste and fashion, and they harshly ridiculed those who did not conform. Moreover, the fashion at the Prussian court was in keeping with the trend toward more modest fashions across the Atlantic world, which ultimately resulted in the demise of the baroque wig and the ubiquity of the military uniform at royal courts everywhere.[79]

Frederick William's reign coincided with the tumultuous early eighteenth-century luxury debates, and we should understand him and his reign in this context. He was not opposed to luxury or opulence in the older moral or religious (Puritan or Pietist) sense.[80] Frederick William was also not "anti-luxury" in the traditional social sense; he was not trying to reinforce or reimpose older social norms of appearance and consumption.

Rather, Frederick William was right in the middle of the contemporary discourse about luxury and money. Frederick William ran afoul of contemporaries like Voltaire who defended luxury based on its civilizing and artistic value, and thus Voltaire and others famously referred to him and his disdain for luxury and the arts as barbaric, savage, miserable, or uncivilized.[81] The King of Prussia was, however, "anti-luxury" in the newer social sense, which was increasingly skeptical of baroque representation. Frederick William saw baroque opulence as "inappropriate acts of display," and his response was to "display a disdain for display," while "the symbolic economy of Old Regime consumption collapsed in the face of a crisis of representation."[82]

It is important to recognize that Frederick William's disdain for baroque representation was also a "display." Frederick William's contempt for baroque opulence was quite public, as he wanted it to be. Frederick William's conspicuous lack of consumption and conspicuous cost-cutting not only legitimized his own rule, but also was an implicit attack on the "spectacular consumption" of other rulers.

Benjamin Marschke is Professor of History at Humboldt State University. His first book was on the Prussian army chaplaincy, and he has published many additional articles on the Prussian monarchy and Halle Pietism. Marschke was also coeditor of *The Holy Roman Empire, Reconsidered* (2010) and *Kinship, Community, and Self: Essays in Honor of David Warren Sabean* (2014). His current research project is centered around the royal court of King Frederick William I of Prussia (1713–40).

Notes

1. Special thanks to the participants and audience of the "Pious Economy, Asceticism, and Criticism of Luxury" and "Grumblers in the Hive" sessions at the 2010 and 2011 German Studies Association conferences, where I presented portions of early versions of portions of this chapter, and to Gadi Algazi, Simon Teuscher, David Sabean, and the other participants in the UCLA/Zürich/Tel Aviv Teleconference Colloquium, where I presented an expanded version of this chapter in November 2011.
2. Regarding the "consumer revolution," see Michael Kwass, "Consumption and the World of Ideas: Consumer Revolution and the Moral Economy of the Marquis de Mirabeau," *Eighteenth-Century Studies* 37, no. 2 (2004): 187–213; Michael Kwass,

"Ordering the World of Goods: Consumer Revolution and the Classification of Objects in Eighteenth-Century France," *Representations* 82 (2003): 87–116; Margot Finn, "Men's Things: Masculine Possession in the Consumer Revolution," *Social History* 25, no. 2 (2000): 133–55. On the "luxury debates," see Maxine Berg and Elizabeth Eger, "The Rise and Fall of the Luxury Debates," in *Luxury in the Eighteenth Century: Debates, Desires and Delectable Goods,* ed. Maxine Berg and Elizabeth Eger (Houndsmills, Basingstoke, Hampshire, 2003), 7–27; Christopher J. Berry, "The Eighteenth-Century Debate," in *The Idea of Luxury: A Conceptual and Historical Investigation* (Cambridge, 1994), 126–76; and John Martin Stafford, *Private Vices, Publick Benefits? The Contemporary Reception of Bernard Mandeville* (Solihull, 1997).
3. Rémy G. Saisselin, *The Enlightenment against the Baroque: Economics and Aesthetics in the Eighteenth Century* (Berkeley, CA, 1992), 32.
4. John Shovlin, "The Cultural Politics of Luxury in Eighteenth-Century France," *French Historical Studies* 23, no. 4 (2000): 577. "Spectacular consumption" is Shovlin's term. This is basically Thorsten Veblen's idea of "conspicuous consumption"; Thorsten Veblen, *The Theory of the Leisure Class* (New York, 1899).
5. "Das Prunken für einen Fürsten eigentlich nur dann Sinn macht, wenn er der einzige ist, der dies tut." Ulf Christian Ewert and Jan Hirschbiegel, "Nur Verschwendung? Zur sozialen Funktion der demonstrativen Zurschaustellung höfischen Güterverbrauchs," in *Luxus und Integration: Materielle Hofkulture Westeuropas vom 12. bis zum. 18. Jahrhundert,* ed. Werner Paravincini (Munich, 2010), 105–21, here 118.
6. On "dignity" and "grace" as defining characteristics of the nobility, see Ronald G. Asch, "What Makes the Nobility Noble?," in *What Makes the Nobility Noble? Comparative Perspectives from the Sixteenth to the Twentieth Century,* ed. Jörn Leonhard and Christian Wieland (Göttingen, 2011), 329–39, here 338–39.
7. "Crisis of representation," see Shovlin, "The Cultural Politics of Luxury," 588; "culture of appearance"; Kwass, "Ordering the World of Goods," 109. We should include the rococo with the baroque. Though Jose Antonio Maravall refers to the baroque as a "structure," an "epoch," a "mentality," and a "total civilization," presumably today he would say "culture." Jose Antonio Maravall, *Culture of the Baroque: Analysis of a Historical Structure,* trans. Terry Cochrane (Minneapolis, MN, 1986). See also Saisselin, *The Enlightenment against the Baroque,* 3–4, 29; and Timothy Hampton, "Baroques," *Yale French Studies* 80 (1991): 1–8.
8. Shovlin, "The Cultural Politics of Luxury," 588.
9. This was the "invention of sincerity." See Lionel Trilling, *Sincerity and Authenticity* (Cambridge, MA, 1972).
10. Jennifer M. Jones, "Repackaging Rousseau: Femininity and Fashion in Old Regime France," *French Historical Studies* 18, no. 4 (1994): 939–67, here 945, 954.
11. Ibid., 944, 948.
12. See Benjamin Marschke, "Competing Post-Baroque Masculinities: Pietist Masculinity and Prussian Masculinity in the Early Eighteenth Century," in *Gender im Pietismus: Netzwerke und Geschlechter-Konstruktionen,* ed. Pia Schmidt (Halle, 2015), 197–210.
13. Saisselin, *The Enlightenment against the Baroque,* 19, 35; Jones, "Repackaging Rousseau," 944, 949, 963; Philip Carter, "Men about Town: Representations of Foppery and Masculinity in Early Eighteenth-Century Urban Society," in *Gender in Eighteenth-Century England: Roles, Representations, and Responsibilities,* ed. Hannah Barker and Elaine Chalus (London, 1997), 31–57; and David Kuchta, "The Making

of the Self-Made Man: Class, Clothing, and English Masculinity, 1688–1832," in *The Sex of Things: Gender and Consumption in Historical Perspective*, ed. Victoria de Grazia and Ellen Furlough (Berkeley, CA, 1996), 62, 64, 69.
14. Kuchta, "The Making of the Self-Made Man," 65.
15. Saisselin, *The Enlightenment against the Baroque*, 25; and Kwass, "Ordering the World of Goods," 113.
16. Shovlin, "The Cultural Politics of Luxury," 602; and Carter, "Men about Town."
17. Jones, "Repackaging Rousseau," 949, 953, 963. Coming full circle, this frivolous "new femininity" was a justification to exclude women from public life, that is, the company of men. Kuchta, "The Making of the Self-Made Man," 66–67.
18. Jones, "Repackaging Rousseau," 947, 959–963; Kuchta, "The Making of the Self-Made Man," 60; and Kwass, "Big Hair: A Wig History of Consumption in Eighteenth-Century France," *American Historical Review* 111, no. 3 (2006): 656–59.
19. Jones, "Repackaging Rousseau," 944; Kwass, "Ordering the World of Goods," 95; and Pierre Bourdieu, *Distinction: A Social Critique of the Judgement of Taste*, trans. Richard Nice (Cambridge, MA, 1984).
20. Jones, "Repackaging Rousseau," 945; and Carter, "Men about Town."
21. Kuchta, "The Making of the Self-Made Man," 72. Peter Burke asks "How it was possible ... ?" Peter Burke, "*Res et verba*: Conspicuous Consumption in the Early Modern World," in *Consumption and the World of Goods*, ed. John Brewer and Roy Porter (London, 1993), 148–61, here 158. "bestand auch keine Möglichkeit zur einseitigen Aufkündigung demonstrativen und andere beeindruckenden Verhaltens." Ewert and Hirschbiegel, "Nur Verschwendung?," 121. Ewert and Hirschbiegel argue that while spending money on such ostentation may not have been really advantageous unless one could set oneself off from one's inferiors (and ideally, one's peers) by doing so, it would have been quite impossible to forego ostentation unilaterally as long as one's peers (and especially one's inferiors) did not do so. Their economic "game" model is too simplistic because it fails to account for differences in taste and fails to see that an actor could forego one form of ostentation and adopt another form, rather than competing directly.
22. Burke, "*Res et verba*," 149.
23. Shovlin, "The Cultural Politics of Luxury," 598–99.
24. Kuchta, "The Making of the Self-Made Man," 56, 60, 71, 72.
25. On the tension between magnificence and parsimony at German courts in the eighteenth century, see Volker Bauer, *Hofökonomie: Der Diskurs über den Fürstenhof in Zeremonialwissenschaft, Hausväterliteratur und Kameralismus* (Vienna, 1997).
26. See Volker Bauer's suggestion that Frederick William's court was the quintessence of the "hausväterliche Hof" ideal type, although Bauer admits that the Prussian court was more an exception than an example, and that the size of Prussia and Frederick William's motivations set it apart from other "hausväterliche" courts. Volker Bauer, *Die höfische Gesellschaft in Deutschland von der Mitte des 17. bis zum Ausgang des 18. Jahrhunderts: Versuch einer Typologie* (Tübingen, 1993), 66–70.
27. On this new anticeremonial style of rule, see Benjamin Marschke, "'Von dem am Königl. Preußischen Hofe abgeschafften *Ceremoniel*': Monarchical Representation and Court Ceremony in Frederick William I's Prussia," in *Orthodoxies and Diversity in Early Modern Germany*, ed. Randolph C. Head and Daniel Christensen (Boston, 2004).

28. Jochen Mattern, "Leopold I. von Anhalt-Dessau: Eine Studie zur Geschichte der politischen Technologie," *Kultursoziologie* 6, no. 2 (1997): 79–96.
29. Kuchta uses the term "inconspicuous consumption," but this does not go far enough, because the point of Frederick William's "symbolic saving" was not at all to be inconspicuous, but quite the contrary, to be conspicuous. Burke's "conspicuous refraining from consuming" is more accurate. Kuchta, "The Making of the Self-Made Man," passim; and Burke, "*Res et verba*," 149.
30. Marschke, "Von dem am Königl.," 228.
31. The impetus and the opportunity for this "early succession" was an economic crisis brought about by an outbreak of the plague in East Prussia and the impending end of foreign subsidies to support Prussian involvement in the war of Spanish succession. Benjamin Marschke, "The Crown Prince's Brothers and Sisters: Succession and Inheritance Problems and Solutions among the Hohenzollerns, From the Great Elector to Frederick the Great," in *Sibling Relations and the Transformations of European Kinship, 1300–1900*, ed. Christopher H. Johnson and David Warren Sabean (New York, 2011), 111–44, here 123–25.
32. Benjamin Marschke, "Princes' Power, Aristocratic Norms, and Personal Eccentricities: *Le Caractère Bizarre* of Frederick William I of Prussia (1713–1740)," in *The Holy Roman Empire, Reconsidered*, ed. Jason P. Coy, Benjamin Marschke, and David Warren Sabean (New York, 2010), 49–70, here 50–51.
33. Friedrich Wilhelm I, "Instruktion König Friedrich Wilhelms I. für seinen Nachfolger [1722]," in *Politische Testamente der Hohenzollern*, ed. Richard Dietrich (Munich, 1981), 221–43, here 223–24. Wolfgang Neugebauer came to similar conclusions, see Wolfgang Neugebauer, "Vom höfischen Absolutismus zum fallweisen Prunk. Kontinuitäten und Quantitäten in der Geschichte des preußischen Hofes im 18. Jahrhundert," in *Hofgesellschaft und Höflinge an europäischen Fürstenhöfen in der Frühen Neuzeit (15.–18. Jh.)*, ed. Klaus Malettke (Münster, 2001), 113–24, here 117; and Wolfgang Neugebauer, "Staatsverwaltung, Manufaktur und Garnison: Die polyfunktionale Residenzlandschaft von Berlin-Potsdam-Wusterhausen zur Zeit Friedrich Wilhelms I," *Forschungen zur brandenburgischen und preußischen Geschichte (FBPG)* 7, no. 2 (1997): 233–57.
34. Neugebauer, "Vom höfischen Absolutismus zum fallweisen Prunk," 117.
35. An original of the 1711–12 court budget survives, and the 1702–3 and 1706–7 court budgets survive as extracts. These are presumably indicative of the expenses during the reign of Frederick III/I. The court budgets from the reign of Frederick William, except 1714–15, have all survived. Geheime Staatsarchiv—Preußischer Kulturbesitz (GStA-PK), Hauptarchiv (HA) I, Repositur (Rep.) 36, "Hofverwaltung," file numbers 64, 66, 69, 70, 78, "Hoffstaats Etat" for 1702–12, 1711–12, 1713–14, 1715–16, and 1723–24.
36. Regarding Frederick William rearranging of the table of ranks in 1713 to give military officers precedence over civilian courtiers, see Benjamin Marschke, "Princes' Power, Aristocratic Norms, and Personal Eccentricities," 51. As was common at other courts, it was impossible to dismiss some high court officials, and the only way to cut their positions (and divert their salaries) was to wait for them to die and then not replace them. Jeroen Duindam, "The Dynastic Court in an Age of Change: Frederick II Seen From the Perspective of Habsburg and Bourbon Court Life," in *Friedrich der Große und der Hof*, ed. Michael Kaiser (Potsdam, 2009), 6.

37. GStA-PK, HA I, Rep. 36, "Hofverwaltung," file numbers 75–78, "Hoffstaats Etat" for 1720–21, 1721–22, 1722–23, and 1723–24.
38. GStA-PK, HA I, Rep. 36, "Hofverwaltung," file numbers 75, 78, and 81, "Hoffstaats Etat" for 1720–21, 1723–24, 1726–27.
39. Regarding food at Frederick William's court, see Elisabeth M. Kloosterhuis, *Soldatenkönigs Tafelfreuden: Die Tafelkultur am Hofe Friedrich Wilhelms* (Berlin, 2009).
40. GStA-PK, HA I, Rep. 36, "Hofverwaltung," file numbers 64 and 69, "Hoffstaats Etat" for 1702–12 and 1713–14.
41. "Effeminating delicacies," see Kuchta, "The Making of the Self-Made Man," 64. Margot Finn has pointed out that porcelain was also gendered feminine; Finn, "Men's Things," 133–55.
42. Regarding wigs, see Kwass, "Big Hair."
43. Bernd Jakob von Arnim, *Von Thalern des Chürfürstlich-Brandenburgischen und Königlich-Preussischen regierenden Hauses* (Berlin, 1788), 241–43; and Bernd Jakob von Arnim, *Von Ducaten des Chürfürstlich-Brandenburgischen und Königlichen-Preussischen regierenden Hauses* (Berlin, 1796), 121–23. Unfortunately, Arnim provides only descriptions, and no pictures of the coins.
44. Frederick William first appeared on a ducat coin in 1716 "mit eigenen Haaren," and then in 1717 on three different ducats "mit Haarzopf," "mit freien Haarlocken," and "in leicht frisirten Haaren." He appeared on a thaler coin in 1718 "in eigenen Haaren und stiefen Zopfe" and then in 1719 "in eigenen frey zurück frisirten Haaren, welche hinten zusammengebunden sind." Arnim, *Von Ducaten*, 121–23; and Arnim, *Von Thalern*, 244–47.
45. Kwass, "Big Hair," 639.
46. Regarding the typical "round" or "bag" wig, see Kwass, "Big Hair," 639, 648.
47. Shovlin, "The Cultural Politics of Luxury," 581.
48. "Vormittag bin ich in die Guarnison-Kirche gefahren; eben da ich nahe an den Kirchen war, sahen mich S.K.M. [Seine Königliche Majestät] und grüßeten gar gnädig, davon ich aber eher nichts wahrgenommen, als bis schon bey denen selben vorbey war." Archiv der Franckeschen Stiftungen zu Halle (AFSt), Hauptarchiv (HA), A 179: 1 "August Hermann Francke Tagebuch, 1 Jan. 1719–31 Dec. 1725," 25 March 1725.
49. "Gestern haben Ihro Majst. der König und der Cron=Prinz keinen andern habit angeleget, alß wie a l'ordinaire nembl. dero tägl. montirungs=rock, wie man es bey den großen Corps trägend," GStA-PK, BPH Rep. 46, W 41, "Journal über die Reise Sr. Durchlaucht des Markgrafen Carl Wilhelm Friedrich zu Ansbach nach Berlin und die daselbst am 30 May 1729 vollzogene Vermählung Höchst dasselben mit mit Ihrer Königl. Hoheit der Prinzessin Friederike v. Preußen vom 11. May–11. Juni 1729."
50. The commemorative literature that recorded such visits typically papered over awkward moments or ceremonial faux pas, and it did so in this case as well, see Marschke, "Princes' Power, Aristocratic Norms, and Personal Eccentricities," 56–57.
51. GStA-PK, HA I, Rep. 36, "Hofverwaltung," Nr. 2950/1, "Einrichtung der Räume im Berliner Schloß sowie Unterbringung des Gefolges während des Besuchs des Königs von Polen in Berlin und Potsdam, 1728."
52. "[Frederick William] ordered all the Provosts (a Sort of Servants to the Executioner) . . . to be dressed in the French Mode, with great Hats, Feathers, their Hair in Bags, and the Cuffs of their Coat-Sleeves turned up with the same Stuff their Waistcoats were made of. Count Rottenbourg, the French Ambassador, who came in his Coach, with

a Retinue of above thirty Persons, to this Review, was surprised to see the Provosts dressed so like himself and his Servants; there being no other Difference, except that the Cuffs of their Sleeves were longer; their Hats larger; and as to their Bags, they seemed rather to be Sacks hanging at their Backs, than Bags for their Hair." Éléazar de Mauvillon, *The Life of Frederick-William I: Late King of Prussia. Containing Many Authentick Letters and Pieces, Very Necessary for Understanding the Affairs of Germany and the Northern Kingdoms*, trans. William Phelips (London, 1750), 229–30.

53. Wilhelm Oncken, "Sir Charles Hotham und Friedrich Wilhelm I. im Jahre 1730: Urkundliche Ausschlüsse aus den Archiven zu London und Wein," *Forschungen zur brandenburgischen und preußischen Geschichte (FBPG)* 7 (1894): 377–407.

54. Regarding Gundling, see Martin Sabrow, *Herr und Hanswurst: Das tragische Schicksal des Hofgelehrten Jacob Paul von Gundling* (Stuttgart, 2001).

55. As Johann Michael von Loen noted in his description of the court in Berlin in 1718: "Ich wolte es keinem rathen, daß er sich an demselben mit bundscheckigten französischen Modekleidern sehen ließ, er muß sich dann gern auslachen lassen: Wie solches einem von meinen guten Freunden begegnet ist, der seine von Paris mitgebrachte Kleider, nachdem er sich einmal damit bey Hof gezeiget, wieder einpacken muste, um den Mißfallen des Königs und dem Gespötte der Höflinge sich zu entziehen; dieser Monarch kann nichts weniger als dergleichen französischen Puppen leiden." Johann Michael von Loen, "Der königlich Preußische Hof in Berlin, 1718," in *Des Herrn von Loen gesammelte Kleine Schrifften, Dritter Abschnitt*, ed. J. C. Schneider (Frankfurt, 1750; reprinted Frankfurt, 1972), 22–39, here 28–29.

56. "An dem Königl Preußischen Hofe wird alle unnöthige Kleider-Pracht durch scharffe Edicta verboten, und die Oeconomie gantz anders, als vorhin, eingerichtet." *Die Europaische Fama, Welche den gegenwärtigen Zustand der vornehmsten Höfe entdecket* 145 (1713–14): 82. Loen even praised the modest style of the clothing at the Prussian court: "Ich habe, so lang ich in Berlin gewesen, kein gantz mit Galonen besetztes Kleid gesehen. Die kostbarsten Kleider haben nicht über etlich und zwantzig Loth Gold oder Silber: sie sind meistentheils gestickt, und dieses so nett, so niedlich und sowohl an den Leib gepaßt, daß man nichts schöners sehen kan." Loen, "Der königlich Preußische Hof," 22–23.

57. Shovlin, "The Cultural Politics of Luxury," 581.

58. Loen, "Der königlich Preußische Hof," 22.

59. "Der König fuhrte bey dem Antritt seiner Regierung eine genaue Haushaltung ein; Er schaffte viele unnöthige Bedienten und Müßiggänger ab." Loen, "Der königlich Preußische Hof," 24. "Dieser *glorieuse* Printz ... hat zwar, was den Pracht des Hofes betrifft, unterschiedenes abgedanckt ... viel unnöthige Bedienten abgeschafft," *Die Europaische Fama* 142 (1713): 789.

60. Regarding keeping servants as status symbols, see Shovlin "The Cultural Politics of Luxury," 581, 603. See also the repeated admonitions that servants be present (but not that they work!) in Irmgard Pangerl, Martin Scheutz, and Thomas Winkelbauer, eds, *Der Wiener Hof im Spiegel der Zeremonial-Protokolle, 1652–1800* (Innsbruck, 2007).

61. This, too, was noted by contemporaries: "Dieser *glorieuse* Printz ... hat zwar, was den Pracht des Hofes betrifft, unterschiedenes abgedanckt, auch so gar einige Lust- und Land-Schlößer inzwischen verpachtet," *Die Europaische Fama* 142 (1713): 789.

62. "Diese Soldaten sind seine Lieblinge ... alle andere Divertissements sind ihm ein Greuel, welches die beyden Königl. Gärten zu Berlin und Oranienburg schon

erfahren: Aus deren Ersterem ein Waffen-Platz zum Exerciren der Soldaten, aus dem andern aber ein gemeiner Obst-Garten, gemacht werden müssen," *Die Europaische Fama* 157 (1714): 39.
63. Saisselin, *The Enlightenment against the Baroque*, 12–14.
64. Andreas Pecar, "Die Imagination von Autonomie, Größe und Dauer: Adelsrepräsentation im 18. Jahrhundert im Schloss- und Gartenbau," in *What Makes the Nobility Noble? Comparative Perspectives from the Sixteenth to the Twentieth Century*, ed. Jörn Leonhard and Christian Wieland (Göttingen, 2011), 255–78, here 273–74.
65. Peter-Michael Hahn, "Die Hofhaltung der Hohenzollern: Der Kampf um Anerkennung," in *Preussische Stile: Ein Staat als Kunststück*, ed. Patrick Bahners and Gerd Roellecke (Stuttgart, 2001), 73–89, here 86.
66. The small size of these palaces, and their remote locations, were also presumably desirable because they engendered the intimate atmosphere of Frederick William's "inner circle."
67. Marschke, "Von dem am Königl.," 247–48.
68. Johann Friedrich Grael and Johann Philipp Gerlach both designed churches for Frederick William.
69. Heinrich Cornelius Hecker claimed that Potsdam's churches were the match of Notre Dame or the Stephanskirche, see [Heinrich Cornelius Hecker], *Das itzt-blühende Potsdam, Mit poëtischer Feder entworffen, Von Bellamintes. Nebst einer Beylage verschiedener Anmerckungen und Nachrichten* (Potsdam, 1727), 42. The dedication of the new Bohemian church was reported in *Die Neue Europäische Fama, Welche den gegenwärtigen Zustand der vornehmsten Höfe entdecket* 21 (1737): 756; 29 (1737): 363.
70. Frederick William was not the first to build new neighborhoods as monarchical self-representation. See, for example, the model city built by the Princes of Anhalt-Dessau at Oranienbaum at the turn of the eighteenth century. See also Liechtenthal outside Vienna, Pecar, "Die Imagination von Autonomie, Größe und Dauer," 259.
71. Regarding Potsdam, see Marschke, "Von dem am Königl.," 247. Regarding Berlin, see Laurenz Demps, "'Intentionen' und Kosten der Berliner Stadtbaupolitik Friedrich Wilhelm I," *Berlin in Geschichte und Gegenwart: Jahrbuch des Landesarchivs Berlin* (2008): 7–26.
72. Demps, "'Intentionen' und Kosten der Berliner Stadtbaupolitik," 8.
73. Ibid., 23; Melanie Mertens, "'Unsern Hiesigen Residentzien . . . in Mehreren Flor und Ansehen zu Bringen': Zur späten Bau- und Kunstpolitik von König Friedrich Wilhelm I," in *Selling Berlin: Imagebildung und Stadtmarketing von der preußischen Residenz bis zur Bundeshauptstadt*, ed. Thomas Biskup and Marc Schalenberg (Stuttgart, 2008), 25–44; and Melanie Mertens, *Berliner Barockpaläste: Die Entstehung eines Bautyps in der Zeit der ersten preußischen Könige* (Berlin, 2003).
74. Demps, "'Intentionen' und Kosten der Berliner Stadtbaupolitik," 11, 13.
75. Ibid., 15; and GStA-PK, HA I, Rep. 36, "Hofverwaltung," file number 94, "Hoffstaats Etat" for 1735–36.
76. "Die Strassen, die vorher gar krum und enge waren,
    Sind, so zu reden, nun ein gleiches Lineal,
    Man kan auf selbigen, ohn' allen Anstoß, fahren
    Dieweil sie überall wie ein geraumer Saal."
    Hecker, *Das itzt-blühende Potsdam*, 63.
77. Demps, "'Intentionen' und Kosten der Berliner Stadtbaupolitik," 23.

78. "Weilen Ihro Majestät gantz anders gesittet, als Dero Vorfahren, und im Regiments-Wesen grosse Reformen gemacht, so hat es allerhand Redens und Schreibens davon gesetzet... Ingleichen trägt man sich mit beykommenden Deutschen Sinn-gedichte, worinnen die *Miraculeuse* Curen des Königs von Preussen, so täglich in Berlin vorgehen, enthalte.

> Die Curen, so der König thut, sind alle wohl gerathen,
> Man setzt nicht mehr so häuffig auf, Pasteten, Torten, Braten.
> Wer grosse Bissen eingeschluckt, dem hilfft Er von dem Steine,
> Wer sich in Kutschen fahren ließ, den bringt Er auf die Beine.
> Dem, der die Kleider immerdar mit Golde ließ bordiren,
> Dem hilfft Er von der Gelbesucht, und lehrt ihn menagiren.
> Die Todten weckt Er wieder auf zu einem neuen Leben,
> Wer allzuviele Dienste hat, dem will Er Ruhe geben.
> Wer sich in Sänfften tragen ließ, der kan nun wieder gehen,
> Wer auf der faulen Seiten lag, beginnet aufzustehen.
> Was ehmahls fast unmöglich schien, bey unsern lieben Alten,
> Geschicht itzt: Denn es lernt der Hof genaue Wirthschafft halten.

Diese Verse hat der König über der Tafel selbsten gelesen, darüber gelacht, und gesaget: Er wolle noch mehr dergleichen Curen thun," *Die Europaische Fama* 157 (1714): 39–40.

79. Regarding the gradual acceptance (or even specification) of military uniforms as appropriate attire at the imperial court in Vienna in the eighteenth century, see Duindam, "The Dynastic Court in an Age of Change," 22; and Pangerl, Scheutz, and Winkelbauer, eds, *Der Wiener Hof im Spiegel der Zeremonial-Protokolle*.

80. Suffice it to say here that Frederick William's conspicuous rejection of luxury and opulence and the Pietism's aesthetic asceticism were largely coincidental and compatible, but hardly the same. It is wrong on several levels to think of Frederick William as a "*Pietist auf den Thron*" as Klaus Deppermann refers to him. Klaus Deppermann, *Der hallesche Pietismus und der preußische Staat unter Friedrich III. (I.)* (Göttingen, 1961). Regarding Frederick William and Pietism, see Benjamin Marschke, "Halle Pietism and the Prussian State: Infiltration, Dissent, and Subversion," in *Pietism in Germany and North America, 1680–1820*, ed. Jonathan Strom, Hartmut Lehmann, and James Van Horn Melton (Aldershot, 2009), 217–28; and Marschke, "Halle Pietism and Politics in Prussia and Beyond," in *A Companion to German Pietism (1600–1800)*, ed. Douglas H. Shantz (Leiden, 2015), 472–526.

81. Kwass, "Ordering the World of Goods," 90.

82. Ibid., 113; Melinda Zook, "The Three-Piece Suit and Modern Masculinity: England, 1550–1850 (review)," *Journal of Interdisciplinary History* 34, no. 3 (2004): 451; Shovlin, "The Cultural Politics of Luxury," 605.

Bibliography

Arnim, Bernd Jakob von. *Von Ducaten des Chürfürstlich-Brandenburgischen und Königlichen-Preussischen regierenden Hauses.* Berlin, 1796.

———. *Von Thalern des Chürfürstlich-Brandenburgischen und Königlich-Preussischen regierenden Hauses.* Berlin, 1788.

Asch, Ronald G. "What Makes the Nobility Noble?" In *What Makes the Nobility Noble? Comparative Perspectives from the Sixteenth to the Twentieth Century,* edited by Jörn Leonhard and Christian Wieland. Göttingen, 2011.

Bauer, Volker. *Die höfische Gesellschaft in Deutschland von der Mitte des 17. bis zum Ausgang des 18. Jahrhunderts: Versuch einer Typologie.* Tübingen, 1993.

———. *Hofökonomie: Der Diskurs über den Fürstenhof in Zeremonialwissenschaft, Hausväterliteratur und Kameralismus.* Vienna, 1997.

Berg, Maxine, and Elizabeth Eger. "The Rise and Fall of the Luxury Debates." In *Luxury in the Eighteenth Century: Debates, Desires and Delectable Goods*, edited by Maxine Berg and Elizabeth Eger, 7–27. Houndsmills, Basingstoke, Hampshire, 2003.

Berry, Christopher J. "The Eighteenth-Century Debate." In *The Idea of Luxury: A Conceptual and Historical Investigation*, 126–76. Cambridge, 1994.

Börsch-Supan, Helmut. "Friedrich Wilhelm I. und die Kunst." In *Der Soldatenkönig: Friedrich Wilhelm I. in seiner Zeit*, edited by Friedrich Beck and Julius H. Schoeps, 207–30. Potsdam, 2003.

Carter, Philip. "Men about Town: Representations of Foppery and Masculinity in Early Eighteenth-Century Urban Society." In *Gender in Eighteenth-Century England: Roles, Representations, and Responsibilities*, edited by Hannah Barker and Elaine Chalus, 31–57. London, 1997.

Demps, Laurentz. "'Intentionen' und Kosten der Berliner Stadtbaupolitik Friedrich Wilhelm I." *Berlin in Geschichte und Gegenwart: Jahrbuch des Landesarchivs Berlin* (2008): 7–26.

Deppermann, Klaus. *Der hallesche Pietismus und der preußische Staat unter Friedrich III. (I.).* Göttingen, 1961.

Duindam, Jeroen. "The Dynastic Court in an Age of Change: Frederick II Seen From the Perspective of Habsburg and Bourbon Court Life." In *Friedrich der Große und der Hof*, edited by Michael Kaiser. Potsdam, 2009.

Ewert, Ulf Christian, and Jan Hirschbiegel. "Nur Verschwendung? Zur sozialen Funktion der demonstrativen Zurschaustellung höfischen Güterverbrauchs." In *Luxus und Integration: Materielle Hofkulture Westeuropas vom 12. bis zum. 18. Jahrhundert*, edited by Werner Paravincini, 105–121. Munich, 2010.

Finn, Margot. "Men's Things: Masculine Possession in the Consumer Revolution." *Social History* 25, no. 2 (2000): 133–55.

Friedrich Wilhelm I. "Instruktion König Friedrich Wilhelms I. für seinen Nachfolger [1722]." In *Politsche Testamente der Hohenzollern*, edited by Richard Dietrich, 221–243. Munich, 1981.

Hahn, Peter-Michael. "Die Hofhaltung der Hohenzollern: Der Kampf um Anerkennung." In *Preussische Stile: Ein Staat als Kunststück*, edited by Patrick Bahners and Gerd Roellecke, 73–89. Stuttgart, 2001.

———. "Hofhaltung und Kulturtransfer nach Berlin-Cölln und Potsdam bis 1740. Zur Rezeption und Imitation höfischer Stilelemente." In *Preussen, Deutschland und Europa 1701–2001*, edited by Jürgen Luh, Vinzenz Czech, and Bert Becker, 253–79. Groningen, 2003.

Hampton, Timothy. "Baroques." *Yale French Studies* 80 (1991): 1–8.

Hecker, Heinrich Cornelius. *Das itzt-blühende Potsdam, Mit poëtischer Feder entworffen, Von Bellamintes. Nebst einer Beylage verschiedener Anmerckungen und Nachrichten.* Potsdam, 1727.

Jones, Jennifer M. "Repackaging Rousseau: Femininity and Fashion in Old Regime France." *French Historical Studies* 18, no. 4 (1994): 939–67.

Kloosterhuis, Elisabeth M. *Soldatenkönigs Tafelfreuden: Die Tafelkultur am Hofe Friedrich Wilhelms.* Berlin, 2009.

Kuchta, David. "The Making of the Self-Made Man: Class, Clothing, and English Masculinity, 1688–1832." In *The Sex of Things: Gender and Consumption in Historical Perspective,* edited by Victoria de Grazia and Ellen Furlough, 54–78. Berkeley, CA, 1996.

Kwass, Michael. "Big Hair: A Wig History of Consumption in Eighteenth-Century France." *American Historical Review* 111, no. 3 (2006): 631–59.

——. "Consumption and the World of Ideas: Consumer Revolution and the Moral Economy of the Marquis de Mirabeau." *Eighteenth-Century Studies* 37, no. 2 (2004): 187–213.

——. "Ordering the World of Goods: Consumer Revolution and the Classification of Objects in Eighteenth-Century France." *Representations* 82 (2003): 87–116.

Loen, Johann Michael von. "Der königlich Preußische Hof in Berlin, 1718." In *Des Herrn von Loen gesammelte Kleine Schrifften, Dritter Abschnitt,* edited by J. C. Schneider, 22–39. Frankfurt, 1750; reprinted Frankfurt, 1972.

Maravall, Jose Antonio. *Culture of the Baroque: Analysis of a Historical Structure.* Translated by Terry Cochrane. Minneapolis, MN, 1986.

Marschke, Benjamin. "Competing Post-Baroque Masculinities: Pietist Masculinity and Prussian Masculinity in the Early Eighteenth Century." In *Gender im Pietismus: Netzwerke und Geschlechter-Konstruktionen,* edited by Pia Schmidt, 197–210. Halle, 2015.

——. "The Crown Prince's Brothers and Sisters: Succession and Inheritance Problems and Solutions among the Hohenzollerns, From the Great Elector to Frederick the Great." In *Sibling Relations and the Transformations of European Kinship, 1300–1900,* edited by Christopher H. Johnson and David Warren Sabean, 111–44. New York, 2011.

——. "Halle Pietism and Politics in Prussia and Beyond." In *A Companion to German Pietism (1600–1800),* edited by Douglas H. Shantz, 472–526. Leiden, 2015.

——. "Halle Pietism and the Prussian State: Infiltration, Dissent, and Subversion." In *Pietism in Germany and North America, 1680–1820,* edited by Jonathan Strom, Hartmut Lehmann, and James Van Horn Melton, 217–28. Aldershot, 2009.

——. "Princes' Power, Aristocratic Norms, and Personal Eccentricities: *Le Caractère Bizarre* of Frederick William I of Prussia (1713–1740)." In *The Holy Roman Empire, Reconsidered,* edited by Jason P. Coy, Benjamin Marschke, and David Warren Sabean, 49–70. New York, 2010.

——. "'Von dem am Königl. Preußischen Hofe abgeschafften *Ceremoniel*': Monarchical Representation and Court Ceremony in Frederick William I's Prussia." In *Orthodoxies and Diversity in Early Modern Germany,* edited by Randolph C. Head and Daniel Christensen, 227–52. Boston, 2004.

Mattern, Jochen. "Leopold I. von Anhalt-Dessau: Eine Studie zur Geschichte der politischen Technologie." *Kultursoziologie* 6, no. 2 (1997): 79–96.

Mauvillon, Éléazar de. *The Life of Frederick-William I: Late King of Prussia. Containing Many Authentick Letters and Pieces, Very Necessary for Understanding the Affairs of Germany and the Northern Kingdoms.* Translated by William Phelips. London, 1750.

Mertens, Melanie. *Berliner Barockpaläste: Die Entstehung eines Bautyps in der Zeit der ersten preußischen Könige.* Berlin, 2003.

———. "'Unsern Hiesigen Residentzien . . . in Mehreren Flor und Ansehen zu Bringen': Zur späten Bau- und Kunstpolitik von König Friedrich Wilhelm I." In *Selling Berlin: Imagebildung und Stadtmarketing von der preußischen Residenz bis zur Bundeshauptstadt,* edited by Thomas Biskup and Marc Schalenberg, 25–44. Stuttgart, 2008.

Paravincini, Werner. "Von materieller Attraktion, adligem Dienst und politscher Macht. Über den tieferen Sinn höfischer Lebensführung: Eine Zusammenfassung." In *Luxus und Integration: Materielle Hofkulture Westeuropas vom 12. bis zum. 18. Jahrhundert,* edited by Werner Paravincini, 271–84. Munich, 2010.

Pecar, Andreas. "Die Imagination von Autonomie, Größe und Dauer: Adelsrepräsentation im 18. Jahrhundert im Schloss- und Gartenbau." In *What Makes the Nobility Noble? Comparative Perspectives from the Sixteenth to the Twentieth Century,* edited by Jörn Leonhard and Christian Wieland, 255–78. Göttingen, 2011.

Sabrow, Martin. *Herr und Hanswurst: Das tragische Schicksal des Hofgelehrten Jacob Paul von Gundling.* Stuttgart, 2001.

Saisselin, Rémy G. *The Enlightenment against the Baroque: Economics and Aesthetics in the Eighteenth Century.* Berkeley, CA, 1992.

Shovlin, John. "The Cultural Politics of Luxury in Eighteenth-Century France." *French Historical Studies* 23, no. 4 (2000): 577–606.

Stafford, John Martin. *Private Vices, Publick Benefits? The Contemporary Reception of Bernard Mandeville.* Solihull, 1997.

Stollberg-Rilinger, Barbara. "Höfische Öffentlichkeit: Zur zeremoniellen Selbstdarstellung des brandenburgischen Hofes vor dem europäischen Publikum." *Forschungen zur brandenburgischen und preußischen Geschichte (FBPG)* 7, no. 2 (1997): 145–76.

Trilling, Lionel. *Sincerity and Authenticity.* Cambridge, MA, 1972.

Veblen, Thorsten. *The Theory of the Leisure Class.* New York, 1899.

Vries, Jan de. *The Industrious Revolution: Consumer Behavior and the Household Economy 1650 to the Present.* Cambridge, 2008.

Wakefield, Andre. *The Disordered Police State: German Cameralism as Science and Practice.* Chicago, 2009.

CHAPTER SEVEN

"Alles Geld gehet immer auf"
Money in an Emerging Consumer and Cash Economy, Göppingen (1735–1860)

DENNIS FREY JR.

In 1782, disaster struck the Swabian hometown of Göppingen. Ignited by a "three-fold lightning strike" on 25 August, fire spread rapidly throughout the city of about 3,500, consuming nearly all domiciles, including that of the *Zeugmacher* (worsted-wool weaver) Ernst Jacob Vayhinger.[1] As he recounted this calamity in his chronicle, he noted that his house had been mistakenly underinsured at "1,300 Gulden (fl.=gulden)" when it should have been valued for "not under 1,800 fl."[2] Vayhinger also bemoaned the slow process of rebuilding: "God help us! Everything is so expensive."[3] A year later, things looked better; indeed, the carpenter in charge of rebuilding his house asked Vayhinger to "strike the first nail," but he refused and passed the hammer onto his sons, proudly describing how the younger one (also named Ernst Jacob) took "twelve strikes to hammer in the nail" and the older one (Andreas) sank his nail "with five blows."[4] Vayhinger's joy proved fleeting, for in the next passage of his chronicle he once again lamented: "With so many costs, I often do not know where I am. All the money continually goes to [them]."[5]

While Vayhinger's emotional up-and-downs certainly catches the eye, so too does his particular attention to money. In fact, the chronicle, which he kept from 1755 to 1784, always included, except for the final two years, a detailed accounting of his household's annual net worth. With an eye so consistently on the bottom line, Vayhinger certainly seems to confirm Mack Walker's argument that "hometownsmen liked money as much as anybody else, and maybe more than most."[6] For Walker, though, the hidebound communal "penumbra" that characterized these hometowns meant that the inhabitants were "kept ... from getting very much [money], and they fiercely resented anybody who did get very much."[7] In this model, money, in particular cash and capital, worked as a destabilizing, outside impulse that hometownsmen strove to stifle and curtail. Preferring stasis and stability to flux and risk, German hometownsmen "stoutly resisted integration into"[8] the modern, bourgeois world by crafting and relying on institutions designed to regulate personal ambition. A close reading of Vayhinger's chronicle suggests, however, that there was more to this than simply tempering of individual avarice and ambition through more powerful socioeconomic and political institutions. A complex understanding of money formed and informed an essential part of Vayhinger's mentalité, and as will be argued, money worked for him simultaneously as "a social relation, a symbolic system, and a material reality."[9] He seemed to intuit money's tangible and intangible forms, and he was not alone in his ability to grasp money as a set of complex meanings. Indeed, analysis of a long series of probate inventories from other artisans in Göppingen reveals a complicated set of patterns, behaviors, and dispositions when it came to money.[10] On one hand, its most tangible form—cash—moved front and center as the *Handwerker* (artisans) became both more consumerist and financially savvy during the late eighteenth and early nineteenth centuries. But, on the other hand, money's intangible nature—represented by and through debt obligations—continued to operate in manifold and meaningful ways, helping Göppingers to negotiate the changing world around them. In order to make this case, a brief exploration of the long-standing tradition and legal systems of partible inheritance in southwest Germany will be followed by further discussion of Ernst Jacob Vayhinger's dispositions toward money as revealed by his chronicle. Then, turning to an analysis of the probate inventories, further light will be shed on the attitudes that ordinary artisan craftspeople in this hometown held about money.

Money in the Eighteenth Century—Institutions and Individuals

The complex nature and understanding of money in Göppingen and more broadly Württemberg stemmed in large measure from the custom of partible inheritance. Dating back to the 1555 *Erstes Landrecht (First Law Code)*, this tradition had a considerable effect on the institutions and culture of the region. Initiated by Duke Christoph in 1551, this code stipulated that the property of anyone who died without a *Testament*, or will, should be fully inventoried. Later iterations of this code in 1567 and 1610 continued the development of what would become an institutional nexus binding ordinary people throughout the duchy to well-trained scribes who were responsible for creating the *Inventuren und Teilungen* (inventories and partitions). As part of this process of institutionalization, authors like Nicodemus Frischlin and Adam Israel Roslin, wrote handbooks for the notaries, and as argued below, these documents provide clear evidence that cash received more and more attention as the eighteenth century transitioned into the nineteenth. The earliest such manual, Nicodemus Frischlin's *Instruction und Bericht* (1605), simply listed fifteen types of currency that should be recorded under the rubric *Bargeld* (cash), before instructing the scribe to summarize the total value.[11] This book would go through six editions over the course of the next 130 years, and with each new one, the list of currencies grew. Indeed, by the last edition in 1733, the manual encouraged scribes to look for and record forty-six different types of coinage.[12] Following in a somewhat similar vein as Frischlin's work, Adam Israel Roslin's *Abhandlung von Inventuren und Abtheilungen* recommended that the notaries should differentiate between "small inheritances," which should be simply summarized in total, and "considerable estates," which deserved more attention to detail through line-listing and conversion rates for the specific currency found.[13]

Manuals written during the nineteenth century took, according to Hildegard Mannheims, a "completely different" approach to cash that was found in an estate.[14] Instead of offering the scribes relatively brief instructions, Albert Heinrich Stein's *Handbuch des Württembergischen Erb-Recht* (1827) and its contemporaries (for example, L. F. John's *Inventur-Büchlein oder Hausstirer* and David Seigle's *Der Württembergische Waisenrichter*) provided more detailed guidelines, including specific conversion rates for the ever-expanding list of currencies and the strong reminder that "the exchange rate of gold is highly variable."[15] Later editions of these manuals also stipulated that paper money should be assessed, and Seigle's 1868 handbook even listed conversion rates for gold and silver coins from the United States: an American "one-dollar piece" was worth, on the average, 4 marks 15–20 pfennig and an American "ten-dollar piece" was valued at between 41 marks 50 pfennig to 42 marks, while one dollar (North American) of one hundred cents was equal to 4 marks 25 pfennig.[16] Clearly by the middle of the nineteenth century, scribes found all types of currencies, even ones from overseas, in the households that they inventoried, and as shown below, at least one artisan household in Göppingen had American dollars among its possessions.

Cash was not, however, the only form of property that the notaries inventoried. Indeed, and dating back to the very beginnings of this institutional nexus in the seventeenth century, notaries were responsible for quantifying and assessing the monetary value of all forms of personal wealth.[17] According to the law code, personal wealth included material items, like real estate and personal possessions, as well as immaterial items, like loans-extended (*Activa*) and debts-incurred (*Passiva*).[18] The law code also stipulated that these assessments should be carried out on the following occasions: marriage (and remarriage), death of the first partner, and death of the remaining partner. When these milestones occurred, a notary usually accompanied by an apprentice would go through the household, line-listing all categories of material and immaterial wealth. By "involving the state directly in private life through the devolution of family property,"[19] partible inheritance and the institutions that grew out of it therefore created an unusual set of circumstances for ordinary Swabians. No matter their gender, at various significant moments in their lives, they met with a scribe and almost certainly watched, if not assisted, him monetize property, both tangible and intangible. From an anthropological perspective, this systematic bringing together of "quantification and money" served to "resacralize exchanges."[20] And, in early modern Württemberg, where most everyone had a personal stake in the orderly exchange of household property, this resacralization manifested itself in the concepts of *Haushaltung* (household management) and *Durchhalten* (persistence).[21]

Consciously or unconsciously, Vayhinger touched on this theme throughout his chronicle. In fact, after presenting his family tree as a sort of introduction, he began the text of his chronicle with the following statement about his marriage to Anna Barbara née Schaupp: "Year 1755. We began our [married] life together. At that time our property was 100 gulden in cash. And on our wedding day we received 30 gulden. So all together it is 130 gulden."[22] In these four sentences, Vayhinger neatly wove together the concept of *Haushaltung* and the centrality of money. These intertwined themes run like red threads through the entire document. For example, when he reconciled accounts for the "year 1764 till 1765," Ernst Jacob noted that an unspecified illness had afflicted him for months, with the consequence that his household had lost fifty gulden.[23] He fared no better in 1766 when his household wealth dropped by another thirty-five gulden to a total of 620. Looking back on these two years of losses, Ernst Jacob grumbled, "I have had great physical infirmities, especially in my chest." He hinted at yet another burden: "there are disturbing difficulties due to my wife, which I will not name."[24] Ten years later in 1776, after calculating a 200-gulden profit, Vayhinger named the difficulties with his wife: "I have suffered much because of my wife's drinking."[25] His wife's predilection for alcohol surfaced once more in Vayhinger's chronicle when he lamented in 1780 that "my *uxor* [wife] had the greatest part" of the seventy-five gulden lost that year.[26] It is striking that Ernst Jacob brought his wife into his chronicle because her apparently heavy drinking restricted the household's accumulation of wealth. She was not fulfilling the most significant role of a spouse: managing the household for future generations (*Haushaltung*). Instead, her behavior jeopardized the primary objective of persistence (*Durchhalten*[27]). Such disputes between spouses frequently wound up, as demonstrated by David Sabean's fine work on the village of Neckarhausen, before the local civil and church authorities; for instance, the wife of Andreas Köpple protested bitterly to the local church consistory about her husband "drinking excessively and not caring for his *Haushaltung*."[28] While the Vayhingers never went before the town magistrates, Ernst Jacob's concentration on the economic implications of his wife's alcoholism—he never mentions it in any other context—suggests that monetizing things, even personal relationships, helped him make sense of the uncontrollable forces in his world.

Not surprisingly, Vayhinger's business interactions also reveal much about his attention to money. In the second year of his chronicle (1756–57), he wrote that he had worked "six *Centner* [hundredweight] of wool; which had come from a ropemaker in Ebersbach" and for which he "had previously given thirty-nine fl. [to the ropemaker]; but because I offered to trade *parr Geld* [cash] for the wool that he brought to my house, he would not trust me and instead took the wool away; finally a good friend, my cousin Michael Vayhinger helped me out with 100 gulden."[29] The ropemaker's mistrust apparently came as a result of Vayhinger either having too little cash on hand or offering coinage that seemed dubious. Vayhinger's status as a newly minted master-weaver with little caché probably also played a role. By bringing not only deeper pockets but also more standing in the community, his cousin thus helped him establish more trust with the ropemaker. This was not the only instance where Vayhinger commented on how money related to trust. Indeed, the most obvious statement came in 1772, when Vayhinger complained that "Johann Georg Kerler, Zeugmacher in Memmingen" had "cheated [him] out of seventy-five fl.," adding that "one does not know anymore, whom one can trust."[30] Unfortunately, our chronicler provided no further details about this swindle: was it cash, services, or goods that the charlatan took from him? Knowing such details would of course be a boon, but here the key is that this instance and others reveal the complex ways in which ordinary Swabians, like Vayhinger, understood that money was more than just metal coinage; it was "trust inscribed."[31]

His complex understanding of money's symbolic nature notwithstanding, Vayhinger certainly retained a healthy respect for hard currency. He had begun his chronicle with a focus on "*Baares Geld*," and near the end of it, as he documented the fire's aftermath, Vayhinger returned to the material nature of coinage. Besides noting the inflation and stress caused by the costs of the disaster, he also discussed the special fire relief fund arranged by the ducal government. According to our chronicler, at least two cash distributions were made from it, and after the second one, he exclaimed: "By God's reward, I received twenty-six fl. forty kr[eutzer]. This good deed was truly well-received, because I had no more *Geld* left."[32] When his chronicle finally came to an end in December 1784, Vayhinger concluded it with a rather fascinating anecdote about seeing "a coin [*Geld*], which a farmer, not from around here, found in his fields. On its face stood: Caesar Tittus [sic] Vespasianus, the emperor who destroyed Jerusalem."[33] Money in all its forms, even ancient Roman coinage, commanded the respect and attention of Vayhinger and, as the ensuing analysis of other sources shows, his fellow Swabians differed little.

Toward a Cash and Consumer-Driven Economy

By the 1770s, most Swabians were experiencing "a growing commercialization of life" and the "new possibilities" that came from the thickening and expanding webs of "a precocious, often unstable, but increasingly potent, world economy."[34] This experience was certainly the case with those living in Göppingen, a city well-positioned between the large, regional centers of Stuttgart and Ulm.[35] Handicrafts, but especially those involved in weaving, dominated the local and regional economies through much of the period.[36] Commercial activity had grown steadily from the mid 1750s to the early 1770s, but stalled thereafter due to various setbacks, including the aforementioned citywide fire and the French Revolutionary Wars.[37] Nonetheless, Göppingen's location showed promise, as observed by Christoph Meiners when he traveled through the town in 1794: "Göppingen comes alive not merely through its flourishing industry, but also through the constant traffic, which flows from or to Ulm, Augsburg, and Italy."[38] In fact, by the 1820s impulses from within and without made Göppingen bustle with activity. Local entrepreneurs established, for instance, twenty manufactories between 1820 and 1844. While the majority of them remained relatively small ventures, one factory owned by Ludwig Bauman employed 115 workers between 1829 and 1832.[39] This plant was, for Karl Kirschmer, a sign that the "second phase of Göppingen's industrialization" had begun, but grand-scale factories like Baumann's remained the exception rather than the rule in the town until at least the 1860s.[40] Alongside these internal catalysts of the nineteenth century came external ones, most notably the opening of a railroad in late 1847 that followed the same path as Meiners had.[41] These developments seemed to put the town on the fast track of economic development, and its population more than doubled, rising from 2,900 to over 7,000 inhabitants between 1730 and 1865.[42] By the 1860s, then, "the pace of intercommunication" along the webs linking central Europe to the Americas had accelerated tremendously.[43]

Through all of this, most artisans continued to rely, as I have argued elsewhere, on the flexible, industrious nature of their patchwork household enterprises.[44] By combining their primary tradecraft with a variety of other economic activities, including but not limited to farming, animal husbandry, and leasing property, the artisans in Göppingen both weathered the period's economic storms and participated in the rising tide of consumerism. As was usually the case, novel behaviors, goods, and tastes, such as drinking coffee, first appeared among the wealthier families around mid century, but it did not take long thereafter for a majority of the townspeople to adopt them. By the 1780s, most artisans had, as evidenced by the clothing, furniture, and household goods listed in their inventories, made their homes more *gemütlich* (cozy) and themselves more *bürgerlich* (bourgeois). The inventories, however, also revealed telling changes in the ways that these artisans related to money. For example, the average and median amounts of gulden found among the artisans oscillated period to period with no glaring trends, other than a relative slow decline over time particularly when considering inflation (see Table 7.1). More clearly discernible was the shift that occurred in the percentage of households keeping cash reserves. Whereas a sizable majority (between 79.6 percent and 83.9 percent) of them had *Bargeld* during the eighteenth century, that figure dropped after the turn of the century to fluctuate between 52.1 percent and 62.4 percent.

Table 7.1. Cash on Hand (*Bargeld*) by 25-Year Periods.

	1738–62 (n = 98)	1763–87 (n = 93)	1788–1812 (n = 119)	1813–37 (n = 101)	1838–62 (n = 147)
Average in fl.	154	97.31	123.88	270.2	143.318
Median in fl.	19	28	12	21.08	10
Households with	78 (79.6%)	78 (83.9%)	62 (52.1%)	63 (62.4%)	83 (56.5%)
Households without	20 (20.4%)	15 (16.1%)	57 (47.9%)	38 (37.6%)	64 (43.5%)

Sources: Stadtarchiv Göppingen, Inventuren und Teilungen.

Closer analysis of some individual inventories reveals even more about this trend. When for instance Justina Weiß, the wife of a tailor named Johannes, died in 1738, the notary who assessed the property of their household listed eight gulden under the rubric of *Bargeld*, but he noted that this money had gone to "*leich Kosten* [burial costs]" and otherwise none was "existing."[45] The inventories of her contemporaries did not differ.[46] Through the mid eighteenth century, a high percentage of households kept cash on hand for the sole purpose of properly burying a deceased member. Beyond that, most families had little to no spare cash.

Several decades later, true reserves of cash began to appear. At his death in 1779, Christian Cammerer, a well-to-do worsted-wool weaver and contemporary of our chronicler, had 208 gulden in cash, aside from the twenty-five fl. that went to his funeral.[47] Similarly, the Widmann household, wealthy tanners, held over 100 gulden in hard currency.[48] Even a middling tailor named Johann Michael Ehmer had spare money (thirty fl.) when he died in 1780.[49] Although Ehmer's cash reserves paled in comparison to those of his wealthy neighbors, at least he had some. And, if Walter Troeltsch's estimate holds true, then thirty gulden equaled about one third of a year's wages; hence, it was no paltry sum.[50] From a consumer's point of view, this cash would have made it easy for Ehmer's household to acquire the latest fashions in clothing (outerwear for men and women was typically valued between one and nine fl.) and in furniture (fashionable double-door wardrobes were valued around four fl.). Reflecting the shift toward a cash- and consumer-driven economy in their town and foreshadowing the instructions found in their guidebooks, the Göppingen notaries at the turn of the century no longer listed *Leichenkosten* under the rubric *Bargeld*. Instead, all funeral costs followed the final accounting as a sort of appendix to the document. The category of *Bargeld* therefore truly meant cash on hand from 1800 onward, and given the declining percentage of households with such reserves, it would seem that more folks were spending their cash than were hoarding it.

Besides documenting the growing cash and consumer economy, the evidence from Göppingen also clarified how the artisans, and not just our chronicler, relied on the symbolic nature of money through debt obligations and networks. Such financial ties featured prominently in Vayhinger's chronicle, and as argued by Sheilagh Ogilvie, Markus Küpker, and Janine Maegraith, they had a long and well-documented history in early modern Württemberg.[51] These scholars conducted an impressive comparative study of marriage and probate inventories from a smaller, more rural settlement than Göppingen, and in doing so, they showed that "ubiquitous borrowing . . . in seventeenth-century Wildberg played a positive role in enabling people to survive as well as they did."[52] In that town, loans were extended for a plethora of reasons, including services rendered, supplies delivered, or simply hard cash. The artisans in Göppingen behaved in much the same way, but subtle and significant changes did occur in their behaviors as they became more cash-oriented over time. One such change appeared when it came to loans-extended (*Activa*). Most of these financial ties during the eighteenth century came without interest. On Andreas Häberle's death inventory from 1742, there was, for example, only one line listed under *Activa*: "Michael Schweizer___5 fl. 30 kr."[53] At some point in time, this middling butcher had loaned, perhaps in cash, goods, or services, five-and-a-half gulden to Schweizer. Likewise, about forty years later in 1780, Johann Michael Ehmer, the same tailor with spending cash, had made prior to his death three consecutive loans (100 fl., 60 fl., and 10 fl.) to "a good friend" with no interest attached.[54] Change was, however, afoot. For instance, among the many *Activa* recorded on his inventory from 1780, the wealthy tanner Widmann made six capital loans bearing explicit rates of interest. Including the premium and the interest, they equaled 620 fl. 45 x [x=kreuzer], or just over a quarter (27.3 percent) of all the loans held by his family.[55] And, when our chronicler's probate inventory was finalized in 1792, the scribe recorded nine capital loans with various terms of interest.[56] Incidentally, both the Vayhinger and Widmann households had been early adopters of the eighteenth century's novel fashions, thus making them trendsetters. By embracing capital loans, they also pioneered a new approach to money that became increasingly commonplace as the eighteenth century neared its end.

Money in the Nineteenth Century—Expanding Networks and Webs

Following the turn of the century, notaries seldom recorded the kind of interest-free loans that had been the norm during much of the eighteenth century. In 1827, when the middle-stratum nail-smith Jakob Friedrich Beeh died, his inventory listed, for example, *Activa* that totaled 1,035 fl. 2 kr., and all came with interest attached.[57] A contemporary of Beeh, the wealthy grandmaster Johann Georg Vayhinger had loaned out nearly 16,000 fl., and interest-bearing "capital" loans accounted for 95 percent of this enormous sum.[58] Thirty-four years later, when Catharina Barbara Greiner died in 1861, her household had extended ten "capital" loans, totaling an impressive 4,900 fl. 29 kr.[59] Interestingly, one of those loans (500 fl.) was extended without interest to Christian Greiner, a "purse-maker in Zanesville, Ohio, North America."[60] Presumably the brother-in-law of Catharina Barbara, Christian very probably borrowed that hefty sum to emigrate to the United States. As the notary went through the possessions of the Greiner household, he discovered "2. American Dollars [each worth] 2 fl. 24 kr."[61] Apparently Catharina Barbara's brother-in-law in Zanesville was slowly, but surely, paying down his debt. In the broader scope of things, however, these two dollars represented much more than simply the repayment of an interest-free loan. On one level, the notary used an exchange rate that matched perfectly the instructions listed in a standard manual.[62] On another level, those dollars further evidenced the widening and thickening of the economic webs, linking markets, societies, and cultures across the Atlantic. On a third level, they represented the ways in which the more material aspects of money—cash and interest-bearing, capital loans—had moved to the forefront of Göppingen's society by the 1860s.

At the same time, Göppingers' attitudes and behaviors toward money's immaterial, symbolic nature shifted ever so slightly. Most notably, as shown in Table 7.2, the portion of households that held no *Activa* or *Passiva* steadily increased. There was evidently a growing tendency among some artisans to avoid debt altogether. For some, this may have been a conscious choice to clear their books before death. For others, it may have come from being locked out of the expanding capital networks. Regardless of which it was, the majority of artisans in Göppingen (at least seven of every ten) continued to participate in the monetized networks of trust that had fueled trade and commerce for generations.[63] Like Vayhinger in the last half of the eighteenth century, nineteenth-century artisans seemed to approach debt management in the careful, judicious fashion dictated by *Haushaltung* and *Durchhalten*, even as they found a way to adopt more financially sensitive approaches to *Activa*. Indeed, as depicted in Figure 7.1, most households, regardless of when, fell at or near zero when it came to balancing their loans and debts. To be sure, a slight majority was always in the red, and the gap between the haves and the have

Table 7.2. Debt Management by 25-Year Periods.

	1738–62 (n = 98)	1763–87 (n = 93)	1788–1812 (n = 119)	1813–37 (n = 101)	1838–62 (n = 147)
Loans-Extended (*Activa*)					
Households with	82 (83.7%)	79 (84.9%)	84 (70.6%)	73 (72.3%)	102 (69.4%)
Households without	16 (16.3%)	14 (15.1%)	35 (29.4%)	28 (27.3%)	45 (30.6%)
Avg fl. per loan	290.51	322.98	453.08	1,078.28	1,360.56
Med fl. per loan	56.41	110	85.07	105	150
Debts-Owed (*Passiva*)					
Households with	92 (93.9%)	85 (91.4%)	97 (81.5%)	89 (88.1%)	111 (75.5%)
Households without	6 (6.1%)	8 (8.6%)	22 (18.5%)	12 (11.9%)	36 (24.5%)
Avg fl. per debt	−162	−268.64	−552.16	−766.32	−929.15
Med fl. per debt	−84.4	−147.28	−279.2	−390.97	−421.98
Credit Balance (*Activa* − *Passiva*)					
Avg fl.	128.58	54.34	−99.08	311.96	431.41
Med fl.	−33.73	−49.5	−120.33	−151.28	−117.9
Households in the red (<0)	57 (58.2%)	55 (59.1%)	77 (64.7%)	65 (64.4%)	83 (56.5%)
Households in the black (≥0)	41 (41.8%)	38 (40.9%)	42 (35.3%)	36 (35.6%)	64 (43.5%)

Sources: Stadtarchiv Göppingen, Inventuren und Teilungen.

nots clearly grew in the nineteenth century, but money in its intangible forms, especially through debt obligations, remained a vital and important part of their daily life. Steeped in a culture and society that emphasized quantification and monetization of all forms of property, good management thereof, and persistence, most artisans intuitively understood the complexity of money, and knowing (consciously or unconsciously) its vagaries meant that most artisans approached money with prudence. However, this did not mean that they were unaware of, or resistant to, money's more capitalistic forms. Thus, their relationship with, and understanding of, money were much more complex than Walker's model implied.

Rather than exhibiting a love–hate relationship with money, fearing its destabilizing effects, and hence relying on institutions to frustrate personal ambition, the artisans, at least in this hometown, shrewdly employed money, knowing that its multiplicity rendered "it supremely suited as a medium of exchange."[64] Employing money's metal, and eventually paper, forms, Göppin-

Figure 7.1. Debt management (Loans minus Debts) of all cases ($n = 558$).

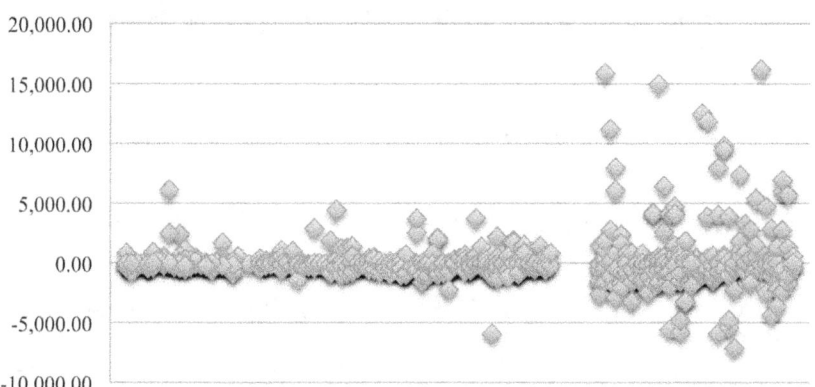

Sources: Stadtarchiv Göppingen, Inventuren und Teilungen.

gers acquired the novel trappings of the bourgeois, consumerist world, thus altering the social space in which they lived. Simultaneously, their enduring involvement with credit networks and the regular monetization of household property confirmed that "money was really about credit, not metal."[65] For most Swabians, these habits, practices, and experiences created a level-headed disposition toward money, captured perhaps best by the old saw, "*schaffe, schaffe, Häusle baue* (work, work, build a little home)."[66] Clearly focusing attention on persistence (*Durchhalten*) and household management (*Haushaltung*), this maxim also reminded folks that money in all its complexity remained central to those goals.

Dennis Frey Jr. has worked at Lasell College since 2004, where he has been teaching mostly world history and first year seminars. After serving two consecutive stints as chair of the humanities department, he moved onto facilitating a faculty task force charged with revising the college's core curriculum. Frey's research borrows heavily from Pierre Bourdieu, with the modest hope of clarifying the dynamic ways in which structures relate to individuals and vice versa. He has published a series of articles on the artisans of Göppingen and how complex socio-economic change affected them.

Notes

1. Karl Kirschmer, *Die Geschichte der Stadt Göppingen* (Göppingen, 1953), 1: 236.
2. Stadtarchiv Göppingen (hereafter: StAG), B.I.1.a., *Hauschronik des Zeugmachers Ernst Jakob Vayhinger*, 52. Unless otherwise noted, all translations are mine. For

additional analysis, see Walter Tröltsch, "Die Göppinger Zeugmacherei im 18. Jahrhundert und das sog. Vayhingerbuch," *Jahrbuch für Gesetzgebung, Verwaltung und Volkswirtschaft im Deutschen Reich*, ed. G. Schmoller (n.p., 1896), 165–87.
3. *Hauschronik*, 60.
4. Ibid., 62.
5. Ibid.
6. Mack Walker, *German Home Towns: Community, State, and General Estate, 1648–1871* (Ithaca, NY, 1971), 134.
7. Ibid., 134, 427–31.
8. Christopher Friedrichs, "But Are We Any Closer to Home? Early Modern German Urban History Since *German Home Towns*," *Central European History* 30, no. 2 (1997): 184.
9. Bill Maurer, "The Anthropology of Money," *Annual Review of Anthropology* 35 (2006): 27.
10. From 3,911 probate inventories, dated 1738 to 1862, I determined that 2,059 of them came from artisanal families and were therefore viable for my study. From these, I selected 558 (or 27.1 percent) for analysis. Lacunae did exist in the series for the following years: 1818–20 and 1822–25.
11. For verbatim copies of these manuals, see Hildegard Mannheim, *Wie wird ein Inventar erstellt? Rechtskommentare als Quelle der volkskundlichen Forschung* (Münster, 1991), 263–384.
12. Ibid., 276.
13. Ibid., 289. Two editions appeared in 1761 and 1780.
14. Ibid., 79.
15. Ibid., 304.
16. Ibid., 329.
17. They used the following: 1 gulden (fl.) = 60 kreuzer (kr., x.) and 1 kreuzer = 6 heller (h.).
18. For more specifics, see Mannheim, *Wie wird ein Inventar erstellt?*
19. Ian F. McNeely, *The Emancipation of Writing: German Civil Society in the Making, 1790s–1820s* (Berkeley, CA, 2003), 22; see also 45–48.
20. Maurer, "The Anthropology of Money," 24.
21. For more details, see Hans Medick, *Weben und Überleben in Laichingen 1650–1800: Lokalgeschichte als Allgemeine Geschichte* (Göttingen, 1997), 157–205 and 532–58; and David Sabean, *Property, Production, and Family in Neckarhausen, 1700–1870* (Cambridge, 1990), 88–123.
22. *Hauschronik*, 8.
23. Ibid., 19.
24. Ibid., 20.
25. Ibid., 36. Evidently Ernst Jacob's embarrassment ran deep, because he switched from his native German to Latin (i.e. "uxor propter bibendum").
26. Ibid., 41. Again, note the use of Latin.
27. For Pietism's influence in this, see Andreas Gestrich, "Pietistisches Weltverständnis und Handeln in der Welt," in *Geschichte des Pietismus*, vol. 4: *Glaubenswelt und Lebenswelten*, ed. Hartmut Lehman (Göttingen, 2004), 556–83.
28. Sabean, *Property, Production, and Family*, 107. See also 101–16 and 174–79.
29. *Hauschronik*, 8. This passage also recorded that "bread cost 10, 12 kreuzer" and that "wine cost 6 for the poor, 8 for the middling, and so forth."
30. Ibid., 32.

31. Niall Ferguson, *The Ascent of Money: A Financial History of the World* (New York, 2008), 31. For more on money, see Rudolf Hilferding, *Finance Capital: A Study of the Latest Phase of Capitalist Development*, ed. Tom Bottomore, trans. Morris Watnick and Sam Gordon (London, 1981).
32. *Hauschronik*, 66.
33. Ibid., 69.
34. Mary Lindemann, *Health and Healing in Eighteenth-Century Germany* (Baltimore, MD, 1996), 19.
35. For more details about Göppingen's significance in the region, see James Allen Vann, *The Making of a State: Württemberg, 1593–1793* (Ithaca, NY, 1984): 180–81; Karl Kirschmer, *Die Geschichte der Stadt Göppingen, I. Teil & II. Teil* (Göppingen, 1953); Tom Scott and Bob Scribner, "Urban Networks," in *Germany: A New Social and Economic History, 1450–1630*, vol. 1, ed. Bob Scribner (London, 1996), 113–43.
36. Kirschmer, *Die Geschichte der Stadt Göppingen*, 217–25. For more details, see Tröltsch, "Die Göppinger Zeugmacherei"; Emil Hofmann, *Die Industrialisierung des Oberamtsbezirkes Göppingen* (Göppingen, 1910); and Alexander Dreher, *Göppingens Gewerbe im 19. Jahrhundert: Veröffentlichungen des Stadtarchivs Göppingen*, vol. 7 (Göppingen, 1971). Last but certainly not least, see also Sheilagh Ogilvie, *State Corporatism and Proto-Industry: The Württemberg Black Forest, 1580–1797* (Cambridge, 1997), 86–112, 129–30, and 308–63.
37. StAG, B.II.7.c. *Commerzienregister, 1754–1824*. For additional details, see Kirschmer, *Die Geschichte der Stadt Göppingen*, vol. 2, 37–50.
38. Christoph Meiners, *Kleinere Länder und Reisebeschreibungen*, vol. 2 (Berlin, 1794), 343.
39. Hofmann, *Industrialisierung*, 6. The oldest manufactory in Göppingen, a paper mill, had been established in 1727 by the Schwarz family, but even in the late 1820s, it employed only ten to twelve workers.
40. Kirschmer, *Die Geschichte der Stadt Göppingen*, 2: 89.
41. For more details on regional developments, see Wilhelm Abel, *Geschichte der deutschen Landwirtschaft vom frühen Mittelalter bis zum 19. Jahrhundert* (Stuttgart, 1962), 312–15.
42. Maarten Prak, ed., *Early Modern Capitalism: Economic and Social Change in Europe, 1400–1800* (London, 2001), 19. For population estimates, see Tröltsch, "Die Göppinger Zeugmacherei," 172, and Dreher, *Göppingens Gewerbe*, 183.
43. J. R. McNeill and William H. McNeill, *The Human Web: A Bird's-Eye View of World History* (New York, 2003), 212.
44. Dennis Frey, Jr., "Wealth, Consumerism, and Culture among the Artisans of Göppingen: Dynamism and Tradition in an Eighteenth-Century Hometown," *Central European History* 46, no. 4 (2013): 1–38, and Dennis Frey, Jr., "Industrious Households: Survival Strategies of Artisans in a Southwest German Town during the Eighteenth and Early Nineteenth Centuries," in *Household Strategies for Survival 1600–2000: Fission, Faction, and Cooperation*, ed. Laurence Fontaine and Jürgen Schlumbohm (Cambridge, 2000), 115–36.
45. StAG, B.II.2.g., *Inventuren & Teilungen*, 1.38–109.5 (1738). In addition to Ernst Jacob Vayhinger, twenty-one other specific case studies were selected from the set of 558 inventories as a way of probing various eras and social strata. An attempt was made to track down all evidence emanating from each case study in the collections of both the *Stadtarchiv Göppingen* and the *Kirchenregisteramt Göppingen*.

46. *Inventuren & Teilungen*, 1.39–4.5 (1739), 4.2–387 (1745), and 1.38–378 (1742).
47. Ibid., 19.2–113.5 (1779).
48. Ibid., 19.2–262 (1780). The exact figure was 113 fl. 40 x. at the time of Johannes's death, and his funeral costs (27 fl.) were listed separately.
49. *Inventuren & Teilungen*, 19.2–457 (1780). As was the convention, the notary listed an additional "14 fl." for his funeral costs separate from *"Baar Geldt."*
50. Walter Troeltsch, *Die Calwer Zeughandlungskompagnie und ihre Arbeiter: Studien zur Gewerbe- und Sozialgeschichte Altwürttembergs* (Jena, 1897), 225. Troeltsch argues that a master weaver in the mid to late eighteenth century earned on average ninety-five fl. "for about 285 days of work." See also Ogilvie, *State Corporatism and Proto-Industry*, where she argues that one gulden was the equivalent of "7–8 days' average earnings for a weaver in ordinary periods," 321.
51. See Sheilagh Ogilvie, Markus Küpker, and Janine Maegraith, "Household Debt in Early Modern Germany: Evidence from Personal Inventories," *Journal of Economic History* 72, no. 1 (2012): 134–67. See also Jürgen Schlumbohm, ed., *Soziale Praxis des Kredits: 16.–20. Jahrhundert*(Hanover, 2007).
52. Ogilvie, Küpker, and Maegraith, "Household Debt in Early Modern Germany," 163.
53. StAG, B.II.2.g., *Inventuren & Teilungen*, 1.38–378 (1742).
54. Ibid., 19.2–457 (1780).
55. Ibid., 19.2v262 (1780). All *Activa* totaled 2,273 fl. 25 kr.
56. Ibid., 24.2–405.5 (1792). For example, *"hierzu kommt Zins auf 20. Wochen___13 fl.* [to this (loan) comes interest from 20 weeks___13 fl.]."
57. Ibid., 239–32b (1827).
58. Ibid., 239–57 (1827). The exact total was 15,912 fl. 50 kr., and his household owed only fifty fl. in *Passiva*. No clear line of descent linked this *Zeugmacher* to E. J. Vayhinger, our chronicler.
59. StAG, B.II.2.g., *Inventuren & Teilungen*, 270–22 (1861).
60. Ibid., 270–22 (1861). Another interest-free loan for 260 fl. was extended to "a goldworker in Eßlingen," named Friedrich Schwarz.
61. Ibid., 270–22 (1861).
62. Mannheim, *Wie wird ein Inventar erstellt?*, 315. The conversion rate of "2 fl. 24 x." appears in L. F. John, *Inventur-Büchlein oder Hausstirer* (n.p.: n.p., 1832).
63. See Peter Kriedte, "Trade," in *Germany: A New Social and Economic History*, vol. 2: *1630–1800*, ed. Sheilagh Ogilvie (London, 1996), 100–33, but especially 110–11; and Sheilagh Ogilvie, *Institutions and European Trade: Merchant Guilds, 1000–1800* (Cambridge, 2011).
64. Martin Holbraad, "Expending Multiplicity: Money in Cuban Ifá Cults," *Journal of the Royal Anthropological Institute* 11, no. 2 (2005): 232–33.
65. Ferguson, *The Ascent of Money*, 53.
66. See Medick, *Weben und Überleben*, passim; and Frederick Marquardt, "'Schaffe, schaffe, Häusle baue': Hans Medick, the Swabians, and Modernity," *Journal of Social History* 32, no. 1 (1998): 197–205. See also Ferguson, *The Ascent of Money*, 232, where he discusses the notion of "safe as houses" and "bricks-and-mortar" investments in the "English-speaking world."

Bibliography

Abel, Wilhelm. *Geschichte der deutschen Landwirtschaft vom frühen Mitteralter bis zum 19. Jahrhundert.* Stuttgart, 1962.
Dreher, Alexander. *Göppingens Gewerbe im 19. Jahrhundert: Veröffentlichungen des Stadtarchivs Göppingen,* vol. 7. Göppingen, 1971.
Ferguson, Niall. *The Ascent of Money: A Financial History of the World.* New York, 2008.
Frey, Dennis, Jr. "Industrious Households: Survival Strategies of Artisans in a Southwest German Town during the Eighteenth and Early Nineteenth Centuries." In *Household Strategies for Survival 1600–2000: Fission, Faction, and Cooperation,* edited by Laurence Fontaine and Jürgen Schlumbohm, 115–36. Cambridge, 2000.
———. "Wealth, Consumerism, and Culture among the Artisans of Göppingen: Dynamism and Tradition in an Eighteenth-Century Hometown." *Central European History* 46, no. 4 (2013): 1–38.
Friedrichs, Christopher. "But Are We Any Closer to Home? Early Modern German Urban History Since *German Home Towns.*" *Central European History* 30, no. 2 (1997): 163–85.
Gestrich, Andreas. "Pietistisches Weltverständnis und Handeln in der Welt." In *Geschichte des Pietismus,* vol. 4: *Glaubenswelt und Lebenswelten,* edited by Hartmut Lehmann, 556–616. Göttingen, 2004.
Hilferding, Rudolf. *Finance Capital: A Study of the Latest Phase of Capitalist Development,* ed. Tom Bottomore, translated by Morris Watnick and Sam Gordon, London, 1981.
Hofmann, Emil. *Die Industrialisierung des Oberamtsbezirkes Göppingen.* Göppingen, 1910.
Holbraad, Martin. "Expending Multiplicity: Money in Cuban Ifá Cults." *Journal of the Royal Anthropological Institute* 11, no. 2 (2005): 232–33.
John, L. F. *Inventur-Büchlein oder Hausstirer.* n.p.: n.p., 1832.
Kirschmer, Karl. *Die Geschichte der Stadt Göppingen, I. Teil.* Göppingen, 1953.
Kriedte, Peter. "Trade." in *Germany: A New Social and Economic History.* Vol. 2: *1630–1800,* edited by Sheilagh Ogilvie, 100–33. London, 1996.
Lindemann, Mary. *Health and Healing in Eighteenth-Century Germany.* Baltimore, MD, 1996.
Mannheim, Hildegard. *Wie wird ein Inventar erstellt? Rechtskommentare als Quelle der volkskundlichen Forschung.* Münster, 1991.
Marquardt, Frederick. "'Schaffe, schaffe, Häusle baue': Hans Medick, the Swabians, and Modernity." *Journal of Social History* 32, no. 1 (1998): 197–205.
Maurer, Bill. "The Anthropology of Money." *Annual Review of Anthropology* 35 (2006): 15–36.
McNeely, Ian F. *The Emancipation of Writing: German Civil Society in the Making, 1790s–1820s.* Berkeley, CA, 2003.
McNeill, J. R., and William H. McNeill. *The Human Web: A Bird's-Eye View of World History.* New York, 2003.

Medick, Hans. *Weben und Überleben in Laichingen 1650–1800: Lokalgeschichte als Allgemeine Geschichte.* Göttingen, 1997.
Meiners, Christoph. *Kleinere Länder und Reisebeschreibungen,* vol. 2. Berlin, 1794.
Ogilvie, Sheilagh. *Institutions and European Trade: Merchant Guilds, 1000–1800.* Cambridge, 2011.
———. *State Corporatism and Proto-Industry: The Württemberg Black Forest, 1580–1797.* Cambridge, 1997.
Ogilvie, Sheilagh, Markus Küpker, and Janine Maegraith. "Household Debt in Early Modern Germany: Evidence from Personal Inventories." *Journal of Economic History* 72, no. 1 (2012): 134–67.
Prak, Maarten, ed. *Early Modern Capitalism: Economic and Social Change in Europe, 1400–1800.* London, 2001.
Sabean, David. *Property, Production, and Family in Neckarhausen, 1700–1870.* Cambridge, 1990.
Schlumbohm, Jürgen, ed. *Soziale Praxis des Kredits. 16.–20. Jahrhundert.* Hanover, 2007.
Scott, Tom, and Bob Scribner. "Urban Networks." In *Germany: A New Social and Economic History,* vol. 1, *1450–1630,* edited by Bob Scribner, 113–43. London, 1996.
Seigle, David. *Der Württembergische Waisenrichter: Grundzüge des ehelichen Güter-, Erb- und Vormundschaftsrechts in Württemberg, und Anleitung zu Behandlung der Beibringens-Inventuren, Eheverträge, Erbschaftstheilungen und Pflegschaftssachen.* Stuttgart: Kohlhammer, 1876.
Troeltsch, Walter. *Die Calwer Zeughandlungskompagnie und ihre Arbeiter: Studien zur Gewerbe- und Sozialgeschichte Altwürttembergs.* Jena, 1897.
Tröltsch, Walter. "Die Göppinger Zeugmacherei im 18. Jahrhundert und das sog. Vayhingerbuch." In *Jahrbuch für Gesetzgebung, Verwaltung und Volkswirtschaft im Deutschen Reich,* edited by G. Schmoller, 1255–77. n.p., 1896.
Vann, James Allen. *Making of a State: Württemberg, 1593–1793.* Ithaca, NY, 1984.
Walker, Mack. *German Home Towns: Community, State, and General Estate, 1648–1871.* Ithaca, NY, 1971.

CHAPTER EIGHT

Status, Friendship, and Money in Hamburg around 1800
Debit and Credit in the Diaries of Ferdinand Beneke (1774–1848)

FRANK HATJE

Money can be perceived from a variety of perspectives. This reality is especially evident in a trading metropolis and financial hub of European and even global rank like Hamburg. A number of advantageous circumstances fueled an almost constant growth both of inhabitants and of wealth from the late sixteenth century onward.[1] This outstanding development was predominantly based on trade and financial services, which caused an affluence among the elite that even Colbert's emissaries considered remarkable when negotiating trade relations with the Hanseatic cities in the 1670s. The degree of conspicuous consumption challenged the city-state's civil society and its moral values more or less throughout the eighteenth century, when Hamburg gradually surpassed Amsterdam as an international commercial center.[2] But on the other hand, utmost poverty and the large numbers of the laboring poor constantly disturbed urban civil society as well. Hamburg responded to these conditions by building costly institutions in the early seventeenth century as well as by endowing private charitable foundations and undertaking two comprehensive poor relief reforms in the eighteenth century, of which the latter—the General Poor Relief established in 1788—was the great "patriotic" enterprise and from the outset belonged to the core of the city-republic's identity.[3]

It goes without saying that having money in abundance or lacking it results in different perspectives on, and attitudes toward, money. Yet, we must keep in mind that the majority of the middling classes was struggling to earn their living, to keep, or if fortunate, to elevate their social status, whereas misfortune or simply old age could easily result in impoverishment. The precariousness of money can be studied in the diaries of Ferdinand Beneke particularly well, not only because these diaries are such a rich, detailed, and multifaceted source for any research related to the German *Bürgertum* between the French Revolution and those of 1848, but also because debit and credit played an important role for the greater part of Beneke's life.[4]

In 1774, Beneke was born in Bremen as a son of a well-to-do merchant. The family associated with the urban elite and, under the auspices of late enlightenment ideals, Ferdinand Beneke was brought up to become a member of the educated middle class. His parents' fortune, however, eroded, and the sixteen-year-old Beneke began studying law under financially difficult circumstances. During his years at the University of Halle, his political thought was profoundly influenced by the ideals and achievements of the French Revolution, and for the rest of his life, Beneke was convinced that a republic was the best form of a polity, not least because it allowed individuals to develop their skills, talents, and intellectual gifts freely and dedicate them to the public benefit, although he also recognized that living up to this ideal was easier with money than without.

After achieving his doctorate at Göttingen, he established himself as an advocate in Hamburg in 1796. With next-to-no money in his pocket, he nevertheless managed to become a highly respected member of the urban elite and began building extensive networks beyond the city walls as well; these connections included Prussian reformers and political elites in Bremen and Lübeck, but also writers like Friedrich Gottlieb Klopstock, Jean Paul, and Friedrich de la Motte Fouqué. Beneke showed an extraordinary commitment to Hamburg's General Poor Relief and in the citizens' assembly (*Bürgerschaft*). He devoted his energy to achieving a modernized rebirth of the Hanseatic League as well as to political reform in Hamburg. Within less than a decade his name came up whenever elections to the city-republic's magistracy (*Senat*) were held. When Hamburg became part of the French empire in 1811, he withdrew from public life, because he opposed Napoleon. During the Wars of Liberation, he organized a sort of government-in-exile (*Hanseatisches Direktorium*) that fought for the liberation of the Hanseatic cities and supported their claims to sovereignty in a future Germany. In 1816, he eventually was elected to one of the most influential offices the city-state had to offer, that of *Oberaltensekretär* (secretary to the constitutionally important council of elders). In office, and until his death in 1848, he neither was a partisan of liberalism nor conservatism, but kept to a reform-oriented republicanism and advocated a political line that tried to reconcile the city-state's sovereignty with what he believed to be the demands of German nation-building.

Beneke's rise in the 1790s and 1800s can be attributed to many factors. One of the most striking is the use he made of the convertability of economic, social, and cultural capital within a mercantile metropolis. It is well worth noting that the phenomena observed in late eighteenth- and early nineteenth-century Hamburg may be regarded as being earlier and more distinct than elsewhere in Germany but they were by no means exceptional, neither with respect to comparable metropoles, nor to the German urban middle classes—and the developing German *Bürgertum*—more generally.[5] Beneke's diaries prove their author to have been an almost seismologically sensitive observer of his time. His diaries allow us to analyze the strategies he adopted as well as their economic, social, and cultural contexts. To comprehend Beneke's perceptions, it is first necessary to understand Hamburg's society in terms of money, trade, and credit relations. Second, with respect to monetary and moral values, it is important to distinguish between the merchant middle classes and the elite formation of the *gebildete Stände* (educated middle classes) in order to perceive correctly the cultural codes on which Ferdinand Beneke built his social, economic, and cultural strategies. We then take a closer look at these strategies themselves.

Money and Credit in a Mercantile Society

Not without good reason, Johann Georg Büsch praised money, or rather the circulation of money, as the essential cause that had raised civil society to its present state of sophistication.[6] Büsch was a professor of mathematics, director of one of the first business colleges in Germany, and an economist whose works were distinguished for being completely based on empirical studies especially in respect to Hamburg.[7] In his *Treatise on the Circulation of Money*, he defined money as the wage (*Lohn*) for reciprocal services with an inherent productive force. Money worked in two ways simultaneously: the prospect of appearing on the market as a supplier stimulated a productivity above the level of self-subsistence, while the prospect of stepping forward as a consumer prompted more extensive work.[8] Hence, money accounted for a generalized deception: people believed that they were pursuing their own benefit by working and earning money, while, in fact, they worked for the benefit of others by doing so.[9] Adam Smith took the division of labor as a starting point for his economic theory, and Büsch emphasized that Smith was not wrong, but had missed an important point. In Büsch's eyes, it was money that invigorated the division of labor to become a powerful force in economy, particularly because it was not the accumulated capital that created national wealth, but the money spent, or rather its circulation, among all members of a society.[10] Consequently, even paupers could be useful members of society, provided they received poor relief support in cash and could therefore participate in the circulation of money. While Büsch strictly keeps to economics in this context, the social implications of his theory can easily be deduced. One can imagine a society without any money at all, but one cannot conceive of its advancement and increasing interconnectedness. Hence, in such a money-less society, neither enlightenment nor education are possible. Immanuel Kant even went a step further in his expectation that commerce would pave the way toward a general keeping of peace.[11]

Turning from theory to the practice Büsch (and presumably Kant) had in mind, we can begin with a simple statement: merchants, particularly when operating internationally, employed highly sophisticated techniques, which required a deep knowledge of markets as much as reliable sources of information about political and economic developments.

Georg Heinrich Sieveking, for example, one of the most intelligent merchants in late eighteenth-century Hamburg, was very much engaged in trade with France and favored the French Revolution. Sieveking realized remarkable gains by speculating in the exchange rates of French *assignats*, which rose and fell at different rates in Paris, Bordeaux, Switzerland, and Hamburg in 1793–94. In 1794, he was the driving force in a consortium that negotiated lifting the embargo against ships from Hamburg in French ports on the condition that the complete sales returns—amounting to 5.8 million livres—would be used to purchase French commodities. This arrangement represented only the beginning of a mass exportation of luxury goods (collections of paintings, libraries, furniture, and the like), which then were auctioned in Hamburg and in part re-exported to countries as distant as Russia and the United States. From 1794 to 1795, Sieveking's profits almost tripled and when both the exchange rates and the prices for French real estate fell dramatically, he invested part of them in French landed estates. In 1795, Sieveking advised the French government how to raise the value of the *assignats*, an augmentation that would have served the needs of France as well as his own interests, had his scheme been put into practice.[12] Sieveking might be regarded as exceptional, but only in the degree of his ability to discern opportunities to make money.

Merchants generally had to take various exchange rates into account and needed to consider the time elapsing between paying (when buying a commodity) and being paid (when reselling it); not to mention that risks had to be calculated and transformed into insurance or interest rates. Moreover, there existed two common ways to mobilize money, which, in contrast to transferring cash or bullion, converted money into a virtual entity at least for a particular period of time, although both eventually had to be backed by cash. Holders of an account at the bank (established in 1619 on the model of its Amsterdam counterpart) could pay each other with money of account, that is, without cash. By extending the opportunities offered by the bank's infrastructure, Hamburg soon became an important hub of international financial networks.[13] While the legal requirements for opening a bank account in practice limited these opportunities to Hamburg's merchants and their associates, bills of exchange were much more commonly used. The elaborate techniques of issuing bills of exchange not only facilitated the transfer of any amount to virtually any place, but also allowed them to be used as a means of cashless payment for a certain period of time, as well as of granting and securing credit.[14]

Credit is, and was, a complex form of transaction involving not only economic, but also social and cultural factors. In this context, estimating the "value" of a person in terms of his or her solvency was as customary in Hamburg as the attempt to conceal one's actual income or capital for the sake of a better competitive position.[15] While by the early 1800s brokers were putting up rating lists on the basis of whatever more or less solid information they could obtain for their specific purposes,[16] reputation and honor under the conditions of social control in a face-to-face society were still the prevailing—and obviously sufficient—basis for judging creditworthiness far into the nineteenth century. We may thereby infer that lacking money, usually in the form of hard cash, was acceptable, whereas not having credit, in the sense of not having the means or the reputation to repay a loan, seems to have been the line separating paupers from the middle classes, at least from a middle-class point of view.

Virtually all of Hamburg's society apparently was pervaded by creditor–debtor relations of some kind or another. The financial crisis of 1799 provides an instructive example of the financial connections that bound various social groups together. The crisis was caused by overheated speculation, unexpected stoppages of shipments, bill jobbing, and an undersupply of coined money and bullion; it triggered a chain reaction of enormous bankruptcies in Hamburg and London with reverberations felt as far away as in the United States and Russia.[17] "The stock exchange has never been so distressed as today, when it only consisted of groups driven together by fear. For it is said that the great house of Popert will stop paying; if it breaks, half of Hamburg will be ruined," Beneke reported.[18] Indeed, the moment of crisis revealed the multitude of credit relations that reached far beyond the circles of internationally operating merchants, as Beneke's diaries indicate and not only in 1799.[19] Beneke himself was affected, too, and in no exceptional way. His clients were either unable or unwilling to pay their fees and his father's business suffered as well; Beneke had to increase his efforts to support him and it turned out to be difficult to bridge the gaps in his budget even by short-term loans.[20] Moreover, and in order to avoid that his name appear in insolvency proceedings, Beneke felt forced to settle an outstanding loan that his friend Gerhard Neckelmann had advanced to him. Beneke made a quick payment to his friend's banker when Neckelmann became insolvent and committed suicide because he had not been able to bear the disgrace of a bankruptcy.[21]

The crisis of 1799, however, marked a watershed concerning the attitudes towards insolvency. While a person declaring bankruptcy still had to resign from all public offices, insolvency no longer meant exclusion from social life. New legal proceedings allowed the bankrupt to begin again, and his credit could be restored within a much shorter period of time.[22] There were two reasons for this sea change in the attitudes toward bankruptcy. First, numerous merchant bankers, who would qualify as "system-relevant" today, were affected by the crisis. Second, an unburdened restitution of one's good name and credit were also essential to preserve social stability.

Because of the interdependent networks of social and business relations in Hamburg, mercantile techniques were also available to people who were not directly engaged in trade. Thus, a lawyer like Ferdinand Beneke was able to obtain a substantial loan by a transaction that involved a finance broker, a "capitalist" (that is, a financier), and a merchant; it operated by employing a bill of exchange and drew on the merchant's bank account. It is worth noting that the capitalist was a business partner of the merchant, as he had previously invested money in the merchant's enterprises. Moreover, the merchant was both a friend and a client of Beneke's.[23] This randomly chosen case also highlights the extent to which the intention of money-making bridged otherwise existing social divides: the broker was Jewish, the merchant was a Mennonite, and Beneke was raised a Lutheran.

Business partners of different religious, cultural, or immigrant backgrounds co-operating in trade and finance had in fact been common practice for generations. The first agreement regulating the settlement and economic activities of the Dutch refugees at the turn of the seventeenth century deliberately left aside all confessional differences.[24] In 1796, Ludwig Robert, Rahel Levin Varnhagen's brother, who had come to Hamburg in order to improve his merchant skills, reported to his sister that the attitudes in the mercantile metropolis differed profoundly from those in Berlin. In Hamburg, he noted, a merchant was primarily regarded as a merchant, while being a Jew was merely considered incidental.[25] Robert's perception might have been too enthusiastic to be generalized. Confessional strife and anti-Jewish sentiments amongst Hamburg's Lutheran citizenry had had bitter effects throughout the early modern period.[26] Yet, the general endeavor to make money through overseas trade, the benefits of co-operating and networking, and the experience of business travel across Europe and the Atlantic, including the indispensable ability to communicate in foreign languages (both in a literal and a metaphorical sense), created a sense of cosmopolitanism.[27] This cosmopolitanism encompassed a certain indifference to religious and confessional divides as well as fostering a mind-set that paved the way for Hamburg to become one of the early centers of the enlightenment in Germany. This development is, at least in part, what Johann Georg Büsch referred to when outlining the effects of money in circulation on the advancement of civil society.

Monetary and Cultural Values among the Urban Elites

An emporium like Hamburg was dominated by the rules of a market economy. Obtaining the largest profit was the ultimate aim of bargaining. But it was counterbalanced by the fact that early modern overseas trade had to combine competition with co-operation to be successful.[28] By the end of the eighteenth century, it seems that the pursuit of profit among Hamburg's merchant and professional elite was tempered further by codes of civility that had resulted from enlightenment discourses on civic virtues, humanity, and respect for one's fellow men, and was partly influenced by literary sentimentalism as well.[29] Some instructive findings in Ferdinand Beneke's diaries support this assumption, although not entirely.

The fact that Beneke considered haggling with a shopkeeper over the price of an item an indecent practice indicates that it nevertheless was common. But when reflecting on the embarrassment he had felt while buying Christmas presents in December 1796 and having to haggle because his slender purse demanded it, he chose significant terms to describe his feeling: he felt constricted by the demands of moral philosophy, his sense of honor, and the generosity expected of him because of his social status.[30]

Likewise, he showed just as much delicacy when it came to billing his legal clients. He found the fees commonly paid in Hamburg unacceptably high and hated to remind his debtors of their delinquent accounts.[31] He also often refused to take money for services that were not associated with advocacy in a strict sense. The ensuing negotiations reveal some insights into the cultural codes underlying the fixing of what could be considered a "just price."

In one instance, he left it to his clients to determine how much they wanted to offer him; this decision led to lengthy deliberations among his clients in his presence over whether his proposal (that is, to leave it to his clients to fix the price) was acceptable or not. They eventually offered him 400 marks. Although he could have asked for 1,000, he accepted the sum "the more joyfully, the less this adequate fee offended my sense of honor."[32] In another case, Beneke successfully mediated a dispute between his friend Johann Andreas August Burmester and Burmester's father-in-law, Beneke's former landlord, Julius Möller. While Beneke felt himself sufficiently compensated by Madame Burmester's cordial kiss, her husband preferred to present his benefactor with a gold coin, a *Portugalöser*, instead of a fee. "It's true," Beneke comments in his diary, "I served him in an important matter and reinstalled peace in his family. But having got my sweetest salary by achieving my aim, I never would have taken money for it, since I had not earned it officio & advocatura. For as a man [*Mensch*] I cannot be paid for a merely humane service. I therefore refused to take any kind of remuneration. But a present offered in such a noble, almost too flattering manner I cannot refuse."³³ In a third case, Beneke had worked painstakingly for a nonresident Jewish merchant banker to save him about 180,000 marks, but there was no fixed fee for his services. The merchant's representative then "indelicately" gave him a louis d'or as an acknowledgement in the presence of others, which Beneke later returned in a letter politely pretending that he had offered his service gratuitously.³⁴

These differing outcomes indicate that something like a code of conduct underlay the exchange of services and remuneration that resembles early modern honor codes,³⁵ partly refashioned according to what late eighteenth-century civility required. The length of the discussion in the first case was crucial to an honorable agreement. In the second and third, it was the choice of the coin and the way it was given that made all the difference. A *Portugalöser* was conventionally used as a present on occasions like baptisms, weddings, or elections, and its symbolic meaning was underlined by the accompanying private letter.³⁶ Yet, a louis d'or was an ordinary means of payment, and it was slipped into Beneke's hand in public, which made it look like a tip given to a domestic servant. In these two cases, the symbolic value of the coin counted more than its material one. The first two examples illustrate that Beneke's clients knew how to play the game of fixing an adequate price. The failure in the third example, in contrast, suggests that the underlying code was peculiar to the Hanseatic societies, with which the nonresident client evidently was unfamiliar.

These three cases, however, do not reveal the whole truth. At the same time, merchants were rumored to possess a particular pride in the profits they made (*Kaufmannsstolz, Geldstolz*) or even to be considered conceited because of the wealth they had allegedly gained through their own skills and industriousness. Merchants were reputed to talk about nothing but money, business, and related topics, to lack refined taste and an appreciation of literature and fine arts, to assess everyone according to his economic prosperity, and to evaluate everything according to its mere monetary value.³⁷

In 1800, an audience, that had assembled in the rooms of a typical enlightenment association in Bremen, the "Museum," listened to a lecture, which cautiously admitted that a merchant tended to judge all things and merits by taking their pecuniary benefits as a yardstick. Further, merchants were used to speculating on the needs of others in order to further their own advantage, a mind-set that molded a merchant's way of thinking beyond the confines of trade itself.³⁸ Some ten years earlier, Georg Heinrich Sieveking read a manuscript to the members of the Hamburg "Patriotic Society" criticizing the general habit of ostentatiously displaying one's wealth by the costly splendor of dinner parties, furniture, or coaches simply because fashion required it, whereas supporting the poor or taking up a commitment for benefitting the public good did not earn a person the same degree of respect or reputation, although both the latter was essential to a republic.[39]

Neither could Beneke help complaining that among the younger generation of merchants, self-interest focused on money matters and a superficially exhibited cosmopolitanism went hand-in-hand with a loss of traditional republican values and was, moreover, detrimental to civic values.[40] In his diaries, Beneke never failed to mock *Kaufmannsstolz*, whenever a person happened to deserve it—be it the financial mogul Georg Friedrich Baur[41] or his landlord Johann Christian Sandberg, who apart from three houses owned a collection of exceptionally expensive books. "We amuse ourselves with these books excellently," Beneke noted, "while in his blessed vanity he [Sandberg] believes himself admired as the *owner* of such splendors. Now and then I look up and offer him new causes of delight by asking: This must have cost a lot?"[42]

Possessing money and being well educated, particularly when in tune with the comprehensive concept of education developed by late enlightenment philosophers and pedagogues, did not necessarily coincide, yet they were expected to, as we may conclude from Beneke's diary entries. Indeed, it was the members of the *gebildete Stände* (educated middle classes or the "genteel") whom Büsch had in mind when thinking of the advancement of civil society and whose cultural codes Beneke referred to when talking about fixing the level of professional remunerations.

The *gebildete Stände* included merchants of varied interests beyond commerce, academically trained professionals, urbane scholars, and open-minded noblemen. They all shared a keen interest in literature and philosophy, a sophisticated culture of communication, a particular sense of "taste," and a familiarity with properly balancing conspicuous consumption and modesty, refinement, and natural simplicity. In short, among the *gebildete Stände*, cultural capital eclipsed economic capital, even when their social and cultural practices could not exist without money.

In Hamburg the *gebildete Stände* formed an elite within the urban elite, although it was a fairly numerous one; the famous Sieveking-Reimarus circle with its vast network of European connections, provides an outstanding example.[43] The families of this circle could afford an expensive lifestyle, but placed more value on their intellectual gifts and their expansive hospitality; they welcomed statesmen as well as poets and young talented clerks.[44] It was this social group that became the vanguard of German *Bürgertum* and to which Beneke wanted to belong. In fact, he became part of Hamburg's urban elite. But how did he manage to with no financial backing of his own or his family whatsoever?

Credit among the Gebildete Stände and Beneke's Rise

Beneke's education is the part of the answer that shall be omitted here, except for stating that it provided him with all he needed to share the values and participate in the sociability of the *gebildete Stände*.[45] The other part of the answer revolves around "credit" in its various aspects: money, trust, and reputation.[46]

In this respect, Beneke's doctorate of law proved significant in two ways, apart from the fact that it was socially prestigious and warranted a privileged rank in the city-state's political bodies.[47] First, earning a doctorate was expensive. At Göttingen the fees amounted to a minimum of 120 thaler. Beneke calculated that he himself had spent 250 thaler on the occasion of obtaining his doctorate, not including another 260 thaler for his subsistence during the seven months of his stay. In comparison, Georg Christoph Lichtenberg's fixed annual salary as a professor ranged from 200 to 460 thaler.[48] Hence, a doctorate indicated a relatively high socioeconomic status. Even if it was not completely paid by one's family, it could be assumed that a doctor of law would have sufficient credit to raise the money he needed and, if he succeeded in persuading others that he was a promising young man, it was to be expected that he would earn enough to repay his debts.[49] In Beneke's case, it was Georg Heinrich Sieveking's support that allowed him to leave Göttingen apparently without debts, whereas his creditors at Halle had to content themselves with kind excusatory letters for years.[50] Second, universities functioned as networking agencies. The law faculties of Göttingen and Halle not only attracted large numbers of students from the Hanseatic cities, but publicly vaunted that also a considerable number of sons of the aristocracy had attended.[51] Therefore, law graduates were generally imputed to belong to a higher social status, and Beneke's diaries reveal that his networks not only included urban elites, but also members of the nobility.

Beneke knew that he had to "make as many acquaintances as possible,"[52] if he wanted to establish himself both as a professional and as a member of Hamburg's elite society. He further realized that he, therefore, had to behave according to the rules of the status to which he aspired. He cautiously concealed the fact that sometimes he was so devoid of means that he could not afford a meal for several days.[53] But as soon as he had some money, he used to dine at the more fashionable restaurants in the city, frequently meeting acquaintances of the elite there. Significantly, although he was suffering from a progressive "consumptiveness of my purse" for weeks, he spent his last shilling smoking a pipe at a coffeehouse frequented by the city's leading merchants.[54] Of course, he joined various clubs and associations, some for the sake of networking, some because of the good dinner, and some with conviction, like the "Patriotic Society." Most of them he abandoned as soon as they no longer served his networking purposes, and not least to save the membership fees.[55]

Despite being in constant need of money, Beneke complied with the attitudes toward money prevailing among the *gebildete Stände*: he expressed a certain disregard for money while showing magnanimity, generosity, and even lavishness at times. Beneke, for instance, had helped Conrad Rücker, offspring of one of the most influential merchant dynasties and a remote relative, with some legal matter without charging him. Rücker believed he owed Beneke a reward appropriate to his gratitude. Beneke's father, on the other hand, owed some 100 marks to Rücker. Beneke had asked Rücker to specify his father's debts in order to pay them and did so a second time when Beneke and Rücker met socially one day. But Rücker "responded, as you offered payment for your father for the first time, I, who am not insensitive towards a child's love, crossed out this debt in my books. . . . But I am still *your* debtor. etc.—Now an argument concerning magnanimity arose, in which I did not yield, of course. Eventually we agreed that I should use the money, which I refused, for philanthropic [*menschenfreundliche*] purposes. Thus I have nice pocket money for indigents and for a long time the pleasure of alleviating sufferings and drying tears for free"[56] Indeed, Beneke was not only extraordinarily committed to the paupers in his poor relief district; he also spontaneously organized substantial help, whenever a person's or family's desperate situation required it.[57] From his successes, we may infer that Beneke's inclination to altruism was well acknowledged by a *Bürgertum* that was compassionate and generous.[58]

Nonetheless, although Beneke's existence depended on the money others were willing to give him, he could not make a claim to the general compassion and generosity of his class if he wanted to be regarded as their peer. He had to choose carefully about whom to ask, when, and how. Here the term "friendship" comes in with all the connotations literary sentimentalism had fashioned. His closest friends and confidants helped him at short notice by sharing their pocket money with him, most willingly giving some louis d'or here and thirty marks there. They were approximately Beneke's age, some of them former schoolmates or fellow students and themselves at the beginning of their careers as merchants, physicians, or clergy.[59]

Helping out a friend with money apparently was regarded as a true proof of friendship, a relationship in which the debtor would carefully consider whether the lender was capable of giving. According to this logic, Beneke, when still in Göttingen, wrote to a former fellow student and rich heir: "I don't *ask* you [for money], but I *demand* it from you as a friend . . . you must take this demand as proof of my friendship and trust. . . . So if you can, you'll wish [to send money], and if you don't [send it], I know you can't."[60]

It is never clear whether these friends expected these debts to be repaid, but undoubtedly Beneke regarded them as loans to be paid off.[61] In a very few cases, interest rates were agreed upon, although Beneke admitted that paying interest lowered the burden of his obligation as it less touched his sense of honor.⁶² But even then a friend might silently write off part of the loan, as Beneke accidentally found out when he discovered that his debit in the above-mentioned Neckelmann's account books only totaled 200 instead of the actual 500 marks owed.⁶³

In order to raise more substantial loans—in 1798 Beneke needed 1,500 marks, in 1801 a short-term amount of 1,200, and in 1803 another 2,000—there were two options: either a *GeldNegoz* with a Jewish banker or a formal loan raised from an acquaintance. Beneke always preferred the latter. For although all three loans were obviously extended on regular conditions (that is, secured by bills of exchange and bearing a 4 percent rate of interest), the act of granting them was couched in phrases of civility and politeness that closely approximated the language of friendship. On one of these occasions, the wealthy lawyer and future senator Dr. Schütze "treated me in such a noble and affectionate way" that the scene "did not go without [the expression of] deep emotions on both parts."⁶⁴

Conclusion

Ferdinand Beneke's diaries reveal the techniques of how to use cultural capital in order to generate social capital and social capital to generate economic capital. Of course, he always reinvested part of his economic capital into his social and cultural obligations. The tools and techniques of trade and finance were widely available in a mercantile metropolis like Hamburg, and its middle class society was pervaded by monetary and—even more importantly—by credit relations as much as it operated a constant exchange of services and remunerations. Against this background, Büsch's theory that the circulation of money generated national wealth and promoted social and cultural progress gains plausibility, particularly since overseas trade increasingly required a widened scope of knowledge beyond the confines of commerce itself, which coincided with the goals of self-education propagated by the enlightenment. The latter, however, was not shared by all members of Hamburg's mercantile and professional elites, but only by the *gebildete Stände*, who formed an elite within the urban elite and did not content themselves with the pursuit of profit. The *gebildete Stände*, with their appreciation of cultural capital, civic virtue, and individual talent, developed the cultural codes that set the framework for Beneke's ability to ascend to the highest ranks in the city-republic, even without the benefit of an inherited or self-made fortune, the normal prerequisite for ascent in early modern Hamburg. These cultural codes, on the one hand, demanded that one conceal a lack of monetary means, show a lavish disregard for money, and be magnanimous toward the lower orders and the needy as well as express a commitment to the public good. But, on the other hand, with their refined sense of honor, their discreteness and delicacy, their civility and particular notion of friendship, the *gebildete Stände* avoided being completely at the mercy of the money market. They were able to maintain their status and credit (in the form of reputation, respect, and acceptance) as long as possible, and, hence, to make full use of the convertability of cultural, social, and economic capital.

Frank Hatje is Director of the Beneke-Edition and Privatdozent at the Historical Seminar of Hamburg University. Apart from studies of the Dutch reformation and the religious and commercial networks of German Pietism and evangelicalism, he has published extensively on the history of the German Bürgertum as well as on poor relief in the early modern period and the nineteenth century.

Notes

1. Frank Hatje, "Libertät, Neutralität und Commercium: Zu den politischen Voraussetzungen für Hamburgs Handel (1550–1900)," in *Überseehandel und Handelsmetropolen: Europa und Asien, 17.–20. Jahrhundert*, ed. Frank Hatje and Klaus Weber (Hamburg, 2008), 213–47.
2. Peter Voss, "'Eine Fahrt von wenig Importantz'? Der hansische Handel mit Bordeaux 1670–1715," in *Niedergang oder Übergang? Zur Spätzeit der Hanse im 16. und 17. Jahrhundert*, ed. Antjekathrin Grassmann (Cologne, 1998), 93–198. The controversies about the opera and the theater and the discourse on "patriotism," republicanism, and civic virtues quintessentially reflected this challenge. See Franklin Kopitzsch, *Grundzüge einer Sozialgeschichte der Aufklärung in Hamburg und Altona*, 2nd ed. (Hamburg, 1990); Mary Lindemann, "Fundamental Values: Political Culture in Eighteenth-Century Hamburg," in *Patriotism, Cosmopolitanism, and National Culture. Public Culture in Hamburg 1700–1933*, ed. Peter Uwe Hohendahl (Amsterdam, 2003), 17–32; Katherine B. Aaslestad, "Old Visions and New Vices: Republicanism and Civic Virtue in Hamburg's Print Culture, 1790–1810," in *Patriotism, Cosmopolitanism, and National Culture: Public Culture in Hamburg 1700–1933*, ed. Peter Uwe Hohendahl (Amsterdam, 2003), 143–66.
3. Mary Lindemann, *Patriots and Paupers: Hamburg, 1712–1830* (New York, 1990); Frank Hatje, "Stiftung, Stadt und Bürgertum: 'Konjunkturen' karitativer Stiftungen vom 16. bis 19. Jahrhundert," *Die Alte Stadt* 33 (2006): 219–48.
4. See Frank Hatje, *Ferdinand Beneke (1774–1848), Die Tagebücher, Begleitband zur ersten Abteilung: Bürger und Revolutionen* (Göttingen, 2012).
5. See Lindemann, "Fundamental Values."
6. Johann Georg Büsch, "Abhandlung vom Geldes-Umlauf in anhaltender Rücksicht auf die Staatswirthschaft und Handlung," in *Sämmtliche Schriften* (Vienna, 1816), vols. 9–11.
7. Johann Georg Büsch, *Theoretisch-praktische Darstellung der Handlung in ihren mannichfaltigen Geschäften*, 3rd ed. (Hamburg, 1808), 1: xiii. See Frank Hatje, "Johann Georg Büsch (1728–1800): Professor academicus et extra-academicus," in *Das Akademische*

Gymnasium: Bildung und Wissenschaft in Hamburg 1613–1883, ed. Dirk Brietzke, Franklin Kopitzsch, and Rainer Nicolaysen (Berlin, 2013), 109–37.
8. Büsch, "Abhandlung vom Geldes-Umlauf," 9: 101–9.
9. Ibid., 112–18.
10. Ibid., 76–87, 91–94.
11. Immanuel Kant, "Idee zu einer allgemeinen Geschichte in weltbürgerlicher Absicht," *Berlinische Monatsschrift* 2, no. 11 (1784): 385–410.
12. Heinrich Sieveking, *Georg Heinrich Sieveking: Lebensbild eines Hamburgischen Kaufmanns aus dem Zeitalter der französischen Revolution* (Berlin, 1913), 117–22, 197, 368–75.
13. Hatje, "Libertät, Neutralität und Commercium," with further references.
14. Büsch, *Theoretisch-praktische Darstellung*, 1: 23–24, 56–120.
15. See Ferdinand Beneke, *Tagebücher*, I/2: 449, I/3: 658; Staatsarchiv Hamburg [hereafter: StAHbg] 622–1/121, C 2, Mappe 5, Beneke to Lavezzari, Hamburg, 18 June 1802.
16. Percy Ernst Schramm, *Kaufleute zu Haus und über See: Hamburgische Zeugnisse des 17., 18. und 19. Jahrhunderts* (Hamburg, 1949), 263–87.
17. Margrit Schulte Beerbühl, "Die Hamburger Krise von 1799 und ihre weltweite Dimension," *Hamburger Wirtschafts-Chronik* 10 (2012): 85–110; Johann Georg Büsch, *Geschichtliche Beurtheilung der großen Handelsverwirrung im Jahre 1799*, ed. H. S. Hertz (Hamburg, 1858).
18. Ferdinand Beneke, *Tagebücher* I/3: 141 (7 October 1799).
19. See e.g. Beneke, *Tagebücher*, I/3: 92–93, 110–11, 129, 132; StAHbg 622–1/121, C 2, Mappe 5, 15 August 1802, 18 September, 3 October 1803.
20. Beneke, *Tagebücher*, I/3: 103, 144.
21. Ibid., 58–59. If Beneke had known of Neckelmann's difficulties, he presumably would have negotiated a rescue operation, as he did in other cases. See ibid., 103, 142, 144.
22. Schulte Beerbühl, "Die Hamburger Krise," 102–5.
23. Beneke, *Tagebücher*, I/3: 164.
24. Alexander Nikolajczyk, "Integriert oder ausgegrenzt? Die Stellung der niederländischen Einwanderer im frühneuzeitlichen Hamburg," *Hamburger Wirtschafts-Chronik* 6 (2006): 7–44.
25. Consolina Vigliero, ed., *Rahel Levin Varnhagen: Briefwechsel mit Ludwig Robert* (Munich, 2001), 13.
26. Joachim Whaley, *Religious Toleration and Social Change in Hamburg, 1529–1819* (Cambridge, 1985); Jutta Braden, *Hamburger Judenpolitik im Zeitalter lutherischer Orthodoxie* (Hamburg, 2001).
27. *Cosmopolitan Networks in Commerce and Society 1660–1914*, ed. Andreas Gestrich and Margrit Schulte Beerbühl (London, 2011); Margrit Schulte Beerbühl and Klaus Weber, "Europäische Zentren deutscher 'Commercial Empires,'" in *Überseehandel und Handelsmetropolen: Europa und Asien, 17.–20. Jahrhundert*, ed. Frank Hatje and Klaus Weber (Hamburg, 2008), 17–59.
28. See *Spinning the Commercial Web: International Trade, Merchants, and Commercial Culture*, ed. Margrit Schulte Beerbühl and Jörg Vögele (Frankfurt, 2004).
29. For the influence of Lessing and Klopstock in Hamburg, see Kopitzsch, *Grundzüge*, passim.
30. Beneke, *Tagebücher*, I/2: 168–69.

31. Ibid., 122.
32. Ibid., 173.
33. Ibid., 331, 339.
34. Beneke, *Tagebücher*, I/3: 149.
35. See Martin Dinges, *Der Maurermeister und der Finanzrichter: Ehre, Geld und soziale Kontrolle im Paris des 18. Jahrhunderts* (Göttingen, 1994); Martin Dinges, "Die Ehre als Thema der historischen Anthropologie," in *Verletzte Ehre—Ehrkonflikte in Gesellschaften des Mittelalters und der Frühen Neuzeit*, ed. Klaus Schreiner and Gerd Schwerhoff (Cologne, 1995), 29–62; Pierre Bourdieu, *Outline of a Theory of Practice* (Cambridge, 1977).
36. E.g. Beneke, *Tagebücher*, I/3: 420, III/6: 369–72; cf. I/3: 625.
37. Ernst Platner, *Philosophische Aphorismen nebst einigen Anleitungen zur philosophischen Geschichte*, 2 vols (Leipzig, 1800), 2: 568–71; Johann Gebhard Ehrenreich Maass, *Versuch über die Leidenschaften: Theoretisch und practisch*, 2 vols (Halle, 1807), 2: 148; Louis Sébastien Mercier, *Neuestes Gemälde von Berlin auf das Jahr 1798* (Kölln, 1798), 148–50. See Beneke, *Tagebücher*, I/1: 216; StAHbg 622-1/121, C 2, Mappe 5, 29 December 1803.
38. Anonymous, "Einfluß des Handels auf die Cultur derer, welche sich damit beschäftigen," *Hanseatisches Magazin* 5 (1801): 177–99.
39. Georg Heinrich Sieveking, "Fragmente, über Luxus, Bürger-Tugend und Bürger-Wohl, für Hamburgische Bürger, die das Gute wollen und können; am 17ten November 1791," in *Verhandlungen und Schriften der Hamburgischen Gesellschaft zur Beförderung der Künste und nützlichen Gewerbe* (Hamburg, 1797), 4: 161–82.
40. Beneke, *Tagebücher*, I/4: 513–23; cf. I/3: 429; I/2: 484.
41. Beneke, *Tagebücher*, I/3: 270.
42. StAHbg 622-1/121, C 2, Mappe 7, 25 September 1805.
43. Sieveking, *Georg Heinrich Sieveking*; Kopitzsch, *Grundzüge einer Sozialgeschichte*; Almut Spalding, *Elise Reimarus (1735–1805), The Muse of Hamburg: A Woman of the German Enlightenment* (Würzburg, 2005).
44. Frank Hatje, "Die private Öffentlichkeit des Hauses im deutschen und englischen Bürgertum des 18. und 19. Jahrhunderts," in *Das Haus in der Geschichte Europas*, ed. Joachim Eibach and Inken Schmidt-Voges (Berlin, 2015), 503–24; cf. Beneke, *Tagebücher*, I/3: 212, 255, 353–54.
45. For details see Hatje, *Ferdinand Beneke*, 101–212.
46. See Mark Casson, *Information and Organization: A New Perspective on the Theory of the Firm* (Oxford, 1997), 146–55, 166–67, 172–77, 191–93; *Vertrauen: Historische Annäherungen*, ed. Ute Frevert (Göttingen, 2003); David Sunderland, *Social Capital, Trust, and the Industrial Revolution, 1780–1880* (London, 2007), 6–12, 15–30, 68–84.
47. Half of the magistrates (*Senatoren*) had to be law graduates. Once elected judge to the lower court (*Niedergericht*), jurists had the right to attend the meetings of the citizens' assembly (*Bürgerschaft*) with a privileged vote, irrespective of the property qualifications otherwise required.
48. *Die Privilegien und ältesten Statuten der Georg-August-Universität zu Göttingen*, ed. Wilhelm Ebel (Göttingen, 1961), 126–33; Beneke, *Tagebücher*, I/1: 467; Hans-Joachim Heerde, *Publikum der Physik: Lichtenbergs Hörer* (Göttingen, 2006), 28; Stefan Brüdermann, *Göttinger Studenten und akademische Gerichtsbarkeit im 18. Jahrhundert* (Göttingen, 1990), 299, 304.

49. See StAHbg 622–1/121, C 2, Mappe 5, 3 August 1802. The advocacy fee of 2,000 marks mentioned here would have more than covered all of Beneke's expenses during his stay at Göttingen, and Beneke used it to repay his debts immediately.
50. Beneke, *Tagebücher*, I/1: 308, 461–62; I/2: 28, 115; I/3: 188, 453.
51. Hatje, *Ferdinand Beneke*, 198–99 with further references.
52. Beneke, *Tagebücher*, I/2: 25.
53. Ibid., I/2: 32–33, 70–71; I/3: 62.
54. Ibid., I/3: 662, cf. I/2: 100.
55. Frank Hatje, "Kommunikation und Netzwerke in den Tagebüchern Ferdinand Benekes," in *Hamburg und sein norddeutsches Umland: Aspekte des Wandels seit der Frühen Neuzeit*, ed. Dirk Brietzke, Norbert Fischer, and Arno Herzig (Hamburg, 2007), 234–53. See Beneke, *Tagebücher*, I/2: 179 (Patriotische Gesellschaft), 484 (Trüdemann); StAHbg 622–1/121, C 2, Mappe 5, 1 November 1802. For social reasons, Beneke did not even refrain from gambling at cards, which used to be part of the sociability. E.g. Beneke, *Tagebücher*, I/2: 54, 148, 155, 158, 201, 250, 402, 451, 504; I/3: 21, 26, 123, 363–64; StAHbg 622–1/121, C 2, Mappe 5, 16, 17, 19 November 1803.
56. StAHbg 622–1/121, C 2, Mappe 5, 1 July 1802.
57. Frank Hatje, "Zwischen Republik und Karitas: Karitative Ehrenamtlichkeit im Hamburg des 18. und 19. Jahrhunderts," *Westfälische Forschungen* 55 (2005): 239–66; Stephen Pielhoff, "Religiosität und Gemeinsinn: Über Ideal und Praxis der Armenpflege bei Ferdinand Beneke (1822–1832)," *Zeitschrift des Vereins für Hamburgische Geschichte* 92 (2006): 33–51.
58. Beneke, *Tagebücher*, I/3: 21–22, 25, 30, 59, 73–74, 96; I/4: 359–60; I/3: 204–6; StAHbg 622–1/121, C 2, Mappe 5, 26 November 1803.
59. Beneke, *Tagebücher*, I/2: 38, 45–46.
60. Beneke, *Tagebücher*, I/1: 374. See Hatje, *Ferdinand Beneke*, 182–83.
61. Beneke, *Tagebücher*, I/2: 46, 155. With Franz Joseph Anton Borger, it was different. He urged Beneke to take his money, whereas Beneke was loathe to ask him because he believed him to be "more noble than rich." Ibid., I/2: 97–98, 155.
62. Beneke, *Tagebücher*, I/2: 371. Dr. Heinrich Lampe, who lent him 1,000 marks, was a lawyer in Bremen and his friend from childhood days.
63. Ibid., I/3: 58–59.
64. Ibid, I/2: 449–50; see also I/3: 103. The other two were Beneke's clients and understandably a bit more polite than affectionate in their responses. Ibid., I/3: 662; StAHbg 622–1/121, C 2, Mappe 5, 9 August 1803, 14 December 1803.

Bibliography

Aaslestad, Katherine B. "Old Visions and New Vices: Republicanism and Civic Virtue in Hamburg's Print Culture, 1790–1810." In *Patriotism, Cosmopolitanism, and National Culture: Public Culture in Hamburg 1700–1933*, edited by Peter Uwe Hohendahl, 143–66. Amsterdam, 2003.

Anonymous. "Einfluß des Handels auf die Cultur derer, welche sich damit beschäftigen." *Hanseatisches Magazin* 5 (1801): 177–99.

Beneke, Ferdinand. *Die Tagebücher: Dritte Abteilung: 1811–1816*. Göttingen, 2016.

———. *Die Tagebücher: Erste Abteilung: 1792–1801*. Göttingen, 2012.
Bourdieu, Pierre. *Outline of a Theory of Practice*. Cambridge, 1977.
Braden, Jutta. *Hamburger Judenpolitik im Zeitalter lutherischer Orthodoxie*. Hamburg, 2001.
Brüdermann, Stefan. *Göttinger Studenten und akademische Gerichtsbarkeit im 18. Jahrhundert*. Göttingen, 1990.
Büsch, Johann Georg. "Abhandlung vom Geldes-Umlauf in anhaltender Rücksicht auf die Staatswirthschaft und Handlung." In *Sämmtliche Schriften*, vols. 9–11. Vienna, 1816.

———. *Geschichtliche Beurtheilung der großen Handelsverwirrung im Jahre 1799*, edited by H. S. Hertz. Hamburg, 1858.

———. *Theoretisch-praktische Darstellung der Handlung in ihren mannichfaltigen Geschäften*, 3rd ed. Hamburg, 1808.

Casson, Mark. *Information and Organization: A New Perspective on the Theory of the Firm*. Oxford, 1997.

Dinges, Martin. *Der Maurermeister und der Finanzrichter: Ehre, Geld und soziale Kontrolle im Paris des 18. Jahrhunderts*. Göttingen, 1994.

———. "Die Ehre als Thema der historischen Anthropologie." In *Verletzte Ehre—Ehrkonflikte in Gesellschaften des Mittelalters und der Frühen Neuzeit*, edited by Klaus Schreiner and Gerd Schwerhoff, 29–62. Cologne, 1995.

Ebel, Wilhelm, ed. *Die Privilegien und ältesten Statuten der Georg-August-Universität zu Göttingen*. Göttingen, 1961.

Frevert, Ute, ed. *Vertrauen: Historische Annäherungen*. Göttingen, 2003.

Gestrich, Andreas and Margrit Schulte Beerbühl, ed. *Cosmopolitan Networks in Commerce and Society 1660–1914*. London, 2011.

Hatje, Frank. "Die private Öffentlichkeit des Hauses im deutschen und englischen Bürgertum des 18. und 19. Jahrhunderts." In *Das Haus in der Geschichte Europas*, edited by Joachim Eibach and Inken Schmidt-Voges, 503–24. Berlin, 2015.

———. *Ferdinand Beneke (1774–1848), Die Tagebücher, Begleitband zur ersten Abteilung: Bürger und Revolutionen*. Göttingen, 2012.

———. "Johann Georg Büsch (1728–1800): Professor academicus et extra-academicus." In *Das Akademische Gymnasium: Bildung und Wissenschaft in Hamburg 1613–1883*, edited by Dirk Brietzke, Franklin Kopitzsch, and Rainer Nicolaysen, 109–37. Berlin, 2013.

———. "Kommunikation und Netzwerke in den Tagebüchern Ferdinand Benekes." In *Hamburg und sein norddeutsches Umland: Aspekte des Wandels seit der Frühen Neuzeit*, edited by Dirk Brietzke, Norbert Fischer, and Arno Herzig, 234–53. Hamburg, 2007.

———. "Libertät, Neutralität und Commercium. Zu den politischen Voraussetzungen für Hamburgs Handel (1550–1900)." In *Überseehandel und Handelsmetropolen: Europa und Asien, 17.–20. Jahrhundert*, edited by Frank Hatje and Klaus Weber, 213–47. Hamburg, 2008.

———. "Stiftung, Stadt und Bürgertum: 'Konjunkturen' karitativer Stiftungen vom 16. bis 19. Jahrhundert." *Die Alte Stadt* 33 (2006): 219–48.

Hatje, Frank. "Zwischen Republik und Karitas: Karitative Ehrenamtlichkeit im Hamburg des 18. und 19. Jahrhunderts." *Westfälische Forschungen* 55 (2005): 239–66.
Heerde, Hans-Joachim. *Publikum der Physik: Lichtenbergs Hörer.* Göttingen, 2006.
Kant, Immanuel. "Idee zu einer allgemeinen Geschichte in weltbürgerlicher Absicht." *Berlinische Monatsschrift* 2, no. 11 (1784): 385–410.
Kopitzsch, Franklin. *Grundzüge einer Sozialgeschichte der Aufklärung in Hamburg und Altona*, 2nd ed. Hamburg, 1990.
Kruse, Jürgen Elert. *Allgemeiner und besonders Hamburgischer Contorist*, 4th ed. Hamburg, 1782.
Lindemann, Mary. "Fundamental Values: Political Culture in Eighteenth-Century Hamburg." In *Patriotism, Cosmopolitanism, and National Culture. Public Culture in Hamburg 1700–1933*, edited by Peter Uwe Hohendahl, 17–32. Amsterdam, 2003.
———. *Patriots and Paupers: Hamburg 1712–1830*. New York, 1990.
Maass, Johann Gebhard Ehrenreich. *Versuch über die Leidenschaften: Theoretisch und practisch*, 2 vols. Halle, 1807.
Mercier, Louis Sébastien. *Neuestes Gemälde von Berlin auf das Jahr 1798*. Kölln, 1798.
Nikolajczyk, Alexander. "Integriert oder ausgegrenzt? Die Stellung der niederländischen Einwanderer im frühneuzeitlichen Hamburg." *Hamburger Wirtschafts-Chronik* 6 (2006): 7–44.
Pielhoff, Stephen. "Religiosität und Gemeinsinn: Über Ideal und Praxis der Armenpflege bei Ferdinand Beneke (1822–1832)." *Zeitschrift des Vereins für Hamburgische Geschichte* 92 (2006): 33–51.
Platner, Ernst. *Philosophische Aphorismen nebst einigen Anleitungen zur philosophischen Geschichte*, 2 vols. Leipzig, 1800.
Schramm, Percy Ernst. *Kaufleute zu Haus und über See: Hamburgische Zeugnisse des 17., 18. und 19. Jahrhunderts*. Hamburg, 1949.
Schulte Beerbühl, Margrit, and Klaus Weber. "Europäische Zentren deutscher 'Commercial Empires.'" In *Überseehandel und Handelsmetropolen: Europa und Asien, 17.–20. Jahrhundert*, edited by Frank Hatje and Klaus Weber, 17–59. Hamburg, 2008.
Schulte Beerbühl, Margrit. "Die Hamburger Krise von 1799 und ihre weltweite Dimension." *Hamburger Wirtschafts-Chronik* 10 (2012): 85–110.
Schulte Beerbühl, Margrit and Jörg Vögele, ed. *Spinning the Commercial Web: International Trade, Merchants, and Commercial Culture*. Frankfurt, 2004.
Sieveking, Georg Heinrich. "Fragmente, über Luxus, Bürger-Tugend und Bürger-Wohl, für Hamburgische Bürger, die das Gute wollen und können; am 17ten November 1791." *Verhandlungen und Schriften der Hamburgischen Gesellschaft zur Beförderung der Künste und nützlichen Gewerbe*, vol. 4. Hamburg, 1797.
Sieveking, Heinrich. *Georg Heinrich Sieveking: Lebensbild eines Hamburgischen Kaufmanns aus dem Zeitalter der französischen Revolution*. Berlin, 1913.
Spalding, Almut. *Elise Reimarus (1735–1805), The Muse of Hamburg: A Woman of the German Enlightenment*. Würzburg, 2005.

Sunderland, David. *Social Capital, Trust, and the Industrial Revolution, 1780–1880*. London, 2007.
Vigliero, Consolina, ed. *Rahel Levin Varnhagen: Briefwechsel mit Ludwig Robert*. Munich, 2001.
Voss, Peter. "'Eine Fahrt von wenig Importantz'? Der hansische Handel mit Bordeaux 1670–1715." In *Niedergang oder Übergang? Zur Spätzeit der Hanse im 16. und 17. Jahrhundert*, edited by Antjekathrin Grassmann, 93–198. Cologne, 1998.
Whaley, Joachim. *Religious Toleration and Social Change in Hamburg, 1529–1819*. Cambridge, 1985.

CHAPTER NINE

Luxury and the Nineteenth-Century Württemberg Pietists

JAN CARSTEN SCHNURR

Luxury, perhaps the most vivid expression of a person's possession of money, has always provoked strong feelings and intense reflection.[1] The condemnation of a luxurious lifestyle has, therefore, a long history. It ranges from classical antiquity through the Christian Middle Ages to early modern Europe. Among the critics were such diverse figures and movements as Pythagoras, the Cynics and Plato, Chinese Taoists, Sallust, Cicero, Seneca and Tacitus, the church fathers, the medieval mendicant orders, Puritanism, Pietism, and Rousseau.[2] In the Middle Ages, *luxuria*, meaning primarily "sexual indulgence,"[3] was regarded as one of the seven deadly sins. Lutheranism did not cherish asceticism as an ideal and was not opposed to all "worldly" pleasures, but it, too, produced warnings and church ordinances that included prohibitions of luxury.[4] Among those critical of "luxury" were also Johann Arndt, the father of seventeenth-century pietistic Lutheran spirituality, and August Hermann Francke, the head of Halle Pietism.[5] Thus, the tradition of deploring luxurious living was long and powerful.

In the course of the eighteenth century, however, something changed: "luxury" became an ambivalent term, rather than a pejorative one.[6] This sea change came about primarily because the Enlightenment had discovered that self-interest, spending, and consumption could be seen not as ethically deficient behavior but instead as healthy ingredients of a prosperous economy. Thinkers such as Bernard Mandeville (1670–1733) stressed that what might be a vice for the individual could be a benefit for the public, namely as a stimulus for economic growth. "If the wants of Men are innumerable," Mandeville wrote, "then what ought to supply them has no bounds."[7] The logic here is that desire and gratification should be affirmed. Voltaire, too, defended luxury by pointing out that the cultural achievements of luxurious Athens had far surpassed those of ascetic Sparta.[8] Especially after 1770, such views were also expressed in Germany.⁹ Although the older *criticism* of luxury remained present in public debate, the term "luxury" had lost a good part of its negativity. This shift explains why it was now possible to publish a periodical such as the German *Journal des Luxus und der Moden* (*Journal of Luxury and the Fashions*), which appeared between 1786 and 1827. Even a cleric like the Enlightenment theologian Andreas Riem (1749–1814) criticized the old Protestant Orthodoxy with the rhetorical question, "Who has forgotten it, the clamor from the pulpits against luxury?"¹⁰ Such clamor no longer appeared relevant to him. The way Riem phrased his question indicates that he was not the only one who held this view. Certainly, by the late eighteenth century, "luxury" had become a term that carried positive as well as negative connotations. While the moral criticism of an expensive, pleasure-loving lifestyle continued to sound, people also saw the aesthetic appeal and economic value of such a lifestyle. In their explanations of the concept, nineteenth-century dictionaries accommodated this ambivalent sentiment about luxury.¹¹

Some Key Nineteenth-Century Württemberg Pietists

Even in the middle of the nineteenth century, however, some people maintained the older criticism of luxury and used the term solely in a negative manner. Among these was a younger generation of Württemberg pastors of a Pietist persuasion who played a vital role in the German evangelical revival (*Erweckungsbewegung*), including, among others, the publisher, author, and Lutheran pastor from Calw, Christian Gottlob Barth (1799–1862); the editor, educator, and pastor, Johann Ludwig Völter (1809–88); and the longtime rector of the Stuttgart Collegiate Church (*Stiftskirche*), Sixt Carl Kapff (1805–79). Several of them had been trained at the *Tübinger Stift*, a college for students of Protestant theology in Tübingen, and they had been inspired by the young revivalist preacher Ludwig Hofacker (1798–1828). They knew each other well. These theologians, who invested their lives in preaching, pastoral care, transnational networking, missionary work, and social action, also produced a number of writings on social and historical issues in which the word *Luxus* frequently appeared.¹² These writings provide much information about how the Pietist Protestants in mid nineteenth-century Württemberg thought and felt about the world. Although we should avoid here far-reaching generalizations, nonetheless, the terms and concepts these authors used appear characteristic of the position the Württemberg Pietists took in regard to the question of luxury and its implications.

Luxury in History and Society

In his *General World History According to Biblical Principles* (*Die allgemeine Weltgeschichte nach biblischen Grundsätzen*), a work of 373 pages published in 1837, which underwent six editions and ten translations, Christian Gottlob Barth describes the rise and fall of empires in terms of their moral and religious qualities.[13] When he describes them as having a tendency toward luxury, this almost always explains their decline. In the early Roman Republic, Barth believes, "Luxury had not yet displaced the old rough simplicity."[14] The *late* Roman Republic, however, suffered from luxury as if it were a "poisonous herb which, slowly but surely, consumed . . . [Rome's] vitality and prepared its fall."[15] Luxury here seems to have a deleterious effect on a nation. Such retrospective criticism of luxury can also be found in Pietist historiographers outside Württemberg,[16] rarely, however, as explicitly as among them,[17] and especially so in the writings of Barth. In his *General World History*, the Phoenicians, Lydians, Carthaginians, Romans, Hellenistic Greeks, Byzantines, medieval Italian city states, and the absolutist monarchy of Louis XIV are all criticized for their cultivation of luxury.[18] The Swiss in the days of William Tell, in contrast, are praised for opening "no door to luxury."[19] When a ruler like Joseph II of Austria "combated luxury with all his strength," he, too, is given credit for his efforts.[20] The emperor Augustus, too, was "an enemy of luxury,"[21] says Barth and adds that the Romans were happy under his rule. A ruler's love of luxury is, thus, almost tantamount to the neglect of his duty to care for his subjects.

Ludwig Völter agreed with Barth. In the case of Duke Christopher of Württemberg (1515–68), however, whom he—like many Pietists—deeply admired, Völter was ready to make excuses. In his textbook *Württemberg: The Land and Its History* (*Württemberg: Das Land und seine Geschichte*), Völter attributes "wisdom, truly that of a father of the nation," to the pious Protestant ruler, but adds, as if for the sake of honesty: "The only thing for which Duke Christopher might be reproached was that he himself was not completely free from a certain inclination to expenditure [*Aufwand*]." Especially, Völter explains, people complained about his "passion for building." However, he immediately rushes to Christopher's defense and argues that this reproach was "not completely justified," for at the time he became duke, "after all, everything was in decay." Finally, he remarks: "Most of all, he beautified Stuttgart through the construction of new buildings."[22] In the end, apparently, the duke's tendency toward expensive living was not so bad after all. The charge of luxuriousness could, thus, be leveled even against the very best of sovereigns, although a beloved ruler could receive a more sympathetic interpretation of his extravagant spending. When a distinction had to be made between a legitimate pleasure on the one hand and luxury on the other, the general assessment of a person, of their character, and their goals in life, became an important factor. Of course, a sovereign was granted a higher standard of living than a lesser nobleman, not to speak of a craftsman or peasant. But this does not change the fact that, in principle, everyone, even the unequivocally Christian ruler, could be accused of indulging in luxurious living. There was, however, always room to make adjustments in evaluating each particular case.

A short anecdote related by Dieter Ising in his great biography of Barth's famous friend and successor as pastor in Möttlingen, Johann Christoph Blumhardt (1805–80), offers an excellent example of such flexibility. In the year 1851, the emotionally disturbed Princess Louise of Prussia, sister-in-law of the Prussian King Frederick William IV, spent several months in Blumhardt's Möttlingen rectory, where she hoped to regain her health or at least improvement of her condition. Blumhardt did not want to accommodate her in his small guest room and instead, after some reflection, let her have the marital bedroom. He also allowed himself—half financed by the royal house—the acquisition of a piano and new furniture. Such "luxury of our house for the royal person" ("Luxus unseres Hauses für die fürstliche Person"), as Blumhardt put it, caused him some inner conflict, however, because the expense was apparently at odds with his regular frugal financial habits. He finally resolved his moral conflict as follows:

> I do not seek luxury . . . but I must guard myself against the obstinacy of not desiring to go beyond what is customary, even though God may lead me thither. If then I receive a princess unsought, it is the duty I owe to every person to ask myself, What can I and what must I do to serve the princess?[23]

For himself, Blumhardt would have considered such costly purchases as indecent. But now, without his having a hand in the matter, a Prussian princess had come to stay at his house. We can presume that Blumhardt did not wish to offer her "luxury." He just realistically expected that what represented luxury for him was probably still modest for the princess, or was, at any rate, only befitting her social status. By refusing to make the renovations, he would have missed the chance to help and to provide a home for someone who was in need and had indeed approached him voluntarily. Blumhardt wanted to offer care and comfort not only to the lower and middle classes, but to the aristocracy as well; hence, as an exception, he justified the unusual expenditure.

The nineteenth-century Pietists, as this example shows, not only considered luxury an evil of former times, but also regarded it as an issue of pressing concern in their own day. According to Barth, contemporary luxury was "in vogue in great refinement."[24] Völter, too, in referring to fashionable dress, believed that luxury had "very much gotten out of hand as of late."[25] Viewed in connection with any social crisis, its detrimental effects were particularly evident to these pietistic critics.

Luxury, Social Crisis, and Revolution

For many Pietists, the revolution of 1848 represented just such a social crisis. Unlike the liberal Rationalists in the Lutheran church of Württemberg, who had welcomed the revolution with great optimism, the orthodox and pietistic Lutherans had, with some exceptions, interpreted the event as catastrophic, and had seen in it a judgment from God.[26] In its aftermath, Sixt Carl Kapff, at the time Lutheran superintendent at Herrenberg, from 1850 prelate at Reutlingen, and who had been a conservative candidate for the National Assembly in 1848, resolved to draft a comprehensive critical analysis of what had happened. The newly established Central Committee for the Inner Mission (*Central-Ausschuß für die innere Mission*) had offered a prize for a Christian evaluation of the "contemporary social concerns" (*sociale Zeitfragen*). Kapff submitted his work, received the reward, and, in 1851, published the text at Johann Hinrich Wichern's *Agentur des Rauhen Hauses* in Hamburg. It bore the title: *The Revolution: Its Causes, Results, and Remedies* (*Die Revolution, ihre Ursachen, Folgen und Heilmittel*). In this book, Kapff describes the recent revolutionary experience as a social tragedy. Among its multiple causes, he especially singles out certain mind-sets and patterns of behavior. Alongside other factors, Kapff blames "excessive luxury in all classes."[27] He accuses all levels of society for cultivating unseemly luxury: the upper classes (such as noblemen or high civil servants) did not content themselves with a high standard of living but always wanted more and thus wallowed in luxury. The lower classes (such as small craftsmen or servants) craved the same pleasures and soon started imitating their betters. "One should give everyone what is right, and to the higher and highest ranks more, even much more, than to the subordinate servants," Kapff concedes, in accordance with the hierarchical order of society, adding "but the excessively high sums only encouraged *luxury* and established it among a great, very influential class so that its general rule even among the lower classes followed as a natural consequence."[28]

Thus, according to Kapff, the poor, before the revolution, imitated the bad example of the rich and aimed for a lifestyle that lay far beyond what was appropriate for their social status, and far beyond their resources.[29] Luxury had become endemic in society. It provoked —as if it were an act of catharsis—the "revolutionary fever" (*Revolutionsfieber*), and therefore inevitably contributed to the political and moral fiasco of 1848.[30] For Kapff, the good of society was at stake in this issue. Some of his Pietist friends may have held a more ambivalent view of the revolution, as Dieter Ising has shown in the case of Blumhardt.[31] Still, they all shared Kapff's assessment of luxury as a crisis phenomenon.

The Pietists' Concept of "Luxury" and Its Roots

But what did Pietists such as Barth, Blumhardt, and Kapff understand by the term "luxury," and why were they so critical of it? Generally speaking, luxury, for them, was a very intense cultivation of beautiful things for the purpose of enjoyment. This description is, of course, expansive and vague. In particular, the Pietists mention pompous architecture, select pieces of furniture, valuable jewelry, extravagant food, champagne, time-consuming and expensive hobbies, and—the classic example—the ever-changing fashions of French female dress: "The girls of the manufacturing classes increasingly prefer French dress to the older, more solid clothes. In our time, an increased luxury of clothing is gaining momentum [especially] in and near cities," in Völter's words.[32] The dislike of expensive imported luxury goods from abroad, especially from France, had already been widespread in the seventeenth century; it was widely shared by nineteenth-century Württemberg Pietists.[33] It seems that some even regarded the import of exotic goods itself as an expression of contemporary discontent with what divine wisdom had allocated to them; a less than enthusiastic opinion of France added weight to their reservations.[34] More generally, luxury, to them, was a pleasure-seeking and idle way of living. It very closely approximated a sin. At any rate, these Pietists linked the term *Luxus* with nouns such as *Sittenverderbniß* ("moral corruption"),[35] *Verschwendung* ("wastefulness"),[36] *Entsittlichung* ("erosion of morals"),[37] and *Unredlichkeit* ("dishonesty").[38] The Pietists conceded that luxury formed part of a cultural sophistication, which they sometimes called *Verfeinerung*, that is, refinement, and, in rare cases, pointed out some positive effects.[39] But the connection to high culture and sophistication did not, for them, provide serious moral justification for the pursuit of luxury.

Several reasons explain this negative assessment. First, luxury, to them, represented an *excess* of something. It goes beyond the legitimate fulfillment of a natural human desire. It stretches desire further and further away from necessity for the sheer sake of momentary pleasure, and thereby makes it unnatural. It delivers a life to an alien master: hedonism. Luxury, or "opulence" (*Ueppigkeit*), as it is also called, is to possess and to strive deliberately for more than one needs in order to live a fulfilled, decent, and godly life.[40] Because it is an excess, it is also a waste—a waste of time, a waste of energy, and a waste of resources. It breaks the ideal of temperance (*temperantia*) and makes a man or woman smug and complacent. In other words, it directs his or her interest toward aesthetics instead of ethics, and toward this world instead of the world to come. Luxury, thus, produces a worldly mind-set. It even fosters addiction: the Württemberg Pietists thought that people could become addicted to ever more superficial pleasures and would soon lose the power to curb their appetites. The term *Genußsucht* (literally, an "addiction to pleasure") was therefore sometimes used as a quasi-synonym for *Luxus*. As Christians, the Pietists regarded such an addiction to pleasure as a big step on the slippery slope toward what the Bible calls the "works of the flesh" (Galatians 5:19), such as sexual immorality, debauchery, and drunkenness. Because luxury consumes large amounts of money, it also easily leads to miserliness and avarice, two further vices condemned by the New Testament. This slippery slope is what Völter hinted at when he asked: "Do not self-indulgence [*Genußsucht*] and luxuriance [*Ueppigkeit*] squander what avarice [*Habsucht*] had gained?"[41] Avarice holds back what should be given; self-indulgence spends what should be kept. Thus, a life of luxury seemed to Pietists like Völter very far from the biblical ideal.

The basis of the Pietist criticism of luxury, however, was not exclusively biblical. A nonreligious preference for simplicity and austerity lay behind it, too. This ideal can be traced far back into antiquity. It can, for instance, be found in the Cynics, in Plato, Tacitus, Cicero, and Seneca.[42] In its modern form, it may in part be traced back to the Biedermeier mentality and to a nineteenth-century middle-class ethic. Some popular writings on lifestyle and manners expressed similar feelings.[43] But an element of Romanticism existed in it, too. Like all romantic-conservative authors of their day, the Pietist pastors believed that the augmentation of bodily desires would lead to cultural decay.[44] A simple, unrefined, and down-to-earth lifestyle seemed to them superior to a civilized, comfortable one that demands little effort and permits every pleasure. Luxury, in the view of the Württemberg Pietists, could quickly develop into the vice of softness (*Verweichlichung*). "Luxury enervates and softens," Barth writes.[45] What he meant by this becomes clear from his praise of the opposite concept, the "old rough simplicity."[46] Barth found this virtue in the ancient Romans, who remained devoted to manual labor and agriculture and eschewed trade. A life of comfort weakens a people's character, so the argument went, it destroys its vitality and reduces its fighting power. People who no longer have to struggle for the bare necessities of life, whose character is no longer strengthened by work and privation, quickly lose their sense of traditions and values, and their practical, sober-minded disposition.[47] They also become alienated from nature. In an 1859 article on the millennium, Barth points out that the Old Testament prophet Micah (4:4) predicted that everyone would one day sit under his own vine and fig tree. He concludes, then, that "current luxurious lifestyles do not correspond to this prophecy; living conditions must once more become much simpler and more in tune with nature. There are, therefore, great changes in the offing."[48] Barth's eschatological expectation almost sounds like a call of "back to nature."

Did the Pietists therefore propagate a bucolic ideal? Did they preach the vision of a primitive life close to nature? Not quite. Significant though it is, the

Romantic element in their thinking must not be overemphasized. The Pietist authors did not advocate cultural primitivism; indeed, they valued civilization. They even, in other contexts, talked about "savage" or "barbarian" nations to describe cultural deficiencies.[49] Unlike *Luxus*, "culture" (*Cultur*) was not a bad word for the "awakened" Württemberg pastors. Many of them, after all, had received a broad education in their youth, which they still appreciated. Also, their own brand of Christianity, and especially its view of original sin, kept them from accepting, or propagating the myth of the noble savage. To quote Barth once more: "the luxury of riches and the innocence of the simple life of a shepherd ... all have in turn been suggested and tried as a cure for mankind, and have not worked."[50] Salvation, for Barth, as for all the Pietists, was not found in a simple lifestyle that harmonizes with nature but in the Gospel of Jesus Christ. None of these writers left any doubt about the primacy of the Christian faith in their thinking. Still, their openness to the romantic sentiment intensified their criticism of luxury; as did their reluctance to welcome the alleged "progress" (*Fortschritt*) that their contemporaries so frequently hailed.[51] People who cannot observe new technological advances without a worried look at the dark side, anti-Christian side effects and the breach with tradition, also usually preserve a good dose of skepticism about the modern comforts and distractions, and the luxury of their age.

Luxury and Pauperism

Social reality seemed to speak in favor of pietistic views. If early industrialization enabled some to afford unlimited luxury, it did not prevent its economic downside: *pauperism*. In spite of technological achievements, the decades before 1850 experienced what historian Heinz-Gerhard Haupt calls "a phase of undernourishment and malnutrition" in Europe.[52] Despite the promise for the future, early industrialization weakened traditional social bonds, worsened working conditions, and could not yet overcome the results of rapid population increase, unemployment, and the poor harvests of the 1840s. Pietists were very much aware of the misery caused by these changes, and many of the Württemberg pastors were actively involved in private charities, orphanages, deaconesses' homes, and other initiatives of the Inner Mission. Pietists recognized that many families lived considerably below the poverty level. In 1845, Völter, a protagonist of the Württemberg *Rettungshaus* (orphanage) movement, wrote an article "On the Causes of the Great Number of Neglected Children in Our Time." In this article, he warned that the widening gap between the rich and the poor might erupt in a new kind of Peasants' War, as it had in the sixteenth century.[53]

Against this background of great social misery, which some Pietists vividly described, luxury seemed all the more shocking and outrageous. Kapff complained:

> Oh, what would have to be told of the *harshness towards the poor*, the stinginess towards the needy, the accumulation of capital in the face of starving and moaning families, the luxury of all kinds alongside half naked people suffering want? . . . Ten gowns are stored in their cabinet, but they refuse the poor man who asks for one.[54]

For the Pietists, such displays of luxury within a context of social misery were nothing less than failure to render assistance to those in need. In their view, society's wealth was limited; those who took more than their share deprived the rest of their needs. Kapff related the story of a nobleman who had sixteen horses and three carriages, and asks, "How many of the poor could eat their fill every day if he had kept only four instead of sixteen horses!"[55]

Kapff did not believe that luxury produced any positive economic effects. Instead, he even regarded it as a cause of the rising number of bankruptcies alongside greed, dishonesty, and stock-market speculation.[56] What Sabine Holtz observes for early modern Protestant sermons also applies to the texts of nineteenth-century Württemberg Pietists examined here: none believed that individual self-interest and luxury might serve rather than harm the common good.[57] Rather, for Pietists, the damage done by luxury to society and to the individual, was unambiguous. It was even harmful to the rich themselves, as the wealthy, indolent baron in Kapff's study of the revolution of 1848 realized:

> Getting up at 10 o'clock in the morning, drinking coffee, reading the newspaper, having lunch, going for a drive, dinner party in the evening—this is my day-to-day routine, and my heart remains empty, and I don't know why I'm here.

"How satisfied," Kapff remarked, "his heart would become if he worked, relieved distress, [and] contributed to the improvement of his people's condition!"[58] The Pietists believed that the rich would be much happier if they shed their luxurious lifestyles. But because they continued to lead destructive indolent and luxurious lives, they stimulated the bad instincts of the poor. Kapff recalled that, during the dearth, a confectioner (*Zuckerbäcker*) was asked how he could still sell his sweets at such a time. The confectioner answered that the begging children were his best customers.[59] They wasted the little that generous people had given them on satisfying their greed. For Kapff, this served as an example of the devastating effects of luxury especially in a time of need. Barth shared this sentiment. Criticizing recent developments in his own congregation in Möttlingen in 1836, he observed that "Impoverishment is on the increase—and so are, in the same degree, the erosion of morals and luxury."⁶⁰ For Barth, pauperization and luxury went hand in hand. Both were symptoms of decline.

Luxury and Eschatology

As Christians interested in salvation history, these authors interpreted such markers of decline in eschatological terms. Referring to a famous New Testament motif (Matthew 16:3), they called them *Zeichen der Zeit*, signs of the time. Among these signs were religious, social, political, and moral tendencies of the day that seemed to indicate the dramatic nature of the present and its proximity to the end times. The cult of luxury was one of them. In a circular correspondence between several of these Pietist pastors, one of Barth's colleagues, in 1844, described the great poverty of one part of humanity alongside the greatest luxury of the other part as a sign of the times.⁶¹ Opponents of the Pietists sometimes mocked them for this concept. The Hegelian Christian Märklin (1807–49), a theological radical and friend of David Friedrich Strauß, wrote a book entitled *Description and Critique of Modern Pietism* (*Darstellung und Kritik des modernen Pietismus*), in which he criticizes Sixt Carl Kapff for lumping diverse modern phenomena together and ascribing an eschatological meaning to them all: Hegel, Goethe, the *Junges Deutschland*, France and its novels, work on Sundays, industrialization, the love of pleasure and luxury. The Pietists traced all these back to the spirit of Antichrist, Märklin observed with noticeable contempt.⁶² According to Märklin, Pietists demonized this world far too much. They even considered art (*Kunst*) to be an "idle, superfluous luxury," he complains.⁶³

Conclusion and Epilogue

This criticism was not altogether untrue; but it was not wholly justified either. The Pietists did not regard all art as luxury, just as they did not regard other worldly pleasures per se as luxury. Enjoyment, they thought, was a part of creation that they accepted, and even valued, as God-given. But they feared that it could easily *become* a luxury, and thereby distort its raison d'être, namely to glorify God. They did not oppose meeting one's needs, but argued that satisfying one's desires as an end in itself, as a philosophy of life, was dangerous. In fact, they thought of this danger sooner than their contemporaries did—hence, their skepticism concerning theater, games, and fashion. It is possible that, by taking this position, the Pietists underestimated the value of earthly pleasures and regarded things as a luxury that could have found their proper place in a worldview based on the Bible and the Reformation. Perhaps luxury did not always begin where they, at times somewhat fearfully or stereotypically, discovered it. One might even wonder if the long-term social impact of the revival movement might not have been even more considerable than it actually was had its stance on the usefulness of art, literature, technology, and some other forms of modern culture been more unambiguously affirmative. Informed though it was, the Pietists' social criticism was not always sophisticated or balanced, and was sometimes overtaken by history. In addition, an in-depth knowledge of economics, especially relating to the interconnectedness of free trade, consumption, economic growth, and living standards, would have enriched and possibly qualified their criticism of luxury.

Nevertheless, it did not require the modern global financial and the eurozone debt crises to understand the appeal of a call to a simpler life of contentment, a life lived in the service of God and others, with a concern not only for earthly, but also heavenly things, as something valuable and worthy of consideration. Despite their political narrowness, these warnings against a hedonistic approach to life and against indifference to other people's misery were not at all far-fetched. In a time of growing impoverishment in Germany, such concerns were quite relevant. Today, too, as we face abject poverty in some parts of the world, a lack of sustainability in our way of living and declining interest in matters of faith in the richer European nations, these warnings may not be irrelevant. The Württemberg Pietists, at any rate, would have seen it this way. This is why they were suspicious of luxurious living. If the individual and if society were not careful, they believed, the excessive pursuit of pleasure would seduce people into setting the wrong priorities. It was above all this strong fear of the disastrous results a pursuit of luxury portended that caused them to speak out so vehemently against it.

Jan Carsten Schnurr earned a BA in Philosophy and Theology at Oxford University (2001), an MA in Modern History and English Literature at the University of Tübingen (2005), and a PhD in Modern History from Tübingen (2009). His project on historiography and historical thought in the Protestant revival in Germany during the post-Napoleonic era was published by Vandenhoeck and Ruprecht in 2011 and was awarded the Johannes-Brenz-Preis of the Verein für württembergische Kirchengeschichte in 2013. He began teaching historical theology at the Freie Theologische Hochschule Gießen as an assistant professor (Wissenschaftlicher Mitarbeiter) in 2008 and then as a Hochschuldozent (from 2011 to present).

Notes

1. First published in German as: Jan Carsten Schnurr, "Luxuskritik in der württembergischen Erweckungsbewegung: Begriffsverwendungen und Argumentationen aus den 1830er bis 1850er Jahren," *Blätter für württembergische Kirchengeschichte* 112 (2012): 131–44.
2. See Horst Muehlmann, "Luxus und Komfort: Wortgeschichte und Wortvergleich" (PhD thesis, Bonn University, 1975); Johan Hendrik Jacob van der Pot, *Die Bewertung des technischen Fortschritts: Eine systematische Übersicht der Theorien* (Assen, 1985), 2: 1019; Mireille Corbier, "Luxus," *Der Neue Pauly* 7 (1999): 534–36; Rainer Bernhardt, *Luxuskritik und Aufwandsbeschränkungen in der griechischen Welt* (Stuttgart, 2003); Ulrich Wyrwa, "Luxus und Konsum: Begriffsgeschichtliche Aspekte," in *Luxus und Konsum: Eine historische Annäherung*, ed. Reinhold Reith and Torsten Meyer (Münster, 2003), 47–60.
3. See Rüdiger Schnell, *Frauendiskurs, Männerdiskurs, Ehediskurs: Textsorten und Geschlechterkonzepte in Mittelalter und Früher Neuzeit* (Frankfurt, 1998), 158, 204–5.
4. See Werner Elert, *Morphologie des Luthertums*, vol. 2: *Soziallehren und Sozialwirkungen des Luthertums* (Munich, 1953), 499.
5. See Martin Brecht, "Das Aufkommen der neuen Frömmigkeitsbewegung in Deutschland," in *Geschichte des Pietismus*, ed. Martin Brecht (Göttingen, 1993), 1: 113–203, here 132; Martin Brecht, "August Hermann Francke und der Hallische Pietismus," in *Geschichte des Pietismus*, 1: 440–539, here 466.
6. See Wyrwa, "Luxus und Konsum," 49–51.
7. See "Luxus," in *Historisches Wörterbuch der Philosophie* (Darmstadt, 1980), 5: 565–69, here 566; John Shovlin, *The Political Economy of Virtue: Luxury, Patriotism, and the Origins of the French Revolution* (Ithaca, NY, 2006), 22; Muehlmann, "Luxus und Komfort," 46–50.
8. See "Luxus," 567.
9. Ibid.; Muehlmann, "Luxus und Komfort," 53, 55.
10. Quoted in Thomas K. Kuhn, *Religion und neuzeitliche Gesellschaft: Studien zum sozialen und diakonischen Handeln in Pietismus, Aufklärung und Erweckungsbewegung* (Tübingen, 2003), 128–287.
11. See Wyrwa, "Luxus und Konsum," 51–53. According to Muehlmann, "Luxus und Komfort," 68–69, editions of the *Brockhaus* encyclopedia between 1797 and 1827 granted luxury an increasingly positive value. Thus, the 1827 edition included the statement, "Luxury is a higher degree of affluence adequate to the state of a people's culture; in its degenerate form, however, pomp and luxuriance. It is a consequence of wealth and springs from the aspiration for the beautification of life." Similarly Ulrich Christian Pallach observes a "gradual de-ethicization" ("langsame Entmoralisierung") of *luxe* around the turn of the same century in France ("Luxe," in *Handbuch politisch-sozialer Grundbegriffe in Frankreich 1680–1820*, ed. Rolf Reichardt and Hans-Jürgen Lüsebrink [Munich, 2000]: 89–114, here 109).
12. It would probably be going too far to call it a key concept in the thinking of Württemberg Pietism of the time since the term does not appear in all of their works. It does appear frequently enough, however, to be noteworthy from the standpoint of European intellectual history.

13. For an interpretation of the work see Jan Carsten Schnurr, *Weltreiche und Wahrheitszeugen: Geschichtsbilder der protestantischen Erweckungsbewegung in Deutschland 1815–1848* (Göttingen, 2011), 197–262.
14. Christian Gottlob Barth, *Die allgemeine Weltgeschichte nach biblischen Grundsätzen bearbeitet für nachdenksame Leser* (Calw, 1837), 92.
15. Ibid., 94.
16. E.g. Heinrich Dittmar, *Die deutsche Geschichte in ihren wesentlichen Grundzügen und in einem übersichtlichen Zusammenhange: Ein Leitfaden für die mittlere historische Lehrstufe in Schulen, wie im Selbstunterrichte*, 2nd ed. (Karlsruhe, 1843 [1st ed. 1840]), 164, 327; Dittmar, *Die Geschichte der Welt vor und nach Christus, mit Rücksicht auf die Entwicklung des Lebens in Religion und Politik, Kunst und Wissenschaft, Handel und Industrie der welthistorischen Völker: Für das allgemeine Bildungsbedürfniß dargestellt* (Heidelberg, 1846), 1: 572. See also Wilhelm Hoßbach, *Philipp Jakob Spener und seine Zeit: Eine kirchenhistorische Darstellung* (Berlin, 1828), 2: 147–48: "[Spener loved] the greatest simplicity and was so far removed from luxury and pomp that he never went by carriage within the city, even when the weather was at its worst, but always went on foot."
17. It is an interesting question whether this finding is mere chance or in any sense connected to the (real or imagined) Swabian penchant for frugality.
18. Barth, *Die Allgemeine Weltgeschichte*, 21, 53, 94, 99, 118, 137, 140, 199–200, 234, 313.
19. Ibid., 213.
20. Ibid., 339.
21. Ibid., 118.
22. Ludwig Völter, *Württemberg: Das Land und seine Geschichte: Ein Lese- und Lehrbuch für Volk und Jugend*, 2nd ed. (Stuttgart, 1847 [1st ed., 1839]), 182–83.
23. Dieter Ising, *Johann Christoph Blumhardt, Life and Work: A New Biography* (Eugene, OR, 2009), 223. The original wording can be found in the German version, Dieter Ising, *Johann Christoph Blumhardt: Leben und Werk* (Göttingen, 2002), 196–97.
24. Barth, *Die Allgemeine Weltgeschichte*, 10.
25. Ludwig Völter, *Geographische Beschreibung von Württemberg, hinsichtlich der Gestalt seiner Oberfläche, seiner Erzeugnisse und Bewohner: Als Grundlage des ersten geographischen Unterrichts, so wie zur Selbstbelehrung* (Stuttgart, 1836), 198.
26. See Stefan J. Dietrich, *Christentum und Revolution: Die christlichen Kirchen in Württemberg 1848–1852* (Paderborn, 1996), 15, 43–50, 60–62.
27. Sixt Carl Kapff, *Die Revolution, ihre Ursachen, Folgen und Heilmittel, dargestellt für Hohe und Niedere* (Hamburg, 1851), 11.
28. Ibid., 32.
29. In a similar fashion, the *Christen-Bote*, published in Stuttgart, already lamented, in 1833, "the great decline in morals in all classes of the people, the rising luxury, the departure of so many from the sphere appropriate to their civil and economic circumstances." "Einige Winke für die gegenwärtige Stände-Versammlung," *Christen-Bote* 3 (1833): 14. Likewise, Ludwig Völter, "Ueber die Ursachen der großen Zahl verwahrloster Kinder in unserer Zeit: Aus einer demnächst erscheinenden Schrift über die württembergischen Kinderrettungsanstalten," *Süddeutscher Schul-Bote* 9 (1845): 97–100, 105–8, here 99, complained that with regard to "pleasure and the luxury of dress," one "even wishes to follow the example of the higher classes."
30. Kapff, *Die Revolution*, 5.

31. For Blumhardt's somewhat changing perception of the revolution, see Ising, *Johann Christoph Blumhardt*, 236–49. On the attitude of Württemberg churchmen (including Kapff) see Dietrich, *Christentum und Revolution*. For several figures of the German evangelical revival from different geographical and ecclesiastical backgrounds (including Barth, Kapff, and Christoph and Wilhelm Hoffmann from Württemberg [212–20]), see Nicholas M. Railton, "Evangelical Reactions to the 1848 Revolution in Germany," *Zeitschrift für Kirchengeschichte* 123 (2012): 195–224.
32. Völter, *Geographische Beschreibung*, 91. See also Kapff, *Die Revolution*, 1851, 28–31; Völter, *Württemberg*, 2nd ed., 183. Manuel Schramm, "Konsumgeschichte," in *Dimensionen der Kultur- und Gesellschaftsgeschichte*, ed. Matthias Middell (Leipzig, 2007), 163–83, here 176, points out that in the nineteenth century, women's dress followed changing fashions more than men's dress, and served as a status symbol.
33. See Alexander Schmidt, *Vaterlandsliebe und Religionskonflikt: Politische Diskurse im Alten Reich, 1555–1648* (Leiden, 2007), 363: "Building on Christian criticism of luxury and a humanistic ideal of national identity, many German authors from the late 1620s on accused foreigners as well as their compatriots of introducing alien, especially French, customs, fashions, and languages. According to them, this had contributed to a decline of morals and good German customs and, above all, to a decline of the sense of unity among Germans."
34. For the way in which representatives of the German evangelical revival perceived France, see Schnurr, *Weltreiche und Wahrheitszeugen*, 235–36, 317–19. These factors are probably more important than the economic fear expressed by Leibniz and others that the luxury of French goods might draw the money out of the country (see "Luxus," 566).
35. Barth, *Die Allgemeine Weltgeschichte*, 137.
36. Völter, "Über die Ursachen," 99.
37. Barth, quoted in Karl Werner, *Christian Gottlob Barth, Doktor der Theologie, nach seinem Leben und Wirken gezeichnet* (Calw, 1866), 2: 328.
38. Kapff, *Die Revolution*, 10.
39. Barth, *Die Allgemeine Weltgeschichte*, 10, 199. Similarly, the inspector of the Basel Mission, a native of Württemberg, Christian Gottlieb Blumhardt, *Versuch einer allgemeinen Missionsgeschichte der Kirche Christi* (Basel, 1828), 1: 509–10.
40. Barth, *Allgemeine Weltgeschichte*, 21, 94; Völter, *Württemberg*, 183; Kapff, *Die Revolution*, 28.
41. Völter, "Über die Ursachen," 99.
42. See Georg Bollenbeck, *Eine Geschichte der Kulturkritik: Von Rousseau bis Günther Anders* (Munich, 2007), 38–39.
43. An example of this in Württemberg were the *Hausregeln* ("house rules") of the pastor and educator Johann Friedrich Flattich (1713–97), which were reprinted in the nineteenth century. On Flattich, see Hermann Ehmer, *Johann Friedrich Flattich, Der schwäbische Salomo: EineBiographie* (Stuttgart, 1997).
44. See van der Pot, *Die Bewertung des technischen Fortschritts*, 2: 1020.
45. Barth, *Die Allgemeine Weltgeschichte*, 53.
46. Ibid., 92.
47. This is one of several reasons why the Pietists had no taste for a bohemian lifestyle. They did not reject intellectual work or creativity as such, as their admiration for several scholars, artists, and musicians reveals.

48. Christian Gottlob Barth, "Ein Blick in das verheißene Friedensreich," *Sammlungen für Liebhaber christlicher Wahrheit und Gottseligkeit* (1859): 225–38, here 234.
49. Barth, *Die Allgemeine Weltgeschichte*, 44, 206–7.
50. Ibid., 363.
51. See Schnurr, *Weltreiche und Wahrheitszeugen*, 174–75.
52. Heinz-Gerhard Haupt, *Konsum und Handel: Europa im 19. und 20. Jahrhundert* (Göttingen, 2003), 35.
53. Völter, "Ueber die Ursachen," 106.
54. Kapff, *Die Revolution*, 31.
55. Ibid., 29.
56. Ibid., 10.
57. Sabine Holtz, *Theologie und Alltag: Lehre und Leben in den Predigten der Tübinger Theologen 1550–1750* (Tübingen, 1993), 228: "This subject is ignored by the preachers."
58. Kapff, *Die Revolution*, 29.
59. Ibid., 21.
60. Quoted in Werner, *Christian Gottlob Barth*, 328.
61. Quoted in Michael Kannenberg, *Verschleierte Uhrtafeln: Endzeiterwartungen im württembergischen Pietismus zwischen 1818 und 1848* (Göttingen, 2007), 300.
62. Christian Märklin, *Darstellung und Kritik des modernen Pietismus: Ein wissenschaftlicher Versuch* (Stuttgart, 1839), 167–68.
63. Ibid., n215.

Bibliography

Barth, Christian Gottlob. *Die allgemeine Weltgeschichte nach biblischen Grundsätzen bearbeitet für nachdenksame Leser*. Calw, 1837.

———. "Ein Blick in das verheißene Friedensreich," *Sammlungen für Liebhaber christlicher Wahrheit und Gottseligkeit* (1859): 225–38.

Bernhardt, Rainer. *Luxuskritik und Aufwandsbeschränkungen in der griechischen Welt*. Stuttgart, 2003.

Blumhardt, Christian Gottlieb. *Versuch einer allgemeinen Missionsgeschichte der Kirche Christi*. Basel, 1828.

Bollenbeck, Georg. *Eine Geschichte der Kulturkritik: Von Rousseau bis Günther Anders*. Munich, 2007.

Brecht, Martin. "Das Aufkommen der neuen Frömmigkeitsbewegung in Deutschland." In *Geschichte des Pietismus*, vol. 1: *Der Pietismus vom siebzehnten bis zum frühen neunzehnten Jahrhundert*, edited by Martin Brecht, et. al., 113–203. Göttingen, 1993.

———. "August Hermann Francke und der Hallische Pietismus." In *Geschichte des Pietismus*, vol. 1: *Der Pietismus vom siebzehnten bis zum frühen neunzehnten Jahrhundert*, edited by Martin Brecht et. al., 440–539. Göttingen, 1993.

Corbier, Mireille. "Luxus." *Der Neue Pauly* 7 (1999): 534–36.

Dietrich, Stefan J. *Christentum und Revolution: Die christlichen Kirchen in Württemberg 1848–1852*. Paderborn, 1996.

Dittmar, Heinrich. *Die deutsche Geschichte in ihren wesentlichen Grundzügen und in einem übersichtlichen Zusammenhange: Ein Leitfaden für die mittlere historische Lehrstufe in Schulen, wie im Selbstunterrichte*, 2nd ed., Karlsruhe, 1843.

———. *Die Geschichte der Welt vor und nach Christus, mit Rücksicht auf die Entwicklung des Lebens in Religion und Politik, Kunst und Wissenschaft, Handel und Industrie der welthistorischen Völker: Für das allgemeine Bildungsbedürfniß dargestellt*. 2 vols. Heidelberg, 1846.

Ehmer, Hermann. *Johann Friedrich Flattich, Der schwäbische Salomo: Eine Biographie*. Stuttgart, 1997.

Elert, Werner. *Morphologie des Luthertums*. Vol. 2: *Soziallehren und Sozialwirkungen des Luthertums*. Munich, 1953.

Haupt, Heinz-Gerhard. *Konsum und Handel: Europa im 19. und 20. Jahrhundert*. Göttingen, 2003.

Historisches Wörterbuch der Philosophie Gesamtwerk, edited by Joachim Ritter and Karlfried Gründer. 13 vols. Darmstadt, 1980.

Holtz, Sabine. *Theologie und Alltag: Lehre und Leben in den Predigten der Tübinger Theologen 1550–1750*. Tübingen, 1993.

Hoßbach, Wilhelm, *Philipp Jakob Spener und seine Zeit: Eine kirchenhistorische Darstellung*. 2 vols. Berlin, 1828.

Ising, Dieter. *Johann Christoph Blumhardt, Life and Work: A New Biography*. Eugene, OR, 2009.

Kannenberg, Michael. *Verschleierte Uhrtafeln: Endzeiterwartungen im württembergischen Pietismus zwischen 1818 und 1848*. Göttingen, 2007.

Kapff, Sixt Carl. *Die Revolution, ihre Ursachen, Folgen und Heilmittel, dargestellt für Hohe und Niedere*. Hamburg, 1851.

Kuhn, Thomas K. *Religion und neuzeitliche Gesellschaft: Studien zum sozialen und diakonischen Handeln in Pietismus, Aufklärung und Erweckungsbewegung*. Tübingen, 2003.

Märklin, Christian. *Darstellung und Kritik des modernen Pietismus: Ein wissenschaftlicher Versuch*. Stuttgart, 1839.

Muehlmann, Horst. "Luxus und Komfort: Wortgeschichte und Wortvergleich." PhD diss., Bonn University, 1975.

Pot, Johan Hendrik Jacob van der. *Die Bewertung des technischen Fortschritts: Eine systematische Übersicht der Theorien*. Assen, 1985.

Railton, Nicholas M. "Evangelical Reactions to the 1848 Revolution in Germany." *Zeitschrift für Kirchengeschichte* 123 (2012): 195–224.

Reichardt, Rolf and Hans-Jürgen Lüsebrink, ed. *Handbuch politisch-sozialer Grundbegriffe in Frankreich 1680–1820*. Munich, 2000.

Schmidt, Alexander. *Vaterlandsliebe und Religionskonflikt: Politische Diskurse im Alten Reich (1555–1648)*. Leiden, 2007.

Schnell, Rüdiger. *Frauendiskurs, Männerdiskurs, Ehediskurs: Textsorten und Geschlechterkonzepte in Mittelalter und Früher Neuzeit*. Frankfurt, 1998.

Schnurr, Jan Carsten. "Luxuskritik in der württembergischen Erweckungsbewegung: Begriffsverwendungen und Argumentationen aus den 1830er bis 1850er Jahren," *Blätter für württembergische Kirchengeschichte* 112 (2012): 131–44.

———. *Weltreiche und Wahrheitszeugen: Geschichtsbilder der protestantischen Erweckungsbewegung in Deutschland 1815–1848*. Göttingen, 2011.

Schramm, Manuel. "Konsumgeschichte." In *Dimensionen der Kultur- und Gesellschaftsgeschichte*, edited by Matthias Middell, 163–83. Leipzig, 2007.

Shovlin, John. *The Political Economy of Virtue: Luxury, Patriotism, and the Origins of the French Revolution*. Ithaca, NY, 2006.

Völter, Ludwig. *Geographische Beschreibung von Württemberg, hinsichtlich der Gestalt seiner Oberfläche, seiner Erzeugnisse und Bewohner: Als Grundlage des ersten geographischen Unterrichts, so wie zur Selbstbelehrung*. Stuttgart, 1836.

———. "Ueber die Ursachen der großen Zahl verwahrloster Kinder in unserer Zeit: Aus einer demnächst erscheinenden Schrift über die württembergischen Kinderrettungsanstalten," *Süddeutscher Schul-Bote* 9 (1845): 97–108.

———. *Württemberg: Das Land und seine Geschichte: Ein Lese- und Lehrbuch für Volk und Jugend*, 2nd ed. Stuttgart, 1847.

Werner, Karl. *Christian Gottlob Barth, Doktor der Theologie, nach seinem Leben und Wirken gezeichnet*. Calw, 1866.

Wyrwa, Ulrich. "Luxus und Konsum: Begriffsgeschichtliche Aspekte." In *Luxus und Konsum: Eine historische Annäherung*, edited by Reinhold Reith and Torsten Meyer, 47–60. Münster, 2003.

CHAPTER TEN

Marx on Money

JONATHAN SPERBER

In January 1851, just a few months after he moved to Manchester to work for his family's business partners, with the aim of supporting himself and his friend and political associate Karl Marx, Friedrich Engels received a note from Wilhelm Pieper, one of the many radical German political refugees in London. A member of Marx's shrinking circle of supporters, and his sometime secretary, Pieper was in a position to report on the activities of the communist leader. Marx, Pieper explained, had been increasingly avoiding political activism and the intense and personally hateful controversies among the refugees of the failed revolutions of 1848. Instead, he was spending his days in the British Museum, reading the works of political economists. "Marx lives very withdrawn," Pieper wrote, "his only friends are John Stuart Mill [and] Loyd, and when one comes to Marx one is greeted not with compliments but with economic categories."[1]

Marx's "friends," the authors he had been studying intensively, included John Stuart Mill, today remembered as a political philosopher, but known to contemporaries primarily as the author of the 1848 *Principles of Political Economy*, the standard mid-Victorian economics textbook, and Samuel Loyd, an expert on monetary issues.[2] This combination of readings does suggest something of the importance Marx gave to monetary matters in his economic thought. Investigations into the nature of money stood at the beginning of his interest in economics; their philosophical implications were considered in the "Paris manuscripts" of 1844, and in Marx's essay on the Jewish question. During the 1850s, when Marx was the European correspondent for the *New York Tribune*, for which much of his work was what we would today call a business and financial columnist, he reported, at some length, on monetary issues. They played an important role in his accounts for the newspaper on the worldwide recession of 1857. Money and monetary questions were not so central to Marx's major economics treatise, *Capital*, appearing in a subordinate position in both volume 1, published during Marx's lifetime, and in the two successive volumes, edited by Engels from Marx's notes and draft manuscripts, and published in the decade after Marx's death. But that was, at least in part, because Marx had already discussed monetary issues in his often-neglected first book on economics, *On the Criticism of Political Economy*, published in 1859, eight years before the initial appearance of *Capital*.

If understanding the economic significance of currency was important for Marx's investigation of capitalism, money also played a role in his vision of a communist future. While Marx, notoriously, refused to lay out a blueprint of a communist society, and made fun of contemporaries who did so, he nonetheless would, on occasion, speculate about what institutions such a society would have, and how they would function. These speculations appeared in the initial draft of *Capital*, written during the late 1850s; the so-called *Grundrisse*, in Marx's 1871 polemic in support of the Paris Commune, *The Civil War in France*; and in his 1875 attack on the ideas of the newly united German social democratic party, *The Critique of the Gotha Program*. Marx's visions of a postcapitalist future included, explicitly or implicitly, accounts of the nature of money under communism, as well as monetary institutions, such as a central bank. Admittedly, money did not play the same crucial role in Marx's economic thought as did the labor theory of value, the idea that commodities' values were determined by the labor time needed for their production or reproduction. But money developed its importance for Marx as a result of its relationship to this basic form of value.

Money in Marx's Early Theoretical Writings

Marx began his systematic study of economics during his first stay in Paris, between October 1843 and January 1845. He read, carefully and extensively, the classics of political economy, the works of Adam Smith, David Ricardo, James Mill, and Jean-Baptiste Say—the Englishmen in French translations, since Marx at the time did not know any English. Marx then interpreted the findings of these authors about the workings of a capitalist economy and society in the light of Hegel's theory of alienation, or more precisely, the application of Hegel's theories of alienation, by his radical followers, the Young Hegelians, to criticize religion.[3]

In doing this, Marx was following in the footsteps of a friend and political associate (later, at times, an enemy and political rival) Moses Hess, who had been emphasizing these points since the late 1830s.[4] For Hess, money was the central expression of human self-alienation under capitalism, as he explained in his essay, *On the Nature of Money* (*Über das Geldwesen*), submitted for consideration in 1844 to the journal edited by Marx and Karl Ruge, the *Deutsch-Französische Jahrbücher*, although ultimately published the following year in the *Rheinische Jahrbücher zur gesellschaftlichen Reform*, which Hess had been instrumental in founding. Hess described humans as species beings (*Gattungswesen*), whose individual existence was expressed in community life and productive cooperation. Under capitalism, Hess went on, individuals were, through competition, self-interest, and production for the market, alienated from each other, and so from their human essence: "the individual has been raised to a goal, the species degraded to a means, that is the reversal of human and, more generally, natural life."[5] This reversal, Hess asserted was articulated in money, "the product of mutually alienated human beings, the externalized and alienated man." The free market turned humans into "social predators, conscious egoists, who, in free competition, the war of all against all . . . in occupational freedom sanction mutual exploitation the thirst for money . . . which is nothing other than the thirst for blood of the social predator." Following the Young Hegelian critique of religion, which perceived God as externalized and alienated human species essence, Hess asserted, "What God is for theoretical life, money is for practical life in the inverted world: the externalized wealth of humans, their life activity which has been bargained away [*ihre verschacherte Lebensthätigkeit*]."[6]

Marx, in his considerations about capitalism, sometimes made similar assertions about money, particularly in his 1844 essay on the Jewish question. He stated that "The god of practical need and self-interest is money . . . Money is the universal value of all things, constructed for itself. . . . Money is the essence of man's labor and of man's existence that has been alienated from him, and this alien being dominates him and he worships it." Marx's linking of this attitude to Jews and Judaism has led to charges that he was an anti-Semite, although it would be fair to note that Hess made similar assertions in his essay.[7]

A version of this analysis also appeared in the so-called Paris Manuscripts of 1844, Marx's chief theoretical contribution during his stay in the French capital. A passage on money in these manuscripts is reminiscent of Hess's ideas, arguing that in capitalist society money could replace basic human characteristics: "The properties of money are my—that is the possessor of money—characteristics and essential powers. That which I am and am capable of is thus in no way determined by my individuality. I am ugly but I can purchase for myself the most beautiful woman. Thus I am not ugly, because the effect of ugliness, its deterrent force, is annihilated by money." Generalizing this point, Marx stated, "The reversal and confusion of all human and natural qualities, the fraternization of impossibilities—the divine power—of money lies in its essence as the alienated, externalized and self-externalizing species essence of human beings. It is the externalized and emptied out wealth [*Vermögen*] of humanity."[8]

As Marx read the major economists of his day and devised his Hegelian critique of their ideas, he developed a somewhat different view of both alienation and the place of money in its expression. In a well-known segment of the Paris Manuscripts, Marx described the three fundamental forms of alienation under capitalism: the alienation of workers from the products of their labor, the workers' alienation in the labor process, and the way that capitalism alienated workers from their human species essence. The nature of the labor process was central to this analysis of capitalist alienation; money was more an epiphenomenon: "As we have, through analysis of the concept of alienated, externalized and emptied out labor, found the concept of private property, so can, with help of both these factors, all the categories of political economy be developed. We will rediscover in each category, i.e., haggling, competition, capital and money, just a determined and developed expression of these initial [conceptual] foundations."[9]

This different attitude is also apparent in Marx's study of economists. The notes he took on their work were very extensive, as Marx's reading notes invariably were, but they were also, somewhat more unusually, not just simple summaries of the works he read and quotations from them. Underlining the significance of the classical economists for Marx's thought, in his notes on their writings Marx argued with them, evaluated them, and articulated his own ideas—among other matters, on the nature of money in capitalism.

Marx copied out Jean-Baptiste Say's distinction between money and precious metals. He noted, emphasized, and summarized in German Adam Smith's observation that national income was either a country's stock of currency, adjusted for the velocity of circulation, or the sum of all consumable materials as well as the latter's attack on mercantilism for emphasizing the possession of precious metals rather than production.[10] Say's and Smith's observations were all directed against the idea of an intrinsic value of money, a value usually connected to precious metals; money's value was, rather, in its ability to command the use of goods that had been produced. It was, as Marx said, commenting on the writings of James Mill (John Stuart's father), opposing "the crude economic superstition of the people and of governments . . . about the absolute value of precious metals, and about the possession of these metals as the sole reality of wealth."

Marx certainly endorsed this viewpoint, as he did so many of the ideas of the classical economists. Yet their insights, Marx asserted, did not go far enough. Economists such as James Mill and David Ricardo "set in place of this crude superstition [of the intrinsic value of precious metals] a refined superstition."[11] They were unable to understand money as the means for the product of alienated labor to circulate and for goods to be exchanged in a capitalist society. In making this remark, Marx was setting up a contrast between money as an alienated measure of value and a potentially more genuine measure of value. The exact nature of that genuine measure and its relation to monetary value remained obscure. Marx's future economic writings would continue both his endorsement of the monetary ideas of economists such as Smith, Ricardo, and the Mills, but also his criticism of them and would feature a refinement of his ideas about differing and contrasting measures of value.

Money in the World Market: Marx on the Global Recession of 1857

Marx made relatively little progress formulating his economic ideas during the second half of the 1840s. He gave intellectual priority to developing a materialist epistemology and a theory of history, working in collaboration with Friedrich Engels on the unpublished manuscripts that have become known, although incorrectly, as "The German Ideology," and then on the *Communist Manifesto*. Marx's time-consuming political activities, first with the Communist League, and then in Cologne during the revolution of 1848–49, also put economics on the back burner. The first decade of Marx's London exile, by contrast, offered, admittedly by default, more opportunities for developing ideas about economics. The 1850s were a period of reaction in continental Europe, following the suppression of the 1848–49 revolutions, leaving Marx with few options for political action. Instead, Marx studied intensively economists' writings in the library of the British Museum. Marx's work as a freelance journalist, especially for the *New York Tribune*, but for other newspapers as well, provided him with an opportunity to try out a wealth of ideas on contemporary politics, society, and, of course, economics, including monetary questions.[12]

These ideas came to the fore in Marx's accounts of the crisis of 1857, the first worldwide recession. In his reporting, Marx persistently argued against the interpretation that the crisis had resulted from a runaway boom, caused by an expansion of the currency beyond the constraints imposed by the supply of precious metals. He stated in 1858:

> There is, perhaps no point in Political Economy, in which there exists more popular apprehension than on the power, which banks of issue are commonly supposed to wield, of affecting general prices through an expansion or contraction of currency. The idea that banks had unduly expanded the currency, thus producing an inflation of prices violently to be readjusted by a final collapse, is too cheap a method of accounting for every crisis not to be eagerly caught at.[13]

Marx noted that the crisis had reached the German city of Hamburg, which had a purely metallic, silver-based currency. He also observed that the Bank of England, following Robert Peel's Bank Act of 1844, had only been able to issue paper currency if it was backed by precious metals. Proponents of the act claimed that such a restriction of currency in circulation would prevent commercial crises—"all monetary crises, as he [Peel] and his partisans observed, would thus be warded off for all time to come." The reality, as Marx sardonically noted, was just the opposite. The monetary policy advocated by Peel and his followers was, as we would say today, pro-cyclical. In a business-cycle downturn, when specie flowed out of the country, this meant an increase in interest rates and a decline in availability of credit, which only reinforced the crisis. Marx quoted favorably John Stuart Mill's testimony before a parliamentary committee that "the condition to be aimed at by a paper currency was not to imitate but to correct and supersede such disastrous vicissitudes." In fact, Marx predicted, the crisis would mean that the 1844 Bank Act would have to be suspended, in order to allow the Bank of England to expand the money supply to deal with the crisis—which, as Marx noted with a fair degree of self-satisfaction, was precisely what happened.[14]

As these remarks suggest, Marx located one of the precipitating elements of the crisis in international financial transactions, occurring through the flow of precious metals. Silver left European countries headed for China; yet even the Opium Wars, Marx observed, could not resolve Europe's balance of payments problems. This created arbitrage possibilities in countries with a bimetallic currency such as France, if the price of silver rose above the rate that the government had fixed for it in relation to gold, leading to a further currency drain. Chinese refusal to buy goods from Europe or European colonies (like Indian opium), accelerating the drain of silver, limiting European countries' money supplies and aggravating the effects of the recession, Marx asserted, "is destined to exercise a far greater influence upon Europe than all the Russian wars, Italian manifestoes and secret societies of that continent."[15]

Marx's journalism of the late 1850s shows him applying the ideas of economists he had first studied in Paris during the previous decade and in the British Museum. In particular, his discussion of the place of international monetary transactions and monetary policy in the origins and course of the global recession of 1857 involved a further development of the ideas about the lack of any intrinsic value of currency he had first considered during the mid 1840s. Marx's sarcastic comments about Sir Robert Peel's Bank Law of 1844 are a particularly good example of this trend in his thought. At the time he did this reporting, Marx was leading an intellectual double life—during the day, correspondent for the *New York Tribune*, at night feverishly working on his economics treatise, which he hoped to have finished before the outbreak of a new wave of European revolutions in the wake of the widespread economic crisis. The new revolutionary wave, of course, never did manifest itself, but Marx did publish, for the first time, a work on economics.

Money in Marx's Mature Economic Theory

This was the *On the Criticism of Political Economy*, which appeared in Berlin in 1859. Today, the work is remembered primarily for its introduction, in which Marx laid out the elements of a social theory, including the ideas of base and superstructure, and the progression of human history through different stages, each characterized by a distinct mode of production, each terminated by a revolution, all ultimately culminating in communism. Generally, not all that much attention has been paid to the rest of the book, and its discussion of economics: commentators are far more likely to go directly to Marx's major economic treatise, *Capital*, or to the very large initial first draft of that work, the *Grundrisse*, from which *On the Criticism of Political Economy* was a small excerpt. Helping this perception along is Marx's own attitude, in particular his extreme frustration about the book's lack of reviews in German newspapers—a fact which he alternated in attributing to a capitalist conspiracy against his ideas and the inability of his Berlin publishers to market the book effectively. As Soviet and East German scholars showed some time ago, this perception was not entirely correct: the book sold out within a year and was reviewed, generally quite favorably, in a number of specialized literary, business, and economics periodicals.[16]

The work was primarily a study of the role of money as means of exchange in a capitalist economy. Marx had three major points to make, two of which reflected his previous studies of the classical economists and his journalism as influenced by these studies. The third point, going beyond the theories of the classical economists, involved a further development of the nascent ideas of 1844 about money as measure of value. These considerations pointed in the direction of Marx's labor theory of value as put forth in *Capital* and also toward his ideas about the place of money in a future communist society.

Marx spent a good portion of the book emphasizing the relationship between money and precious metals. He pointed out, expanding on his journalistic observations for the *New York Tribune*, that only one precious metal at a time could form the basis for currency. The rise in the global price of silver meant that French owners of that metal preferred to sell it abroad for gold, rather than to exchange it for gold at the official and lower rate, so that France's bimetallic standard was de facto a gold standard. Marx also discussed the relationship between precious metals and price. He observed that the price relationships or the "exchange value" (*Tauschwert*), as he said, between different goods remained constant, regardless of which precious metal was used as basis of a currency. If one commodity were four times as expensive as another, it would be so whether prices were expressed in gold or silver coins. However, Marx went on, since different precious metals themselves had different prices, the prices of individual goods would be different, depending on which metal was the basis for currency. The confusion of these two points, Marx noted, "has brought forth the craziest theories," in particular the idea that products have an intrinsic value in gold.[17] In making these observations, Marx was, once again, reiterating the ideas of classical economists about the lack of an intrinsic value of money.

A second major issue in the book connected money and price levels. Marx was skeptical of the idea that the quantity of money determined prices. He pointed out that post-Ricardian English political economists, particularly Thomas Tooke, the author of a history of prices, had ascertained just the opposite: "Prices are thus not high or low, because more or less money circulates; rather more or less money circulates because prices are high or low."[18] Circulation of money depended, Marx noted, not just on the amount of money present—whether coins made from precious metals, or banknotes—but also on the money's velocity of circulation. And that in turn depended on "the total character of the mode of production, the size of the population, relationship of city and country, development of means of transportation, of greater or lesser development of labor, credit, etc., in short circumstances, which all lie outside the simple circulation of money and are just reflected in it."[19] With this notion as well, Marx was adding to the skepticism he had articulated in his journalism about excessive monetary expansion as the cause of the 1857 recession. Indeed, he had some sharp words for the idea that monetary phenomena could be understood as the cause of commercial crises.[20] Rather than changes in money supply causing a commercial crisis, Marx understood such a crisis as affecting the money supply, because businessmen then wanted to hold cash rather than goods: "for instance in London and Hamburg, during certain moments of the 1857–58 commercial crisis, [there were] actually more buyers than sellers of one commodity, namely money, and more sellers than buyers of all other kinds of money, namely goods."[21]

The third major feature of the book was Marx's discussion of money as a means of exchange, making it possible to trade different and otherwise incommensurable goods. Marx expressed this idea using the symbolic expression C – M – C, that is, the sale of a commodity for money, and use of that money to purchase another commodity. Money in that understanding is a measure of value, making exchange possible. But Marx asserted, here once again following the ideas first stated by Adam Smith and David Ricardo, that the value of goods was given by the amount of labor time necessary for their production. It was labor time that, ultimately, acted as a homogenizing agent, providing a common valuation for different goods and making their exchange possible. But goods were exchanged, not in terms of labor time, but at a market price, given in money, as a result of supply and demand. How was it possible to reconcile these two measures of value?[22]

This was a complex issue with which Marx would wrestle for most of the rest of his life. In *Capital*, he provided two answers to this question. One involved turning his diagrammatic exposition of exchange around, beginning with money rather than with goods: M – C – M, in Marx's notation, rather than C – M – C. Turning money into capital required the second "M" in that formulation to be larger than the initial one. This, in turn, led to Marx's version of the labor theory of value, in which workers sold their labor power to capitalists, receiving its value from them, but the labor embodied in the labor power they sold increased the value of the commodities to which it was applied. This answer was a central element of the published volume 1 of *Capital*. The other answer, unpublished in Marx's lifetime, was what has come to be known as the "transformation problem," the means by which the value of goods, determined by the amount of labor embodied in their production, gets expressed in market exchange as money prices.[23]

Marx's analysis of these points emphasized the labor theory of value; the accounts of money in *Capital* were less central and less original, tending just to reiterate what Marx had already discussed in his previous book on economics.[24] Common to all these considerations is the idea that a characteristic feature of capitalism is the dualism between value determined by labor time and market value expressed in prices. A major feature of Marx's speculations about a future communist society was the abolition of this dualism.

Speculations about Money in a Communist Society

Early communist thinkers in both France and England had considered the possibility of founding a bank that would issue notes denominated not in money but in labor time, thus creating a currency that would express the genuine values of goods. In *On the Criticism of Political Economy*, Marx had some sarcastic words to say about the Scottish socialist John Gray, who had written pamphlets in the 1830s and 1840s proposing such a bank. He noted that Gray's scheme amounted to the "pious wish" that "Products should be produced as commodities [that is, in capitalist labor relations] but not exchanged as commodities."[25] In his unpublished economic writings of the time, Marx took a somewhat more favorable attitude toward this scheme. In a capitalist economy, the exchange rates of these bank notes denominated in labor time with the money currency would not remain stable, but would fluctuate with the market, so, in effect, subordinating the currency based on labor value to the currency based on money. To change this state of affairs would either require a government to create a legally fixed and inalterable exchange rate—a prospect which Marx, considering his views on bimetallic currency, would have found dubious—or the bank would have to be "a board which keeps the books and does the calculations for a society working communally." In other words, such a bank could only be created as an institution of a postcapitalist, communist regime.[26]

Almost two decades after these initial speculations, Marx again took up the question of a communist currency in *The Critique of the Gotha Program*. He explained that at least in the initial stages of a communist regime, workers would be paid with notes denominated in labor time. Wages would consist of the amount of time an individual worked, less deductions to a "common fund," to be used for investment; prices of goods for sale would also be expressed in labor time. Value expressed in currency and in labor time would finally coincide. "The same quantum of labor that he [the worker] gives society in one form, he receives back in the other."[27]

Although Marx did not expressly assert it, one might imagine that the notes would be issued by a bank similar to the one imagined in the *Grundrisse*. This line of speculation can be taken a bit further. Marx's great polemic, *The Civil War in France*, written in 1871, right after the violent suppression of the Paris Commune by the army of the new Third French Republic, contained an account of a future communist society, ostensibly modeled on the Commune. This communist regime was a highly decentralized one, where decisions about production were made primarily by local communes. Marx did note that there would be a central authority of sorts, whose members would be selected at a local level and subject to immediate recall, if their voters were displeased with them. This was a vision of communism quite unlike twentieth-century communist governments, with their very elaborate, extremely centralized, top-down planning apparatuses. Marx did not explain just how "united cooperative societies," would "regulate national production upon a common plan" in his decentralized communist future, or whether there would be any central economic agencies at all.[28] One does have to wonder, though, in view of Marx's other discussions of the economics of communism, if this decentralized planning might have been facilitated by a central bank issuing notes denominated in labor time.

Marx's Monetary Theories in Their Nineteenth-Century Context

In all of Marx's views on money, running from his youthful philosophical critiques of capitalism, to his middle-aged empirical investigations of the workings of a capitalist economy, to his speculations late in life about a communist future, two features remained constant. One was a reiteration of the ideas of the classical political economists, such as Smith, Ricardo, Say, and the Mills.[29] Marx took up and endorsed their ideas about the value of money consisting of its ability to purchase goods and services for sale, its facilitation of the exchange of produced commodities, and their denunciation of the idea of an intrinsic value of money linked to precious metals. This viewpoint was articulated in Marx's own discussion of the monetary origins and consequences of the 1857 global recession, which was, in many ways, his most detailed and best investigated account of the nature of capitalist crises.

If Marx's expositions of monetary questions showed him to be a pupil of the classical economists, they also showed that he could point out what seemed to be weaknesses and contradictions in their work. In particular, he noted that they held two very different ideas about the value of goods produced and exchanged in a capitalist economy—value expressed in terms of the labor time needed for production, and value expressed in monetary terms, the price of market exchange. A central feature of his economics was showing how these two features of value were related, and how the latter was, ultimately, an articulation of the former. In a communist society, Marx thought, the two versions of value would be merged, since money itself would take the form of banknotes denominated in labor time. All these points show how Marx's economic ideas were rooted in the theories and practices of the nineteenth century.

Jonathan Sperber received his PhD from the University of Chicago, where he studied with Leonard Krieger, William H. Sewell Jr., and John Boyer. Since 1984, he has been in the department of history at the University of Missouri, since 2003 as the Curators' Professor of History. Sperber has written extensively on nineteenth-century German and European history. Among his books are *Popular Catholicism in Nineteenth Century Germany* (1984); *Rhineland Radicals: The Democratic Movement and the Revolution of 1848–49* (1991); *The European Revolutions, 1848–1851* (1994; 2nd ed., 2005); *The Kaiser's Voters: Electors and Elections in Imperial Germany* (1997); *Revolutionary Europe, 1780–1850* (2000; 2nd ed., 2017); *Property and Civil Society in Southwestern Germany, 1820–1914* (2005); *Europe, 1850–1914: Progress, Participation and Apprehension* (2009); and, most recently, *Karl Marx: A Nineteenth Century Life* (2013), which has been published in a German-language edition, *Karl Marx: Sein Leben und sein Jahrhundert*. Spanish, Brazilian, Slovenian, Chinese, Japanese, Turkish, French and Iranian editions have also appeared. Sperber is currently working on a new and different scholarly project, a global history of the second half of the twentieth century.

Notes

1. *Karl Marx Friedrich Engels Gesamtausgabe* (Berlin, 1975), 3/4: 17. On Marx's work in the British Museum, ibid., 3/4: 140.
2. On Samuel Loyd, Baron Overstone, and Marx's opinion of his theories concerning the money supply and interest rates, ibid., 2/4.2: 484–500, 1388–89.

3. On Marx's stay in Paris, 1843–45, see Jonathan Sperber, *Karl Marx: A Nineteenth Century Life* (New York, 2013), 108–52.
4. Concerning Hess and his influence on Marx, see Zwi Rosen, *Moses Hess und Karl Marx. Ein Beitrag zur Entstehung der Marxschen Theorie* (Hamburg, 1983), 142–58 and passim.
5. Moses Hess, "Über das Geldwesen," in *Philosophische und Sozialistische Schriften 1837–1850*, ed. Auguste Cornu and Wolfgang Mönke (East Berlin, 1961), 329–48, quote on 333.
6. Ibid., 334–35, 345.
7. "Zur Judenfrage," *Karl Marx Friedrich Engels Gesamtausgabe*, 1/2: 166. More generally concerning this essay, Sperber, *Karl Marx*, 127–34.
8. *Karl Marx Friedrich Engels Gesamtausgabe*, 2/1: 436–37.
9. Quote from ibid., 1/2: 374, part of Marx's analysis of alienated labor on 363–75.
10. Ibid., 4/2: 308–9, 345, 373. Marx's notes on James Mill also emphasize the velocity of circulation: ibid., 442–43.
11. Ibid., 4/2: 449; more broadly, Marx's discussion on 447–59.
12. On Marx during the 1850s, Sperber, *Karl Marx*, 291–325.
13. "Commercial Crises and Currency in Britain," *New York Daily Tribune*, 28 August 1858, in *Karl Marx Friedrich Engels: Collected Works*, 50 vols (New York, 1975–2004), 16: 8–9. Series 1 of *Karl Marx Friedrich Engels Gesamtausgabe*, reprinting Marx's writings, has not yet reached this period, so I will use the English-language edition of Marx's works to cite the journalism he originally wrote in (a very Teutonic) English.
14. "The English Bank Act of 1844," *New York Daily Tribune*, 23 August 1858, *Karl Marx Friedrich Engels, Collected Works* 16: 5–6; "The Bank Act of 1844 and the Monetary Crisis in England," *New York Daily Tribune*, 21 November 1857, *Karl Marx Friedrich Engels, Collected Works* 15: 379–84; other relevant articles in *Karl Marx Friedrich Engels, Collected Works* 15: 385–91, 404–9, 16: 33–36. Marx was making these observations as early as 1855: "Finanzielles," *Neue Oder-Zeitung*, 22 May 1855, *Karl Marx Friedrich Engels Gesamtausgabe*, 1/14: 340–42.
15. "The Causes of the Monetary Crisis in Europe, *New York Daily Tribune*, 27 October 1856, *Karl Marx Friedrich Engels, Collected Works* 15: 117–22; "The Monetary Crisis in Europe—From the History of Money Circulation," *New York Daily Tribune*, 1 November 1856, *Karl Marx Friedrich Engels, Collected Works* 15: 123–29.
16. Inge Schliebe and Ludmilla Kalinina, "Rezensionen des Marxchen Werkes: 'Zur Kritik der politischen Ökonomie aus dem Jahre 1859,'" *Beiträge zur Marx-Engels-Forschung* 1 (1977): 103–23.
17. *Karl Marx Friedrich Engels Gesamtausgabe*, 2/2: 140–49, quote on 145.
18. Ibid., 2/1: 173; also, 243–45.
19. Ibid., 2/1: 173; cf. 217–49. Ironically, Marx's emphasis on the combination of the amount of money in circulation and its velocity of circulation sounds a lot like the so-called money equation, $MV = PQ$, or money in circulation (M) times velocity of circulation (V), equals prices (P) times total goods and services (Q), a favorite idea of the twentieth-century libertarian, Chicago School of economics.
20. Ibid., 2/1: 241; more broadly, 233–40, one of the few times Marx criticized David Ricardo, an economist whose views Marx greatly esteemed.
21. Ibid., 2/1: 166. This viewpoint is actually quite similar to one expressed by John Stuart Mill, in his criticism of Say's law, that supply and demand are always in

equilibrium: cf. http://delong.typepad.com/sdj/2010/11/delong-smackdown-watch-walras-law-and-says-law-edition.html, accessed 20 December 2013.
22. Ibid., 2/1: 139, 158–66.
23. Relevant passages are ibid., 2/8: 163–91; 2/15: 144–98. A discussion of these points in Sperber, *Karl Marx*, 429–30, 444–46.
24. *Karl Marx Friedrich Engels Gesamtausgabe*, 2/8: 119–62; 2/15: 461–583.
25. Ibid., 2/1: 156.
26. Ibid., 2/2: 86–89.
27. Ibid., 1/25: 14–15.
28. Ibid., 1/22: 140–43, quote on 143. Marx understood quite well that the actual Paris Commune was not any kind of communist regime, so his account of a communist future, while citing the commune as a model, was an articulation of this own ideas. See Sperber, *Karl Marx*, 381–82.
29. Marx rarely had much to say about German economists. Although he was very much immersed in the German cultural and political worlds throughout his life, his thoughts on economics were distinctly oriented around English and French economists. On this point, cf. Jonathan Sperber, "Karl Marx the German," *German History* 31 (2013): 383–402.

Bibliography

Hess, Moses. "Über das Geldwesen." In *Philosophische und Sozialistische Schriften 1837–1850*, edited by Auguste Cornu and Wolfgang Mönke, 329–48. East Berlin, 1961.

Karl Marx Friedrich Engels: Collected Works. New York, 1975–2004.

Karl Marx Friedrich Engels Gesamtausgabe. Berlin, 1975.

Rosen, Zwi. *Moses Hess und Karl Marx. Ein Beitrag zur Entstehung der Marxschen Theorie.* Hamburg, 1983.

Schliebe, Inge, and Ludmilla Kalinina. "Rezensionen des Marxchen Werkes: 'Zur Kritik der politischen Ökonomie aus dem Jahre 1859.'" *Beiträge zur Marx-Engels-Forschung* 1 (1977): 103–23.

Sperber, Jonathan. *Karl Marx: A Nineteenth Century Life.* New York, 2013.

———. "Karl Marx the German." *German History* 31 (2013): 383–402.

CHAPTER ELEVEN

Modernism, Relativism, and the *Philosophy of Money*

ELIZABETH S. GOODSTEIN

Georg Simmel's *Philosophy of Money* may well be the twentieth century's most significant mostly unread theoretical text. Upon its publication in 1900, its author was already a mainstay of Berlin's modernist intellectual culture, internationally famous in academic circles and beyond.[1] Gustav Schmoller welcomed the work as a brilliant reimagining of the boundaries of scholarship that had "blazed new paths through a previously unexplored primeval forest": "anyone who wants to elucidate the general significance of the money economy in the future will have to build upon it," for Simmel's purpose was nothing less than "to determine what the money economy, especially the modern one of the nineteenth century, has made out of human beings and society, their relations and institutions." Yet Schmoller also wrote to Simmel's publisher, "certainly no more than a hundred people in Germany will read it, even if more buy it."[2]

In fact, the *Philosophy of Money* enjoyed considerable success—notably, according to his wife Marianne, it was one of the first works Max Weber read after his nervous breakdown. A second, slightly expanded, edition would appear at the beginning of 1907. Burned by the Nazis in 1933, it was reissued in 1958 and has remained in print in German, since 1989 in a critical edition; by then, it had been translated into Polish, Italian, French, Spanish; since 1989 it has also appeared in Hungarian, Serbian, Slovenian, Chinese, and Japanese. Although it has been canonized as the first sociology of modernity, the *Philosophy of Money* is better understood as a work of modernist philosophy that reframes the resources of the philosophical tradition through a sophisticated and historically self-reflective relativist theory of value.

Rejecting "abstract philosophical system-construction," with its reifying "distance from individual phenomena, particularly of practical existence," in a gesture that even today has not lost its transgressive power, the *Philosophy of Money* sets out to overcome that (apparent) distance between the everyday and the profound by "cast[ing] a guideline from the surface of economic events into the ultimate values and meanings of everything human."[3] Simmel's modernist reworking of the trope of synecdoche makes possible a pathbreaking style of cultural theorizing that brings sociological, psychological, and historical analysis to bear on philosophical questions.

Simmel does not simply elevate money into the realm of philosophical significance. Through his innovative strategy for attending to and representing the multiplicity of lived experience, he demonstrates that value and meaning cannot be thought in abstraction from (the historical and cultural institution of) money. Because money is "so to speak, indifference itself, insofar as its entire meaning and purpose lies not in itself, but only in its conversion into other values,"[4] the *Philosophy of Money* becomes an exploration of the way meaning is created in human (historical, cultural) life. Simmel unfolds his relativist theory of value through an overtly modernist account of the historical and cultural evolution of knowledge practices in the *"Kulturprozeß,"* the cultural process revealed by the vicissitudes of money.

The *Philosophy of Money* self-consciously addresses the ways reflection on social and cultural phenomena was becoming fragmented and disconnected from philosophical inquiry as the disciplinary organization of the modern academy emerged. Simmel's magnum opus thereby poses questions—concerning the interpretation of phenomenal reality and the creation of value; the impact of technological and sociological developments on human experience; the direction and significance of cultural and historical change—that have lost none of their philosophical and theoretical import since 1900. While it is impossible to do justice to this work in a brief essay, I hope to persuade my readers to turn (or return) to a text whose significance for theorizing money is but one of its many virtues, and to give the *Philosophy of Money* the patient, serious, and thorough reading it deserves.[5]

Relativism as Method

At over 700 pages, the *Philosophy of Money* is remarkable for its breadth of culture; for its author's philosophical discernment; and for a density and complexity of argumentation not amenable to easy summary. A text not simply open to manifold readings but distinctly resistant to the closure of definitive interpretation, the book advances a methodological relativism that exposes the philosophical limits of the longing for such closure. By demonstrating the viability of multiple, conflicting interpretations, as Simmel described it in his book announcement, the *Philosophy of Money* set out to show that vis à vis every grounding of intellectual or moral, religious or artistic existence in the forces and vicissitudes of the material stands the possibility of excavating for the latter a further foundation and grasping the course of history as an interplay between the material and the ideal factors in which none is the first and none the last.[6]

From this point of view, there is no ultimate, nonrelativizable foundation. Simmel declared in the preface that for "cognitive practice" (*die Praxis des Erkennens*) to grasp the complex unity of lived reality, materialist and idealist interpretations must proceed in an unceasing dialectic, via "alternation and absorption" and "in endless mutuality on "into infinity."[7] Writing from a perspective at once Kantian and Nietzschean, Simmel presents distinctions between material and ideal, historical and transhistorical, life and form, as dialectically constituted ways of describing a reality that exceeds our conceptual grasp, yet remains open to being approached and understood in multiple ways, from intersecting, indeterminately bounded disciplinary and philosophical perspectives.

The *Philosophy of Money* thereby redefined the tasks of philosophical reflection for a world where all that was solid had already melted into air—where, Simmel had come to believe, it was no longer possible to secure a reliable philosophical foundation in the face of the "contemporary dissolution of everything substantial, absolute, eternal into the flux of things, into historical mutability, into merely psychological reality."[8] New philosophical strategies were called for, and Simmel set out to show that philosophy could, as it were, learn from money how to think historically and sociologically.

Money can do such heavy theoretical lifting because it is so deeply imbricated with the ways we think, live in society, and reflect upon and communicate with one another about the world. The *Philosophy of Money* traces those connections in order to reveal their philosophical significance. By establishing a self-reflexive perspective on the increasing pervasiveness and power of psychological, historicist, naturalizing, and other antifoundationalist accounts of human life, culture, and experience, Simmel developed a modernist strategy for philosophizing in a world where value is understood as relative to human (social, cultural) existence—a world, that is, without ultimate foundations.

Although it may seem paradoxical, Simmel had come to believe that the only way to avoid nihilism, to prevent the slide into bottomless "subjectivism and skepticism," was to embrace the flux by accepting the apparently universal contingency and historicity of truths and the multiplicity and perspectivalism that beset value. From this point of view, he writes,

> The central concepts of truth, of value, of objectivity, etc. appeared to me as reciprocalities [*Wechselwirksamkeiten*], as contents of a relativism that now no longer signified the skeptical dissipation of all that is solid but precisely protection against this via a new concept of solidity.[9]

This new way of thinking about thinking found direct expression in the *Philosophy of Money*'s strategy for interweaving ideal and material explanations and interpretations of human experience and (individual and collective) existence.

Money, "relativity itself that has become substance,"[10] provided the basis for Simmel's reconceptualization of foundations as such. He turns the sociological (but also historical and anthropological, economic, and psychological) matter that makes up much of the 723 pages of the *Philosophy of Money* into the mode or vehicle for presenting his new, modernist vision of philosophy. Moving from concrete—historically, culturally located—particulars to reflection on their global, spiritual significance by making phenomenological connections between surface and depth, appearance and essence, "between what is apparently the most external and inessential and the most interior substance of life," thereby became a performative demonstration of his relativist strategy for overcoming the dichotomy between materialist and idealist explanation.[11] More than a century later, the *Philosophy of Money* remains a work of enduring theoretical and philosophical interest both within and beyond the social sciences.

Philosophical Modernism

The *Philosophy of Money* is a book of intricate byways as well as grand highways. The conceptual range and interdisciplinary breadth of Simmel's project is daunting, and to call its mode of argumentation challenging to the reader understates the matter considerably. To write a philosophy of money is both to illustrate or exemplify and to address the philosophical and historical significance of the fact that value, like human existence itself, is both a historical and super- or transhistorical phenomenon.

As Simmel shows in Chapter 1, money is intricated with the category of value as such; its ambiguous status as both substance and function, discussed in Chapter 2, helps account both for the increasing complexity of the "techniques [*Technik*] of life" and for the felt loss of meaning in modern societies since, as he shows in Chapter 3, money fosters the hypertrophy of means over ends and of quantitative over qualitative modes of valuation. These chapters, which taken together form a compelling analysis of what would come to be known as the reified world, make up the "analytic part" of the *Philosophy of Money*. The second, "synthetic" part of the book explores the "intertwining of the monetary principle with the developments and valuations of inner life."[12] Its three chapters parallel the arguments of the first three, focusing respectively on money and individual freedom, on the transmutation of personal value into monetary equivalents, and on the overall impact of money on the style of life. If the analytic illuminates the philosophical significance of money as such, the "essence and meaning of its existence" through an exploration of "the conditions and relations of life in general," the synthetic part reverses perspectives, interpreting "the essence and formation [*Gestaltung*] of the latter through the effectiveness of money."[13]

The dialectical tension between Simmel's philosophical ambition for the *Philosophy of Money* and its self-reflexive perspectivism is the hallmark of his distinctive and largely unrecognized contribution to twentieth-century thought: the inauguration of a modernist mode of philosophizing.[14] In one of the most sustained methodological statements in his oeuvre, Simmel's preface offers a brief yet highly illuminating account of what is at stake in these innovative strategies of thought and writing. He sets out his vision of a philosophy of money as at once "prior to and beyond the economic science of money" in its concern with money's "substantial meaning and significance" in and for human life: "its effects upon the inner world, upon individuals' feeling for life, upon the linkage of their fates, upon culture in general."[15]

In asking what the (historical, cultural) phenomenon of money reveals about human existence and about the conditions of reflection on that existence, the *Philosophy of Money* rejects the proprietary logic of the disciplines. Incorporating evidence from history, psychology, anthropology, sociology, law, political economy, Simmel approaches money as the paradigmatic cultural medium—as at once element and emblem of the symbolic exchange that constitutes the foundation of human collective life. While economics addresses itself to "most practically interesting . . . most exactly representable" aspect of "the phenomena of valuation and selling, exchange and means of exchange," in reality, he writes, "there is no such thing" as an act of exchange whose "content would be exhausted by its economic image [*nationalökonomischen Bilde*]."[16] As Simmel underlines, the epistemic and methodological point holds quite generally: "Just as a poem is not only a literary-historical fact but also an aesthetic, a philosophical, a biographical one . . . the standpoint *of one* science [*Wissenschaft*], which is always a specialized [*arbeitsteilige*] one, can never exhaust the totality of a reality."[17]

The philosophical perspective on economic "facts" reveals dimensions of life that economics cannot dream and leads to a hermeneutic model of far-reaching theoretical significance. In Simmel's phenomenological approach, money thereby becomes the

> means, material, or example for representing the relations that exist between the most external, most realistic, most contingent phenomena and the most ideal powers of existence, the most profound currents of individual life and of history. The meaning and purpose of the whole [book] is only this: to cast a guideline from the surface of economic events into the ultimate values and significances of everything human.[18]

Grasped philosophically, money points the way to an overcoming of the instrumental logic it embodies and exemplifies, for such reflection exposes the limits of the narrowed, quantitative understanding of value of which it is, in Simmel's terms, both bearer and symbol.

What money most fundamentally is—to translate the point into more modern terminology, its signifying power—cannot be explained in the reductive and instrumental quantitative terms money itself imposes upon all it touches. As the purest product of the human activity of meaning-making, money is a (lived, instantiated) metaphor for the power of signification, for the specifically human (that is to say, trans-individual, cultural and historical) power of creating a world of value distinct from the world of nature. Money is thus the perfect "means, material, or example for representing the relations" between the material and the ideal, making the link "from the surface of economic events into the ultimate values and significances of everything human." Indeed, because it embodies the greatest possible tension "between what is apparently the most external and inessential and the inner substance of life," if "this particular reveals itself as not only, bearing and being borne, woven into the entirety of the spiritual world, but also as the symbol of its most essential forms of movement," it would amount to a paradigmatic reconciliation of the opposition between phenomenon and essence.[19]

Approaching money as both product and medium of human historical, cultural, social activity thus made it possible for Simmel to pose new sorts of philosophical questions altogether and to pose old questions in new ways. By exploring the meaning, value, and operations of a phenomenon that is mediation incarnate—"so to speak, indifference itself"—the *Philosophy of Money* develops a new perspective for reflection on the social-cultural world and forms of life money both epitomizes and perpetuates.[20]

For Simmel, money is not simply an example; it is the example of examples—or more precisely, the synecdoche of synecdoches. Its operations turn out to reveal the (relativist) mechanisms of valuation, of signification, as such. The *Philosophy of Money* exposes those mechanisms via the analysis of money's concrete operations: by focusing on the actual practices through which it enables (objective) meaning and value to be created and perpetuated in human historical, cultural, psychic, and social—*geistige*—life. For Simmel, "the philosophical significance of money" lies in its making practically visible the "formula of being in general, according to which things find their meaning *in one another* and in the mutuality of relations" that makes them what they are.[21]

The *Philosophy of Money* is not, then, concerned with the sociohistorically conditioned, culturally evolved practices or mechanisms or institutional arrangements of the money economy *per se*. The work has a formal or methodological rather than a substantive mode of cohesion: reflection on money reveals meaning-making as a lived process of negotiating surface and depth, ideal and material, particular and universal. As Simmel emphasized, his undertaking was unified not by a disciplinary effort to prove "a proposition about a singular content of knowledge" but rather by a speculative end: "the possibility (which is to be demonstrated) of finding in every particular of life the totality of its meaning."[22] In my terms, as the synecdoche of synecdoches, money both instantiates and symbolizes the human power of signification. Its historical vicissitudes illuminate human being and knowing in general.

Money is the philosophical object par excellence. By enabling reflection on the constituted, perspectival qualities of knowledge as such, it reveals philosophy itself as relativistic—that is to say, poised between lived reality and the abstract account to which thought aspires in the pursuit of scientific (not empirical or quantitative but self-reflexively assured, reliable) knowledge of reality. As a modernist, Simmel both builds upon and breaks with the dialectical tradition, exposing the philosophical limits of the longing for hermeneutic closure by demonstrating the viability of multiple, conflicting interpretations of the phenomena that make up human (sociocultural, historical, psychological) life.

Integrating attention to the phenomena of everyday social and cultural life with nuanced reflection on their philosophical and historical significance, Simmel renders human self-determination visible through a performative philosophical praxis that represents and enacts, demonstrates and reflects, his relativist strategies of thought. As a modernist text, the *Philosophy of Money* demands readers do more than simply follow a discursive or logical path: readers who self-consciously submit to an experience of reflection that aims to change their self-understanding as thinkers and as human beings. Philosophizing about money involves actively engaging with the central dilemma of post-Nietzschean thought: what constitutes thinking in a world without secure foundations, where subjectivity itself has entered into flux?

The *Philosophy of Money* thereby strategically reframes very old philosophical questions—about life and knowledge, about the relation between value and history, about human freedom—in ways that are, even today, palpably relevant. Embracing an epistemic situation that forecloses appeals in both individual and collective life to absolute, transcendent truth or values, this work makes theoretical contributions whose significance is by no means limited to the social sciences Simmel helped bring into being. By developing new, modernist strategies for approaching epistemological, metaphysical, and ethical questions, it resituates philosophy as a discipline (*Wissenschaft*) in relation to historical and social life as a whole.

Money and the "Cultural Process"

From Simmel's relativist perspective, understanding human cognitive activity requires a phenomenological (which for him also means historical, cultural, and psychological) account of human embodied, cultural, social existence. The *Philosophy of Money* performatively and self-reflexively situates philosophical inquiry in the historical-evolutionary context of what he calls the *Kulturprozeß*, the cultural process: the ongoing interactive and trans-subjective historical form of human life in and through which value and meaning are created and perpetuated (or destroyed). In that process, human beings generate, refine, and propagate what Simmel sometimes called "objective culture": our social, historical, and psychological worlds, the interactively created and sustained environments that orient human life toward the dimension of value. Understanding the phenomena that emerge in and through these symbolically mediated forms of existence—subjectivity, objectivity, value, meaning, art, law, science—requires multidimensional analyses that can encompass a nuanced, nonreductive awareness of the relativity of these lived frameworks to what Simmel elsewhere calls the "forming productivity"[23] of human (cultural, historical, social spiritual) life as such.

Grasped philosophically, the phenomenon of money illuminates that specifically human, generative, history-making power. As Simmel shows, money facilitates the cultural process both by enabling abstraction from concrete particularity and also by embodying and representing the forms of value thereby created. Because it is so deeply intertwined both theoretically and practically with human (cultural) existence as such, reflection on its operations helps reveal how need, desire, and exchange are related and elaborated into the super-subjective, super-natural structures and institutions that make up the human, cultural world. The *Philosophy of Money* thus illuminates how meaning and value arise in and through the (historical) cultural process.

From a philosophical perspective, Simmel writes, the "economic system" is based on an abstraction: on distinguishing "the reciprocal relation of exchange [*Tausch*]" from "the actual process" of its realization, which is in reality "inextricably merged into foundation and result: into desires and enjoyments."[24] As in the other "areas into which we dissect the totality of appearances for the purposes of our interests," on an experiential level, the "form of existence" of exchange melds the subjective and objective. What makes economic values independent and objective is a second-order abstraction: the trans-individual, super-subjective validity (*Gültigkeit*) that value acquires in and through exchange itself.[25] Thus the "economic form of value provides one of the clearest justifications for the equation: objectivity = validity for subjects as such."[26] In Hegelian terms, objective value is the (recognized) desire of the other.

Exchange is, then, a paradigmatic cultural or life-form. According to Simmel, "most relations among human beings can be considered as exchange; it is at once the purest and most heightened reciprocal interaction [*Wechselwirkung*]"; moreover, "every reciprocal interaction may also be regarded as an exchange."[27] In exchange, the living subject that confers "the form of its own unity" on the sensorially given apprehends "the naturally given rhythms of our existence" and organizes its elements into a meaningful connection.[28] From Simmel's phenomenological point of view, "the economy is a special case of the universal form of life of exchange" through which the realm of value—that is, culture—comes into being.[29] Economics points beyond itself, equally to that quasi-transcendental world of meaning and value and to the material a priority of the inter- and trans-subjective life situation of human being and knowing.

If money is only a means or example, it is thus one of particular philosophical significance. As the bearer of the process of abstraction or rationalization, it plays a key role in the historical development of cultural life and thereby both invites and enables reflection on the historical, cultural, and philosophical significance of its own operations. To recall Simmel's remark in the preface, money does not simply exemplify "the indifference of pure economic technique [*Technik*] but is, so to speak, indifference itself insofar as its entire purpose lies not in itself but in its conversion into other values."[30] As the synecdoche of synecdoches or (as Simmel puts it later on) because money is "itself nothing other than the representation of the value of *other* objects" in quantitative terms that enable "virtually unlimited" division and addition, money "provides the technical possibility for exact equation among exchange values."[31]

In its very purity as means, as the *techne* of quantification par excellence, money facilitates the intersubjective representation, translation, and manipulation of qualitative differences. It thereby fosters cultural development and stabilizes difference by mediating among individual desires. Monetary exchange in general thus provides a formal solution to what Simmel calls "the great cultural problem" that ensues once (things of) value have been created in the first place: how to generate new values by turning "objectively given quanta of value into a higher quantum of subjectively felt value via a mere change in bearer."[32] That is, to rephrase his point in more contemporary language, to the problem of how to make values (objects) signify. "Exchange is the essential social way of solving this problem . . . in money, exchange itself has become a body."[33]

If value cannot be located in the (natural) object as such, neither is it purely a function of subjective desire. Only as "the foundation or matter of a—real or imagined—exchange" does an object's desirability (or better, desiredness: *Begehrtheit*) turn it into a value.[34] Indeed, to be precise, "it is always the relation of desires [*Begehrungen*] to one another first realized in exchange that makes its objects into economic values."[35] This distinction between the natural and the social existence of objects is culture's condition of possibility. Within human society, "the value of an object depends on its being desired, but on a desiring that has lost its absolute instinctuality [literally, drive-character, *Triebhaftigkeit*]."³⁶ For human sociocultural existence to achieve higher degrees of complexity and refinement, it is thus necessary both that objects achieve a certain independence and that desiring itself be regulated and socially structured.

Value dwells in intersubjectivity and is a function of the super-individual dimension that is the condition of possibility for subjectivity and objectivity alike. Exchange, the paradigmatic form of human interaction, thereby reveals the metaphysical significance of *Vergesellschaftung*, association or becoming-social as

> the most immediate illustration [*Veranschaulichung*] of relativity in the material of humanity: society is the super-singular formation that is yet not abstract . . . the universal that also has concrete vitality [*Lebendigkeit*]. Hence the unique significance for society of exchange, as the economic-historical realization of the relativity of things: it elevates the individual thing and its significance for the individual person out of its singularity, yet not into the realm of the abstract but rather into the vitality of reciprocal interaction [*Wechselwirkung*] that is at the same time the body [*Körper*] of economic value.³⁷

Exchange is embodied sociality: the expression of the concrete reality of the super-singular yet nonabstract existence of human historical association, the symbolic cultural mode in which value properly speaking dwells. Viewed in another way, exchange is the medium for the mediation of desire—and hence the creation and elaboration of objectivity and subjectivity alike.

Money enriches the lived world. It makes visible the creation of value, enabling human beings to weave complex webs of symbolic interrelations and mediations in which subjective and objective effects are intricately intertwined. As a pure representation of value, it is a spiritual-intellectual *techne* in the widest sense: money's very being is inextricably tied up with the historical-cultural evolution of human life.

There can be no (coherent) economics without philosophical reflection, for it is human social relations that constitute objects as objects. Money's philosophical significance is not outside or different from its sociocultural existence but rather emerges with and through it. The need for a philosophy of money arises from reflection on the conditions of possibility and consequences of money's historical reality and effectiveness; such reflection directly ties questions of money's subjective and cultural significance to its most basic operations.

Philosophizing and Money

As philosophical object, money enables us to achieve reflective awareness of the value-creating dialectic between human beings and world, the process of mediation that socializes and objectifies (the experience of) desire so that it loses its "absolute drive-character." Moreover, as "exchange itself become a body," it is the name for the representation of that universality—a manifestation of the super-singular yet concretely lived actuality of human interdependence. As the signifier of value, money is thus at once substance and function, element and symbol of human sociality. "The significance of money," as Simmel puts it, "is to represent in itself the relativity of the things desired, [that] through which they become economic values."[38]

Money, the synecdoche of synecdoches, takes on its exemplary function in the cultural process through the same doubling that makes it philosophically significant: by enabling the transformation of objects of desire and consumption into things of independent meaning and value, money renders visible how human symbolic practice as such operates. In the very purity of its relativity, as exchange incarnate, money thereby makes it possible to recognize and reflect upon the distinctive "forming productivity" of human "spiritual" (not disembodied but super- or trans-subjective, historical, cultural) existence.

Simmel's argument that money makes visible the qualities of being in general thus takes a self-reflective and performative, modernist form. Native to the boundary zones of interaction where concretion gives way to reflection, capable (to pick up the text of the book's preface once again) of redeeming the "most external and inessential" phenomena by linking them to life's most profound depths, money is revealed as the "symbol of the essential forms of movement" proper to "the spiritual world."[39] Simmel's doubled inquiry into the philosophical and historical significance of money leads, then, to meta-reflection on the historical and cultural process by which meaning as such is produced and perpetuated. In clarifying the origins and growth of objectivity, this inquiry not only illuminates the vicissitudes of subjectivity. As a cultural phenomenon, money also sheds light on the relations between thought and positive knowledge more generally. Since meaning emerges in and through the ongoing process that can retrospectively be characterized as the historical evolution of culture, the philosophical investigation of money generates reflection both on the foundations and limits of knowledge as such and on how foundations and valuations come into being and evolve historically.

At the end of the chapter on "Value and Money," Simmel returns to his account of money as the synecdochic instantiation of the interactive spiritual-historical, sociocultural process by which value emerges and persists—by which things gain objective meaning—from a slightly different perspective. Here money again appears as a body, but one of a peculiarly ghostly sort. "The gap that drove the subjective and the objective out of their original unity with one another has so to speak become embodied in money," which enables human beings to bridge and performatively overcome the resulting distance in exchange.[40] Cultural history shows that despite the vast variety of objects that have served as money,[41] money as such tends to abstractness: tends to lose its meaning as substance and become simply the signifier of its social function. Over time, naturalia "cease to be money or to be able to be money in proportion as money ceases to be a use-value."[42] This dynamic is internal to the cultural process: "Money becomes ever more an expression of economic value because this is itself nothing other than the relativity of the things as exchangeable with one another." Relativity thereby comes to dominate and suppress "all other qualities" so that money itself eventually becomes "nothing other than relativity itself that has become substance."[43] Money evolves socially, historically, culturally from substance to function, object to sign.

Money's philosophical significance lies in this synecdochic being without qualities. Again, it is that site "within the practical world" that renders most visible "the formula of being in general, according to which things find their meaning *in one another* and in the mutuality of relations" that makes them what they are.[44] As the purest and clearest expression of the intersubjective relations through which meaning and value come into being, persist, and circulate, money is the paradigm of reification, but also of sublation: we experience the coin or bill not as metal or paper but as the instantiation of value. Philosophizing about money means not just (cognitively) recognizing the social and cultural foundations of these experiences of value but encountering ourselves as engaged in world-making even as we confront the desubstantialization of meaning. The tendency to abstraction that subtends the cultural process thereby fosters new forms of subjective awareness. Both representing and embodying the fact that meaning is a function of the (social) relativity of beings to and among one another, money is the synecdoche of synecdoches.

As the symbolic form of exchange, that is to say, of interaction as such, money is revealed as both representing and expressing human spiritual-cultural existence in all its complexity as the trans-individual source and ground of value and meaning. We live not in a world of things in themselves but in a dense historically, socially, and culturally constituted, inter- and trans-subjective network of symbols, meanings, and value. Only by grasping the phenomena of cultural life—ultimately, the coherency of the world—as the product of human endeavor can we understand ourselves *qua* human beings. Reflection upon money as the symbol and bearer of very material processes of abstraction is uniquely suited to fostering insight into the relation between human praxis and signification: insight into the genesis but also the limits of meaning and value as functions of human (social, cultural) being.

As culture grows more complex and differentiated, money gains an increasingly universal signifying power—in Simmel's terms, it becomes "the most extreme (since beyond all qualities and intensities) configuration [*Gebilde*] of spirit" itself.⁴⁵ As "the absolute means that thereby ascends to the psychological significance of an absolute end," money is "the strongest and most immediate symbol" of the (apparently) absolute relativity of things: "it is the relativity of economic value in substance, it is the meaning of every particular that it has as a means for acquiring another, but really only this mere *significance* [*Bedeutung*] as means disconnected from its singular concrete bearer."⁴⁶ Money's cultural and sociohistorical importance for human existence lies in this infinitely extensible, because abstract, power of representation: "The significance of money is that it is a unity of value that cloaks itself in the multiplicity of values" and thus enables us to perceive (Simmel uses the verb *empfinden*, to feel or sense in general) "qualitative differences among things" in the form of the "quantitative differences of homogenous currency [*einheitliches Geld*]."⁴⁷

Money thus embodies and exemplifies what Hegel called the "monstrous power of the negative": the capacity of signifying practices to turn everything human beings encounter into conceptual shadows. Comparable, Simmel writes, to language, "which likewise lends itself to the most divergent directions of thought and feeling, supporting, clarifying, working them out," money "belongs to those powers whose singularity [*Eigenart*] consists precisely in their lack of singularity."⁴⁸ Money is as ambiguous as thought itself; it embodies the dialectical capacity of intensifying opposites.⁴⁹ Its historical and cultural as well as philosophical importance are tied up with this seemingly unlimited power to divide and unite, to render unlike things indifferently equivalent, to convert quality into quantity, but also to dematerialize life's most material aspects.

While not the source of value per se, money is a means of expressing, intensifying, transforming, multiplying, converting, and generally increasing the forms of value generated in, by, and through human interaction. Its historical, cultural, sociological, and psychological effects are intertwined with very fundamental features of human existence. Thus, as the "techniques of life," money enables and enhances grow ever more complex, so too does the hegemony of the quantitative form of valuation of which it is (in a favorite phrase of Simmel's) "both bearer and symbol." As the cultural means by which particularity of all sorts is represented and thereby interrelated—in practical terms, the *techne* for socializing difference by making all objects of desire exchangeable—money comes to permeate human existence as a whole, "as the means of means, as the most universal technique of external life [*die allgemeinste Technik des äußeren Lebens*], without which the individual techniques [*Techniken*] of our culture would never have come into being."⁵⁰

Simmel's relativist effort to think the historicity of the philosophical problems being lived in and through the cultural changes exemplified and borne by the historical ascendance of the money economy remains provocative. He insists that the subjective effects of modern forms of life, the sociopolitical and cultural problems that arise as a consequence of industrialization and urbanization—and, we might add, globalization and the aftermath of colonialism—cannot be understood in purely materialist terms. Conversely, the peculiarly modern intensity of the subjective crisis already manifested (as Simmel often noted) in the rebellion against the ideal of reason and the turn to the category of life (both intensified by the ascent of naturalistic and evolutionary paradigms beginning in his lifetime) cannot be explained without reference to very material transformations. By juxtaposing and linking these seemingly opposed dimensions, the *Philosophy of Money* plumbs the depths of an experience of crisis Nietzsche had called the death of God as a cultural and historical process with very tangible phenomenal manifestations.

Elizabeth S. Goodstein is Professor of English and the Liberal Arts at Emory University; she is also affiliated with the departments of comparative literature, history, and philosophy. She is the author of *Experience without Qualities: Boredom and Modernity* and *Georg Simmel and the Disciplinary Imaginary*, both Stanford University Press.

Notes

1. Despite holding his lectures before overflow crowds in the largest halls of the university, Simmel (1858–1918) had until that very year remained a Privatdozent in the Berlin Philosophische Fakultät, where he had taken his doctorate and habilitated, and where he would remain as an unremunerated Professor Extraordinarius until finally receiving a professorship in Straßburg in early 1914, just a few years before his death.
2. Gustav Schmoller, "Simmels Philosophie des Geldes," in *Georg Simmels Philosophie des Geldes: Aufsätze und Materialien*, ed. Otthein Rammstedt, with Christian Papilloud, Natàlia Cantó Milà, and Cécile Roi (Frankfurt, 2003), 297, 282. Schmoller's letter to Carl Giebel of 8 May 1901 is cited in Otthein Rammstedt, ed., *Georg Simmel Gesamtausgabe* (Frankfurt, 1989–2015), vol. 22, 380–81. All translations are my own.
3. All citations from Simmel follow the critical edition, David P. Frisby and Klaus Christian Köhnke, eds, *Georg Simmel Gesamtausgabe Band 6: Philosophie des Geldes* (Frankfurt, 1989), 12–13.
4. Ibid., 12.
5. This essay draws on my book, *Georg Simmel and the Disciplinary Imaginary* (Stanford, CA, 2017).
6. Frisby and Köhnke, *Georg Simmel Gesamtausgabe Band 6*, 719.
7. Ibid., 13.
8. Georg Simmel, "Fragment einer Einleitung," in *Georg Simmel Gesamtausgabe Band 20: Postume Vëroffentlichungen. Ungedrucktes. Schulpädagogik*, ed. Torge Karlsruhen and Otthein Rammstedt (Frankfurt, 2004), 304–5; here, 304. The provenance and

dating of Simmel's autobiographical text, first published by Kurt Gassen and Michael Landmann, *Buch des Dankes an Georg Simmel* (Berlin, 1958), is uncertain; see Klaus-Christian Köhnke, *Der junge Simmel in Theoriebeziehungen und sozialen Bewegungen* (Frankfurt, 1996), 31 and passim.
9. Karlsruhen and Rammstedt, *Georg Simmel Gesamtausgabe Band 20*, 304–5.
10. Frisby and Köhnke, *Georg Simmel Gesamtausgabe Band 6*, 134.
11. Ibid., 12.
12. Ibid., 10.
13. Ibid., 10–11.
14. Simmel's image as a thinker has evolved considerably in recent years as the full range of his writing has become available. He was a modernist in both the sociopolitical and cultural senses whose diverse theoretical contributions must be seen in conjunction with the engagement with modernist art and culture that runs through writings. In characterizing him as a modernist philosopher, I am proposing a way of integrating what are still too often treated as distinct "kinds" of work in a way that expands our theoretical as well as historiographical perspective on Simmel himself and thereby helps foster a more encompassing understanding both of modernist literary and aesthetic innovation and of the sociopolitical and cultural context in which the modern social science disciplines emerged. On Simmel's engagement with various forms of modernist cultural activities, including those associated with the new social movements of his day, see especially Lichtblau; Köhnke, *Der junge Simmel in Theoriebeziehungen*; and Ralph Matthew Leck, *Georg Simmel and Avant-Garde Sociology: The Birth of Modernity, 1880–1920* (Amherst, MA, 2000), who documents Simmel's impact as a teacher and writer on a modernist avant-garde that included politically radical figures such as Kurt Hiller and first-wave feminists such as Marianne Weber and Helene Stöcker. Simmel's active participation in modernist cultural production is also exemplified in the literary texts that appeared in the Art Nouveau journal *die Jugend* (see Karlsruhen and Rammstedt, *Georg Simmel Gesamtausgabe Band 20*; and Thomas M. Kemple, trans., "Selections from Simmel's Writings for the Journal *Jugend*," *Theory, Culture and Society* 29 [2012]: 263–78).
15. Frisby and Köhnke, *Georg Simmel Gesamtausgabe Band 6*, 10.
16. Ibid., 11.
17. Ibid., 11.
18. Ibid., 12.
19. Ibid., 12.
20. Ibid., 12.
21. Ibid., 136.
22. Ibid., 12.
23. As he described "human spiritual freedom" in the 1907 edition of the *Problems of the Philosophy of History*; Georg Simmel, *Georg Simmel Gesamtausgabe Band 9: Kant Die Probleme der Geschichtsphilosophie, 1905/1907* (Frankfurt, 1997), 231.
24. Frisby and Köhnke, *Georg Simmel Gesamtausgabe Band 6*, 58.
25. Ibid., 58–59.
26. Ibid., 59.
27. Ibid., 59.
28. Ibid., 60.
29. Ibid., 67.
30. Ibid., 12.

31. Ibid., 388.
32. Ibid., 388–89.
33. Ibid., 389.
34. Ibid., 77.
35. Ibid., 83.
36. Ibid., 43. Here Simmel's philosophical analysis converges with a Freudian perspective in an interesting way. I pursued the implications of this convergence in relation to the problem of fetishism in Elizabeth Goodstein, "'Eine specifisch moderne Begehrlichkeit': Fetischismus und Georg Simmels Phänomenologie der Moderne," *Die Philosophin* 13 (May 1996): 10–30.
37. Ibid., 91.
38. Ibid., 138.
39. Ibid., 12.
40. Ibid., 136.
41. Indeed, for Simmel, all commodities may be regarded as being "in a certain sense money" (ibid., 133).
42. Ibid., 134.
43. Ibid., 134.
44. Ibid., 136.
45. Ibid., 299.
46. Ibid., 307.
47. Ibid., 589–90.
48. Ibid., 654.
49. As he puts it later, "the objectivity of money" does not stand outside the dialectical process as "something beyond the antitheses . . . this objectivity signifies from the outset the service of both sides of the opposition" (ibid., 694).
50. Ibid., 676.

Bibliography

Dahme, Heinz-Jürgen, and Otthein Rammstedt. *Georg Simmel und die Moderne: Neue Interpretationen und Materialien*. Frankfurt, 1984.

Frisby, David P., and Klaus Christian Köhnke, eds. *Georg Simmel Gesamtausgabe Band 6: Philosophie des Geldes*. Frankfurt, 1989.

Gassen, Kurt, and Michael Landmann. *Buch des Dankes an Georg Simmel*. Berlin, 1958.

Goodstein, Elizabeth. "'Eine specifisch moderne Begehrlichkeit': Fetischismus und Georg Simmels Phänomenologie der Moderne." *Die Philosophin* 13 (May 1996): 10–30.

———. *Georg Simmel and the Disciplinary Imaginary*. Stanford, CA, 2017.

———. "Georg Simmels Phänomenologie der Kultur und der Paradigmenwechsel in den Geisteswissenschaften." In *Aspekte der Geldkultur. Neue Studien zu Georg Simmels Philosophie des Geldes*, edited by Willfried Geßner and Rüdiger Kramme, 29–62. Berlin, 2002.

———. "Style as Substance: Georg Simmel's Phenomenology of Culture." *Cultural Critique* 52 (2002): 209–34.

Karlsruhen, Torge, and Otthein Rammstedt, eds. *Georg Simmel Gesamtausgabe Band 20: Postume Veröffentlichungen. Ungedrucktes. Schulpädagogik*. Frankfurt, 2004.
Kemple, Thomas M., trans. "Selections from Simmel's Writings for the Journal Jugend." *Theory, Culture and Society* 29 (2012): 263–78.
Klaus, Christian Köhnke. *Der Junge Simmel in Theoriebeziehungen und Sozialen Bewegungen*. Frankfurt, 1996.
Leck, Ralph Matthew. *Georg Simmel and Avant-Garde Sociology: The Birth of Modernity, 1880–1920*. Amherst, MA, 2000.
Lichtblau, Klaus. *Kulturkrise und Soziologie um die Jahrhundertwende. Zur Genealogie der Kultursoziologie in Deutschland*. Frankfurt, 1996.
Rammstedt, Otthein, ed. *Georg Simmel Gesamtausgabe*. Frankfurt, 1989–2015.
Schmoller, Gustav. "Simmels Philosophie des Geldes." In *Georg Simmels Philosophie des Geldes: Aufsätze und Materialien*, edited by Otthein Rammstedt, with Christian Papilloud, Natàlia Cantó Milà, and Cécile Roi, 282–99. Frankfurt, 2003.
Simmel, Georg. "Fragment einer Einleitung." In *Georg Simmel Gesamtausgabe Band 20: Postume Veröffentlichungen. Ungedrucktes. Schulpädagogik*, edited by Torge Karlsruhen and Otthein Rammstedt, 304–5. Frankfurt, 2004.
———. *Georg Simmel Gesamtausgabe Band 6: Philosophie des Geldes*, edited by David P. Frisby and Klaus Christian Köhnke. Frankfurt, 1989.
———. *Georg Simmel Gesamtausgabe Band 9: Kant. Die Probleme der Geschichtsphilosophie (1905/1907)*. Frankfurt, 1997.
———. *Georg Simmel Gesamtausgabe Band 22: Briefe, 1880–1911*, edited by Klaus Christian Köhnke. Frankfurt, 2008.
———. "*Philosophy of Money* von Prof. Dr. G. Simmel (Berlin)." In *Gesamtausgabe Band 6: Philosophie des Geldes*, edited by David P. Frisby and Klaus Christian Köhnke, 719–23. Frankfurt, 1989.

CHAPTER TWELVE

A Narrative in *Notgeld*
Collecting, Emergency Money, and National Identity in Weimar Germany

ERIKA L. BRIESACHER

The phrase "emergency money" conjures up a variety of possible scenarios, from a secret "stash" or "rainy day fund" an individual or institution may squirrel away to circumstances that require hiding funds in a mattress amid economic turmoil to governmental ventures introduced to fund specific programs. German emergency money, or *Notgeld*, embodied all of these scenarios, and it was introduced as a temporary measure during World War I to combat growing wartime costs on the homefront. By the early 1920s, it represented the persistence of economic catastrophe, wartime defeat, and cultural dislocation, and its value was more rooted in its collectability. As artifact and material culture, currency is the type of cultural expression that is often taken for granted, and the "very commonness [of objects such as currency] is one reason why they are so slippery and tend to drop out of traditional philosophical discourse."[1] As early as 1921, collector groups and practices took over the exchange of *Notgeld*. Collectors essentially subordinated *Notgeld*'s monetary value to its cultural value, and the ways in which they organized and displayed their collections demonstrated narratives of national, social, and cultural identity.

Notgeld production and use after the abdication of the kaiser demonstrated intense fragmentation; the system itself was unregulated and multilayered.[2] While there *was* a central institution in the *Reichsbank*, it had little power to prevent regions, municipalities, and private businesses from printing and utilizing their own currencies. Emergent during World War I as an emergency measure to keep German society functional, there was also an impulse toward an overarching nationalist narrative, one that was, on the one hand, distinct from the imperial past but also, on the other hand, built on traditional foundations that echoed across the country. *Notgeld*, especially *Serienscheine* (series notes), displayed cultural iconography and imagery. They were at times regionally specific. In other cases, they spoke to the region's place within a broader German context. This variety represented an attempt to "reconcile conflicting views on the shape of national community," including political, economic, and cultural identity.[3] Everyday Germans participated in this reconciliation not only through expanded political activity but also through more passive means: collecting objects carrying nationalist and cultural messages. Currency in general, and *Serienscheine* in particular, demonstrates the cultural aspect of economic structures, especially in the realm of consumption, art, and meaning, even becoming an object of consumption itself.[4] This is especially clear when considering the role collecting and display plays in identity formation.

Constructing a nationalist narrative in the wake of World War I in ways that were aligned with expressions of personal identity involved concomitant phenomena in Germany. One was a constantly evolving and recast national identity and nationalism manifested in a variety of media including currency. There was also the effect that the extreme devaluation of the economy, particularly represented by the printing and dissemination of *Notgeld*, had on the collective memory of Germans. Last, the rise of contemporary collector groups and exhibitions showcased *Serienscheine* in particular, tying identity and the meaning of objects together in a concrete way.

Culture, Nationalism, and the Construction of Meaning

The very existence of a national economy represents a way in which to exchange goods, ideas, and messages, all with a (relatively) fixed value assigned to them. The idea that an object has a fixed price is subject to cultural variation. Just as an object may be "worth" more in one country than another, so to an object is often valued more by one socioeconomic class or cultural group than another. This has been conceptualized as "taste," articulated by Pierre Bourdieu in his work *Distinction*, demonstrating the active construction of "cultural capital"—an accumulation of power or influence through education, social standing, and cultural adeptness, whether these attributes are accompanied by material wealth or not. This was especially important in the context of inflation and/or depression, when currency exchange rates fluctuated and the purchasing power individual Germans had was inconsistent at best and nonexistent at worst.

The immediate postwar years in Germany were lean ones, and memories of the "Turnip Winter" from 1916–17 persisted, especially since conditions did not improve much once the war was over. Many Germans found their savings completely wiped out, swept away in war loans that were never paid back by a defunct monarchy and a nation in defeat.[5] The solution to the money shortage was not increased use of credit; instead, businesses, regions, and even the national government began printing more and more money, driving down the value of currency and inflating prices while income remained stagnant. Rather than face mounting unemployment, government officials chose inflation, which quickly spiraled out of control. In response, French and Belgian troops occupied the Ruhr valley in 1923, prompting general strikes and work stoppages, which exacerbated the monetary crisis.

In Weimar Germany, particularly during the inflationary years, capital accumulation, banking, and savings accounts were turned upside down by extreme currency devaluation. As the bottom dropped out of the German Mark, traditional methods of determining social class and the cultural elite became decentered, especially because purchasing power no longer functioned as it had in the past. Success depended on those who wielded cultural capital as well as (or despite a lack of) material accumulation. Bourdieu commented that taste itself operated as a social and cultural act designed to affirm identity, often based on the cultural norms already inculcated into an individual.[6] Collecting *Notgeld* (and the choices individual collectors made) demonstrated a commentary on German identity, turning a failing currency into a culturally valuable—yet culturally and socially malleable—material. A variety of choices and meanings were situated within this broad collectability according to social status, local and regional identity, and cultural capital.[7] The *act* of collecting *Notgeld*, a largely worthless economic implement, injected cultural value into the notes themselves.

Collecting helped forge a shared experience and solidify national ties between citizens, which was embodied by individual collections housed in albums, boxes, and, later, museums.[8] At the same time, the accumulation of cultural capital was a way to engage the discourse about Germanness and identity in a time when few citizens were able to control economic or political structures in everyday life, even affecting the way Germans viewed economics or the iconography on the notes. The concert of Europe was a set of distinct, though interconnected, national identities. Bourdieu's notion of displayed cultural identity and capital can be adapted to the European continent after World War I, demonstrating how Germans expressed their unique role and identity within the larger scope of Europe as a performance of cultural identity.[9]

The link between systems of cultural capital and the formation of German national identity becomes convincing due to the forms of mass printing, including currency, that "provided the technical means for 're-presenting' the *kind* of imagined community that is the nation."[10] Implicit in the use of print is the notion that a national context is somehow bound together so that the message can get through; language is one example, but a sense of a common history and shared experience also provide a foundation upon which to build the framework of the nation-state. World War I, although it problematized the German past, also provided shared circumstances of defeat and rebuilding, and the inflationary period of the Weimar Republic is yet another example of experience that contributed to the national narrative.

Notgeld, and more specifically *Serienscheine*, was printed currency that contained cultural messages for a large and varied collector market. Currency especially reinforces national ideals through the use of imagery, iconography, and even national mottos or phrases (e.g. *E pluribus unum*). In this way, the collection of *Serienscheine* demonstrates the formation of a specific national story, despite the fragmentation of the system. Collectors were encouraged by clubs to focus on several towns or regions in one part of the country, amassing a storyline about how those cities or regions fit into the national context or affected German history (see Figure 12.1).

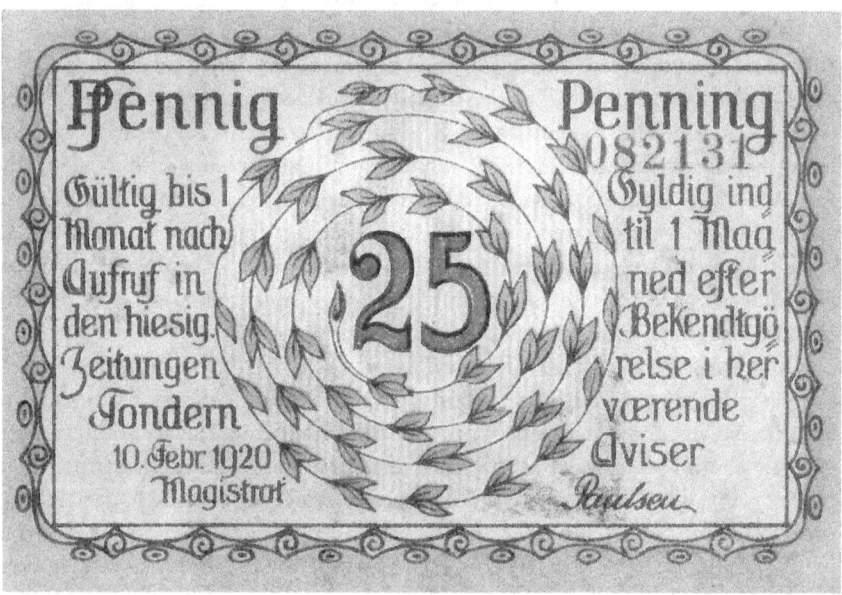

Figure 12.1. 25 Pfennig note, 10 February 1920. This note detailing the Schleswig Plebescite emphasized the border state of Schleswig-Holstein and its unique German-Danish populations. Courtesy of The Permanent Collection, the University Museum, Southern Illinois University Edwardsville.

The similarities that existed between images, regardless of geographic or historical distance, emphasized the shared heritage of the nation in subtle ways. Often, images or subject matter focused on the role of religion, literature, music, and even traditional political fragmentation from place to place, making Germany a nation of culturally similar but independently minded people. The collection of specific pieces, then, demonstrated individual choice to emphasize particular aspects of national and social identity. At the same time, this was evidence of participation in the formation of a self-imposed identity within the German context as a whole.

The importance of *Notgeld* as a cultural construct goes beyond mere iconography. The very existence of the system connoted important things. First, it demonstrated the belief that a centralized bank in the Weimar Republic could not adequately control spiraling inflation. It was therefore up to individual regions and cities to continue the day-to-day activities of the nation, especially in the realm of economics. Additionally, economic confidence was tied up, in some cases, in cultural norms such as national identity and social mores. Last, evidence of system devaluation was located in the fact that an entire portion of the *Notgeld* system—*Serienscheine*—was related less to circulation and more to an increasingly thriving collector market.

The act of collecting provided a forum in which artists, firms, and even cities could express cultural goals or fears. In addition, collection, especially overseas, represented economic prospects; collector groups circulated magazines dedicated to issues brought to the forefront by collecting, bringing in subscription fees, entrance fees for exhibitions, and purchase of collectable notes, and businesses entered the market to provide albums and display options for *Notgeld* and related ephemera. While the capital injected into the system did not rectify Germany's economic woes, everyday Germans, even those living abroad, could create individual archives of how the inflationary period affected them and their nation.[11]

The Collection of *Notgeld*

Widespread collecting of German *Notgeld* emerged after the end of World War I, although the concept of emergency money was not a new one. The German national economy fractured as early as 1917 due to the necessity of funding the war effort; issuing emergency money, beginning with private issues meant to alleviate the strain of war mobilization on the home front, was one strategy employed by the *Kaiserreich* to address the serious economic issues generated by the war. By 1919, the appearance of collector magazines such as *Das Notgeld* and price guides listing the values of individual notes indicated that there was a market for the currency itself, both within German borders and internationally.[12] Within this community, *Notgeld* dealers, appraisers, and collectors wielded authority and, more importantly, reputation.

Guides and pamphlets such as *Wie sammelt man Notgeld? (How Does One Collect Notgeld?)* appeared for purchase, often published by leading figures in the numismatic movement who specialized in collection. The audience for such pamphlets, though, was certainly not expert, and the prose was often informal. For example, *Wie sammelt man Notgeld?* presented a fictionalized debate between the author "Karl" and his "Onkel Rechnungsrat" at the kitchen table. The "uncle," described as a family friend of young Karl's parents, attempts to convince his young nephew of the value and complex nature of collecting *Notgeld*:

> "Yes, completely, uncle," Karl argued, "but you digress from my point which was that the collecting of so-called emergency money was still stupid!" "Be nicer to your old uncle. Consider my opinion," said Uncle, "and now on to my reply. I would like your remark, which is not too polite, to be in a little different form. Calmly ask rather: Why does one collect emergency money?" "Oh dear Uncle, yes, you have cut to the core, this would actively interest me," noted Karl. "Such a simple question, such a complicated answer" Uncle continued counsel in his fatherly tone.[13]

Collectors attempted to legitimize *Notgeld* as a collectable artifact, despite the nature of the currency. The nature of collecting *anything* as a hobby was analyzed by these pamphlets, if only to demonstrate that *Notgeld* was as worthy a collectable as stamps, knickknacks, or other objects. In the pamphlet *Einiges über Notgeld* (*Some Things about Notgeld*), Victor Engelmann argued that "It is something peculiar to start to collect as a hobby. What has not been already collected! One does not need to speak of the stamps and coined money of earlier decades, because this sport has proven authority of collectors. No reasonable person will argue that coins and stamps do not have enormous value."[14]

Arnold Keller, already recognized as a leading authority on numismatics and *Notgeld*, wrote extensively for *Das Notgeld*, arguing that it was the worldwide crisis of World War I that ushered in the necessity for paper-based emergency money and brought together a larger *Notgeld*-collecting community.[15] It was because of this widening group of collectors, he claimed, that a magazine specifically geared toward a *collecting* sensibility was necessary, protecting the market from false issues and fraudulent notes.[16] Keller also produced a series of price guides, widely regarded as authoritative in an era when such publications became commonplace. The introductions to his guides, released in several volumes, included a history of *Notgeld*, the periods associated with issues, and *Serienscheine*. Interestingly, Dr. Keller evaluated *Serienscheine* as inferior and not true *Notgeld* at all, siding with the view that notes produced almost exclusively for collectors were a misappropriation of resources, further weakening the economy. At the same time, the appearance of *Serienscheine* highlighted the appeal of the community beyond traditional collectors of coins and issues of centralized banks.

Notgeld collection was viewed as different from traditional coin or money collecting. In the first place, it was a currency that did not have a fixed value relative to other currencies; traditionalists who viewed *Notgeld* as inferior to "real" money viewed collecting it as a worthless pastime. In *Wie sammelt man Notgeld?*, Onkel Rechnungsrat derisively comments that the general public only collects money that has appreciative value; the only way for *Notgeld* to have or retain any value was to keep it properly, especially since "the war made emergency money necessary; afterward it was not quite so necessary."[17] One can see here the connection to Bourdieu's notion of taste and display; the value in collecting *Notgeld* could not simply be calculated monetarily.

Proponents of collecting for cultural reasons attempted to combat the notion that collections were largely to accumulate wealth, attempting to interest *all* sectors of society in collecting as a pastime and for its own sake, rather than courting only socioeconomic elites. An inherent barrier to this, of course, was that collecting required money to purchase albums, price guides, and notes, and the weak economy meant that the number of people with disposable income enough to collect was limited. It is not clear, however, to what degree *knowledge* of *Notgeld* and its imagery was constrained.

Authors attempted to reinforce the notion that *Notgeld* was indeed money, especially during the later years of World War I and immediately following:

> Emergency money was the true money of municipalities and cities, but it was also about beauty and ugliness. Despite a number of biased bureaucrats, the people came to it, making the point for beauty and development of local patriotism. Reflected in the emergency money were the war and its consequences as well as the peculiarities and idiosyncrasies of the homeland [*Heimat*].[18]

This passage illustrates several points. In the first place, it acknowledges layered notions of identity from local patriotism to a broader concept of *Heimat*. Second, this shows that collectors actively promoted their pursuits as cultural activity, related in a lot of ways to the already established community of stamp collectors. In an article for the newsletter *Der Notgeldmarkt* (*The Notgeld Market*) from Hanover, Ehrfried Siewers addressed the question of why there was a collector market for *Notgeld* by referencing stamp collecting:

> A strange question. With the same rights and reasons that one collects stamps, postal stationery, bookplates, exhibition marks, artist postcards. In stamp collecting, for example, one talks so much of general enrichment of geographical and historical knowledge, behind which lies nothing tangible.[19]

Indeed, collector magazines and exhibitions spoke of *Notgeld* and stamp collecting as particularly related, listing resources for both. This reveals the function of both *Notgeld* and stamps: retaining a concrete or utilitarian purpose while simultaneously presenting highly symbolic images that contributed to a cultural narrative. It gave an air of authenticity and authority to the collection of something as volatile and uncertain as *Notgeld*.

Collecting representations of narrative meant that people who could not invest monetarily in a consumer society could invest in a shared national heritage. *Notgeld* was a temporary measure that did not appreciate in economic value over time. *Serienscheine* had more debatable value and was rarely circulated in the same way typical currency operated. "Serious" collectors exemplified by people like Dr. Keller paid little attention to it for that reason. It was, however, valuable as a purely cultural artifact. Siewers addressed this notion as well in his editorial, arguing that *Notgeld* collection was essentially a way to ensure the "memory of a stormy period of our country and our hope for better living circumstances for our children and grandchildren," by handing collections down from generation to generation.[20]

The link between stamp and *Serienscheine* collection was clear, especially in terms of artistic trends and the demonstrated cultural narrative to be understood. One example of such documentation is a stamp-collecting page that noted the spiraling inflation entitled "*Dokumente einer irrsinnigen Zeit!* [Documents of an insane time!]" produced in the early 1920s.[21] Several versions of the mounting sheet exist, printed and distributed by the stamp dealer (*Briefmarkenverstand*) Friedrich Peter of Würzburg. In addition, he also provided a mounting sheet for a series of stamps to commemorate territories or colonies lost to Germany after World War I with the caption, "Never forget! Commemorative stamps to mourn the 19 areas stolen from Germany!"[22] This particular object was much more like *Serienscheine* in that the stamps for this collection were clearly never meant for circulation; they featured the names of colonies or territories overlaid with a black border, some with a German commercial flag at half-mast. Given prominence was the stamp for Alsace, which was surrounded by exhortations to "never forget."[23] These mass-produced collecting sheets provided a standardized framework within which to collect, rather than the intensely personalized practice of individual collecting.

In this way, one can see how collecting could take on political or propagandistic overtones, appealing to a sense of both nationalism and shared bitterness. *Notgeld* was also a recognized way to promote or disseminate a specific message. In the magazine *Der Notgeld-Schein-Werfer*, Franz Grewe discussed how *Notgeld* operated as a first line of propaganda, especially for festivals and organizations. He referenced, in particular, two festivals: *Kultur- und Sport Woche* (Culture and Sport Week) in Hamburg in 1921 (see Figure 12.2) and *Deutsche Amerika-Woche* (German America Week) to be held in Bremen in 1923. Grewe especially noted that, with "perhaps hundreds of thousands of collectors, proof that *Notgeld* collectors of all strata and all age groups operate with seriousness and joy," the advance release of a festival's *Notgeld* presented specific ideas to be promoted by the festival.[24] The phrase "*Seefahrt ist not!* [Seafaring is necessary!]," which appeared on the reverse of the notes for *Kultur- und Sport Woche*, also included the black, white, and red flag of commercial

Figure 12.2. One Mark note, 12–24 August 1921, *Kultur- und Sportwoche*, Hamburg. This series promoting Hamburg's festival included references to "black-white-red" and body culture in the Weimar Republic. Courtesy of The Permanent Collection, the University Museum, Southern Illinois University Edwardsville.

and right-wing nationalist groups and phrases such as "Be united! United! United! (*Seid einig! Einig! Einig!*)."[25] These notes simultaneously advertised the festival itself and its message, often propagandizing a specific point of view.[26]

Advocates of *Notgeld* collecting continually claimed wide audiences and appealed to a drive to establish a national narrative, particularly in the wake of World War I. Even though *Notgeld* itself was not centrally regulated, authors cited "*deutsche Notgeld*," rather than referencing municipalities as they produced "cultural history meditations" on the subject.[27] Catalogues and magazines included articles and lists grouped by nation, with regions and cities as subcategories. In part, the *Notgeld* system itself determined the way it was advertised. Yet, while organizing guides in this way seems a foregone conclusion, it was yet another subtle way to assure that notes were considered *German*, differentiated from those of other nation-states.[28]

Magazines and price guides also included advertisements of dealers, who listed what notes they had for sale or trade. The focus was on completing a collection, however the collector framed it, and dealers were often collectors themselves. At times, articles appeared, such as "*Wie lege ich meine*

Kriegsnotgeldsammlung an? [How do I create my collection of war *Notgeld?*]," demonstrating a framework within which a reader could begin his or her collection. Pages of classified ads hawked rare issues, notes depicting specific cities, or issues of large and small denominations (*Großgeld* or *Kleingeld*), often dwarfing the number of pages dedicated to articles or analysis of the collecting market.[29]

Often, pamphlets about collecting emphasized correct storage and display. For example, advertisements differentiated albums for beginning, amateur, and serious collectors whose *Notgeld* utilized a variety of media (such as coins, porcelain, or silk in addition to paper).[30] This indicated, in addition, that there was a preferred method to display and care for the objects. According to one author, museums and people with large collections would be best served to keep two of the same note side by side, in order to show both sides, in an album, organized by geographic region, and further contained in a cardboard box.[31] This extended to even the mind-set the collector needed to have: "One must collect with a brisk desire to understand the language which these little slips of paper cannot dress in words; one must collect with a sense of order and economy, and therefore, recognize this hobby as an ideal end in itself to develop for himself [sic]."[32]

Notes or *Notgeld* albums were advertised by firms such as the International *Notgeld* and Stamp Mail-Order House in Lübeck as "the nicest Christmas present [*Das Schönste Weihnachts-Geschenk*]," while also claiming that they were "The finest work of German art and culture, the best investment, historically very valuable. The most beautiful adornment for every reception room. First rate geographic and historical teaching resource for German youth."[33] Advertisements such as this show how fully culture and economic issues were intertwined. It is important to point out that *Serienscheine* (as well as other *Notgeld* issues) were clearly meant to be displayed as well as collected, assuming that the general audience would understand the cultural import of the objects. Indeed, as Manfred Mehl pointed out, notes most often ended up "in the albums of the collector" rather than in circulation, again reinforcing the display function of *Notgeld*.[34]

Individuals were not the only targets of the collecting sensibility. Magistrates and city archives recognized the cultural and historical value of collecting *Notgeld*, though those collections were generally local in scope and with an eye on preserving a specific city's experience during inflation. A notable example is the city archives of Kiel, which solicited uncirculated examples of *Notgeld* produced by the city's firms and private banks to be stored for posterity.[35] The preservation of such local history was important for future considerations of the larger German context. Even during the Nazi period, preservation methods were incorporated to present a more complete picture regarding the German experience during hyperinflation.[36] An emphasis on this era could be used to mobilize both public opinion and the political interpretation of history; in this way, the meaning of material objects, as in an exhibit or show, was manipulated to support a particular view of society as well as affect the way an event or era—in this case hyperinflation—was remembered.

Notgeld Exhibitions

Another important facet of the *Notgeld* collecting community was the prevalence of conventions or trade shows [*Messe*]. At these shows, often organized by a local collecting group or group of dealers, collectors brought their collections for sale or trade. One such convention, held 26–28 February 1922 organized by the Hamburg chapter of the *Internationalen Notgeldshändler Verbandes EV* (International *Notgeld* Traders' Association), was advertised as the "first German *Notgeld* trade show [*1. Deutsche Notgeld-Messe*]."[37] These shows made it possible for collectors and traders to discuss issues of collecting as well as supplement their collections at the booths of retailers or other private collectors.

Exhibitions occurred throughout Germany, with dealers and collectors traveling and advertising nationwide. Advertisements for dealers' booths, such as Hans Tripp & Company of Nuremberg, took up entire inserts in collector magazines, hoping to draw crowds to these conventions, which aided the local economy, especially industries associated with tourism: the food, drink, and lodging concerns. The selection of collections available for trade widened if large numbers of collectors attended, reinforcing the collecting market. These conventions allowed municipalities to put themselves on display, essentially selling themselves as convention centers, places for tourism, and cultural destinations. Kiel, in its promotion of its annual *Nordische Messe*, argued that exhibitions of this sort, whether dominated by trade shows or not, could create relationships that were "economically beneficial without the risk of inefficient fragmentation."[38]

Exhibitions could provide an organizing theme that motivated potentially competing factions to work together. In the case of the *Nordische Messe* in Kiel, it fostered collaboration between the Chamber of Commerce, commercial and trade unions, and the newly formed *Nordische Messe in Kiel GmbH*. Often, the display or collection at the center of the exhibition was sponsored by a specific organization, such as a 1921 exhibition at the Silesian Museum for Decorative Arts and Antiquities in Breslau (*Schlesischen Museum für Kunstgewerbe und Altertümer in Breslau*), featuring a pamphlet printed by the Silesian League for Homeland Security (*Schlesische Bund für Heimatschutz*).[39]

In addition to cultivating these relationships, exhibitions were put on to reinforce the notion that *Notgeld* was worth collecting. One such exhibition in Hanover invited well-known contemporary numismatists in an effort to challenge the opinion that collecting *Notgeld* was unjustified. Rather, the community argued, collecting notes required commitment and a sense of history. Indeed, *Das Notgeld* reported that the exhibition "persuaded [a great number] ... to create a collection; new life will enter the *Notgeld* movement."[40] Similarly, the exhibition in Nuremberg contained a collection that traced Austro-Hungarian paper money throughout its history, demonstrating a crafted set of objects that told the story of a defunct empire.[41] Potential collectors were wooed by evidence of what collectors did, which in turn increased the readership of collector magazines.

The collection and display of *Notgeld* provided a unique opportunity for Germans in the early years of the Weimar Republic. On the one hand, collectors, regardless of their socioeconomic status in Germany itself, virtually could create a narrative about what Germany meant to them. This was not only a performance of nationalism but also a demonstration of the cultural role they played in Germany as citizens. Germans, who understood the culture of worthless currency, formulated material statements on what it meant to be German and, at times, actively displayed their membership in the national community through their collections. On the other hand, though, Germans who had access to more material resources and wealth clearly had a greater opportunity to shape the narrative arc. Notes that were viewed as more popular or in-demand could be replicated by future issues. This influenced how German culture was perceived both inside and outside Germany, effectively denoting a broad conception of taste.

In addition to the participation of Germans in formulating identity, the collector communities crafted ways in which cultural and social discourse interacted with the economic system—exhibitions. Exhibitions were multifaceted in that each collector framed his or her own story. This narrative could be sponsored by a cultural institution, such as a museum focused on preserving local history or a more general collector group concentrating on the promotion and expansion of collecting as an intellectual activity that affected cultural capital. The notion that everyday people had their identities invested in their collections of *Notgeld* or *Serienscheine* points to a facet of identity creation: the public performance or display of it.

Erika L. Briesacher is Assistant Professor in the Department of History and Political Science at Worcester State University. She holds a doctorate from Kent State University and is completing a manuscript on the intersections of economy, identity, and cultural festivals in the Weimar Republic and postwar West Germany.

Notes

1. Susan M. Pearce, *Museums, Objects, and Collections: A Cultural Study* (Washington, DC, 1992), 21. Pearce's work deals with objects in general, but the overarching concept is that physical objects are often given short shrift as concrete expressions of contexts, especially relating to particular time and space.
2. *Notgeld* was used as a system by 1917 in a variety of ways. Some notes were produced by the authority of the *Reichsbank*, while others were produced by municipalities and firms to combat scarcity during the war and immediately following it. Though it was meant to be a temporary measure, the persistence of economic hardship beyond 1919 meant that the system continued to perpetuate itself despite attempts to end the exchange of *Notgeld* locally.
3. Konrad H. Jarausch and Michael Geyer, *Shattered Past: Reconstruction German Histories* (Princeton, NJ, 2003), 232–33.
4. James Carrier, "Reconciling Commodities and Personal Relations in Industrial Society," *Theory and Society* 19, no. 5 (1990): 579–98. See also James Carrier and Josiah McHeyman, "Consumption and Political Economy," *The Journal of the Royal Anthropological Institute* 3, no. 2 (1997): 355–73.
5. For a broader discussion of the persistence of defeat and the inadequacy of the social system to deal with it (especially regarding the populations directly affected by the war, such as veterans), see Robert Weldon Whelan, *Bitter Wounds: German Victims of the Great War, 1914–1939* (Ithaca, NY, 1984).
6. Pierre Bourdieu, *Distinction: A Social Critique of the Judgement of Taste*, trans. Richard Nice (Cambridge, MA, 1984), 6–7.
7. This was juxtaposed against a moment when consumption patterns were disrupted, leading to official rhetoric combatting "hoarding," and collectors often combatted that label which carried nationalist and economic implications. Susan Pearce tackles the line between hoarding, accumulating, and collecting in "The Urge to Collect," in *Interpreting Objects and Collections*, ed. Susan M. Pearce (London, 2012), 159.
8. Historians and scholars of material culture have pointed to the act of collecting as an expression of the desire to possess, generally from a Freudian standpoint. For this reason, I focus on the *act* of collecting generally, rather than individual collections. Further research is needed to focus particularly on individual collections themselves, as data regarding personal collections is incomplete.
9. Though I am correlating cultural and national identity in the context of Europe after World War I, it must be noted that within the consolidating German identity were dynamic social relations. Clearly, upper-class Germans demonstrated their national and cultural identity differently than working-class or naturalized Germans. However, I am beginning from the standpoint that there were practices Germans of every social class could understand, even if they could not fully participate.
10. Benedict Anderson, *Imagined Communities: Reflections on the Origin and Spread of Nationalism*, rev. ed. (London, 1991), 25.
11. Personal collections are often considered in the context of individual motivation, which render challenges to the researcher. Insightful studies analyze collecting from psychological, literary, or antiquity contexts, such as the impact of heirlooms and inheritance as a connection between generations, especially in an aging population in Sheldon S. Tobin, "Cherished Possessions: The Meaning of Things," *Generations* 20,

no. 3 (1996): 46. One example of a literary perspective is Yomota Inuhiko, "In Praise of the Collecting Act," *The Literary Review* 39, no. 2 (1996): 162.

12. Manfred Mehl, in his authoritative price guide *Deutsche Notgeld von 1918–1922*, claimed that as many as twenty different *Notgeld*-collecting magazines existed during the 1920s, perhaps more; see Manfred Mehl, *Deutsche Serienscheine von 1918–1922* (Regenstauf, 1998), 11.
13. Karl Skowronnek, *Wie sammelt man Notgeld?* (Munich, n.d.), 3–4 [Qf 128, Archiv der Kulturgeschichte (hereafter AdK), Altonaer Museum für Kultur und Kulturgeschichte (hereafter AMfKK)].
14. Victor Engelmann, *Einiges über Notgeld*, (Kiel, 1921), 1. [Qf 127, AdK, AMfKK]
15. Arnold Keller, "Vorwort," *Das Notgeld: Zeitschrift für Notgeldkunde Offertenblatt* 3, no. 1 (1922): 3 [Qf 138, 1–3, AdK, AMfKK]. Keller's influence has persisted even in more recent price and collecting guides, such as Courtney L. Coffing, *A Guide and Checklist of World Notgeld 1914–1947 and Other Local Issue Emergency Monies* (Iola, WI, 1988) and Kai Lindman, *Das deutsche Notgeld: Katalog der Serienscheine, Spendenquittungen und Bausteine 1918–1922* (Sassenburg, 1989). Lindman produced many price guides, based on geography and chronology.
16. Keller, "Vorwort," 4.
17. Skowronnek, *Wie sammelt man Notgeld?*, 3, 5.
18. Victor Engelmann, "Merkbuch für Notgeldsammler," *Einiges über Notgeld*, 10.
19. Ehrfried Siewers, "Warum sammelt man Notgeld?," *Der Notgeldmarkt Hannover* 2, no. 22 (1922): 260 [Qf 136, AdK, AMfKK].
20. Siewers, "Warum sammelt man Notgeld," 260.
21. The Friedrich Brauer Papers (MS 060), Box 4, Folder 4, Manuscript Collection, Special Collections Department, University of North Carolina at Wilmington. This object is evidence of the desire to pass on previous generations' experiences to younger generations, almost like an inheritance of experience that aided in modern German identity.
22. MS 060, Box 4, Folder 4.
23. Some versions of the mounting sheet utilize a quote from a poem by Goethe often called "Feiger Gedanken"; "In spite of all power,/never bend,/show strength,/calling up the arms of the gods." Translation mine from the original German: "Allen Gewalten/ zum Trotz sich erhalten,/ Nimmer sich beugen,/ Kräftig sich zeigen,/ rufet die Arme/der Götter herbei!" Interestingly, this quote has been linked with the White Rose resistance group.
24. Franz Grewe, "Notgeld und Propaganda," *Der Notgeld-Schein-Werfer: Organ für Alle Notgeld Angelegenheiten* 1, no. 3 (1922): 1.
25. Hamburg, 1 Mk, "Kultur- und Sport Woche," 12–24 August 1921. The Permanent Collection, the University Museum, Southern Illinois University Edwardsville. "Seefahrt ist not!" references a novel of the same name from 1913 by Gorch Fock, who wrote with great pride about the lives of deep-sea fishermen of Hamburg and resort islands. Fock's diaries were later published by JF Lehmann, which published many National Socialist and pseudoscientific works.
26. "Notgeldscheine der Kultur- und Sportwoche Hamburg," *Lübeckische Anzeiger* no. 349 (29 Juli 1921) [Hansestadtarchiv Lübeck, Handelskammer zu Lübeck 275: Nordische Woche in Lübeck (Allgemeines)]

27. One major example is Gustav Prange, *Das Kriegs-Notgeld: Eine kulturgeschichtliche Betrachtung*, advertised in price and collector guides such as Engelmann's *Einiges über Notgeld*.
28. One example was the *Notgeld*-like system in post-World War I Austria or other nations' currencies.
29. *Der Notgeldmarkt Hannover*, 2, no. 22 (1922): 262. [Qf 136, AdK, AMfKK]
30. Victor Engelmann, *Einiges über Notgeld*, [Qf 127, AdK, AMfKK]
31. J. C. Martin, "Wie lege ich meine Kriegsnotgeldsammlung an?," *Das Notgeld: Zeitschrift für Notgeldkunde* 3 (1922): 28 [Qf 138 1–3, AdK, AMfKK]
32. Skowronnek, *Wie sammelt man Notgeld?*, 16 [Qf 128, AdK, AMfKK].
33. Ibid., 266.
34. Mehl, *Deutsche Serienscheine*, 11
35. Letter from Dr. Gundlach, 11 March 1924 (Tgb. Nr. 2080) [Stadtarchiv Kiel (hereafter SAK), Kieler Notgeld 1917–54].
36. Letter from G. Steinmann, 29 March 1943 [SAK, Kieler Notgeld 1917–54]; this letter references the 1937 founding of a commission for "preservation of contemporary records" by Dr. Goebbels, including a record of city emergency money collections from 1914 through 1924.
37. *Der Notgeld-Schein-Werfer*, 11. This type of convention is much like organizations such as the Coca-Cola Collectors Club, which hosts national conventions for collectors to buy, sell, and trade with other collectors.
38. Dr. H. Meyer, "Nordische Messe in Kiel. Ein Geleitwort," in *Nordische Messe in Kiel Messkatalog 1921* (Kiel, 1921), 13 [SAK, Nordische Messe 6898/2].
39. Hanns Reinbach, "Die Notgeldausstellung im Schlesieschen Museum für Kunstgewerbe und Altertümer in Breslau," in *Das Notgeld* (Sondernummer zur Messe in Hannover und Ausstellung in Bad Nauheim), n.p.
40. "Die Notgeldausstellung in Hannover," *Das Notgeld*, 55.
41. Arnold Keller, "Das Notgeldausstellung in Nürnberg," *Das Notgeld*, 81.

Bibliography

Anderson, Benedict. *Imagined Communities: Reflections on the Origin and Spread of Nationalism*, rev. ed. London, 1991.

Archiv der Kulturgeschichte, Altonaer Museum für Kultur und Kulturgeschichte. Qf 127, 128, 136, and 138.

Arnim, Otto. *Von Rathenau zu Barmat: Der Leidensweg des deutschen Volkes*. Stuttgart, 1925.

Bourdieu, Pierre. *Distinction: A Social Critique of the Judgement of Taste*. Translated by Richard Nice. Cambridge, MA, 1984.

Carrier, James. "Reconciling Commodities and Personal Relations in Industrial Society." *Theory and Society* 19, no. 5 (1990): 579–98.

Carrier, James, and Josiah McHeyman. "Consumption and Political Economy." *Journal of the Royal Anthropological Institute* 3, no. 2 (1997): 355–73.

Chancellor, Edward. *Devil Take the Hindmost: A History of Financial Speculation*. New York, 1999.

Coffing, Courtney L. *A Guide and Checklist of World Notgeld 1914–1947 and Other Local Issue Emergency Monies*. Iola, WI, 1988.
Inuhiko, Yomota. "In Praise of the Collecting Act." *The Literary Review* 39, no. 2 (1996): 162–79.
Jarausch, Konrad H., and Michael Geyer. *Shattered Past: Reconstruction German Histories*. Princeton, NJ, 2003.
Lindman, Kai. *Das deutsche Notgeld: Katalog der Serienscheine, Spendenquittungen und Bausteine 1918–1922*. Sassenburg, 1989.
Mehl, Manfred. *Deutsche Serienscheine von 1918–1922*. Regenstauf, 1998.
Meyer, H., ed. *Nordische Messe in Kiel Messkatalog 1921*. Kiel, 1921.
Pearce, Susan M. *Museums, Objects, and Collections: A Cultural Study*. Washington, DC, 1992.
———. "The Urge to Collect." In *Interpreting Objects and Collections*, edited by Susan M. Pearce, 157–59. London, 2012.
The Permanent Collection, Southern Illinois University Edwardsville Museum.
Roth, Alfrons. *Die Aufwertung*. Berlin, 1925.
Skowronnek, Karl. *Wie sammelt man Notgeld?* Munich, n.d.
Tobin, Sheldon S. "Cherished Possessions: The Meaning of Things." *Generations* 20, no. 3 (1996): 46–48.
Whelan, Robert Weldon. *Bitter Wounds: German Victims of the Great War, 1914–1939*. Ithaca, NY, 1984.

CHAPTER THIRTEEN

Predatory Speculators, Honest Creditors
Money as Root of Evil or Proof of Virtue in Weimar Germany

MICHAEL L. HUGHES

Since antiquity, people have been concerned with the moral implications of money. The *Bible* declares that "the love of money is a root of all kinds of evil." Medieval Christian theologians argued, based on the doctrine "do unto others as you would have them do unto you," that prices should be based on fairness, and that it was immoral to demand a higher price just because the buyer was in desperate need: it was immoral to profit from monetary manipulation. The eighteenth-century English crowd defended a "moral economy" rooted in the idea that in setting prices, the marketers of grain and bread were entitled to a "fair allowance" but no more. In the current Euro crisis, creditors and policy makers often stigmatize debtors who cannot or will not repay their debts as morally inferior, and those who warn against the "moral hazard" of letting "irresponsible" debtors off the hook have dominated the discussion. Vociferous, politically charged debates about the relationship of money and morality have been perennial.[1]

Germans in the 1920s also clashed over the moral implications of money, with creditors (those who had saved by securing monetary assets, e.g. by loaning money on mortgage, buying private or government bonds, having a savings account) pitted against debtors and "speculators." Most Germans suffered, some horribly, amid the economic chaos of the early 1920s, as hyperinflation disrupted economic activity and destroyed utterly the value of the monetary assets creditors had accumulated. Other Germans, though, took advantage of the volatile monetary conditions to accumulate substantial wealth. A subsequent vehement debate about whether creditors were entitled to a revaluation of the debts, their repayment in gold marks or gold mark equivalents, generated a flood of pamphlets, petitions, letters, articles, and debates (available in archives and libraries across Germany) that illuminate attitudes toward money. Suffering creditors vociferously denounced those winners as speculators or profiteers whose wealth consisted of ill-gotten gains from "dishonest" manipulation amid monetary chaos. Their money was a consequence of evil. Meanwhile, those same creditors characterized themselves as particularly honorable individuals whose monetary assets constituted well-earned rewards for virtuous, productive, and indeed patriotic, efforts. When commentators noted that in a free-market economy any investment is a speculation, creditors did not respond directly—but they did repudiate free markets and capitalists. They demanded a socioeconomic system in which accumulated money resulted only from virtuous activity by inherently virtuous people and not from rapacious speculations in unregulated markets. Ultimately, they asserted a kind of property right, based on their virtue, to their social status. And money—depending on its source—was a key marker of moral status.[2]

The inflationary policies that German governments pursued from 1914 to 1923 were not immoral ploys to privilege some Germans at the expense of others, although they sometimes had that effect. While not indifferent to moral concerns, German governments had other priorities that they viewed as being more important than preserving the value of creditors' assets.

During World War I, the German government's highest priority was total victory. Even when Germany's military position was strong, the government refused to negotiate with its enemies because it thought an overwhelming victory was necessary for securing its expansionist war aims and preserving the authoritarian domestic regime. That meant privileging production of war materiel at the expense of consumer goods while accepting the consequences of a British blockade that deprived Germany of vital imports, especially food. The forces of supply and demand then led to substantial inflationary pressures. The need to maintain popular support for the war effort induced the government to introduce price and rent controls as well as rationing, so that the government effectively acknowledged the moral claims of Germans desperate for access to food. Nonetheless, the sheer insufficiency of calories and nutrients in the blockaded wartime economy meant that the government could not actually provide enough foodstuffs for all civilians to survive, and perhaps 700,000 died from malnutrition.[3]

After the war, the priorities of the governments of the new Weimar Republic included managing the massive war debt the collapsed empire had left behind, reviving the economy, dealing with the demands of the best-organized groups (e.g. business owners), and building legitimacy for a new constitutional order that many Germans rejected. As early as 1919, some experts recognized that the state could manage the war debt through inflation, which would lower the real burden of repaying the debt at the expense of creditors. The proposal, which the government rejected, revealed early on the possible advantages of manipulating the value of money and the potential conflict between fairness to creditors and economic recovery. Moreover, an awareness that the government could not afford to repay its debt in real terms influenced monetary and fiscal policy thereafter. German industrialists did not embrace inflation although many of them saw its utility: the depreciating paper mark (PM) enabled German business to regain lost markets and to repay old and any new debts in increasingly worthless paper. Moreover, many Germans were convinced that reparations imposed by the Allies were impossible to fulfill, so that stabilization of the currency could only come with a less onerous reparations settlement. And because Germans did not accept reparations as legitimate, attempts at stabilization were also complicated by the fact that virtually no German was open to tax increases or budget cuts because they could seem merely inordinate pain to pay unjust reparations.[4]

Germans were increasingly aware of the disastrous consequences of the inflation for those who held monetary assets denominated in PM. Already in 1921, before hyperinflation, legal scholars had begun debating sharply the legitimacy of the statutorily established principle mark = mark, i.e. a PM repaid in 1921 or later was equivalent for all legal purposes to a gold mark borrowed in 1913. Legally, that principle was unimpeachable under Germany's prevailing doctrine of legal positivism—that law was whatever the statutes said. However, some legal scholars pointed to the obvious. The PM, effectively, was not fulfilling two of its three tasks as money. As a measure and as a store of value, a 1921 PM was not equal to, indeed was worth dramatically less than, a 1913 gold mark. Forcing a creditor to accept increasingly worthless paper was hence clearly grossly inequitable and unjust. Efforts to address this problem were challenged by those who pointed out that Germany simply could not afford to pay off its war debt and simply could not reverse years of economic developments by fiat. Meanwhile, as public debate over protecting creditors' assets grew, many debtors, from fear of their own economic vulnerability or from cold calculation, decided to pay their debts with devalued PM while they could. Creditors could now see (often wealthy) debtors deliberately and "unscrupulously" acting to evade their moral obligation to repay their debts at full value. Germans were increasingly aware of the moral implications of inflationary policies and of money, but attempts to deal with those implications remained stymied by the perception that doing so would prove economically catastrophic.[5]

By some measures, the German hyperinflation of the 1920s was only the fourth worst in world history. Nonetheless, with an overall inflation rate of 100 trillion percent between 1914 and 1923, it was severe enough to destroy the value of all paper assets. Around 100,000 marks in mortgages or savings deposits or bonds could in 1913 generate enough interest to support a modest but secure middle-class existence. In 1924, with a loaf of bread costing 200 billion marks, those same 100,000 marks in assets literally could not buy a crumb of bread. While the 1914 exchange rate had been 4.2 marks to 1 dollar, the government finally stabilized the currency, in late 1923, at PM 4.2 trillion to 1 U.S. dollar. It issued a new currency at a rate of PM 1 trillion for 1 new Rentenmark.[6]

This inflation meant that millions of Germans effectively lost their life savings. As prices rose and eventually soared, the interest from monetary assets remained the same in nominal terms but shrank in real terms. Eventually, it would become inadequate to provide even subsistence. Many creditors then sold off their assets, more or less gradually, to cover living expenses. Others still held their monetary assets (a savings account, a bond, a mortgage), but it was worth only one trillionth of what it originally had been. Millions of Germans who had worked hard and saved diligently, often all their lives, saw the value of their assets obliterated. These creditors came from almost all social classes, but those for whom revaluation of debts was a vital issue were those who had saved enough to be able to support themselves in case of disability or old age, primarily urban lower-middle-class and middle-class citizens (especially civil servants, white-collar workers, professionals, and rentiers) who had depended on or who had expected to depend on their savings but who now faced a plunge into poverty. Their desperation and anger sparked a years-long battle to secure a revaluation of debts, their repayment at least partially in gold mark equivalents instead of worthless PM.[7]

While most Germans suffered, often piteously, from inflation and hyperinflation, some did manage to profit from the prevailing confusion and the available opportunities. Doing so was widely seen as profiteering (*Wucher*) or speculation, which in this context Germans defined as attempting to profit from shifts in prices, with attendant risk, rather than attempting to preserve capital for future use or to finance a productive investment. Although not all who invested during the inflation and hyperinflation were seeking to profit from price shifts, inflation certainly provided many opportunities to do so. Such practices were not without risk. Some speculators, Hugo Stinnes and the Barmat brothers, for example, lost everything after the mark's stabilization. Others, though, flourished during the inflation and continued to do well after stabilization. The underlying assumptions among many Germans were that if these people were getting richer, someone else must have gotten poorer, and that if so many honest Germans faced economic misery, then only dishonesty could enable anyone to make money amid the chaos of inflation. Hence, many Germans viewed any success in profiting monetarily during the confusions of inflation as inherently suspicious if not patently immoral. As one embittered creditor wrote, one was left with "the feeling that, by misusing momentary constitutional power and fleeting financial misery, one takes from the one [individual] in order to give to another [individual who is] often the morally, intellectually, and spiritually lower standing," and that those who ignored Germany's needs during the war "are able to take advantage of the favorable occasion only because they know to use their economic ruthlessness at just the right moment."[8]

Feeling ran extremely high against speculators and inflation profiteers. For example, Käthe Kollwitz produced for the Reich's food control authorities three leaflets against *Wucher* (profiteering), showing impoverished, emaciated, sickened mothers and children who had suffered because of soaring food prices, putatively driven up by unscrupulous speculators. The Association against Profiteering and Price Gouging called for a determined struggle against speculation, price gouging, capital flight, tax evasion, and luxurious living. Creditor leader Georg Best, in attacking inflation profiteers, thundered, "The criminal who steals, robs, or defrauds from necessity, stands morally far higher than the one who enriches himself unscrupulously through the ruin of honorable savers." One Bavarian creditor group, in a resolution passed during a mass meeting, denounced the "gluttonous speculation-hyenas and parasitic speculator-louts."[9]

Some Germans, though, defended the speculators and speculation, arguing that both were inherent to market economies and were or at least could be beneficial, so that both were implicitly moral. Roland Schacht, in 1922, published a piece in the voice of a speculator. The protagonist pointed out that his "illegal" sales (in contravention of wartime price controls and rationing and postwar regulations) had always had a ready purchaser. He insisted that he actually prevented starvation by making foodstuffs available to people who desperately needed them, even if at high prices. Schacht's speculator also insisted that he worked hard for his money. He was asserting for himself a morally admirable role, both by putatively helping people secure food and by working hard. Offering a pragmatic argument, the Board of the Berlin Stock Exchange rejected proposals to limit "speculatively" purchased government bonds to a worse revaluation than bonds held by original purchasers, insisting that "an economically useful speculation is indispensable for the placing of larger amounts of bonds."[10]

More disturbing for the creditors was the reality that in a market economy, every investment is a speculation, in the sense that no investment can ever be completely secure. In choosing any investment vehicle, one is taking a risk. Shares of stock, whose prices fluctuate daily, are obviously risky, but to varying degrees every sort of investment is. Farmers and landlords can default on their mortgages; corporations can default on their bonds; even sovereign states have been known to default on their obligations. Most importantly, as Alfons Roth put it in 1925, any investor in monetary assets is running a "natural risk" that money will decline in value, a risk that is "inherent to the nature of a [market] economy." Industrialist Oskar Funcke bluntly asserted, "These people [PM creditors] speculated on the preservation of the body politic as a guarantee of the mark.... Their state succumbed in the revolution. It may sound harsh and severe, but it remains true that they suffered a not entirely undeserved fate when the loss arose."[11]

The German government had compounded confusion because already in the nineteenth century it had approved some investments as *mündelsicher*, as safe enough to serve as investments for a trustee acting for a minor. The government also required certain other trustees and some classes of investors, for example, life insurance companies, to invest only in *mündelsicher* assets. Implicitly, the government asserted that these investments (for example, mortgages, mortgage bonds, government bonds) were not "speculative" but were instead more or less risk-free. Creditors touted the *Mündelsicherheit* of their assets as though that guaranteed that those investments would not lose *any* value. Nonetheless, *mündelsicher* assets proved no more secure against the risks of inflation than non-*mündelsicher* ones, even as creditors argued vehemently that their *mündelsicher* assets deserved better treatment than more "speculative" assets.[12]

Creditors fighting for a revaluation of their inflation-devastated assets faced almost universal opposition from debtors. Such debtors included many farmers, small businessmen, and building owners who had borrowed on mortgage, and creditors were angry at the behavior of fellow members of the lower-middle and middle classes. Nonetheless, they focused on big business, big agriculture, and the government—the debtors most vociferously opposed to revaluation and with the most influence on policy outcomes. Almost without exception, these individuals, firms, and governments had already paid or intended to pay their debts with legal tender—worthless PM. And given the parlous economic situation of Germany and many businesses in the 1920s, these debtors had no trouble asserting, and perhaps even convincing themselves, that they could not repay debts at 1913 values and that forcing them to do so would seriously undermine the already weakened German economy.[13]

Creditors came to associate "big capital" with speculation and inflation profiteering. A creditor periodical, *Der Sparerschutz*, denounced "großkapitalistischen Eigennutz und parasitenhaften Schieberunwesen [big-capitalist self-servingness and parasitic speculator-trickery/-reprehensible deeds]." A retired cheese wholesaler, whose assets had been devastated by inflation, repeated the widespread rumor that the inflation had been deliberately implemented in order to shift wealth to "big capitalists, speculators, and profiteers." The logic here was compelling for many 1920s Germans: the inflation was a time of confounding confusion; so any profits made then could only be inherently speculative; but speculative profits were inherently dishonest; so those big capitalists who had profited must be dishonest too; and if such folk were dishonest enough to have profiteered, then they were dishonest enough to have planned the whole thing.[14]

Denunciations of speculators by creditors increasingly became denunciations *tout court* of big capitalists, international capital, and free markets. These traditionally conservative middle-strata citizens certainly wanted *their* old capital back. However, they had long feared and resisted the creative destruction of free markets, and the role of big capitalists in profiting from inflation and opposing revaluation powerfully reconfirmed the deep suspicions that creditors had of the existing free-market system and its supporters. The Hamburg local of the Hypothekengläubiger und Sparer Schutzverband (HGSSV), the main creditor interest group, wrote to Center party leader Wilhelm Marx, "Among the people the view is widely held that our current government is just a willing tool of big capital, of big industry." Creditor activist Reinhard Wüst asserted that the mainstream political parties had proved that they "no longer stand strictly on the basis of *Recht* [law, justice] and in fact only or predominantly represent the interests of certain capitalist economic circles that stand behind them and that are incompatible with the principles of a true people's community." One HGSSV local wrote, "These inflation profiteers believe that they can introduce a new economic method, one that is both communist and big capitalist." The main creditor newspaper, *The Revaluation*, printed in bold type the slogan, "The power of big capital can only be broken through the power of the masses!" That a group seeking to protect (the value of) its private property could appeal for support with a slogan echoing socialist and communist rhetoric reveals how desperate its members were and how disillusioned with capitalism—with free-market economics—they had become.[15]

Attacks on speculators and capitalism could be closely associated with anti-Semitism, but, surprisingly, few creditors arguing for revaluation expressed such attitudes explicitly. *Völkisch* and anti-Semitic writers would characterize speculators as Jewish or as permeated by a Jewish spirit of Mammonism and avarice. In one political cartoon, for example, they could present an anti-Semitic caricature of a Jewish businessman crushing a presumably productive "Aryan" worker with stock exchanges, speculation, and—notably—the "money economy." When the (Jewish) businessman Julius Barmat was arrested for fraud and bribery in relation to loans secured from the Prussian Staatsbank, anti-Semites had a field day presenting him as typical of "*Ostjuden* [Jews who had immigrated into Germany from Eastern Europe and were hence double outsiders]," who were supposedly prone to dishonest speculations and greed. Creditors, in lobbying for a revaluation, tended not to engage in open anti-Semitism, probably because they recognized that their main enemies were governments and big business and agriculture, which were overwhelmingly controlled by Christians. Nonetheless, their rhetoric did often echo anti-Semitic prejudices (e.g. the reference to a "communist/big capitalist economic method" and references to the Barmat affair), so that they were certainly trading in anti-Semitic rhetoric for political purposes.[16]

On one level, the creditors were simply protecting their economic interests. If debtors got their way and blocked a revaluation, creditors would be left with effectively worthless pieces of paper, whether PM, bonds, mortgages, savings passbooks, or some other vestige of the prewar economy. They had every reason to attack the influence of the economic interests that had enriched themselves at creditor expense and that were fighting vigorously to keep their arguably ill-gotten and not hard-earned gains. Yet creditors were operating on the basis of more than mere economic self-interest. Their *Weltanschauung* also involved moral values. And they, not surprisingly, emphasized the latter.[17]

Creditors were not modest about depicting themselves in virtuous terms. They regularly characterized themselves as superior to most Germans. *Der Sparerschutz* described creditors as "the most virtuous, order-loving stratum of citizens." Other creditor groups characterized themselves as "the most indispensable bearers and supports of the German state," as coming from "not the worst but the best group in society," or simply as "the best Germans." People want to think well of themselves, and they want to present themselves as deserving when seeking support for their policy positions. Yet the assertions of superiority here are unusually categorical and frequent.[18]

More specifically, creditors saw themselves as embodying certain virtues that they believed were necessary to society's survival and development and that entitled them to their property and status. These virtues were both social and personal. Creditors emphasized that they were the patriotic, honorable, and loyal Germans. They were the lovers of order within the society. They were the thrifty, the trustworthy, and the hard-working Germans. Their monetary assets, they proclaimed, resulted from the virtuous, socially beneficial effort they put forth, unlike speculators, whose filthy lucre derived from no productive contribution. Within a widely shared nationalism, they posited a vision of the world in which the nation could only flourish, indeed could only survive, because a critical mass of the population engaged voluntarily, out of virtue, in the productive efforts and state-supporting behavior necessary for the effective operation of economy, society, and polity—rather than pursuing rank self-interest through monetary manipulation.[19]

Creditors vehemently rejected proposals to meet their demands for revaluation with social payments based on need. They had worked and saved to support themselves independently in the event of disability or old age. They distinguished themselves from the proletariat they disdained by their claim to independence. Hence, as one creditor put it, "We also consider ourselves citizens with equal rights, just as much as the owners of real property; we too want to be able to pay taxes again and not to be fed from the soup kitchen." As a political pamphlet put it, the creditors did not want to "remain in the, for them, unbearable and shameful role of welfare recipients." The creditors' status pretensions were certainly at stake here, but so too was their vision of a society built on independent, virtuous citizens and an economy where money was a reward for that virtue.[20]

Because creditors based their claim to revaluation on the putatively virtuous nature of their acquisition of assets, they generally opposed any revaluation of assets held by morally suspect speculators. They defined the latter in this context as those who had sought monetary gain by purchasing depreciated war or prewar era assets at some date after the inflation took off in the early 1920s. The HGSSV made plain its determination to punish "speculators" who had acquired revaluable assets after 1 April 1924 by proposing to allow them only one quarter of the revaluation creditors normally would get (albeit, with an exemption for heirs and those required to acquire *mündelsicher* assets). The *Deutsche Handelswacht*, a periodical for white-collar workers (most of whom would have been small creditors), applauded the unfavorable treatment in revaluation legislation of "speculatively" acquired government bonds because the speculators had bought the bonds not to support the German Reich but merely in hopes of "wangling special profits." Money could be good or evil depending on the means and motive of acquisition.[21]

The creditors' disdain for, indeed often hatred of, speculators put them in an apparently hypocritical position. Creditors based their demand for revaluation of their monetary assets on law and property rights. Yet their policy proposals toward speculators involved depriving the latter of their legally established property rights in the monetary assets they had purchased. That this expropriation would deny only "speculatively" secured profits and be to the benefit of the creditors or the German state did not make it, in formal terms, any less an uncompensated expropriation.

Creditors, though, held to a concept of substantive rights. They demanded the reestablishment of *Recht*—not their statutory formal property rights in their (now worthless paper) assets but their morally substantive right to the values, the real purchasing power and the moral honor, that a PM asset had embodied. Sometimes creditors could simply insist that the establishment of *Recht* was the precondition for economic recovery or at least for the reestablishment of the desire to save and hence of new investment credit for the economy. More importantly, creditors often argued that because forcing them to accept PM in repayment was a gross injustice, Germany could reestablish its character as a *Rechtsstaat* and indeed any popular support for itself only by revaluing debts according to the principles of equity and of good faith in contractual relationships. Notably, a number of politicians and civil servants expressed similar concerns about loss of faith in the state and the law if the state chose to ban revaluation, particularly as the new Weimar democracy was struggling to establish itself.[22]

As they grappled with the effects of inflation on their monetary wealth and social position, creditors often demanded an alternative economic system to the Weimar Republic's free-market economy. As Dr E. Bendix proclaimed in November 1923, all the recent attempts to deal with hyperinflation through the courts "are incompatible with the individualist-capitalist principles of our civil code because they stem from a wholly different social—or if one does not like this word—*comradely* [*genossenschaftlichen*] *spirit of a community of fate of all members* of the hard-pressed German *Volk*." Creditors wanted a recognition that the saving, production, and purchasing power of upstanding members of the middling strata of German society were just as important to a flourishing economy as the big capitalists. And they especially wanted economic and legal systems that worked together to protect the value of their monetary assets, and the social status that those assets supported, against any economic difficulties that life might present. Ultimately, though, they wanted a moral socioeconomic order that rewarded virtue and punished vice and that guaranteed them an economic and social status commensurate with (their perception of) their inherent virtue and value.[23]

Millions of German creditors in the 1920s saw their economic activities, and in particular the monetary assets they had accumulated, in moral terms. They were convinced that money gained by the kind of careful, productive activity they had engaged in was a marker of virtuous behavior and moral superiority. They were also convinced that the money that "speculators" had accumulated through risky, manipulative activity was a marker of ethical misbehavior and moral inferiority. Such speculators were hence to be despised, indeed to be punished. Moreover, because businessmen, capitalists, had also accumulated or at least preserved wealth through the hyperinflation, that wealth was tarred with the same brush of immorality. Creditors hence became anticapitalist, in that they rejected the free-market economic system of the Weimar Republic as inherently unjust and in that they sought a more "comradely" and, from their perspective, moral alternative. By the early 1930s, many of them and their heirs would think they had found it—in Hitler's National Socialism.

Michael L. Hughes, Professor of History and Bryant/Groves Faculty Fellow at Wake Forest University, received his PhD from the University of California, Berkeley in 1981. He has published extensively on inflation and debt revaluation in Weimar Germany, on the equalization of burdens in West Germany after World War II, on victim identities in postwar West Germany, on the West German currency reform, and on democratic values in Weimar and West Germany. He is currently researching conceptions of political citizenship in Germany, 1888–1993 by looking at public demonstrations and protests.

Notes

1. 1 Timothy, 6:10, *Bible*; Daryl Koehn and Barry Wilbratte, "A Defense of a Thomistic Concept of the Just Price," *Business Ethics Quarterly* 22, no. 3 (2012): 501–2; E. P. Thompson, "The Moral Economy of the English Crowd in the Eighteenth Century," *Past and Present* 50 (1971): 83, passim; for Euro crisis see, e.g. Marion Fourcade et al., *Moral Categories in the Financial Crisis, maxpo discussion paper* # 13/1 [accessed 3 December 2013, url: www.maxpo.eu/pub/maxpo_dp/maxpodp13-1.pdf]; Olaf Storbeck, "'Moral hazard' wird überschätz," *Handelsblatt* (21 June 2011) [accessed 4 December 2013, url: http://www.handelsblatt.com/politik/oekonomie/wissenswert/euro-schuldenkrise-moral-hazard-wird-ueberschaetzt/4310932.html]; Hubert Thaler, "Euro-Krise: Wenn Moral auf Prinzipien trifft," *Das Investment.com* (15 June 2012) [accessed 4 December 2013, url: http://www.dasinvestment.com/nc/investments/maerkte/news/datum/2012/06/15/euro-krise-wenn-moral-auf-prinzipien-trifft/.
2. Eric D. Weitz, *Weimar Germany. Promise and Tragedy* (Princeton, NJ, 2007), 136–40.
3. Fritz Fischer, *World Power or Decline. The Controversy over Germany's War Aims in the First World War,* trans. Lancelot L. Farrar et al. (New York, 1974), 82–92, passim; Wolfgang Mommsen, *Imperial Germany 1867–1918. Politics, Culture and Society in an Authoritarian State,* trans. Richard Deveson (London, 1998), 209–14; Belinda Davis, *Home Fires Burning: Food, Politics, and Everyday Life in World War I Berlin* (Chapel Hill, NC, 2000), 61–75, passim; Belinda Davis, "Homefront. Food, Politics, and Women's Everyday Life during the First World War," in *Home/Front. The Military, War and Gender in Twentieth-Century Germany,* ed. Karen Hagemann and Stefanie Schüler-Springorum (Oxford, 2002), 117–21; Gerald D. Feldman, *The Great Disorder. Politics, Economics, and Society in the German Inflation, 1914–1924* (New York, 1993), 56–66; Hans-Ulrich Wehler, *Das deutsche Kaiserreich 1871–1918* (Göttingen, 1973), 200–7.
4. Feldman, *Great Disorder,* 151–52, 252–53, 465–67, 514, 518–19, 666, 670–71, passim; Theo Balderston, *Economics and Politics in the Weimar Republic* (Cambridge, 2002), 34–60.
5. Feldman, *Great Disorder,* 515–20, 682–84; Oskar Mügel, "Gesetzliche Maßnahmen aus Anlaß der Geldentwertung," *Juristische Wochenschrift* 50, no. 20 (1921): 1270–71; G. Best, "Goldmark und Papiermark," *Juristische Wochenschrift* 51, no. 23 (1922): 1670–71; Michael L. Hughes, *Paying for the German Inflation* (Chapel Hill, NC, 1988), 23–25; petitions in Bundesarchiv Berlin Lichterfelde (hereafter, BA-L), RJM, Nr 781–84.
6. Carl-Ludwig Holtfrerich, *Die deutsche Inflation* (Berlin, 1980), esp. 195–318; Feldman, *Great Disorder,* 780–95, passim.
7. Hughes, *Paying for the German Inflation,* 2–9, 13–16, passim; Martin H. Geyer, *Verkehrte Welt. Revolution, Inflation und Moderne: München 1914–1924* (Göttingen, 1998), 205–22, 358–59.
8. For Stinnes, see Feldman, *The Great Disorder,* 6, 284–300, passim; Otto Arnim [Alfred Roth], *Von Rathenau zu Barmat. Der Leidensweg des deutschen Volkes* (Stuttgart, 1925), iii–v, 60–89; for quotation, "Zeitgemäße Glossen zur Aufwertungsfrage, eine Warnung," in *Spiegel der deutschen Inflation,* ed. Rechtsanwalt Dr. Oelenheinz (Leipzig, 1928), 38.
9. For Kollwitz pamphlets see Feldman, *The Great Disorder,* 247, and see also 245, 553, passim; Bund gegen Wucher und Teuerung to Reichskanzler, Bundesarchiv Koblenz,

R43 I/1246, Bl. 348–49; Otto Kühn to Reichswirtschaftsminister Neumann, 30 Jan. 1925, BA-L, Reichswirtschaftsministerium, Bd. 15423, Bl., 235; Dr. Georg Best, "Wie die Regierung die Aufwertung denkt," [ca. 20 Apr. 1925], Bayerisches Hauptstaatsarchiv (hereafter BayHStA), MJu 15335; Schutzverband der Hypotheken-Pfandbrief- und Obligationsgläubiger in Bayern, "Entschließung," 10 Feb. 1924), BA-L, RWM 15423, Bl. 18; Rechtsanwalt Dr. Oelenheinz, "Aufruf der Geusen," *Spiegel,* 15 Apr. 1924, 93.

10. Roland Schacht, "Verteidigung des Schiebers," *Die Weltbühne* 18 (14 December 1922): 618–20; "Pressenotiz aus dem Büro der Industrie und Handelskammer zu Berlin," BA-L, Reichskommissar bei der Berliner Börse, #666. Bl. 32; Edward Chancellor, *Devil Take the Hindmost. A History of Financial Speculation* (New York, 1999), ix–xiv.

11. Julius Lehmann, "Zur Aufwertungsfrage," *Bankarchiv* XXIII, no. 7 (1924): 67–68; Alfons Roth, *Die Aufwertung* (Berlin, 1925), 9, 16; Oskar Funcke, "Von der Markstabilisierung zu Brüning," 6, Nachlass Funcke, Deutsche Industrie-Institut, Köln.

12. Hughes, *Paying for the German Inflation,* 10, 16; S. Kaut, "Zur Aufwertungsfrage der Lebensversicherungen," *Mercuria* 44, no. 4 (1924); W. Groening to Reichskanzler, 16 January 1924, BA-L, Reichsjustizministerium, Bd. 788, Bl. 240; Oskar Mügel, *Geldentwertung und Hypothek* (Berlin, 1924), 4–5; Ernst Neckarsulmer, *Der alte und der neue Reichtum* (Berlin, 1925), 167–69.

13. Hughes, *Paying for the German Inflation,* 16, 84–87, 120–25.

14. "Zum Geleit," *Der Sparerschutz* 1:1 [ca. 1 May 1924], BayHStA, MA 103775; Wilhelm Linnow, "Gutachten zur Aufwertung der Hypotheken!" BA-L, RWM 15424, Bl. 54; Reichsbund für Aufwertung, "Sparer! Arbeiter! Frauen!" Geheimes Staatsarchiv Preußischer Kulturbesitz (hereafter GehStA), XII. Hauptabteilung, Zeitgeschichtliche Sammlung III; "Die Aufwertungsvorlage [letter to editor]," *Der Beamtenbund* 9, no. 40 (1925); "Aufruf!" *Gläubiger und Sparer* 2, no. 42 (1926); cf. Martin Geyer, "Der Barmat-Kutisker Skandal und die Gleichzeitigkeit der Ungleichzeitigen in der politischen Kultur der Weimarer Republik," in *Politische Kultur und Medienwirklichkeiten in den 1920er Jahren,* ed. Ute Daniel (Munich, 2010), 69–70.

15. HGSSV Hamburg to Wilhelm Marx, 20 Apr. 1925, Historisches Stadtarchiv Köln, NL Marx, #205; Reinhard Wüst, *Beiträge zur Aufwertungsfrage* (2nd ed.), in Bundesarchiv Koblenz (hereafter BA-K), NL Dietrich #295, Bl. 74; HGSSV, Landesverband Mecklenburg, "Die Aufwertungsfrage vom wirtschaftlichen Standpunkt aus betrachtet," BA-L, RWM 15423, Bl. 342; *Die Aufwertung* 1, no. 19 (1924).

16. "Barmat," *Sigilla Veri. Ph. Stauff's Semi-Kürschner* (Erfurt, 1929), 395–98; Arnim [Alfred Roth], *Von Rathenau zu Barmat,* iii, v, 6, 35–36, 60–93; Neckarsulmer, *Der alte und der neue Reichtum,* 6–7; Geyer, "Der Barmat-Kutisker," 51, 56–57, 64, 68–69; Martin Geyer, "Contested Narratives of the Weimar Republic. The Case of the 'Kutisker-Barmat Scandal,'" in *Weimar Publics/Weimar Subjects. Rethinking the Political Culture of Germany in the 1920s,* ed. Kathleen Canning et al. (New York, 2013), 215–17, 220–25.

17. Cf. E. Bendix, "Geldentwertung und Rechtsfindung," *Juristische Wochenschrift* 52, no. 21/22 (1923): 916.

18. "Zum Geleit,"*Der Sparerschutz* 1:1 [ca. 1 May 1924], BayHStA, MA 103775; Schutzverband Hypothekengläubiger, Ortsgruppe Burghausen a. S. to Bayerische Regierung, 2 July 1924, BayHStA, MA 103780; Hypothekengläubiger Schutzverband für die beiden Mecklenburg, "Die Verschiebung der deutschen Vermögen," [ca. 28 Feb.

1924], BayHStA, MA 103775; "Entschließung und Forderungen der heute gegründeten Ortsgruppe Hamburg des HGSSV," 14 Apr. 1924, Staatsarchiv Hamburg [StAHbg], Cl I Lit T #15b, Vol. 70, Fasc 7.
19. Siegfried Hirth, "Die Inflationslüge," Oct. 1924, BayHStA, MJU 15334; Schutzverband Hypotheken, "Bayerische Sparer in Stadt und Land," Jan. 1925, BayHStA, MJU 15334; "Die Frage der Aufwertung," Der Arbeiter 35, no. 7 (1924); "Aufwertung und Anleihe-Ablösung," Die Handels- und Büroangestellte 30, no. 9 (1925); Prof. Dr. Köhler-Stettin to Reichspräsident, Spiegel (8 June 1926): 47; Alfred Stuckert (Fabrikdirektor) to Erkelenz, 5 Sept. 1924, BA-K, NL Erkelenz #32, Bl. 296; "Wiedergutmachung am eigenen Volk," StAHbg, Cl I Lit T #15b, Vol. 70, Fasc 1.
20. Bayerisches Statistisches Landesamt, Die Verelendung des Mittelstandes, Heft 106 der Beiträge zum Statistik Bayerns (Munich, 1925), 53; J. Rose, "Wieder die Aufwertungsfrage," Germania 54, no. 204 (1924); Thomas Childers, "Inflation, Stabilization, and Political Realignment in Germany, 1919–1928," in Die deutsche Inflation, ed. Gerald Feldman (Berlin, 1982), 427; "Graf Posadowsky sprach in Erfurt," Gläubiger und Sparer 1, no. 23 (1925).
21. HGSSV, "Plan zur Verzinsung von Reichsanleihen," 17 Jan. BA-L, RWM 15469, Bl. 4; Schutzverband Hypothekengläubiger, "Kundgebung," 11 Nov. 1924, BayHStA, MA 103775; "Die gesetzliche Lösung der Aufwertungsfrage," Deutsche Handelswacht 32, no. 8 (1925): 409; Fr. Collier-Weserlingen, "Zur Aufwertungsfrage," Der Beamtenbund 9, no. 28 (1925); Bayerische Handelsbank Bodenkreditanstalt, "Aufwertung der Pfandbriefen und Deckungshypotheken der Hypothekenbanken," 15 Feb. 1924, BayHStA, MiWi 491.
22. Osnabrück HGSSV to Generalstaatskommissar Dr. v. Kahr, 13 Dec. 1923, BayHStA, MA 103775; Schutzverband Hypothekengläubiger, Ortsgruppe Mindelsheim, to Held, 20 Sept. 1924, BayHStA, MA 103775; A. Bauser, "Aufgaben des Sparerbundes," in Für Wahrheit und Recht (Stuttgart, 1927), 88; Ludwig Küppers, Chairman, Rheydt HGSSV, "Zur Hypothekenaufwertungsfrage," Jan. 1925, Stadtarchiv Köln, NL Marx #203; Dr. M. Silberstein, "Ist das Deutsche Reich noch ein Rechtsstaat?," 8 Uhr Abendblatt 76, no. 287 (1923); Preußischer Justiz Minister to Herrn Minister Präsident und sämtlichen Staatsministern, 15 Nov. 1923, GehStA, Rep 84a #5885, Bl. 520, 524.
23. Dr. E. Bendix, "Geldentwertung und Rechtsfindung," Juristische Wochenschrift 52, no. 21/22 (1923): 916; Dr LG, "Kapitalsnot und Kredithilfe," Handels- und Industriezeitung der Leipziger Neuesten Nachrichten, 20 May 1924, in BA-L, RWM 15423, Bl. 86; HGSSV, Landesverband Mecklenburg, "Die Aufwertungsfrage vom wirtschaftlichen Standpunkt aus betrachtet," [ca. 7 Mar. 1925], StAHbg, Cl I Lit T No 15b, Vol. 70 Fasc 5; Denkschrift der Reichsarbeitsgemeinschaft der Aufwertungs-, Geschädigten- und Mieterorganisationen (Berlin, 1927), 70, 83; cf. also "zu Reichskanzler 926,[25]" 19 Feb. 1925, BA-K, R 43, I/2455, Bl. 109–10.

Bibliography

"Aufruf!" Gläubiger und Sparer 2, no. 42 (1926).
"Die Aufwertungsvorlage [letter to editor]," Der Beamtenbund 9, no. 40 (1925).
Balderston, Theo. Economics and Politics in the Weimar Republic. Cambridge, 2002.
"Barmat," Sigilla Veri. Ph. Stauff's Semi-Kürschner, 395–98. Erfurt, 1929.

Bendix, E. "Geldentwertung und Rechtsfindung." *Juristische Wochenschrift* 52, no. 21/22 (1923).
Best, G. "Goldmark und Papiermark." *Juristische Wochenschrift* 51, no. 23 (1922).
Chancellor, Edward. *Devil Take the Hindmost. A History of Financial Speculation.* New York, 1999.
Childers, Thomas. "Inflation, Stabilization, and Political Realignment in Germany, 1919–1928." In *Die deutsche Inflation,* edited by Gerald D. Feldman, 409–31. Berlin, 1982.
Davis, Belinda. *Home Fires Burning: Food, Politics, and Everyday Life in World War I Berlin.* Chapel Hill, NC, 2000.
———. "Homefront. Food, Politics, and Women's Everyday Life during the First World War." *Home/Front. The Military, War and Gender in Twentieth-Century Germany,* edited by Karen Hagemann and Stefanie Schüler-Springorum, 113–37. Oxford, 2002.
Feldman, Gerald D. *The Great Disorder. Politics, Economics, and Society in the German Inflation, 1914–1924.* New York, 1993.
Fischer, Fritz. *World Power or Decline. The Controversy over Germany's War Aims in the First World War.* Translated by Lancelot L. Farrar, Robert Kimber, and Rita Kimber. New York, 1974.
Funcke, Oskar. "Von der Markstabilisierung zu Brüning." Nachlass Funcke, Deutsche Industrie-Institut. Cologne.
"Die gesetzliche Lösung der Aufwertungsfrage," *Deutsche Handelswacht* 32, no. 8 (1925): 409.
Geyer, Martin H. "Der Barmat-Kutisker Skandal und die Gleichzeitigkeit der Ungleichzeitigen in der politischen Kultur der Weimarer Republik." In *Politische Kultur und Medienwirklichkeiten in den 1920er Jahren,* edited by Ute Daniel. Munich, 2010.
———. "Contested Narratives of the Weimar Republic. The Case of the Kutisker-Barmat Scandal." In *Weimar Publics/Weimar Subjects. Rethinking the Political Culture of Germany in the 1920s,* edited by Kathleen Canning, Kerstin Barndt, and Kristin McGuire. New York, 2013.
———. *Verkehrte Welt. Revolution, Inflation und Moderne: München 1914–1924.* Göttingen, 1998.
Holtfrerich, Carl-Ludwig. *Die deutsche Inflation.* Berlin, 1980.
Hughes, Michael L. *Paying for the German Inflation.* Chapel Hill, NC, 1988.
Kaut, S. "Zur Aufwertungsfrage der Lebensversicherungen," *Mercuria* 44, no. 4 (1924)
Koehn, Daryl, and Barry Wilbratte. "A Defense of a Thomistic Concept of the Just Price." *Business Ethics Quarterly* 22, no. 3 (2012): 501–26.
Mommsen, Wolfgang. *Imperial Germany 1867–1918. Politics, Culture and Society in an Authoritarian State.* Translated by Richard Deveson. London, 1998.
Mügel, Oskar. *Geldentwertung und Hypothek.* Berlin, 1924.
———. "Gesetzliche Maßnahmen aus Anlaß der Geldentwertung." *Juristische Wochenschrift* 50, no. 20 (1921).

Neckarsulmer, Ernst. *Der alte und der neue Reichtum.* Berlin, 1925.
Oelenheinz, Dr. "Aufruf der Geusen," *Spiegel,* 15 April 1924.
Silberstein, Dr. M. "Ist das Deutsche Reich noch ein Rechtsstaat?," *8 Uhr Abendblatt* 76, no. 287 (1923).
Storbeck, Olaf. "'Moral hazard' wird überschätz," *Handelsblatt* (21 June 2011) [accessed 4 December 2013: http://www.handelsblatt.com/politik/oekonomie/wissenswert/euro-schuldenkrise-moral-hazard-wird-ueberschaetzt/4310932.html]
Thaler, Hubert. "Euro-Krise: Wenn Moral auf Prinzipien trifft," *Das Investment.com* (15 June 2012) [accessed 4 December 2013: http://www.dasinvestment.com/nc/investments/maerkte/news/datum/2012/06/15/euro-krise-wenn-moral-auf-prinzipien-trifft/
Thompson, E. P. "The Moral Economy of the English Crowd in the Eighteenth Century." *Past and Present* 50 (1971): 76–136.
Wehler, Hans-Ulrich. *Das deutsche Kaiserreich 1871–1918.* Göttingen, 1973.
Weitz, Eric D. *Weimar Germany. Promise and Tragedy.* Princeton, NJ, 2007.
"Zeitgemäße Glossen zur Aufwertungsfrage, eine Warnung." In *Spiegel der deutschen Inflation,* edited by Rechtsanwalt Dr. Oelenheinz, 38. Leipzig, 1928.

CHAPTER FOURTEEN

Mobilizing Citizens and Their Savings
Germany's Public Savings Banks, 1933–39

PAMELA E. SWETT

Under the Nazi government, Germans were continually asked to make deposits into a raft of collection boxes. The Nazi Party's People's Welfare organization ran a winter relief campaign among others that collected hundreds of millions of Reichsmarks (RM) every year, as well as used clothing, shoes, and other household items.[1] Children were also mobilized to collect for winter relief and other campaigns through the Hitler Youth. In addition to membership dues and uniform expenses, mass organizations like the Sturmabteilung (SA) and the Women's League also encouraged their members to purchase a variety of reading materials at a small (but persistent) cost. Alongside these "voluntary" drives, employed adults had new mandatory fees to pay to the German Labor Front (Deutsche Arbeitsfront, DAF) and the myriad of other professional and trade associations under its control. The list goes on and on. A range of responses can be found to these calls for funds. Some percentage of citizens undoubtedly supported the mobilization of individual incomes for what they believed to be the common good. However, many others saw the constant prodding for donations as a thinly veiled tax or, more bluntly, as extortion. Informers for the Social Democratic Party of Germany in Exile (SOPADE) regularly reported grumbling among the population about the pressures to participate in what was referred to as the "donation-economy."[2]

In this context of mobilizing private funds to achieve the public agenda of the state and Nazi party after 1933, which was chiefly the preparation for and waging of war, there was no factor more significant than the deposits made by Germans into their accounts in the country's *Sparkassen*, or communal savings banks. Moreover, in contrast to the resentment engendered by the constant calls for donations to other public causes, most Germans seem to have accepted the encouragement to save their money. By the end of the 1930s, roughly every German household possessed at least one savings account, and a large proportion had more than one. While the National Socialist leadership used the language of sacrifice and duty to the nation to encourage deposits into these accounts, these were not the only ideas communicated to Germans, even after 1939. As demonstrated below, contributing to individual savings accounts was presented to Germans by the public banks and local and state officials as an essential way to achieve both personal and national goals. Through their savings, Germans would provide support for farmers and small businessmen, and expand the possibilities for homeownership and other individual consumer purchases. According to supporters of the regime, making deposits in the local *Sparkasse* also helped fight "Jewish capital" and "foreign domination"—in other words, "saving money" was a practice that gave shape to life in the *Volksgemeinschaft*.

The Most "German" Banks

Germany's first public savings banks, or *Sparkassen*, were founded before 1848. Their number grew dramatically in the years after the founding of the German Empire in 1871, thanks to industrialization, urbanization, and new technologies and laws that made banking more secure and more efficient. In addition to retaining savings deposits and issuing mortgages and municipal loans, after 1908 the savings banks were also able to handle cashless transactions through networks of giro associations.[3] Communally owned and dependent on local governments, savings banks were political from the start. Local notables held sway over how these private-turned-public funds would be spent, including investments in economic development and public infrastructure. By encouraging deposits from "small savers," individuals whose deposits had been considered "hitherto virtually valueless as investments,"[4] Germans of lesser means could be engaged in the growth of their hometowns. Even if savers had little say in which communal projects received funding, their participation in saving was seen by local notables as part of their education in the conservative values of thrift and long-term planning.

By 1900, there were about fifteen million individual savings accounts in Germany valued at roughly RM 9 billion, and the public banks remained a critical player in commercial and public investment in the early twentieth century.[5] While savings remained their mainstay, the inflationary period after World War I led the *Sparkassen* to increase the number of short-term loans they handled. Business returned to an emphasis on savings deposits as well as long-term loans to individuals and municipalities after the currency reform of 1924, but it is clear that by the end of the decade, the *Sparkassen* had become formidable rivals to the big private banks. They offered all the same services, but they paid no national taxes because of their status as public institutions.[6] While there was significant variation in the regulation of banks among the Western nations in this era, growing public confidence in opening savings accounts was not particular to Germany. "World Savings Day" began in 1924, with the first congress meeting in Italy. The following year, Germany's republican government began coordinating promotional efforts with the nation's savings banks to mark the day (30 October). The occasion was renamed "National Savings Day" in 1933 by the new Nazi leadership.

Following the banking crisis of 1931, bankers and public officials began discussions about possible new regulations for the banking sector.[7] In the meantime, the depression led to the closure of some branches, while others were consolidated. A new wave of promotional literature intended to buttress flagging public trust in the savings banks was also put forth. In places where National Socialists made early gains in local elections, this restructuring provided the opportunity to implement pro-Nazi human resource management. In Coburg, Bavaria, for example, the Coburger *Sparkasse* began layoffs of 43 of its 131 staff in 1930, including 4 managers. By the start of 1932, the bank had rebounded slightly, employing 103 men and women. Analysis of the surviving personnel files of those staff members who stayed on through the depression shows that about 84 percent joined the Nazi party or one of its mass organizations by 1938.[8] Even more striking is the fact that all 15 new employees hired by 1932 were already members of the Nazi Party or one of its affiliated organizations when they joined the bank.

Eventually, a new federal regulatory law, the *Reichsgesetz über das Kreditwesen*, or Banking Act, was passed in December 1934,[9] but the private banks' goal of using the crisis to push the *Sparkassen* out of some areas of lending was turned back. Those representing the savings banks with ties to the left wing of the Nazi party, however, also had their dreams of a nationalization of the private banks rejected. Reichsbank President and Economics Minister Hjalmar Schacht pursued a path that was far more moderate than either of these proposals, ensuring under the new law that the central bank gained far greater oversight over lending practices. All banks had to be licensed by and report to a new supervisory board, which had the ability to set minimum liquid reserve requirements. According to Adam Tooze, the three largest private banks (Deutsche, Dresdner, and Commerzbank) were the chief "losers" of the crisis and the recovery that followed. While the assets controlled by these titans of the financial system rose by 15 percent between 1932 and 1939, the communal savings banks welcomed an increase of 102 percent over the same period.[10] By 1938, there were 14,000 *Sparkassen* deposit sites in the country staffed by about 56,000 men and women.[11] In that same year, the association of public banks trademarked the blocky red

"S" that still stands today as the visual symbol for the vast network of *Sparkassen* in Germany.[12]

While this shift in fortunes under the new regime has multiple explanations, it does not come as any real surprise. National Socialists had always had a rather difficult relationship with large private banks, which they frequently lambasted as part of the international Jewish conspiracy that preyed upon the German nation. One can find many examples of National Socialist writings that discuss alleged Jewish infiltration of global financial markets as the cause for Germany's economic woes in the Weimar era. The Nazi economist Gottfried Feder, for example, began his 1933 book on the "Functional Meaning of the Monetary and Credit Systems" by tracing historically the development of "Jewish lending" and "Aryan" attempts since the Middle Ages to thwart its advance. As Feder put it most simply, "The idea to control a people through money and with money accords perfectly with the mentality of the Jews."[13]

As public institutions, however, savings banks were immune from this taint and were lauded after 1933 as homegrown establishments that supported the advancement of all members of the *Volk*. Public banking offered a counterweight, in Feder's eyes, to the "liberal economic-mindset" that motivated the owners of the private banks. While the party did nothing to end private banking after it came to power, party leaders did trumpet the *Sparkassen* as authentic representative institutions of the *Volksgemeinschaft*.[14] As Feder again explained, "The savings banks are the oldest and proudest bearer; one can go so far as to call them the cornerstone of the German credit system. They have not only brilliantly withstood the encroachments of recent years, they have continued to progress in their development." He added that "the collection of the savings of workers" and its "proper utilization in service of the community" was among "the highest and most significant work" of the National Socialist state.[15]

Seeing saving as a fundamentally German virtue was not a Nazi invention, but the new government, its supporters, and the managers of the savings banks emphasized the perceived Germanness of these institutions as well as the practice of saving. *Sparkassen* administrators, for example, encouraged the use of quotations by "great German men" like Kant and Goethe about the German virtue of thrift in *Sparkassen* advertisements.[16] Another official also emphasized the links between past and present, declaring that the foundation for public banking had been laid by the "men of Old Prussia" (Frederick William I and Frederick the Great), but that their dream would be realized by the *Sparkassen*'s "new patron," the National Socialist regime.[17] Interior Minister Wilhelm Frick referred to frugality and industry as the "most noble of German virtues," adding in 1933 that "the savings banks have fostered and protected [these virtues] since their founding, even in the hardest of times."[18] The long tradition of serving the community was also celebrated in *völkisch Sparkassen* anniversary festivities and poetry.[19] During the mid 1930s, traditional symbols of hard work and community spirit like bees and beehives continued to be used in advertisements and as common motifs in *Sparkassen* interior decoration such as wall murals and ironwork, even as new technologies changed the way banking was carried out, and some new branch openings reflected a more modern aesthetic.

"Saving Makes Happiness"

In the first two years of the dictatorship, advocates of a greater role for *Sparkassen* in the "national reawakening" focused on the role individuals could play in helping their unemployed "national comrades." The regime urged people to deposit their earnings in the communal banks so as to stimulate job creation. The *Sparkassen* could then lend this money to fund capital projects initiated by municipal governments, or offer credit to local businesses hoping to expand or withstand the difficult times. In the mid 1930s, the *Sparkassen* did indeed see healthy gains in deposits over the depression years. From the low point of the economic crisis to the middle of 1937, for example, the Berliner *Sparkasse* more than doubled its deposits from RM 253 million to RM 595 million.[20] Although it could be argued that early increases resulted from fear that unemployment might return, the National Socialist leadership saw it differently. Savings levels were understood to be a litmus test of the regime's popularity and trustworthiness. Party leaders proclaimed that increased levels of saving among the *Volk* signified growing support for the regime. As one observer wrote, "The national socialist state promotes saving not least through its reestablishment and solidification of trust in state leadership, its economic policies and the stability of the currency. That this [has been achieved] is obvious and proven by the fact that this branch of national capital-generation is coming along so well."[21]

Despite such confidence among supporters of the regime, there were rumors of inflation in 1934 that led individuals to seek nonliquid assets. Deposits into savings accounts slowed, and those who could afford to purchase land did so, while Germans of lesser means stocked up on items like textiles and rubber tires.[22] These inflationary fears subsided as the economic recovery gained ground in the middle part of the decade, thanks to the massive shift to rearm. As unemployment dropped, so did job creation as a central element in the literature about the importance of saving, though the banks continued to remind citizens that their deposits helped support farmers and small businesses through the credit provided by *Sparkassen*.[23]

Although the importance of job creation was receding, the regime's desire to promote savings during the mid 1930s was stronger than ever before. On the one hand, deposits were needed to help finance rearmament. The government ensured deposits would be used this way by forcing *Sparkassen* to buy high levels of Reich debt. On the other hand, the government was also conscious of the necessity of removing excess funds from the pockets of its citizens, because with the shift to arms manufacturing, the level of consumer items available for purchase had fallen. Knowing that men and women still desired these goods, the language around saving emphasized the preparation for purchase—that saving up was the rational, responsible way to attain the things one most wanted. Such arguments bought the regime time.[24] In order to channel saving (and thereby spending) in ways the regime could manage and even take credit for, certain purchases were prioritized. The party's Strength through Joy (*Kraft durch Freude*) office ran saving programs for home radios, holiday travel, and the Volkswagen automobile, but the rhetoric of individual fulfillment through saving for desired goods was much more widespread than these famous projects.[25]

Another promotional focus of long-term saving was the goal of homeownership. As economist Heinrich Hunke explained to an association of homeowners in 1935, the republican era's rent freezes and subsidized housing had discouraged new building. Germans, in Hunke's opinion, "had gambled away their property and had all become proletarians." He advocated for policies that would reverse this development and affirm the place of property ownership in National Socialist Germany, because "it means for the individual a home [*Heimat*] born out of effort and work." The savings banks cheered such comments, agreeing with Hunke that a mortgage "rooted" the individual, making him a "firm member of the community."[26] In reality though, home construction remained severely limited in the prewar years, and the idea of homeownership was far beyond the financial reality of most families.[27]

Those who could not afford a mortgage were not left behind. The *Sparkassen* "created saving-opportunities for the everyman," including the "economically weak," "in the fight against proletarianization."[28] The banks were right not to forget Germans of lesser means. In 1936, three quarters of all savings books were attached to accounts that held less than RM 300, and over 50 percent of accounts held between RM 20 and 100.[29] While most accounts were small, savings books were held by about thirty-five million German men, women, and children in 1938, or roughly half the population.[30] While deposits increased annually, the positive trends in bank balance sheets were magnified by a decrease in the levels of withdrawals, as opportunities for spending dried up.[31] So the question arises: what did Germans think they were saving for?

As noted above, thousands of Germans made regular small contributions toward holiday travel packages sponsored by the DAF's Strength through Joy program. It was reported that in 1937 alone RM 15.18 million were deposited into savings accounts for this purpose, though this sum was but a tiny fraction of the hundreds of millions of Reichsmarks finding their way into *Sparkassen* accounts.[32] Beyond this example of *Zielsparen* (targeted saving), which made up only a tiny fraction of total savings, families also commonly saved for dowries, apprenticeships, other education expenses, and Christmas presents. A small number of middle-class Germans were also still able to plan for the purchase of other larger ticket items, like household appliances. It may come as a surprise that despite the work done by the Reich government to dampen consumer spending, advertisements for saving did not shy away from slogans that embraced consumption too. Even in 1938, slogans such as "Saving makes buying easy," "Save in order to buy," and "First save, then buy" were common.[33] Although the promotion of individual consumption was never abandoned, there was an acknowledgement that saving should take precedent. Moreover, Germans were encouraged to value the process of saving. Promoters of saving extolled the comfort the individual could draw from one's account booklet, like a personal diary that records the ups and downs of life: "By diligent saving the saver sees the accumulation of his wealth, sees how . . . he has achieved goals, and sees ultimately how [his wealth] rebounds after it has been spent rationally. His own production, success, bad times and good, come to light to him through his savings book."[34] While the regime continued to champion this personal perspective on savings, officials maintained that the life story of the *Volk* should also be represented this way. As individuals made deposits into their own accounts, they contributed to the "capital accumulation of the whole" nation, and could participate in its rise to greatness and protect it from calamity.[35] Slogans promoting saving could be read as offering a salve to the individual and nation alike: "Saving keeps worries away. Saving makes happiness."[36]

"Hidden Money Is Dead Money"

While Richard Evans was right that in Nazi Germany "people were remorselessly exhorted to save, save, rather than spend, spend, spend,"[37] his statement would have been more precise had he noted that housewives were regarded with particular attention by bank advertisers and state officials, because they recognized that women made more of the decisions about how to spend family income. In fact, the statistic that "two thirds of the national income goes through the hands of housewives" was a common refrain among those promoting savings banks.[38] One essay went so far as to call the housewife "the finance minister of the family."[39] Women, as mothers, also set the standard of model behavior for the next generation.[40] If daughters (and sons) saw their mothers saving steadily and shopping rationally, so the thinking went, they were more likely to develop the same values. *Sparkassen* managers, party ideologues, and those working in the economics ministry could all agree that it was imperative to convince women of the necessity to invest an increasing amount of family resources into savings accounts during the last years of peace. How-to pamphlets and exhibits aimed at the "clever housewife" were offered; free budgeting books and small coin banks were handed out; print ads were run in magazines; and short films spoke to the issue in theaters—even clocks that would only run for twenty-four hours and required a coin deposit to get restarted were made available.[41] Savings banks helped by assigning employees the work of visiting outlying homes on a weekly or monthly basis to pick up deposits from families who could not readily visit the branches in town.[42] Leaving no stone unturned, promoters of saving also recognized that "not all women marry.... We find women behind the counter, in front of the typewriter, in artisanal workshops, and many, many other careers. These earners are savers, or can be won as such."[43]

Children too were thought to be able to contribute to their families and by extension to the nation in this way. And while mothers were seen as critical conduits for lessons about saving, the school savings bank (*Schulsparkasse*) also promised to help spread the virtues of saving among children who did not have good models in this regard at home. Indeed, children who soaked up the value of saving at school were relied on to bring home the message and teach their parents.[44] The school savings bank was not a new concept in 1930s Germany; the earliest examples can be found in the 1820s, and the idea spread substantially in the 1920s. They were, however, made mandatory in 1933, but slower-than-wished-for adoption led to an additional decree from the Reich Education Ministry in 1936 to strengthen oversight and uniformity. By year's end, roughly 60 percent of all schools had opened *Schulsparkassen*.[45]

The aim of saving at school was not simply to raise money but also to teach pupils a sense of "community and social utility." This cocurricular service was understood as central to the mandate of schools, alongside teaching about dental care and providing cultural excursions.[46] While young Germans were taught to save through their daily actions, by taking care not to ruin or lose clothes or school materials for example, making regular deposits of spare change was also seen as important. Children were instructed that "hidden money was dead money." In other words, squirreling away coins at home under the proverbial mattress benefited no one—certainly not the *Volksgemeinschaft*. Depositing those funds at the *Sparkasse* allowed the money to come alive in service to the nation.[47] And yet there was also concern that too much saving could lead to "life-hating miserliness." Some "phantasies and desire to play" had to be satisfied, particularly among growing (male) youths. As one official from the Reich Education Ministry explained, "We do not live to save; rather we save so that we can live better, more secure and worry-free lives."[48] The most frequently noted examples of positive "targeted saving" for schoolchildren were collections to fund class trips. However, school saving also contributed to community projects like building homes for "children-rich families."[49]

Men were not targeted by the state or bank propaganda as frequently as women or children. In part, this can be explained by the tendency to subsume saving under the domestic decisions of the housewife. There was also a longstanding belief that women were more vulnerable to spending irrationally or compulsively, and therefore warranted more educational training to strengthen their resolve against wasteful spending. This is not to say, however, that men were wholly ignored by the campaigns to fill public coffers. Germany had a longstanding tradition of *Werksparkassen* (factory savings banks), in which employees deposited some of their earnings into an account held and invested by the employer, often back into its own operations. New legislation in 1934 called for the dissolution of these institutions by 1940, because of the risk that a bankrupt company would mean unemployment and the loss of savings for the firm's unfortunate workers. The regime spoke less of its other motivation for ending this practice—workers' savings invested in these accounts held by private companies were beyond the reach of the state. Books and pamphlets on the subject of *Werksparkassen* dissolution, however, were sure to stress the importance of moving the funds to local public banks, rather than paying out savings in cash to workers who might spend or hide the windfall.[50] Once the assets had been shifted to local *Sparkassen*, those banks were encouraged to set up branches at large factory sites, so that future deposits could easily find their way into existing accounts.[51] "Savings-cabinets" and other forms of automatic deposit machines were also installed at smaller work sites and even in some public meeting halls.[52]

Not to be forgotten, men in the Wehrmacht were also tapped as potential "savers." Officers admitted that "soldiers and saving" didn't seem an obvious match, but they were convinced that the virtues of saving one's money could be nurtured among this growing cohort of young men. On the practical side, soldiers were reminded (in peacetime) that at the end of their two-year compulsory service stint, they would be returning to civilian life and needed to prepare to purchase "a new wardrobe, linens and much more." In some cases, there would be expenses related to regaining civilian work. Even those who decided to stay on in the military were reminded that uniforms were costly and that planning for a future family made sense. In addition to these considerations, "the position of the soldier, who wears the nation's uniform, demands that his actions are exemplary not only on duty but in his private life as well." Saving his money was one way to model the ideals of the nation: "Even if one's holdings are small, they provide some economic independence and fortitude in the case of unforeseen events."[53]

Of course, not all soldiers engaged in model behavior. The *Sparkassen* in Breslau reported that the local commander was very supportive of setting up a bimonthly mobile branch for his men at the barracks, because otherwise "they wouldn't think of saving their earnings, choosing to spend them instead at the cantina." The commander's motivations for providing saving opportunities to his men were clear: soldiers with less spare change were sober soldiers, and sober soldiers caused fewer headaches for their commanding officers. While its services were called the "saving hour," the mobile branch that visited the base also handled payments for rent and utilities for those officers who lived elsewhere, accepted contributions to Strength through Joy accounts held by civilian employees at the base, and even permitted "small withdrawals" for servicemen.[54]

By the time the war began in September 1939, the *Sparkassen* had played their role in suppressing individual consumption and financing public consumption to great effect. In the months before the war, withdrawals from savings accounts shot up, as families sought to lay in stocks of food and other household items. But following this spike, it was the rate of deposits that saw a dramatic increase. Already successful, the messages of the prewar period continued thereafter at a heightened pace. Individual consumption continued to drop—in 1941 it was down 18 percent over 1938—leading to higher levels of "excess" income. By 1941, Adam Tooze reports, more than RM 1 billion were being added to the country's savings banks each month—savings that were channeled into the "silent" war financing. Tooze calculates that RM 8 billion from *Sparkassen* savings were redirected toward the war effort in 1940 alone—a figure that climbs to RM 12.8 billion in 1941.[55]

These measures worked remarkably well in the first half of the war and meant that most families were not faced with higher taxes, a point that the regime was fond of mentioning.[56] The only significant change was that messages in support of saving became explicit about the role individual deposits played in financing the war, such as in the following speech by economics minister Walther Funk to mark the second "War Savings Day," 30 October 1940: "Every war requires substantial financial means. This is particularly true in a war of destiny (*Schicksalskampf*), as the German nation is waging at present to secure its life and future. Every German must be aware of this: that saving in this grand hour is a serious duty to the fatherland, and that each Mark put aside helps attain victory."[57] In this sense, the "silent" financing was anything but.[58] This is an important point because it speaks to individual Germans' awareness that *Sparkassen* funds were syphoned off by the state to pay military expenditures.[59]

And, yet, taking a longer view of the *Sparkassen* across the 1930s allows us to see that these monetary institutions also played a significant role in state efforts to foster a *Volksgemeinschaft* before the war. More precisely, it becomes clear that the popularity of saving in these years was as closely linked to reaching personal aims as it was to ideas of sacrifice. And therein lies the dual aspects of the Nazi racial community.[60] On the one hand, these institutions were lauded as a cornerstone in the foundation of a new order that prioritized community and sought to combat "selfish" individualism, decried by National Socialists as "parasitic" and "Jewish." On the other hand, deposits were not donations to the state or party. Promotional efforts encouraging saving never shied away, even during the war, from reminding citizens that this money was theirs—that saving helped them reach their private goals. *Volksgemeinschaft* as a concept made room for both: a racial war and personal dreams of prosperity. The majority of Germans felt comfortable supporting that national vision, while watching their savings accounts grow and dreaming of future spending. Only in the latter stages of the war, as rumors of runaway inflation, taxes on savings, and compulsory saving made their way across the country, did many Germans start to worry about their money.

Pamela E. Swett is Professor and Chair of History at McMaster University. She is the author of *Selling Under the Swastika: Advertising and Commercial Culture in Nazi Germany* (2014) and *Neighbors and Enemies: The Culture of Radicalism in Berlin, 1929–1933* (2004). She is also coeditor of the volumes *Pleasure and Power in Nazi Germany* (2011) and *Selling Modernity: Advertising in Twentieth Century Germany* (2007). Her current research project is entitled "Citizen Soldiers: Military Service in Divided Germany."

Notes

1. We should not forget as well the mobilization of people's time that is represented in these massive drives for donations. Men, women, and children were involved: knocking on doors, cooking meals, organizing, and distributing. The impact of these actions is discussed in Claudia Koonz, *The Nazi Conscience* (Cambridge, 2003), Chapter 4.
2. See for example SOPADE (Social Democratic Party of Germany in Exile), *Berichte aus Deutschland*, September/October 1934, 530–35, and August 1936, 1068–77. The latter report refers to the "donation- and dues-economy."
3. As savings banks were public institutions, after 1908 municipal authorities in each German state formed giro associations for the savings banks in the area to process checks. These associations then partnered to establish centralized giro institutions to serve as clearing centers for the banks under their mandate. In 1918, a national headquarters was founded, the Deutsche Girozentrale, bringing all the savings banks of the Reich into one network. Karl Erich Born, *International Banking in the 19th and 20th Centuries*, trans. Volker R. Berghahn (New York, 1983), 247–48.
4. Paul Thomes, "German Savings Banks as Instruments of Regional Development up to the Second World War," in *The Evolution of Financial Institutions and Markets in Twentieth-Century Europe*, ed. Youssef Cassis, Gerald D. Feldman, and Ulf Olsson (Aldershot, 1995), 143.
5. Ibid., 144. Also Jens Piorkowski, *Die deutsche Sparkassenorganisation 1924 bis 1934* (Stuttgart, 1997), 65.

6. Jürgen Mura, *Entwicklungslinien der deutschen Sparkassengeschichte* (Stuttgart, 1987), 110–12.
7. One significant immediate step taken was the introduction of the concept of *Gewährträgerhaftung* through emergency decree in 1931, by which *Sparkassen* deposits were guaranteed by local authorities. Christian Lütke-Uhlenbrock, *Bewertung öffentlich-rechtlicher Sparkassen* (Wiesbaden, 2007), 11.
8. Frank Finzel, *Spuren: 175 Jahre Sparkasse Coburg: Hauptwege, Nebenwege, Irrwege* (Stuttgart, 1996), 341–42. Fifty-one of eighty-eight personnel files of those working in the bank in 1930 and stayed on survived the war. The percentage noted in the text comes from these files. While it was not mandatory to join the NSDAP, one oral history taken from a staff member at the *Sparkasse* Coburg noted in 1951 that the bank manager strongly encouraged his staff to do so. The Nazi *Gleichschaltung* of the *Sparkassen* was extensive, beginning with the law to "cleanse" the civil service of all Jews and political opponents to Nazism issued on 7 April 1933, but also included changes to administrative structures and regulations. In addition, the "Aryanization" of private banks between 1932 and 1939 accounts for most of the decline in this sector from 1,350 down to 520 institutions. Many other non-*Beamten* staff also lost their positions at the public and private banks that wished to fall into line. See Eckhard Wandel, "Das deutsche Bankwesen im Dritten Reich (1933–1945)," in *Deutsche Bankengeschichte*, ed. Gunther Aschhoffer et al. (Frankfurt, 1983), 178–82; Hans Pohl, *Wirtschafts- und Sozialgeschichte der deutschen Sparkassen im 20. Jahrhundert* (Stuttgart, 2005), 165–71.
9. Piorkowski, *Die deutsche Sparkassenorganisation*, 121–26.
10. Adam Tooze, *Wages of Destruction: The Making and Breaking of the Nazi Economy* (New York, 2006), 110. For a brief overview of the place of German banks within the Nazi economy see Dieter Ziegler, "'A Regulated Market Economy': New Perspectives on the Nature of the Economic Order of the Third Reich, 1933–1939," in *Business in the Age of Extremes: Essays in Modern German and Austrian Economic History*, ed. Hartmut Berghoff, Jürgen Kocka, and Dieter Ziegler (Cambridge, 2013), 139–52.
11. Rudolf Lencer, "Der Mitarbeiter in der Sparkasse als Träger der Sparidee," *Die Deutsche Volkswirtschaft*, no. 15 (1938): 551.
12. Norbert-Christian Emmerich, *Die Deutsche Sparkassenwerbung, 1750–1981* (Stuttgart, 1983), 168–69. Emmerich reports that the trademark was originally designed by Lois Gaigg.
13. Gottfried Feder, *Die funktionelle Bedeutung des Geld- und Kreditwesens* (1933), 6. For another example of the same sort of praise for the history of public banking in Germany, in contrast to "Jewish" private banking, see Arthur Herrmann, *Zweihundert Jahre öffentliches Bankwesen* (Berlin, 1935).
14. On 1 July 1933, the NSDAP leadership announced that the banking for the regional party administration (*Gauverwaltungsapparates*) would be handled through public banks like the *Sparkassen*, and a number of the party's affiliated associations followed suit; Pohl, *Wirtschafts- und Sozialgeschichte*, 151.
15. Feder, *Die funktionelle Bedeutung*, 11.
16. "Grosse deutsche Männer über das Sparen," *Sparkassen Werbedienst* 1, no. 1 (1 April 1935): 120–21.
17. Herrmann, *Zweihundert Jahre öffentliches Bankwesen*, foreword. See also 85–88 and 114–17.
18. BA-Berlin, NS6/492, Special edition of the *Deutsche Sparkassen-Zeitung*, 3 October 1933.

19. Nuremberg's Oberbürgermeister, Willy Liebel, was the editor of one such collection: *Kleines Lesebuch vom Sparen: Eine Dichtergabe für jung und alt* (Nuremberg, 1941).
20. Herbert Krafft, *Immer ging es um Geld. Einhundertfünfzig Jahre Sparkasse in Berlin* (Berlin, 1968), 160.
21. Franz Neuwirth, *Nationalsozialistische Sparkassenpolitik* (PhD diss., University of Vienna, 1941), 9.
22. Such "fear shopping" was motivated by concerns of inflation and new policies, which made consumer items that were dependent on imported resources increasingly scarce and hence more valuable. Pamela E. Swett, *Selling under the Swastika: Advertising and Commercial Culture in Nazi Germany* (Stanford, CA, 2014), 140. These rumors also made their way into discussions within the Reichsbank, where it was decided that propaganda campaigns to quell concerns about inflation would only exacerbate the situation. BA-Berlin, R3101/16613 Memo from the Reichsbank Direktorium, 25 May 1934.
23. *Die Deutschen Sparkassen und ihre Organisation*, 1938, 34.
24. The need to wait for a time in the future without shortages is discussed quite plainly in writings about saving. See for example, Das Deutschen Sparkassen und Giroverband, ed., *Das Gefolgschaftssparen: Ein Handbuch für die Sparkassenpraxis* (Berlin, 1939), 7. The granting of credit to small businesses and communities by *Sparkassen* fell overall between 1933 and 1939, owing to the political and economic prioritization of rearmament. Personal credit remained flat before 1939 and declined markedly after the onset of war. New mortgages also declined throughout the decade. See Pohl, *Wirtschafts- und Sozialgeschichte*, 212–22.
25. For further reading on Strength through Joy travel programs and the *Volksprodukte*, including the Volkswagen, see Shelley Baranowski, *Strength through Joy: Consumerism and Mass Tourism in the Third Reich* (New York, 2004) and Wolfgang König, *Volkswagen, Volksempfänger, und Volksgemeinschaft: "Volksprodukte" im Dritten Reich* (Paderborn, 2004). On the private sector's attempts to remain profitable in this period, see Swett, *Selling under the Swastika*; and S. Jonathan Wiesen, *Creating the Nazi Marketplace* (New York, 2010).
26. "Der nationalsozialistische Eigentumsbegriff," *Die Deutsche Sparkassen-Zeitung*, no. 13 (31 January 1935): 3.
27. Tooze, *Wages of Destruction*, 157–61.
28. T. Heckmann-Schwege, "Vertrauen," *Die Deutsche Sparkassen-Zeitung*, no. 19 (14 February, 1935): 3.
29. Thomes, "German Savings Banks as Instruments of Regional Development," 148. For the breakdown of this data, see the table in Rudolf Schraut, "Das Kleinsparwesen— eine bedeutsame Quelle für die Sammlung nationalen Sparkapitals," *Die Deutsche Volkswirtschaft*, no. 15 (1938): 581.
30. "Entwicklung der Spareinlagen der deutschen Sparkassen von 1924–1937," *Die deutschen Sparkassen und ihre Organisation* (1938): 10.
31. See "Deutsche Sparkassen," which includes a table that sums up these findings between 1934 and 1937 in *Die Deutsche Volkswirtschaft*, no. 10 (1938): 348.
32. Schraut, "Das Kleinsparwesen," 581.
33. Emmerich, *Die Deutsche Sparkassenwerbung*, 170.
34. *Die Deutschen Sparkassen und ihre Organisation*, 18.
35. Ibid., 18.
36. Hans Vorwerk, "Wir werben um die Frau," First Continuation, *Sparkassen Werbedienst* (1937): 161.

37. Richard J. Evans, *The Third Reich in Power* (New York, 2006), 411.
38. "Hausfrauen-Sparwerbung," *Sparkassen Werbedienst* 1 (1935): 88–89.
39. Vorwerk, "Wir werben um die Frau," 137.
40. "Hausfrauen-Sparwerbung," *Sparkassen Werbedienst* 1 (1935): 88–89.
41. Advertising for banks was regulated by the Nazi Ad Council, which worked under the authority of the Propaganda Ministry. See for example the rules about ads to mark the annual *Spartag*, or National Savings Day in 1936 in Hunke Nachlass, Landesarchiv Nordrhein-Westfalen, Abteilung Ostwestfalen-Lippe, Karton 7–2. The "saving-clock" is mentioned in Schraut, "Das Kleinsparwesen," 581–82. On advertising public banks more generally, see Emmerich, *Die Deutsche Sparkassenwerbung*, 156–75 as well as Peter Borscheid, "Sparsamkeit und Sicherheit. Werbung für Banken, Sparkassen und Versicherungen," in *Bilderwelt des Alltags*, ed. Peter Borscheid and Clemens Wischermann (Stuttgart, 1995), 316–25.
42. Ernst Joachim Haas, *Stadt-Sparkasse Düsseldorf, 1825–1972* (Berlin, 1972), 242.
43. Vorwerk, "Wir werben um die Frau," 161.
44. Dr Galandi, "Schulsparwesen und Unterrichtsverwaltung," *Die Schulsparkasse im Dienst von Volk und Staat*, ed. Deutschen Sparkassen- und Giroverband (Berlin, 1939), 19.
45. Gerhard Schnackenburg, "Vom Werden und Wirken der deutschen Schulsparkassen," *Die Schulsparkasse im Dienst von Volk und Staat*, ed. Deutschen Sparkassen- und Giroverband (Berlin, 1939), 21–25.
46. Galandi, "Schulsparwesen und Unterrichtsverwaltung," 9.
47. Ibid., 14–15.
48. Ibid., 13.
49. Schnackenburg, "Vom Werden und Wirken der deutschen Schulsparkassen," 29.
50. Das Deutschen Sparkassen- und Giroverband, *Das Gefolgschaftssparen*, 15–16.
51. Ibid., 19.
52. Haas, *Stadt-Sparkasse Düsseldorf*, 243.
53. Major Bleyer, "Das Sparen in der Wehrmacht," *Deutsche Sparkassen-Zeitung*, no. 122–23 (28 October 1938): 4.
54. "So spart die Wehrmacht," *Sparkassen-Werbedienst. Leitgedanken und Wege der Sparkassen-Werbung* 3, no. 2 (April 1937).
55. Tooze, *Wages of Destruction*, 354–55, including Figure 15 on 355.
56. "Die Kriegsfinanzierung Deutschlands," *Deutsche Sparkassen-Zeitung*, no. 95 (24 August 1940).
57. Walther Funk, Speech on the Occasion of the Second "Kriegspartag," 30 October 1940 in *Deutsche Sparkassen-Zeitung*.
58. See also the reports on "War-saving" in SOPADE, *Berichte aus Deutschland* VII (March 1940): 186–91.
59. Philipp Kratz discusses the difficulty of using rates of saving as an indicator for public support for the regime during the war in Philipp Kratz, "Sparen für das kleine Glück," in *Volkes Stimme. Skepsis und Führervertrauen im Nationalsozialismus*, ed. Götz Aly (Frankfurt, 2006), 59–79.
60. This point is similar to the one made by Andreas Wirsching that "the regime and its propaganda advocated *fighting* but promised *normality*" in Andreas Wirsching, "Volksgemeinschaft and the Illusion of Normality from the 1920s to the 1940s," in *Visions of Community in Nazi Germany: Social Engineering and Private Lives*, ed. Martina Steber and Bernhard Gotto (Oxford, 2014), 149–56, here 152.

Bibliography

Baranowski, Shelley. *Strength through Joy: Consumerism and Mass Tourism in the Third Reich*. New York, 2004.

Bleyer, Maj. "Das Sparen in der Wehrmacht." *Deutsche Sparkassen-Zeitung*, 28 October 1938.

Born, Karl Erich. *International Banking in the 19th and 20th Centuries*. Translated by Volker R. Berghahn. New York, 1983.

Borscheid, Peter. "Sparsamkeit und Sicherheit. Werbung für Banken, Sparkassen und Versicherungen." In *Bilderwelt des Alltags*, edited by Peter Borscheid and Clemens Wischermann, 294–349. Stuttgart, 1995.

"Deutsche Sparkassen." *Die Deutsche Volkswirtschaft*, no. 10, 1938.

Das Deutschen Sparkassen und Giroverband, ed., *Das Gefolgschaftssparen. Ein Handbuch für die Sparkassenpraxis*. Berlin, 1939.

"Der nationalsozialistische Eigentumsbegriff." *Die Deutsche Sparkassen-Zeitung*, 31 January 1935.

Emmerich, Norbert-Christian. *Die Deutsche Sparkassenwerbung, 1750–1981*. Stuttgart, 1983.

"Entwicklung der Spareinlagen der deutschen Sparkassen von 1924–1937." *Die deutschen Sparkassen und ihre Organisation*. Berlin, 1938.

Evans, Richard J. *The Third Reich in Power*. New York, 2006.

Feder, Gottfried. *Die funktionelle Bedeutung des Geld- und Kreditwesens*. Berlin, 1933.

Finzel, Frank. *Spuren: 175 Jahre Sparkasse Coburg: Hauptwege, Nebenwege, Irrwege*. Stuttgart, 1996.

Funk, Walther. "Kriegsspartag," *Deutsche Sparkassen-Zeitung*, 30 October 1940.

Galandi, Dr. "Schulsparwesen und Unterrichtsverwaltung." *Die Schulsparkasse im Dienst von Volk und Staat*, ed. Deutschen Sparkassen- und Giroverband, 5–20, Berlin, 1939.

"Grosse deutsche Männer über das Sparen." *Sparkassen Werbedienst*, 1935.

Haas, Ernst Joachim. *Stadt-Sparkasse Düsseldorf, 1825–1972*. Berlin, 1972.

"Hausfrauen-Sparwerbung," *Sparkassen Werbedienst*, 1935.

Heckmann-Schwege, T. "Vertrauen." *Die Deutsche Sparkassen-Zeitung*, 14 February 1935.

Herrmann, Arthur. *Zweihundert Jahre öffentliches Bankwesen*. Berlin, 1935.

König, Wolfgang. *Volkswagen, Volksempfänger, und Volksgemeinschaft: "Volksprodukte" im Dritten Reich*. Paderborn, 2004.

Koonz, Claudia. *The Nazi Conscience*. Cambridge, 2003.

Krafft, Herbert. *Immer ging es um Geld. Einhundertfünfzig Jahre Sparkasse in Berlin*. Berlin, 1968.

Kratz, Philipp. "Sparen für das kleine Glück." In *Volkes Stimme. Skepsis und Führervertrauen im Nationalsozialismus*, edited by Götz Aly, 59–79. Frankfurt, 2006.

"Die Kriegsfinanzierung Deutschlands." *Deutsche Sparkassen-Zeitung*, 24 August 1940.

Lencer, Rudolf. "Der Mitarbeiter in der Sparkasse als Träger der Sparidee." *Die Deutsche Volkswirtschaft*, no. 15, 1938.

Liebel, Willy. *Kleines Lesebuch vom Sparen. Eine Dichtergabe für jung und alt*. Nuremberg, 1941.
Lütke-Uhlenbrock, Christian. *Bewertung öffentlich-rechtlicher Sparkassen*. Wiesbaden, 2007.
Mura, Jürgen. *Entwicklungslinien der deutschen Sparkassengeschichte*. Stuttgart, 1987.
Neuwirth, Franz. *Nationalsozialistische Sparkassenpolitik*. PhD diss., University of Vienna, 1941.
Piorkowski, Jens. *Die deutsche Sparkassenorganisation 1924 bis 1934*. Stuttgart, 1997.
Pohl, Hans. *Wirtschafts- und Sozialgeschichte der deutschen Sparkassen im 20. Jahrhundert*. Stuttgart, 2005.
Schnackenburg, Gerhard. "Vom Werden und Wirken der deutschen Schulsparkassen." In *Die Schulsparkasse im Dienst von Volk und Staat*, edited by Deutschen Sparkassen- und Giroverband, 5–32. Berlin, 1939.
Schraut, Rudolf. "Das Kleinsparwesen—eine bedeutsame Quelle für die Sammlung nationalen Sparkapitals." *Die Deutsche Volkswirtschaft*, no. 15, 1938.
"So spart die Wehrmacht." *Sparkassen-Werbedienst. Leitgedanken und Wege der Sparkassen-Werbung*, 3, no. 2, April 1937.
Swett, Pamela E. *Selling under the Swastika: Advertising and Commercial Culture in Nazi Germany*. Stanford, CA, 2014.
Thomes, Paul. "German Savings Banks as Instruments of Regional Development up to the Second World War." In *The Evolution of Financial Institutions and Markets in Twentieth-Century Europe*, edited by Youssef Cassis, Gerald D. Feldman, and Ulf Olsson. Aldershot, 1995.
Tooze, Adam. *Wages of Destruction: The Making and Breaking of the Nazi Economy*. New York, 2006.
Vorwerk, Hans. "Wir werben um die Frau." *Sparkassen Werbedienst*, 1937.
Wandel, Eckhard. "Das deutsche Bankwesen im Dritten Reich (1933–1945)." In *Deutsche Bankengeschichte*, edited by Gunther Aschhoff, Günter Ashauer, Karl Erich Born, Wolfram Engels, Ernst Klein, Rosemarie Kolbeck, Manfred Pohl, Wilhelm Treue, Herbert Wolf, and Gerhard Zweig, 149–99. Frankfurt, 1983.
Wiesen, S. Jonathan. *Creating the Nazi Marketplace*. New York, 2010.
Wirsching, Andreas. "Volksgemeinschaft and the Illusion of Normality from the 1920s to the 1940s." In *Visions of Community in Nazi Germany: Social Engineering and Private Lives*, edited by Martina Steber and Bernhard Gotto, 149–56. Oxford, 2014.
Ziegler, Dieter. "'A Regulated Market Economy': New Perspectives on the Nature of the Economic Order of the Third Reich, 1933–1939." In *Business in the Age of Extremes: Essays in Modern German and Austrian Economic History*, edited by Hartmut Berghoff, Jürgen Kocka, and Dieter Ziegler, 139–52. Cambridge, 2013.

CHAPTER FIFTEEN

"One Would Not Get Far Without Cigarettes"
The Cigarette Economy in Occupied Germany, 1945–48

KRAIG LARKIN

In his 1959 study of the American occupation, historian Eugene Davidson characterized Germany as a "nation of bowed heads."[1] That assessment, however, should not be understood as a commentary on collective guilt or shame in the wake of military defeat or revelations regarding Nazi crimes. Rather, the description of downward-looking Germans testified to the thriving *Zigarettenwährung*, as Germans directed their gaze at the ground in the hopes of discovering discarded cigarette butts. *Kippensammlung* or *Stummeling*, the practice of scrounging for partially consumed cigarettes in street gutters, ashtrays, dustbins, or practically anywhere, emerged as a common practice during the occupation years, because collectors could combine the remnants of cigarettes together to fashion a new one. Germans of diverse social backgrounds and ages engaged in this behavior to cope with chronic tobacco shortages in a situation where tobacco functioned as currency on the black market.[2] Access to cigarettes, in particular, proved vital to surviving in the ruins of Germany, especially in urban centers. Cigarettes, whether professionally manufactured or refashioned from butts, constituted economic power. Or, as a young widow suggested in a May 1947 *Die Welt* article, "one would not get far without cigarettes."[3]

Germans, displaced persons (DPs), and occupation personnel used an array of economic behaviors to navigate a postwar landscape characterized by scarcity. Shortages necessitated the development of a "harsh discipline" to make do, but the material circumstances and thriving black market helped shape the social and political relations of the occupation era.[4] Paul Steege has shown how postwar Berliners actively shaped their own experiences of the black market to create a framework for interpreting and negotiating Cold War political struggles.[5] Laura Hilton and Malte Zierenberg have both examined how Germans employed the discourses and practices of black marketing to construct narratives of victimization, which functioned as distractions from addressing questions of guilt and complicity tied to the recent past.[6] Examining the deployment of strategies to contend with tobacco scarcity, including private cultivation, *Kippensammlung*, and efforts to regulate illicit trading in the American zone, offers insight into the nature of everyday life for those operating in the shadow economy. These practices also remind us that economic exchanges are also social exchanges that could be used to express power and communicate attitudes. As Erving Goffman noted in his 1961 study of asylums, "in any actual social situation the process of economic exchange will be modified by the influence of additional social arrangements."[7] Until the introduction of the Deutsche Mark in June 1948, occupiers, Germans, and DPs redefined what constituted acceptable forms of economic exchange to suit their needs. In the process, they determined exchange value through their behavior, which in turn was shaped by the social and economic conditions they encountered on a daily basis. In this context, not only did tobacco products emerge as *ersatz* currency, but the *Zigarettenwährung* "powered the country."[8]

The Zigarettenwährung

A September 1947 anecdote in the *Fränkische Presse* attributed to General Joseph T. McNarney, the former Military Governor of the American zone of occupation, described how a single American cigarette given to a GI's *Fräulein* could be traded six times before finally being smoked. McNarney's tale suggested that a typical cigarette could be given to a cobbler for shoe repair, bartered for coal, passed along to a butcher for extra pieces of meat, handed to a plumber for services rendered, before finally landing in the hands of a farmer who received it in exchange for some produce. The "journey of an American cigarette" culminated in the well-stocked home of the farmer, the only character in the story, besides the GI, who enjoyed the "luxury of smoking a real cigarette." The five people who formed the links in the chain connecting the GI and the farmer may have been tempted to light up and smoke, but elected to forego pleasure in order to pay for valuable services or to acquire scarce foodstuffs. The farmer, by contrast, could satisfy a nicotine craving while he "peacefully settles between his nice furniture, genuine Persian rugs and Swiss clocks," which he acquired through barter. Though this anecdote exaggerates the exchange value of a single cigarette, it illustrates how cigarettes acquired economic functions in the immediate postwar era.[9]

The inflation of tobacco goods was already visible before war's end, stemming from a combination of war-related disruptions in production and Nazi policies that sought to discourage tobacco consumption in order to protect the race.[10] German smokers encountered "nearly bare" shelves and lengthy queues by late 1939.[11] Wartime rationing, introduced in 1940, entitled males over eighteen and women over twenty-one to purchase tobacco, although the regime raised the age limit for females to twenty-five in 1942 due to persistent shortages.[12] Fearing an unsatisfied population at home could sap morale, local authorities in Berlin mandated that tobacconists remain open throughout the day to increase shoppers' opportunities to purchase rations.[13] Domestic production had declined from over 38,000 tons of tobacco at the start of the war to only 6,500 tons by 1945.[14] Factory closures exacerbated shortages, prompting the regime to permit citizens to grow their own tobacco. In exchange for a licensing fee of RM 48, home growers could harvest up to 200 plants, which could potentially produce ten kilos of raw tobacco under perfect conditions.[15] Harvested leaf, however, could not be earmarked for personal use; rather it had to be delivered to professional manufacturers, in part to meet the demands of the armed forces, which received priority over civilian usage.[16] The cumulative effect of scarcity ultimately produced a "nicotine-starved society" and an inadequate supply to meet continually growing demands.[17]

The constrained consumption of the war years continued well into the postwar period and was particularly pronounced when the Office of the Military Government of the United States (OMGUS) introduced a temporary prohibition on tobacco imports, thereby exacerbating an already existing shortage of tobacco products in Germany. American officials in Germany monitored the tobacco situation closely, but OMGUS rejected calls to import large quantities of tobacco into the American zone of occupation until 1948, electing to concentrate on food relief and on other materials required for postwar reconstruction. The relative absence of tobacco imports, combined with the practically nonexistent domestic production during the war and the disruptions to the global tobacco trade, created profound shortages in quantity as well as quality.[18] A 1947 request from German trade officials to import raw tobacco into the American and British zones argued that "cigarettes and other tobacco products will not be eliminated as a 'sham currency,'" and tax revenues would continue to be lost to black-market exchanges unless tobacco imports resumed immediately.[19] Cigarettes represented the ideal "sham currency" because they were relatively uniform, transportable, and recognizable, which helped to facilitate exchanges between groups from different linguistic and cultural backgrounds.[20] Unlike many other forms of commodity-currencies, black marketers could also theoretically control for inflation simply by using the cigarette as originally designed, although the sight of Germans smoking cigarettes often raised eyebrows. Jokes about cigarettes growing stale because they were traded too often before being smoked were commonplace. Zierenberg notes the cigarette emerged as the "collective symbol of the black market era" because of its status as the preferred form of black-market tender.[21]

The actual exchange value of cigarettes varied considerably during the occupation. Fluctuations in pricing stemmed from a variety of factors: country of origin, proximity to the original source of supply, and the impact of occupation policies on production, importation, or distribution of tobacco goods. American brands, for instance, were considerably more popular and in greater demand than Russian cigarettes, while various efforts to combat the black-market trade in tobacco products generally had the effect of raising rates by cutting into the available supply. General Lucius D. Clay, McNarney's successor, understood that production limitations and other pressing needs meant OMGUS could not "swamp Germany with cigarettes" to undercut their worth on the underground economy.[22] Occupation personnel profited, especially nonsmokers, as it was possible to sell a carton for as much as $150 in the six months following VE-Day.[23] Single packs of the more popular American brands, such as Chesterfields, could fetch as much as $90 by the end of the first year of the Allied occupation.[24] Between Christmas 1945 and the middle of 1946, the going price of a single American cigarette, or *Ami*, reportedly quadrupled.[25] Vladimir Petrov estimated that occupation personnel could earn as much as USD $12,000 per year by selling their cigarette rations on the shadow economy.[26] Others traded cigarettes for souvenirs and heirlooms, prompting a German journalist to caution readers against letting occupation soldiers use their "powerful butts" to rob the nation of its valuables.[27] Inflated rates and the appeal of big profits encouraged thieving, tampering, and counterfeiting. An American relief worker in the French zone declared that "a few cigarettes will do wonders" when one needed to navigate the ruins of the postwar economy; they could open closed doors, procure food, medical, or housing supplies, and even facilitate social and sexual relationships.[28] Given the prominent role of the underground economy, German satirist Thaddäus Troll surmised it was impossible to "live a life free from the black market" prior to currency reform in June 1948.[29]

The black market was not a new phenomenon in the postwar years, but it was distinct due to its size and, more importantly, its relative openness. Sociologist Hilde Thurnwald discovered a Berlin family erected roadside signs in 1947 boldly declaring their desire to exchange tobacco products for food, while shipping companies in the United States advertised their ability to transport large quantities of cigarettes into the American zone, even after the imposition of a formal import ban.[30] Local black-market operators occasionally pirated radio frequencies in order to publicize the going rates for popular black-market commodities, with prices often announced in cigarettes as opposed to RM.³¹ Black marketeering represented one type of economic behavior used to address needs that legal means could not always satisfy. City residents packed trains headed for the countryside on "hamster trips" to barter household objects for food, while Archbishop Josef Frings sanctioned petty thefts meant to feed the hungry, giving birth to the term *fringsen*. The severity of the deprivations allowed for a degree of moral ambivalence.³² Germans active on the black market often framed their trade as essential, unlike the exploitative transactions conducted by greedy Americans, DPs, or organized criminal syndicates.³³

Powerful Butts

Those who enjoyed regular access to tobacco supplies enjoyed a privileged position within postwar society, a fact recognized by occupation authorities responsible for overseeing the reconstruction of the German economy. As "one of the most important if not the most important form of an incentive good," cigarettes represented a powerful tool for occupation authorities and employers to use in recruiting healthy and able-bodied workers. Nowhere was this more evident than in the coal mining industry, where officials sought to use American cigarettes as a means to reverse a "completely hopeless" situation by attracting workers and stimulating coal production.³⁴ In 1947, the U.S. and British occupation governments, along with industry leaders, instituted a points-based incentive system that rewarded workers for attendance and productivity. Points could be exchanged for cigarettes, coffee, soap, and other scarce commodities.³⁵ The inclusion of cigarettes was crucial for attracting miners, because the "insufficient supply of tobacco for the working population" formed "an essential factor in the unsatisfactory efficiency of a population generally known as being very industrious."³⁶ Other jobs that struggled to recruit personnel also turned to tobacco. Britain's Reparations, Deliveries, and Restitution Division used confiscated cigarettes as a reward for German employees engaged in industrial dismantling programs, while American authorities unsuccessfully sought to provide extra rations to defense lawyers and related personnel in war crimes trials.³⁷ In light of its heightened economic value, it is hardly surprising that occupation authorities used increased access to cigarettes and other tobacco products as an incentive to boost production in a variety of fields.

Growing tobacco at home, in gardens, or fields harkened back to the establishment of private gardens during both world wars to address food shortages; it represented a significant means of augmenting one's supply and thus one's power on the black market.³⁸ Following the war, both the American and British occupying governments preserved aspects of the Nazis' own system of restricting how much tobacco one was permitted to plant or harvest. Beginning in 1947, occupation authorities limited licensed growers to twenty-five plants (or 1.5 kilos), trying to prevent most of the harvested tobacco from finding its way to the black market rather than to legitimate manufacturers.[39] According to Christoph Maria Merki, private tobacco operations produced twenty-two times more tobacco than professional tobacco farmers in 1946.[40]

Perhaps the best indicator of private cultivation's relative importance in the initial postwar era is the plethora of guides published on how to grow tobacco at home. These pamphlets, presumably geared toward personal consumption, served as a space in which Germans could openly acknowledge their frustrations with years of protracted shortages and insufficient rations. Tony Kellen's *Tabak im Garten* informed readers that queues and empty shelves at the local tobacconist's shop would quickly become a thing of the past by following his detailed instructions.[41] Another guide intimated that readers who adhered to the instructions and successfully grew their own crop could augment meager tobacco rations in a manner far more respectable than black marketing and *Kippensammlung*.[42] Although growing-it-yourself provided individuals a semblance of power, this method could not always guarantee quality. Most pamphlets acknowledged consumers might have to settle for an inferior smoking experience and not expect "much in terms of quality." Yields from small plots could have a "pleasant taste" and "good combustibility," but would not replicate the effect of nicotine from professionally manufactured cigarettes.[43] Kellen's pamphlet simply set the standard for success at producing something of "smokeable quality."[44]

Kippensammlung, however, continued to be a far more common means of supplementing rations than private tobacco gardens, since it did not require access to land, was less time intensive, and could be performed by practically anyone, regardless of age or social status. Stub collecting developed into such a normalized behavior that trolley passengers were unfazed when the conductor stopped the vehicle to collect a "Gross Stomp" from the gutter.[45] The struggle for butts often proved intense, particularly in regions where GIs congregated. Competition could degenerate into physical conflict and, as such, symbolized not only its importance as a survival strategy but also the depths of Germany's decline as a civilized nation. Director Rainer Werner Fassbinder incorporated a *Kippensammlung* scene into his *Die Ehe von Maria Braun* (1979), when an American soldier gleefully tossed a butt to the floor in a train station, prompting a half dozen or so Germans to pile upon one another in the hopes of securing the valuable stub.[46] A satirical cartoon entitled "Dream of the German Who Grows His Own Tobacco" published in a Bavarian newspaper two years into the occupation inverted the power relationship reflected in such scenes by portraying two American soldiers chasing after a well-dressed German smoker.[47]

Naturally, those who lived or worked in close proximity to occupation personnel enjoyed an advantage in the battle for butts. Julian Bach Jr., a correspondent for *Life*, claimed that a study of cafés along the popular Kurfürstendamm in Berlin revealed that ashtrays would typically be emptied of their contents within a minute of the patrons' departure.[48] *Stars & Stripes* reported that waiters in Viennese cafés frequented by GIs or their dependents earned "the equivalent of a $1,000-a-week-income" selling cigarettes created from the contents of ashtrays. Waiters in restaurants generally capitalized upon their opportunity to secure partly smoked cigarettes, although their counterparts at popular clubs often faced stiff challenges from young Germans who would storm the premises in order to seize ashtrays from tables or butts from the floor.[49]

Kippensammlung proved common enough to warrant advice columns in local papers. Editor Walter Kloeck, for instance, wrote a series of articles offering tips for prospective stub-collectors, using his own experiences of searching for cigarettes each night as evidence of his credibility, noting that his day job and nightly habit gave him a split personality *a la* Dr. Jekyll and Mr. Hyde. Unlike many who engaged in *Kippensammlung*, Kloeck explained that his involvement stemmed not from a desire to sell reconstituted cigarettes on the black market, but rather to supplement his tobacco rations so he would be able to offer dinner guests the opportunity to smoke. Most of Kloeck's recommendations focused on location; he suggested readers direct their energies to roads frequented by GIs rather than the actual destinations popular among soldiers, as "butts of very respectable length fly out" of American vehicles and "may lie up in the gutter for up to 15 seconds." More to the point, concentrating on the route as opposed to cafés, restaurants, and clubs would allow those looking for butts to avoid competition from the "street urchins [who] simply can't be beat."[50]

In addition to functioning as a coping mechanism, *Kippensammlung* was also a type of performance that revealed much about power and identity within the context of the occupation. The rituals, behaviors, and act of stub collecting created a forum, one that enabled both occupied personnel and Germans to communicate with one another. Many American accounts of *Kippensammlung* either emphasized frustration with German aggressiveness in the pursuit of stubs or criticized occupiers' callousness in toying with collectors. A member of the Women's Auxiliary Army Corps complained about bellicose waiters who prematurely snatched lit cigarettes from ashtrays, while GIs used the "B-Bag" section of *Stars & Stripes* to criticize the "undemocratic" Germans whose hounding of soldiers smoking cigarettes meant that GIs did not have the freedom to be left alone in public spaces.[51] In contrast, an American journalist stationed in Berlin recounted how one GI deliberately flaunted his act of smoking so as to attract a "circle of children, able-bodied men, and whiskered old men, all waiting to dive for the butt."[52] Although some soldiers advised field stripping cigarettes so that the remaining tobacco could be scattered about and local German Youth Activities clubs created spaces and opportunities for recreational and educational pursuits in city centers to discourage delinquent behavior, *Kippensammlung* remained a "universal practice" for several years after the war.[53]

The manner in which Americans discarded their cigarette butts shifted over the course of the occupation, particularly as new soldiers replaced combat veterans. Soldiers who had fought against the Wehrmacht expressed contempt for Germans through a very public and ritualistic destruction of cigarettes, typically by grinding the butt into the ground or disposing of them in water.[54] *Kippensammlung* provided fodder for cartoonists writing for *Stars & Stripes*. In one case, a hand enters the frame from the left in order to pick up a discarded butt, unaware of the fact that the cigarette stub had been placed there by a devious GI who attached it to a fishing wire; it was a trick clearly modeled after the dollar-bill-on-a-line prank familiar to those who grew up in Depression-era America.[55] These types of behavior reportedly declined in frequency over time, possibly because the new occupying personnel had not engaged German forces in armed combat during the war and thus felt less hostility toward the Germans that older occupiers did. Such a noticeable decline in the expression of animosity seems consistent with Atina Grossmann's arguments regarding the triangulated relationship between American occupiers, Germans, and DPs. Grossmann notes that in the two years just following the war, GIs often found it easier to relate to Germans than DPs, because DPs lived in camps, were seen as unhygienic, and were accused of controlling the black market.[56]

How soldiers disposed of cigarettes was not lost on the Germans. Several Germans who experienced the occupation as children recalled distinct differences between how American and French soldiers smoked. The French stationed in Erzingen "smoked cigarettes down to nothing" and would use needles as cigarette holders to ensure they smoked "the last bit until nearly nothing remained," forcing collectors to follow other "foreign visitors."[57] Such tactics denied loitering Germans the opportunity to scoop up the butt and, by extension, money. In contrast, German children in the U.S. zone remembered American GIs as being decidedly more generous. Whereas the French consumed practically the entire cigarette as a form of punishment and "German men smoked their cigarettes until they burned their fingers," the Americans in Bavaria "took a few puffs and then threw away their cigarettes."[58] The American method left "more than half of their cigarettes," which was a "real find."[59] Although such differences in smoking habits may have been a reflection of the material conditions and limited access to tobacco on the part of French soldiers or German civilians, many young Germans assigned meaning to these consumption and disposal practices, in large part because of the inflated economic and social importance of cigarettes and smoking in the occupation era. They viewed the Americans as generous because their abundance permitted improvidence; the French as vengeful given the deliberate nature of their tobacco consumption; and the Germans as poor in light of the fact that they could not afford to let any tobacco go to waste.

Countering the Cigarette Economy

Combating the black-market value of tobacco products became vital for reconstructing the German economy, since American occupation authorities believed illegal economic exchanges encouraged worker absenteeism, deprived legal markets of goods and consumers, and discouraged taxable economic transactions. Officials feared that the illicit economy's persistence could foster social and political instability, an uncomfortable possibility in the early stages of the Cold War. To prevent this, the occupation government introduced a broad array of countermeasures, ranging from intermittent raids of popular black-market sites and education campaigns discouraging personnel from bartering illegally to experiments with barter centers in larger cities. At the barter marts, established in Frankfurt, Stuttgart, and Berlin, Germans and occupation personnel could swap goods through a mediator. The barter marts represented the appropriation of black marketing, but relocated these social and economic encounters to a regulated space that held scheduled hours of operations and offered the military government a semblance of control. Appraisers assigned point values to the goods that Germans or Americans wished to trade and gave receipts to the supplier, which they then used to purchase commodities available in the barter mart. Proponents of the system heralded the barter centers' ability to create a "controlled medium of exchange between Americans and Germans," one that would be equitable given the role of the professional appraisers.[60] Germans would presumably acquire necessities, while Americans could purchase cameras, porcelain, and other souvenirs without risking arrest. Critics, however, feared that the barter marts simply offered convenient cover "for German and American black marketeers" who could thus effectively launder their illegal profits through official channels.[61]

Cigarettes posed a significant problem for the organizers and proponents of barter centers. Descriptions of barter marts often drew attention to the large congregations of people that gathered just outside of the facility, similar to how Germans and DPs flocked toward PX stores and commissaries in order to contact potential American suppliers. A member of the Hessian State Ministry for Economics and Price Control was critical of the Frankfurt center's impact, noting that he believed it had "enormously invigorated the black market."[62] The fact that GIs' cigarettes brought to the barter marts wound up on the black market was an open secret by late 1946 and prompted OMGUS to contemplate the possibility of prohibiting tobacco products altogether.[63]

Yet, as a potential alternative to black-market channels, the barter marts had to attract patrons, which would not happen if the centers did not accept cigarettes. Officials, moreover, feared Germans would not use the barter marts without the opportunity to acquire cigarettes through legitimate means and at a more reasonable price than the black market offered.[64] Hence, OMGUS felt compelled to accept tobacco products to lure Germans and Americans alike away from the black market. Nonetheless, their willingness to carry out exchanges in the sanctioned centers reinforced the use of cigarettes as a form of currency and appeared to have a negligible effect on black marketing.

In May 1947, OMGUS issued Ordinance No. 20, which prohibited all tobacco shipments into the U.S. zone, a measure driven by the ineffectiveness of the marts. The draconian regulation also empowered authorities to inspect and confiscate any shipment suspected of containing tobacco products. Guilty parties risked a five-year prison sentence and a fine of RM 100,000.[65] Despite concerns that the import ban might have violated civil liberties and the absence of any direct reference to the black market in the actual ordinance, General Clay hoped the move would "kill the heart" of the underground trade in cigarettes.[66] Advertisements from commercial shipping companies eventually disappeared, but enterprising participants found alternative means of smuggling tobacco into the U.S. zone. More importantly, prohibition encouraged black marketers to hoard their supplies, which, within three months, dramatically increased the black market cost of cigarettes, so much so that some felt they could "make enough on one killing to retire."[67]

Many Germans interpreted Ordinance No. 20 as a form of punishment and a potential threat to developing German-American relations. Surveys in Bavaria revealed that Germans of diverse social and political backgrounds were equally critical of the new measure. Church officials, local leaders of the Social Democrats, and newspaper editors all questioned the legitimacy and intent of the import ban. The *Süddeutsche Zeitung* characterized Ordinance No. 20 as OMGUS's deliberate attempt "to deprive the German people of every pleasure."[68] Clay insisted he "fully understood the importance of tobacco in the mind of the average German," but this did not prevent OMGUS from denying petitions submitted by individual Germans requesting the release of confiscated tobacco goods.[69] Petitioners typically emphasized war-related hardships or claimed the confiscated cigarettes were merely a gift and destined to be consumed rather than bartered on the black market.[70] Despite the general unpopularity of the ordinance, some praised the measure, including a Munich lawyer who attributed excessive black marketing to the working class. The ban, in his mind, would require workers to "cease to think in terms of cigarettes" and finally "have more regard for money."[71]

Thirteen months after the imposition of the import ban, the American and British military governments introduced the Deutsche Mark to "withdraw excess money from circulation, to eliminate the black market, and to create an incentive to produce."[72] The introduction of the new currency was accompanied by a relaxation of rationing and most price controls, in part to reduce the supposed necessity of the black market. Though currency reform was heralded as the beginning of the *Wirtschaftswunder* in West Germany, these economic measures did not result in the immediate availability of previously scarce goods or eliminate the black market in cigarettes.[73] Instead, the nature of black market transactions underwent a significant transformation with the appearance of the Deutsche Mark. What had been conducted out in the open was once again clandestine and increasingly associated with organized rackets, suggesting ordinary Germans no longer saw the cigarette economy as socially acceptable. The street price of cigarettes, meanwhile, was quite volatile in the immediate aftermath of currency reform. Within weeks of the Deutsche Mark's introduction, the black-market value of cigarettes dramatically dropped from DM 10 in late June to as low as DM 4 by the middle of July 1948.[74] The decreased black-market rates reflected a gradual increase in the overall supply of tobacco in Western Germany, as well as a change in the cigarette's basic role on the black market. No longer a principal form of black-market currency, cigarettes were now smuggled into Western Germany as part of criminal efforts to circumvent tobacco duties and sell cigarettes to consumers below retail prices.[75]

The postwar cigarette economy not only illustrated how differing amounts of access to tobacco products determined economic power, but also highlights the historically contingent nature of money and exchange values. Although black marketing had lost its status as a normalized behavior, the experience of privation and participation in the cigarette economy played important roles in shaping the early Federal Republic. The "mentality of scarcity" that emerged in the initial postwar period forced Germans and DPs to develop strategies to navigate shortages, which in turn contributed to a desire for normalcy that helped facilitate the transition to the social market economy in West Germany.[76] Although the occupation era left an indelible mark on the psyche of West German consumers in the 1950s, the new legal tender in 1948 gradually restored overall confidence in the Federal Republic's economic reconstruction.[77] Western Germany's social and economic transformation meant that the cigarette was once again seen primarily as a commodity designed to be consumed as opposed to an *ersatz* currency.

Kraig Larkin is Associate Professor of History at Colby-Sawyer College in New Hampshire. His research explores the connections between public health and consumer culture in modern Germany and America, with a particular emphasis on cigarette smoking.

Notes

1. Eugene Davidson, *The Death & Life of Germany: An Account of the American Occupation* (Columbia, MO, 1959), 85.
2. The term black market is used here to refer to a broad range of trades, including black marketing, bartering, trade-in-kind, and racketeering. Contemporaries often distinguished between such activities based upon the parties involved, the size of trades, and the objectives of the trading parties. See Paul Steege, *Black Market, Cold War: Everyday Life in Berlin, 1946–1949* (Cambridge, 2007), 50.
3. The National Archives of the United Kingdom (TNA): Public Records Office (PRO) FO 1034/43, "Die Welt," 13 May 1947.
4. Manfred J. Enssle, "The Harsh Discipline of Food Scarcity in Postwar Stuttgart, 1945–1948," *German Studies Review* 10, no. 3 (1987): 481–502.
5. Steege, *Black Market, Cold War*.
6. Laura J. Hilton, "The Black Market in History and Memory: German Perceptions of Victimhood from 1945 to 1948," *German Studies Review* 28, no. 4 (2010): 479–97; and Malte Zierenberg, *Stadt der Schieber: Der Berliner Schwarzmarkt, 1939–1950* (Göttingen, 2008).
7. Erving Goffman, *Asylums: Essays on the Social Situation of Mental Patients and Other Inmates* (Chicago, 1961), 265. Also see Georg Simmel, *The Philosophy of Money*, trans. Tom Bottomore and David Frisby (New York, 1990).
8. Thaddäus Troll, "Vom Schwarzen Markt," in *So lebten wir . . . : Ein Querschnitt durch 1947*, ed. Hans A. Rümelin (Stuttgart, 1997), 65.
9. "General McNarney's German Story," *Fraenkische Presse*, 15 September 1947; Fraenkische Press (FP); Scrutiny Reports of German Newspapers, 1945–1949 (SR), Records of the Press Branch (PB), Records of the Information Control Division (ICD); Records of the U.S. Occupation Headquarters, World War II, Record Group 260 (RG 260); National Archives at College Park, Maryland (NACP).
10. Robert N. Proctor, *The Nazi War on Cancer* (Princeton, NJ, 1999); Christoph Maria Merki, "Die nationalsozialistische Tabakpolitik," *Vierteljahrshefte für Zeitgeschichte* 46 (1998): 19–42; and Jonathan Lewy, "A Sober Reich? Alcohol and Tobacco Use in Nazi Germany," *Substance Use & Misuse* 41 (2006): 1179–95.
11. John Raleigh McCutcheon, *Behind the Nazi Front* (New York, 1940), 274–75.
12. William L. Smyser, "Rationing Cards for Tobacco Products," 12 November 1941; and Harrison Lewis, "German Economic Notes: Control System Introduced for Distribution of Tobacco Manufacturers," 6 March 1942; Narrative Reports 1950–1954 (NR); Records of the Foreign Agricultural Service (FAS); RG 166; NACP.
13. Sam E. Woods, "Tobacco Shops Required to Keep Open in Berlin," 19 May 1940; NR 1920–1941; RG 166; NACP.
14. Christoph Maria Merki, "Die amerikanische Zigarette—das Mass aller Dinge: Raucher in Deutschland zur Zeit der Zigarettenwährung," in *Tabakfragen: Rauchen aus kulturwissenschaftlicher Sicht*, ed. Thomas Hengartner and Christoph Maria Merki (Zürich, 1996), 62–63.
15. "Tobacco Situation," 10 March 1947; General Records of the Industry Branch (IB), Records of the Economic Division (ED); RG 260; NACP.
16. Walter Bähr and Hans W. Bähr, eds., *Kriegsbriefe Gefallener Studenten, 1939–1945* (Tübingen, 1952), 26–27.

17. Kurt Pohlisch, *Tabak: Betrachtungen über Genuss- und Rauschpharmaka* (Stuttgart, 1954), 168.
18. Maurice W. Altaffer, "Tobacco Industry in Western Germany," 12 October 1946; Germany: Requests-Tobacco; NR; FAS; RG 260; NACP.
19. "Application for Approval of Raw Tobacco Imports from Abroad," 22 July 1947; Records of the Bipartite Control Office; RG 260; NACP.
20. R. A. Radford, "The Economic Organization of a P.O.W. Camp," *Economica* 12, no. 48 (1945): 189–201; and Paul W. Meyer, *Die Zigarette als Generaltauschware im deutschen Schwarzen Markt 1945 bis 1948: Ein Beitrag zur Geldgeschichte und Geldtheorie* (Augsburg, 1984), 8–9.
21. Zierenberg, *Stadt der Schieber*, 280.
22. Jean Edward Smith, ed., *The Papers of General Lucius D. Clay: Germany, 1945–1949*, 2 vols (Bloomington, IN, 1974), vol. 2, 336.
23. "Stateside Newspaper Ponders Puzzles of Cigaret [sic] Currency," *Stars & Stripes*, 1 September 1946, 2.
24. Joel Sayer, "Letter from Berlin," in *The New Yorker Book of War Pieces* (New York, 1947), 505–6.
25. "Black Markets Underground in Bavaria," *Stars & Stripes*, 16 December 1945, 1.
26. Vladimir Petrov, *Money and Conquest: Allied Occupation Currencies in World War II* (Baltimore, MD, 1967), 205–6.
27. Arno Scholz, "Die Macht der runden Stäbchen," *Telegraf* 163, no. 2 (1947), 3.
28. Joel Carl Welty, *The Hunger Years in the French Zone of Divided Germany, 1946–1947* (Beloit, WI, 1993), 26. On fraternization, see Perry Biddiscombe, "Dangerous Liaisons: The Anti-Fraternization Movement in the U.S. Occupation Zones of Germany and Austria, 1945–1948," *Journal of Social History* 34, no. 3 (2001): 611–47; Suzanne zur Nieder, "Erotic Fraternization: The Legend of German Women's Quick Surrender," in *Home/Front: The Military, War and Gender in Twentieth-Century Germany*, ed. Karen Hagemann and Stefanie Schüler-Springorum (New York, 2002), 297–310; and John Willoughby, *Remaking the Conquering Heroes: The Social and Geopolitical Impact of the Post-War American Occupation of Germany* (New York, 2001).
29. Troll, "Vom Schwarzen Markt," 63.
30. Hilde Thurnwald, *Gegenwarts-Probleme Berliner Familien: Eine Soziologische Untersuchung an 498 Familien* (Berlin, 1948), 81–83. For shipping, see Lt. Col. G. H. Garde to Chief of the Civil Affairs Division, undated; General Correspondence (GC), Office of the Adjutant General (OAG), Executive Office (EO); RG 260; NACP. The black-market trade in cigarettes was also extensive in the Soviet zone of occupation. Most of the trade was organized by the Rasno Export agency, which was backed by the Soviet military occupation and sought to use the high demand for tobacco products as a means of collecting foreign currencies. See J. P. Nettl, *The Eastern Zone and Soviet Policy in Germany, 1945–1950* (New York, 1951), 227; Norman Naimark, *The Russians in Germany: A History of the Soviet Zone of Occupation, 1945–1949* (Cambridge, MA, 1995), 34; and Jörg Roesler, "The Black Market in Post-War Berlin and the Methods Used to Counteract It," *German History* 7, no. 1 (1989): 92–107.
31. Supplement to Weekly Intelligence Report No. 7 for Week Ending 18 February 1949; Office of the Military Government, Bavaria (OMGB), Records of the Control Office (CO); RG 260; NACP.
32. Alan Kramer, "Law-Abiding Germans? Social Disintegration, Crime and the Reimposition of Order in Post-War Western Germany," in *The German Underworld:*

Deviants and Outcasts in German History, ed. Richard J. Evans (New York, 1988), 238–60; and Enssle, "The Harsh Discipline," 492.
33. Atina Grossmann, *Jews, Germans, and Allies: Close Encounters in Occupied Germany* (Princeton, NJ, 2007), 162–76; Michael Berkowitz, *The Crime of My Very Existence: Nazism and the Myth of Jewish Criminality* (Berkeley, CA, 2007), 188–94; and Hilton, "The Black Market in History and Memory," 482–83.
34. Werner Abelshauser, *Der Ruhrkohlenbergbau seit 1945: Wiederaufbau, Krise, Anpassung* (Munich, 1984), 7.
35. Ernst Deissmann, "Report submitted to the German Executive Committee on the Miners' Point Scheme," March 1947; General Records of the Consumer Goods Section, 1946–49, ED; RG 260; NACP.
36. G. Schmidt to Bipartite Economic Control Group, 20 May 1947; Subject: Gift Parcel Cigarette Service; IB, ED; RG 260; NACP.
37. TNA: PRO FO 1046/243, Reparations, Deliveries & Restitution Division to Revenue Branch, 10 November 1947; G. H. Garde to Commanding General, 7 January 1947; GC, OAG, EO; RG 260; NACP.
38. Michael Wildt, *Der Traum von Sattwerden: Hunger und Protest, Schwarzmarkt und Selbsthilfe* (Hamburg, 1986), 87–90.
39. John M. Warde, "Report of Discussion Held with Mr. A. M. Spears, Tobacco Expert, Handicrafts and Economic Inspectorate, CCG, at Minden," 24 March 1947; BECG (US) Tobacco; GR, IB, ED; RG 260; NACP.
40. Merki, "Die amerikanische Zigarette—das Mass aller Dinge," 62–63.
41. Tony Kellen, *Tabak im Garten: Anbau und Fermentation für jedermann* (Stuttgart, 1946), 6.
42. F. A. Dieckmann, *Tabak aus heimischen Kräutern: Anleitung zur Sammlung und Zubereitung von Kräutertabak* (Berlin, 1946), 3.
43. Alfred Emil Lattinger, *Der Tabak-Eigenbau* (Graz, 1946), 3; Dieckmann, *Tabak aus heimischen Kräutern*, 3–4.
44. Kellen, *Tabak im Garten*, 6.
45. "Now You Tell One . . ." *Red Circle News*, 27 September 1945, 2; OMGB/Intel/"Bavarian" (Newspaper) 27 Sep 45–31 Jan 46 (Bav.); OMGB; CO, EO; RG 260; NACP.
46. *The Marriage of Maria Braun*, directed by Rainer Werner Fassbinder (1979; New York: Criterion Collection, 2003), DVD.
47. *Trend: A Report of Political Analysis and Public Opinion*, No. 47, 29 October 1947 (13–30 October 1947); 13/142–3 10a Trend Bavaria 1946/1948 #28–54 (Trend Bav.); Records of the Land Director (LD); Reports, Division Publications & Related Records, 1945–49; OMGB; RG 260; NACP.
48. Julian Bach Jr., *America's Germany: An Account of the Occupation* (New York, 1946), 69–70.
49. Arthur Noyes, "Cigarette Butts Make Waiters Rich in Vienna," *Stars & Stripes*, 6 January 1946, 3.
50. "Collecting of Stubs," FP, 27 August 1947; FP; SR, PB, ICD; RG 260; NACP.
51. Major Anne E. Alinder, Bulletin No. 4, 2 November 1945; Research Center, Wisconsin Veterans Museum; T/5 Philip C. Howse, 9th Inf. Div., "Let GI Maintain His Own Self-Respect," *Stars & Stripes*, 6 December 1946, 2.
52. Sayer, "Letter from Berlin," 505–6.

53. "Bremen Boys Club: A U.S. Sergeant Finances a Lesson in Democracy," *Life*, 9 December 1946, 46–47.
54. Walter C. Krause, *So I Was a Sergeant: Memoirs of an Occupation Soldier* (Hicksville, NY, 1978), 36.
55. Shep, "Occupation," *Stars & Stripes*, 16 July 1946, 2.
56. Grossmann, *Jews, Germans, and Allies*, 175–78.
57. Wolfgang W. E. Samuel, *The War of Our Childhood: Memories of World War II* (Jackson, MS, 2002), 241–42.
58. Ibid., 31.
59. Ibid., 242.
60. Smith, *The Papers of General Lucius D. Clay*, 276–79.
61. Lt. Col. James E. O'Steen to the Director, Office of Military Government, Hesse (OMGH), Irregularities Connected with the Frankfurt Barter Market, 24 September 1947, 2; GC, OAG, EO; RG 260; NACP. Also see Frank Grube and Gerhard Richter, *Die Schwarzmarktzeit: Deutschland Zwischen 1945 und 1948* (Hamburg, 1979), 79.
62. Schulte to Dept. Trade; Barter Centers; OMGH; GR, EB; Bipartite Liaisons Division; RG 260; NACP.
63. "Army is Battling Cigarette Barter," *The New York Times*, 27 December 1946, 8; Herbert M. Bratter, "An Economy Based on Cigarettes," *Nation's Business* (June 1947), 42.
64. Madlen Lorei and Richard Kirn, *Frankfurt und die drei wilden Jahre: Ein Bericht* (Frankfurt, 1962), 142–44.
65. Ordinance No. 20: Prohibition Against the Import of Cigarettes and Other Tobacco Products; OMGUS Directive AG 010.6 (LD) 22 November 47; Foreign (Occupied) Area Reports; Operations Branch, Administrative Services Division; RG 407; NACP.
66. Meyer, *Die Zigarette als Generaltauschware*, 17.
67. Russell Jones, "Cigaret [sic] Market in Berlin Rises Slowly After Drop: Operators Waiting for Top Price," *Stars & Stripes*, 12 August 1947, 3; "EES Reports Theft of 750 Cartons," *Stars & Stripes*, 12 August 1947, 3.
68. *Trend: A Report of Political Analysis and Public Opinion* 40, 19 June 1947 (Trend 40); Trend Bav.; LD; OMGB; RG 260; NACP.
69. "Ban on Cigarets in EC to Remain, Clay Tells Press," *Stars & Stripes*, 4 June 1947, 1.
70. Letter to General Clay, AG 439 Tobacco; GC, OAG, EO; RG 260; NACP.
71. *Trend: A Report of Political Analysis and Public Opinion* 40, 19 June 1947.
72. Dennis L. Bark and David R. Gress, *A History of West Germany: From Shadow to Substance, 1945–1963* (Cambridge, 1989), 198.
73. Mark E. Spicka, *Selling the Economic Miracle: Reconstruction and Politics in West Germany, 1949–1957* (New York, 2007), 26–48.
74. Saul Kagan to Burnett, 19 August 1948; Currency Reform Vol. III 1948 (Currency Reform); GC, OAG, EO; RG 260; NACP.
75. This shift is comparable to the black marketeering in cigarettes that occurred in Germany at the end of the twentieth century, where higher retail prices fostered illegal transactions at lower rates. See Klaus von Lampe, "Explaining the Emergence of the Cigarette Black Market in Germany," in *The Organised Crime Economy: Managing Crime Markets in Europe*, ed. Petrus C. Van Duyne et al. (Nijmegen, 2005), 209–29.
76. Manfred J. Enssle, "Five Theses on German Everyday Life after World War II," *Central European History* 26, no. 1 (1993): 15.

77. Michael Wildt, "Continuities and Discontinuities of Consumer Mentality in West Germany in the 1950s," in *Life After Death: Approaches to a Cultural and Social History of Europe During the 1940s and 1950s*, ed. Richard Bessel and Dirk Schumann (Washington, DC, 2003), 214.

Bibliography

Abelshauser, Werner. *Der Ruhrkohlenbergbau seit 1945: Wiederaufbau, Krise, Anpassung*. Munich, 1984.

"Army Is Battling Cigarette Barter." *The New York Times*, 27 December 1946, 8.

Bach, Julian, Jr. *America's Germany: An Account of the Occupation*. New York, 1946.

Bähr, Walter, and Hans W. Bähr, eds. *Kriegsbriefe Gefallener Studenten, 1939–1945*. Tübingen, 1952.

"Ban on Cigarets [sic] in EC to Remain, Clay Tells Press." *Stars & Stripes*, 4 June 1947, 1.

Bark, Dennis L., and David R. Gress. *A History of West Germany: From Shadow to Substance, 1945–1963*. Cambridge, 1989.

Berkowitz, Michael. *The Crime of My Very Existence: Nazism and the Myth of Jewish Criminality*. Berkeley, CA, 2007.

Biddiscombe, Perry. "Dangerous Liaisons: The Anti-Fraternization Movement in the U.S. Occupation Zones of Germany and Austria, 1945–1948." *Journal of Social History* 34, no. 3 (2001): 611–47.

"Black Markets Underground in Bavaria." *Stars & Stripes*, 16 December 1945.

Bratter, Herbert M. "An Economy Based on Cigarettes." *Nation's Business*, June 1947, 41–42 and 77.

"Bremen Boys Club: A U.S. Sergeant Finances a Lesson in Democracy." *Life*, 9 December 1946, 46–47.

Davidson, Eugene. *The Death & Life of Germany: An Account of the American Occupation*. Columbia, MO, 1959.

Dieckmann, F.A. *Tabak aus heimischen Kräutern: Anleitung zur Sammlung und Zubereitung von Kräutertabak*. Berlin, 1946.

"EES Reports Theft of 750 Cartons." *Stars & Stripes*, 12 August 1947, 3.

Enssle, Manfred J. "Five Theses on German Everyday Life after World War II." *Central European History* 26, no. 1 (1993): 1–19.

———. "The Harsh Discipline of Food Scarcity in Postwar Stuttgart, 1945–1948." *German Studies Review* 10, no. 3 (1987): 481–502.

Goffman, Erving. *Asylums: Essays on the Social Situation of Mental Patients and Other Inmates*. Chicago, 1961.

Grossmann, Atina. *Jews, Germans, and Allies: Close Encounters in Occupied Germany*. Princeton, NJ, 2007.

Grube, Frank, and Gerhard Richter. *Die Schwarzmarktzeit: Deutschland Zwischen 1945 und 1948*. Hamburg, 1979.

Hilton, Laura J. "The Black Market in History and Memory: German Perceptions of Victimhood from 1945 to 1948." *German Studies Review* 28, no. 4 (2010): 479–97.

Jones, Russell. "Cigaret [sic] Market in Berlin Rises Slowly After Drop: Operators Waiting for Top Price." *Stars & Stripes*, 12 August 1947, 3.
Kellen, Tony. *Tabak im Garten: Anbau und Fermentation für jedermann*. Stuttgart, 1946.
Kramer, Alan. "Law-Abiding Germans? Social Disintegration, Crime and the Reimposition of Order in Post-War Western Germany." In *The German Underworld: Deviants and Outcasts in German History*, edited by Richard J. Evans, 238–60. New York, 1988.
Krause, Walter C. *So I Was a Sergeant: Memoirs of an Occupation Soldier*. Hicksville, NY, 1978.
Lampe, Klaus von. "Explaining the Emergence of the Cigarette Black Market in Germany." In *The Organised Crime Economy: Managing Crime Markets in Europe*, edited by Petrus C. Van Duyne, Klaus von Lapme, Maarten van Dijck, and James L. Newel, 209–29. Nijmegen, 2005.
Lattinger, Alfred Emil. *Der Tabak-Eigenbau*. Graz, 1946.
"Let GI Maintain His Own Self-Respect." *Stars & Stripes*, 6 December 1946, 2.
Lewy, Jonathan. "A Sober Reich? Alcohol and Tobacco Use in Nazi Germany." *Substance Use & Misuse* 41 (2006): 1179–95.
Lorei, Madlen, and Richard Kirn. *Frankfurt und die drei wilden Jahre: Ein Bericht*. Frankfurt, 1962.
The Marriage of Maria Braun. Directed by Rainer Werner Fassbinder. 1979. New York: Criterion Collection, 2003. DVD.
McCutcheon, John Raleigh. *Behind the Nazi Front*. New York, 1940.
Merki, Christoph Maria. "Die amerikanische Zigarette—das Mass aller Dinge: Raucher in Deutschland zur Zeit der Zigarettenwährung." In *Tabakfragen: Rauchen aus kulturwissenschaftlicher Sicht*, edited by Thomas Hengartner and Christoph Maria Merki, 57–82. Zürich, 1996.
———. "Die nationalsozialistische Tabakpolitik." *Vierteljahrshefte für Zeitgeschichte* 46 (1998): 19–42.
Meyer, Paul W. *Die Zigarette als Generaltauschware im deutschen Schwarzen Markt 1945 bis 1948: Ein Beitrag zur Geldgeschichte und Geldtheorie*. Augsburg, 1984.
Naimark, Norman. *The Russians in Germany: A History of the Soviet Zone of Occupation, 1945–1949*. Cambridge, MA, 1995.
Nettl, J. P. *The Eastern Zone and Soviet Policy in Germany, 1945–1950*. New York, 1951.
Nieder, Suzanne zur. "Erotic Fraternization: The Legend of German Women's Quick Surrender." In *Home/Front: The Military, War and Gender in Twentieth-Century Germany*, edited by Karen Hagemann and Stefanie Schüler-Springorum. 297–310. New York, 2002.
Noyes, Arthur. "Cigarette Butts Make Waiters Rich in Vienna." *Stars & Stripes*, 6 January 1946, 3.
Petrov, Vladimir. *Money and Conquest: Allied Occupation Currencies in World War II*. Baltimore, MD, 1967.

Pohlisch, Kurt. *Tabak: Betrachtungen über Genuss- und Rauschpharmaka.* Stuttgart, 1954.
Proctor, Robert N. *The Nazi War on Cancer.* Princeton, NJ, 1999.
Radford, R. A. "The Economic Organization of a P.O.W. Camp." *Economica* 12, no. 48 (1945): 189–201.
Roesler, Jörg. "The Black Market in Post-War Berlin and the Methods Used to Counteract It." *German History* 7, no. 1 (1989): 92–107.
Samuel, Wolfgang W. E. *The War of Our Childhood: Memories of World War II.* Jackson, MS, 2002.
Sayer, Joel. "Letter from Berlin." In *The New Yorker Book of War Pieces.* New York, 1947.
Scholz, Arno. "Die Macht der runden Stäbchen." *Telegraf,* 16 July 1947, 3.
Shep. "Occupation." *Stars & Stripes,* 16 July 1946, 2.
Simmel, Georg. *The Philosophy of Money.* Translated by Tom Bottomore and David Frisby. New York, 1990.
Smith, Jean Edward, ed. *The Papers of General Lucius D. Clay: Germany, 1945–1949,* 2 vols. Bloomington, IN, 1974.
Spicka, Mark E. *Selling the Economic Miracle: Reconstruction and Politics in West Germany, 1949–1957.* New York, 2007.
"Stateside Newspaper Ponders Puzzles of Cigaret [sic] Currency." *Stars & Stripes,* 1 September 1946, 2.
Steege, Paul. *Black Market, Cold War: Everyday Life in Berlin, 1946–1949.* Cambridge, 2007.
Thurnwald, Hilde. *Gegenwarts-Probleme Berliner Familien: Eine Soziologische Untersuchung an 498 Familien.* Berlin, 1948.
Troll, Thaddäus. "Vom Schwarzen Markt." In *So lebten wir . . . : Ein Querschnitt durch 1947,* edited by Hans A. Rümelin, 62–66. Stuttgart, 1997.
Welty, Joel Carl. *The Hunger Years in the French Zone of Divided Germany, 1946–1947.* Beloit, WI, 1993.
Wildt, Michael. "Continuities and Discontinuities of Consumer Mentality in West Germany in the 1950s." In *Life After Death: Approaches to Cultural and Social History of Europe During the 1940s and 1950s,* edited by Richard Bessel and Dirk Schumann, 211–29. Washington, DC, 2003.
———. *Der Traum von Sattwerden: Hunger und Protest, Schwarzmarkt und Selbsthilfe.* Hamburg, 1986.
Willoughby, John. *Remaking the Conquering Heroes: The Social and Geopolitical Impact of the Post-War American Occupation of Germany.* New York, 2001.
Zierenberg, Malte. *Stadt der Schieber: Der Berliner Schwarzmarkt, 1939–1950.* Göttingen, 2008.

CHAPTER SIXTEEN

When the Deutsch Mark Was in Short Supply
Reconstruction Finance between Currency Reform and "Economic Miracle"

ARMIN GRÜNBACHER

The Wirtschaftswunder Myth

In (West) German public memory, the currency reform of 20 June 1948 is seen as the single pivotal moment that ended the economic woes of the immediate postwar years and heralded the beginning of the "Economic Miracle" and West Germany's meteoric economic recovery. However, the economic reality was quite different, and in 1948, the outcome of Minister of Economics Ludwig Erhard's neoliberal experiment was far from certain.[1] While the currency reform was necessary to stabilize the West German currency, not least so that the three western zones of occupation (which were soon to be transformed into the Federal Republic of Germany) could successfully participate in the Marshall Plan, the currency reform had also huge short-term drawbacks. The downsides to the currency reform included negative social effects for large parts of the population and a massive reduction in monetary supply that had detrimental impacts for the reconstruction.

Nazi war finance had completely wrecked sound fiscal policy, and government debt had increased almost forty-fold from RM 11 million (Reichsmarks) in 1932 to RM 380 million in 1945; only the continued use of wartime economic controls by the allied military governors prevented rampant inflation and further economic decline in the immediate postwar years.[2] The American-led currency reform converted the Reichsmark in circulation into the new Deutsche Mark on the basis of 10:1, the most severe conversion rate in German history.[3] Overall, money supply was reduced by 93.5 percent, but what people remembered was the issuing of a per capita quota (*Kopfgeld*) of DM 40 to each person on the day of the reform, which helped to establish the myth that "we all started out with DM 40."

The severe reduction in money supply, together with Erhard's *Leitsätze Gesetz*, which abolished all rationing as well as price controls except for rent, basic foodstuffs, and basic commodities (fuel, electricity, steel, and coal) had an immediate, not least psychological, effect.[4] Overnight, shop windows were full again with goods that had not been on sale for years. Werner Abelshauser sarcastically noted that after the reform, "even the cows gave more milk" because goods previously withheld for black-market trading or hoarded in anticipation of the reform reappeared.[5] Companies and traders were now able to sell with considerable profit the goods they had hoarded prior to the currency reform to a population that had been starved for years of everything from basic consumer goods to foodstuffs; many people were prepared to pay high prices for these newly available goods. The resulting economic flurry led to a profit inflation in which working-class people and refugees struggled to pay the prices charged for all but the basic foodstuffs.[6] With prices rising but wages still fixed, the situation deteriorated so much that the trade unions called for a twenty-four-hour general strike against profiteering, which took place on 12 November 1948.[7] Because of the growing social inequality, Erhard faced and only narrowly survived two votes of no-confidence in the Economic Council, the quasi-parliamentary body of the combined Anglo-American occupation zone.[8]

The other most obvious negative effect of the currency reform was a sharp rise in unemployment. In the face of scarce liquidity, companies began to lay off workers whom they had kept on when they had been able to pay them in practically worthless but plentiful old Reichsmark. Unemployment rose from 3.2 percent in the second quarter of 1948 and reached a peak of 12.2 percent, or two million people out of work in February 1950, putting considerable pressure on the new West German federal government, which responded half-heartedly by initiating a cobbled-together work creation scheme.[9]

Not least because of the rising unemployment and the profit inflation, the value of the Deutsche Mark dropped on the international money markets, and the Bank deutscher Länder (BdL) had to tighten borrowing as a countermeasure.[10]

Despite the inflation, it was actually the scarcity of the new currency that had a severe detrimental impact on reconstruction, which was exacerbated by BdL monetary policy. Within the first six months after the currency reform, money in circulation increased massively, from just over DM 6 billion in June to more than DM 14.3 billion in December 1948, and bank credits rose from practically zero to DM 5.2 billion. Nonetheless, this volume of money was still only a fraction of the amount of old Reichsmark that had been in circulation.[11]

Worse, hardly any of this money was available for long-term loans, which were necessary for a successful reconstruction program. In 1949, free liquid bank reserves in West Germany were a mere DM 300 million.[12] During the first year of the Deutsche Mark, 77 percent of all investments were financed by short-term loans or company self-financing.[13] With such a tight money supply, it is not surprising that by the end of 1948, profit inflation gave way to deflation due to a lack of consumer spending and because of the BdL's money tightening.

These structural impediments to West German economic reconstruction resulted, ironically, from the currency reform and Erhard's subsequent *Leitsätze Gesetz*. In order to reestablish sound finances, the Americans thought that a 10:1 conversion of Reichsmark to the new Deutsche Mark was necessary but by applying such a harsh ratio, they reduced the amount of investment finance available for economic reconstruction. Both the *Leitsätze Gesetz* and Erhard's general economic policies exacerbated the situation. Erhard believed that the economic recovery should be based on the consumer goods industries, and he therefore reversed Anglo-American strategies that the military governments had introduced after the winter crisis of 1946–47. Their policy had put all available resources into the basic industries, in particular coal, in an attempt to get the disrupted economy back to normal again by providing sufficient basic materials. With consumer goods industries' prices freed but those of the basic industries still fixed at relatively low levels—not least in order to support the consumer industries with lower input prices—banks preferred to give the little investment money they had as short-term credits to the light and consumer industries instead of long-term loans to the basic industries in the expectations of faster and higher returns.[14]

The Nazi war economy with its insufficient investment and the accepted running down of equipment and assets, as well as the damage caused by the war, meant that the basic industries had a huge backlog of urgent capital investments that simply could not be satisfied by the German capital market in the years after the currency reform. Months before the reform, Erhard had been fully aware that West Germany's investment capital would be inadequate for the huge task ahead. In a speech to trade union representatives in February 1948, he admitted as much but explained that he expected to raise all the capital necessary for reconstruction from foreign sources so that the German GDP could be used exclusively for consumption.[15] It is not clear if Erhard really believed that foreign funds, and he was referring most likely to Marshall Plan counterpart funds, would be sufficient for this task, or if he was simply stoking the unrealistically high expectations the Germans had for the European Recovery Program (ERP), as the Marshall Plan was officially called. In light of other comments, Erhard made around this time in his capacity as chairman of the *Sonderstelle Geld und Kredit*, the German body which planned for the currency reform, it is clear that he believed that reconstruction should be based on the consumer industries and not on heavy industry. In order to implement this idea, he explained, that he was prepared to accept a delay of the reconstruction process by five to ten years.[16] Such a dogmatic and ideological approach would very soon come to haunt the Minister of Economics; his intention to finance the long-term investment necessary for the reconstruction with Marshall Plan counterpart funds did not materialize before the autumn of 1949 due to lack of funds. The myth of the Wirtschaftswunder thus developed in three stages: the first one was visible immediately with the currency reform and the full shop windows when previously hoarded goods or those traded on the black market became available again. The second stage was the August 1949 general election result, which, due to Erhard's Düsseldorf Principles and despite significant economic setbacks, resulted in a narrow Christian Democratic Union victory. This allowed Erhard not only to stay in office but with the help of his excellent press contacts and sponsoring from industry, to continue a massive propaganda campaign for the social market economy in the mass media.[17] When the economic boom arrived by 1952–53, it was export driven and not really of Erhard's making, but it served as German exculpation from the Nazi crimes and the emergence of the *Wir-sind-wieder-wer* mentality. There was little interest in the collective memory to remember the "bad times" before 1945 or the devastation 1945–50, as neither fitted the image of "good Germans" and the heroic legend of German economic recovery from ruins.

The Kreditanstalt für Wiederaufbau

American military governor and Marshall Plan administrators were disappointed and annoyed with the German reliance, even fixation, on Marshall Plan funds. In his frustration, General Clay, the U.S. military governor in Germany, went so far as to call the existence of the Marshall Plan counterpart funds the "biggest evil" for the German economy because, as he explained, he had not seen a single German reconstruction proposal that was not based on those funds.[18] However, Marshall Plan deliveries to West Germany during 1948 were so slow to materialize that the Marshall Plan advisor to the bizonal Economic Council had to write two reports at the end of 1948. The "official" report for the public presented sugar-coated figures in order to keep up public morale; a confidential report that contained the real figures was for the administration's internal use only.[19] It was only in December 1949 that the first sizable sum from the counterpart funds, just over DM 1 billion, was authorized by the Marshall Plan administration for release to German authorities.[20] The counterpart funds arose from German companies having to pay the Deutsche Mark equivalent of the dollar value of the goods they received under the Marshall Plan into special accounts (ERP Counterpart Accounts) held at the

Bank deutscher Länder. With the permission of the ERP Administration, these funds were then lent by the German government as revolving investment funds at 5.5 percent interest for reconstruction projects.[21]

The most important of the German reconstruction agencies was the Kreditanstalt für Wiederaufbau (KfW), a bank set up through bizonal legislation in November 1948. Initially financed by the German *Länder* and the Economic Council in equal parts to the sum of DM 1 million, the KfW was the brain child of Hermann Josef Abs, a former (and eventually again after 1957) director of Deutsche Bank who also became deputy director of the KfW's supervisory board and was its central figure. Abs had also been the driving force in drafting the KfW bill.[22] The foresight he displayed in the process would become essential for the bank's operation and thus, despite all problems and limitations, for the successful running of reconstruction finance, as shown below by way of example of the coal industry.

In the late 1940s, West Germany was confronted with a massive reconstruction project: construct six million housing units for refugees and bombed-out civilians; repair, rehabilitate, and in some cases, replace, industrial plants; rebuild destroyed civil infrastructure. In the face of insufficient investment capital, the work of the KfW, which was called "a characteristic German arrangement" by Andrew Shonfield for its cooperation between public authorities and private business, became a crucial tool in the reconstruction period.[23]

A further reason for the delayed release of the counterpart funds to the KfW (other than the slow accumulation of the funds) had been American demands for the provision of German funding as well. Those U.S. expectations proved very quickly to be unrealistic. In March 1949, the Munich-based newspaper *Die Neue Zeitung* reported that of the expected DM 100 million *Pfandbrief* issue, which was part of an overall attempt to raise DM 1 billon for reconstruction purposes, only DM 30 million were signed.[24] The KfW also experienced a practically nonexistent capital market in West Germany when it tried to issue bonds in September 1949. The assumption that a 3.5-percent tax-exempt bond would raise some DM 300 million, designated solely for housing construction, turned out to be wishful thinking. Bonds worth a mere DM 8 million could be placed, despite the fact that the military governments had allowed the use of blocked saving accounts for the purchase of these bonds. Similarly, a tax-reduced, 5.5-percent bond achieved a placement of DM 50 million overall, but only because Abs had been able to receive a guarantee from banks for this sum. The actual sale on the open market brought a mere DM 22 million, with the banks' guarantee covering the remaining DM 28 million. Even the KfW called this result "measly." The situation proved wrong those banking representatives on the KfW's supervisory board, who had opposed the issuing of the bonds with the argument that the KfW would scoop West Germany's capital market, to the detriment of the traditional banks.[25] To put the scale of the problem into perspective, between the currency reform and the end of 1953, the German capital market was able to raise only a total of DM 7 billion.[26] It was therefore not surprising when in their first annual report, published in March 1950, the Kreditanstalt stated in very plain language that the German capital market was nonfunctional. The relatively small investment funds available from counterpart funds had therefore to be used to counterbalance the existing market distortions (which had arisen in part because of Erhard's economic policy); their release and utilization had to follow for the foreseeable future a "predetermined plan" and could not be left to be decided by market forces.[27]

In view of the gigantic task of rebuilding West Germany's national economy after the most devastating war in history, it was quite clear that Erhard's claim of funding all investment from outside funds, i.e. Marshall Plan counterpart funds, was sheer fantasy. According to calculations by Egon Baumgart, some DM 81.1 billion were spent in West Germany for reconstruction and investment from 1949 to 1952, the amount growing to DM 226 billion by 1956.[28] Until December 1952, only DM 5.35 billion had accumulated in the Marshall Plan counterpart fund accounts.[29] Nevertheless, during the 1949 to 1951 period, the reconstruction finance from counterpart funds contributed a small, but significant share to the overall reconstruction finance (see Table 16.1).

The effect of the counterpart funds for basic industry was considerably bigger than the figures suggest, and the funds had a significant multiplier effect for the rest of the economy since these sectors, particularly the coal industry, were strategic bottleneck sectors on which the reconstruction process as a whole was dependent. It was estimated in 1948–49 that the coal mining industry would need DM 1.5 billion over the next three years to be able to meet its investment requirements. Because Erhard wanted to subsidize the consumer goods industries with cheap energy prices through a low price of coal, he did not press the Allies, who were ultimately in charge of the coal price,

Table 16.1. Share of ERP Loans in Gross Capital Investments in the Federal Republic 1949–56† (in percent).

	1949	1950	1951	1952	1953	1954	1955	1956
Total	5.8	7.8	4.1	2.1	1.9	1.3	1.6	1.1
Commercial Enterprises	6.4	8.6	4.5	2.3	2.1	1.4	1.8	1.3
Industry‡	7.1	13.3	4.6	2.3	2.0	1.9	2.1	0.6

† Without Berlin.
‡ Without building industry, electricity industry, and small businesses.

Source: Baumgart, *Investitionen*, 50.

for a further increase (although he had supported a small increase in August 1948). With coal prices remaining well below real-market prices, investments in the pits could not come from the sale of coal.[30] Instead, a quarter of all counterpart funds released in 1949 for reconstruction went into coal mining, where they provided a staggering 47 percent of all capital investment, while in 1950, 13.2 percent of counterparts released provided still a considerable 40 percent of all investments in that sector.[31]

The high share of counterparts for investment into the crucial coal mines came about because "normal" banks were not willing to lend significant sums of money to the coal mines while their ownership status and future company structure were still to be decided by the Allies. Until this had happened, the coal mining companies had very little collateral that they could offer as security for their loans. As a matter of fact, of a total of DM 570 million given to the pits from the counterpart funds via the KfW by the end of 1951, less than DM 38 million had any security at all.[32] Some of these loans were actually used to pay for the purchase of equipment that had come into the country under the Marshall Plan because the pits could not get other credit.[33] During 1949, the need for loans to the coal mining industry had become so great and available funds so limited that because of the insufficient funds available, the KfW had to resort to a system of financing the coal mines that was not dissimilar, except for its scale, to the *Mefo* system the Nazis had used to finance their rearmament program.[34] The KfW accepted bills of exchange issued by the coal mines, which were then offered to banks but without any obligation by the banks to prolong them, leaving any default risk with the KfW. Even senior German officials felt very uncomfortable with such arrangements. Indeed, the only "security" the KfW received were Allied assurances that it would be the first to make a mortgage claim against the collieries once those were released from Allied control. When the Economic Cooperation Administration (ECA), as the Marshall Plan administration was officially called, released the first DM 150 million for the coal mining industries, one third of this sum had to be used immediately to redeem those bills of exchange. German authorities, in particular Bank deutscher Länder, which ultimately had to authorize and sanction the scheme, had gone along with the plan only in anticipation of the large-scale release of counterpart funds.[35]

Table 16.2. Production Output of Industry and Coal Mining, 1946–51 (1936 = 100).

	1946	1947	1948	1949	1950	1951
All Industry	34	44	63	90	130	141
Coal Mining	51	65	81	96	109	116

Source: Grünbacher, *Reconstruction*, 133.

The consequences of Erhard's policy of favoring consumer goods and investment goods industries over basic industries became visible rather quickly, as the growth in output demonstrates (see Table 16.2).

Because of the Allies' efforts to raise Ruhr coal production, which was also essential for wider European reconstruction, output growth for all industries had considerably trailed those in the coal industry for the period 1946 to 1948. However, the effects of Erhard's policy, insufficient investments in coal production, and the new possibilities after the currency reform for tax depreciation for light and consumer industries (which allowed large-scale self-financing), meant that by 1950, positions had reversed, and coal output and supply could not keep pace with industrial growth and demand.[36]

The Korean War and the Investitionshilfe Gesetz

Initially, the effect of this development went unnoticed, but when the Korean Conflict broke out on 25 June 1950, the negative impact was demonstrated quickly and with strong impact. Immediately world raw material prices increased on average by 25 percent. This amplified West Germany's balance of payment deficit, which had been barely covered by Marshall Plan imports, to a crisis point because the country's export industries, which were still in the process of recovery, were unable to earn enough foreign currency to pay for the increased cost of raw material imports. By February 1951, West Germany's trade liberalization measures had to be suspended, and the European Payment Union (EPU) had to grant the Federal Republic a special line of credit to keep the country trading, while the central bank tightened the availability of credit and reduced foreign trade licenses.[37] Furthermore, the Americans demanded, very much to the anger of Erhard and Chancellor Adenauer, that the German economy had to bear some of the costs of the Western war effort—and if they were not willing to do so would suffer suspension of Marshall Aid.[38] The third big impact, the resulting coal shortages, was the most embarrassing for Erhard and caused serious problems for his economic policy. With the outbreak of the war in Korea, Western countries switched their industrial production from reconstruction back to armaments, which lead to short supply in all areas of civilian and investment goods. The only country that had spare production capacities and was able to fill the shortfall was West Germany. The resulting expansion in output in the investment and consumer industries was so rapid that the lack of investment into the basic industries became fully exposed, a situation most noticeable in the coal industry because output could not keep up with the increased demand.[39] Despite the KfW's loans to the mining industry, coal was the most pressing topic on the government's cabinet agenda during 1951. Insufficient supplies of coal caused secondary bottlenecks in the steel industry and in electrical power supply, so much so that electricity had to be rationed for a short period during the 1950–51 winter.[40]

The previously insufficient funding for the pits made it necessary to import large amounts of expensive American coal, which of course increased West Germany's balance of payment crisis.[41] Both German industrialists and the economics minister were desperate to avoid the reintroduction of economic controls and *Wirtschaftslenkung*, so Erhard was happy to accept a proposal from the Bundesverband der deutschen Industrie (BDI, Federation of German Industry), which offered to raise DM 1 billion from German commercial businesses by issuing interest-bearing bonds to fund investments into coal, iron, and steel; and electricity. Because many small and medium-sized businesses outside the three sectors felt subject to a policy of enforced participation, they contested the idea, and it had to be passed into law and rushed through parliament in early 1952 as the *Investitionshilfe Gesetz*. Because of the KfW's good reputation with industry, it was once again asked to handle the funds.[42] Initially, each of the three sectors was supposed to receive DM 300 million, with another DM 100 million for the Ruhr industries' water supply. As it turned out, by the end of 1953, coal mining had received the smallest share of money among the big three beneficiaries, DM 186 million out of a total of DM 624 million paid out.[43] Eventually, coal was to receive DM 228 million, with the largest sum going to the steel industry (DM 296.5 million).[44] A considerable larger impact on investment than the DM 1 billion raised came from the law's articles 36 and 37. Under article 36, basic industries were allowed tax depreciation on investments of up to 50 percent annually. In this way, the basic industries could write off DM 3.2 billion, three times as much as had been raised by the loan. Finally, article 37 empowered Erhard to raise basic industry's fixed prices without needing authorization from parliament, but he rarely used this power because he continued to support a policy of low coal prices.[45] All in all, the coal industry was able to finance 14 percent of their investment up to 1955 from *Investitionshilfe* fund loans, compared with 59 percent from "own funds," which meant mainly depreciations under article 36 of the law.[46]

After the "Korea Crisis" turned into the "Korea boom" from mid 1951 onward, West Germany's balance of trade had turned positive, and it continued to grow with the ongoing expansion of international trade during the 1950s.[47] This does not mean that the capital shortage within the Federal Republic had ended by this time, or even, as Tooze suggests, that "1952 marks the true end point of reconstructions."[48] For example, of the estimated shortfall of 6 million dwellings in 1948, less than 1.3 million, or about 20 percent, had been built by the end of 1952.[49] Long-term investment capital, especially for reconstruction in the politically crucial housing sector or the rationalization and modernization of industry remained scarce because the German capital market continued to be unable to raise the required funds.

The reconstruction process would be slow as long as investment capital from abroad was unavailable on a large scale. As Tooze rightly suggests, 1952 was a year in which important decisions had been made and developments put in place that would accelerate German reconstruction. The most important of these decisions led to West Germany signing the London Debt Agreement in 1953, which settled the pre-World War II debt of the German Reich as well as West Germany's postwar debt stemming from Allied aid. Christoph Buchheim has shown that foreign capital investment in West Germany in 1954 increased more than tenfold compared with the previous postwar peak in 1952, with a tripling of foreign direct investment.[50] The increase is even more astounding in light of the fact that both the BDI and the BdL were either very cautious of, or outright hostile to, the idea of new foreign debt.[51] Despite this strong opposition, which most likely came from the fear of repeating past mistakes and indebtedness abroad, foreign investment in the Federal Republic continued to grow and accelerate the reconstruction process.

Summary

"The heroic legend of the German reconstruction as a spontaneous upsurge of aggressive private enterprise" in the wake of the currency reform is a myth, as Shonfield argues.[52] Contrary to this myth, in 1948–49, the "success of the Deutschmark . . . was not preordained."[53] One can easily argue that in the climate of the Cold War, the Americans would have prevented a total failure of the experiment, most likely by interfering with and ending Erhard's economic strategy, because of the negative political fallout it would have caused. However, despite all his rhetoric, Erhard himself was not really true to the pure creed of neoliberalism. The biggest challenge the Bizone and then the young Federal Republic faced in economic terms during the early reconstruction period from 1948 onward was the totally insufficient capital market; without appropriate funds, the rebuilding of the country could proceed only to a small degree and with huge frictions: the system of self-financing of companies after the currency reform meant that valuable assets for the reconstruction were misdirected into branches of industry that were nonessential.

The Marshall Plan counterpart funds were an important tool to counterbalance the misdirection of funds and help those sectors of the economy that were vital but which suffered from a lack of investment. Although counterpart funds were at best moderate in size, the way they were used (providing partial funding for crucial bottleneck projects) and the psychological impact they had (enticing banks to provide further funding for the companies) made the difference. The best example for the latter is the optical company Zeiss: relocated from the Soviet to the American occupation zone, all the company had left in the West was its reputation and technical know-how. Abs, who used to be on the Zeiss supervisory board, organized a KfW loan, which then encouraged banks to give additional loans to the company despite its lack of collateral.[54]

The revolving utilization of the funds provided an additional benefit because the repaid loans and the interest they had yielded could be reinvested in key industries (in 1954, for instance, the KfW had scheduled DM 320 million for investment, which derived from repayments and interest).[55] The existence of the counterpart funds had the additional psychological advantage that the German authorities could claim that reconstruction was financed with the offshoots of the Marshall Plan, which, in the grand scheme of the reconstruction, was only true to a very small part.

The "Korean crisis" of 1950–51 demonstrated that Erhard's economic policy had considerable weaknesses—or that the West German economy generally, and the capital market in particular, was simply not able to cope with additional strain caused by increased orders. The 1952 *Investitionshilfe Gesetz*, born out of desperation (but crucial for the rehabilitation of German big business) was regarded by many at the time as the belated financial compensation for the basic industries;[56] but in the end, it was only the signing of the London Debt Agreement in 1953, which brought foreign investment capital to West Germany—against the wishes of the BDL and the BDI—and eventually helped to end the drought in the German capital market.

Armin Grünbacher is Senior Lecturer in Modern History at the University of Birmingham. His publications include *West German Industrialists and the Making of the Economic Miracle: A History of Mentality and Recovery* (2017), *The Making of German Democracy: West Germany during the Adenauer Era* (2010) and *Reconstruction and Cold War in Germany: The Kreditanstalt für Wiederaufbau: 1948–1961* (2004).

Notes

1. From March 1948 to September 1949, when he became officially Minister for Economics, Erhard's position and title had been Director for Economics at the *Verwaltungsrat für Wirtschaft des Vereinigten Wirtschaftsgebietes*.
2. Werner Abelshauser, *Wirtschaftsgeschichte der Bundesrepublik Deutschland 1945–1980* (Frankfurt 1983), 46.
3. Ibid., 50.
4. Ibid., 50–51.
5. Ibid., 51.
6. Armin Grünbacher, *The Making of German Democracy: West Germany during the Adenauer Era, 1945–1965* (Manchester, 2010), 83–84.
7. Abelshauser, *Wirtschaftsgeschichte*, 53.

8. Armin Grünbacher, *Reconstruction and Cold War in Germany: The Kreditanstalt für Wiederaufbau 1948–1961* (Aldershot, 2004), 13–14; Institut für Zeitgeschichte und Deutscher Bundestag, eds, *Wörtliche Berichte und Drucksachen des Wirtschaftsrates des Vereinigten Wirtschaftsgebietes 1947–1949* (Munich, 1977).
9. Abelshauser, *Wirtschaftsgeschichte*, 64; Grünbacher, *Reconstruction and Cold War*, 84–85.
10. Monika Dickhaus, *Die Bundesbank im westeuropäischen Wiederaufbau* (Munich, 1996), 65–66.
11. Abelshauser, *Wirtschaftsgeschichte*, 53.
12. Carl-Ludwig Holtfrerich, "Monetary Policy under Fixed Exchange Rates," in *Fifty Years of the Deutsche Mark: Central Bank and Currency in Germany since 1948*, ed. Deutsche Bundesbank (Oxford, 1999), 307–401, 312; Grünbacher, *Reconstruction*, 14.
13. Heiner R. Adamsen, *Investitionshilfe für die Ruhr: Wiederaufbau, Verbände und soziale Marktwirtschaft, 1948–1952* (Wuppertal, 1981), 257.
14. Grünbacher, *Reconstruction*, 14.
15. Bundesarchiv Koblenz BA Z 32/10, cited in Abelshauser, *Wirtschaftsgeschichte*, 54.
16. Adamsen, *Investitionshilfe für die Ruhr*, 41.
17. Christian L. Glossner, *The Making of the German Post-War Economy: Political Communication and Public Reception of the Social Market Economy after World War Two* (London, 2010), 55–56.
18. Kreditanstalt für Wiederaufbau, Historisches Archiv (henceforth KfW HA), VS 65, memo on a meeting with the Military Governors, 13 April 1949.
19. Gerd Hardach, *Der Marshall Plan: Auslandshilfe und Wiederaufbau in Westdeutschland 1948–1952* (Munich, 1994), 255 for the American side; 262–63 for the German action.
20. Grünbacher, *Reconstruction and Cold War*, 67.
21. See Armin Grünbacher, "Cold War Economics: The Use of Marshall Plan Counterpart Funds in Germany 1948–1960," in *Central European History* 45, no. 4 (2012): 697–716.
22. Grünbacher, *Reconstruction and Cold War*, 15–50; for Abs's biography, see Lothar Gall, *Der Bankier Herman Josef Abs* (Munich, 2004). For the continuing significance of the KfW for the German economy, see Eric Owen Smith, *The German Economy* (London, 1994), passim.
23. Andrew Shonfield, *Modern Capitalism: The Changing Balance of Public and Private Power* (London, 1965), 277.
24. *Die Neue Zeitung*, Munich, 10 March 1949.
25. Grünbacher, *Reconstruction and Cold War*, 90.
26. Shonfield, *Modern Capitalism*, 277.
27. Kreditanstalf für Wiederaufbau, *1. Jahresbericht 1949*, translated in: Grünbacher, *The Making of German Democracy*, 94.
28. Egon Baumgart, *Investitionen und ERP Finanzierung* (Berlin, 1961), 47.
29. Federal Minister for the Marshall Plan, ed., *Twelfth, Final Report of the German Federal Government on the Progress of the Marshall Plan* (Bonn, 1953), 25.
30. Grünbacher, *Reconstruction and Cold War*, 127; 129.
31. Baumgart, *Investitionen und ERP Finanzierung*, 122–23.
32. Kreditanstalt für Wiederaufbau, *Jahresbericht 1951*, 53.

33. KfW HA Prot 10-1, Protokoll der 5. sitzung TOP 5, Grünbacher, *Reconstruction and Cold War*, 128.
34. The *Metallurgische Forschungsgesellschaft* (Mefo) was a dummy company set up by the Reichsbank and the Reichswehr ministry. The company issues bills of exchange which, with the endorsement of the Reischsbank, were accepted by commercial banks who paid out cash for those bills. Ultimately, RM 12 billion were created in this way out of nothing and injected into the real economy to finance rearmament.
35. Grünbacher, *Reconstruction and Cold War*, 129.
36. For an example of the impact of the *DM Eröffnungsbilanz Gesetz* and the tax depreciation it offered see Grünbacher, *The Making of German Democracy*, 85.
37. Adam Tooze, "Reassessing the Moral Economy of Post-War Reconstruction: The Terms of the West German Settlement in 1952," *Past and Present* 210, no. 6 (2011): 47–70, 66–67.
38. Werner Abelshauser, "Ansätze 'korporativer Marktwirtschaft' in der Koreakrise der 50er Jahre. Ein Briefwechsel zwischen dem Hohen Kommissar John McCloy und Bundeskanzler Adenauer," *Vierteljahrshefte für Zeitgeschichte* 30 (1982): 715–56.
39. Adamsen, *Investitionshilfe für die Ruhr*, 84; Grünbacher, *Reconstruction and Cold War*, 164.
40. Hans Booms, ed., *Die Kabinettsprotokolle der Bundesregierung* 4, 1951 (Boppard, 1988), passim; Knut Borchard and Christoph Buchheim, "Die Wirkung der Marshall Plan Hilfe in Schlüsselbereichen der deutschen Wirtschaft," *Vierteljahrshefte für Zeitgeschichte* 35, no. 3 (1987): 317–47, 331.
41. Kreditanstalt für Wiederaufbau, *Jahresbericht 1951*, 19.
42. Grünbacher, *Reconstruction and Cold War*, 99–102.
43. Adamsen, *Investitionshilfe für die Ruhr*, 140; Kreditanstalt für Wiederaufbau, *Jahresbericht 1953*, 49.
44. Adamsen, *Investitionshilfe für die Ruhr*, 264.
45. Grünbacher, *Reconstruction and Cold War*, 102.
46. Adamsen, *Investitionshilfe für die Ruhr*, 270.
47. Tooze, "Reassessing the Moral Economy," 66. Herbert Giersch, Karl-Heinz Paque, and Holger Schmieding, *The Fading Miracle: Four Decades of Market Economy in Germany* (Cambridge, 1994), 89.
48. Tooze, "Reassessing the Moral Economy," 68.
49. Grünbacher, *Reconstruction and Cold War*, 187.
50. Christoph Buchheim, "Das Londoner Schuldenabkommen," in *Westdeutschland 1945–1955. Unterwerfung, Kontrolle, Integration*, ed. Ludolf Herbst (Munich, 1986), 219–29, esp. 227; Hans-Peter Schwarz, ed., *Die Wiederherstelllung des deutschen Kredits: Das Londoner Schuldenabkommen* (Stuttgart, 1982).
51. Bundesverband der Deutschen Industrie, Historisches Archiv, HGF Pro 785/3 'Kundgebung und 4. Mitgliederversammlung des Bundesverbandes der Deutschen Industrie in Wiesbaden vom 17. bis 19. Mai 1953'; Buchheim, "Das Londoner Schuldenbakommen," 228.
52. Shonfield, *Modern Capitalism*, 276.
53. Tooze, "Reassessing the Moral Economy," 47.
54. Deutsche Bundesbank, Historisches Archiv B330/3338, Protokoll zur 6. Sitzung des KfW Kreditbewilligungs-Ausschusses, TOP 1.
55. Kreditanstalt für Wiederaufbau, *Jahresbericht 1953*, 44.
56. Shonfield, *Modern Capitalism*, 275.

Bibliography

Abelshauser, Werner. "Ansätze 'korporativer Marktwirtschaft' in der Koreakrise der 50er Jahre. Ein Briefwechsel zwischen dem Hohen Kommissar John McCloy und Bundeskanzler Adenauer." *Vierteljahrshefte für Zeitgeschichte* 30 (1982): 715–56.

———. *Wirtschaftsgeschichte der Bundesrepublik Deutschland 1945–1980*. Frankfurt, 1983.

Adamsen, Heiner R. *Investitionshilfe für die Ruhr: Wiederaufbau, Verbände und soziale Marktwirtschaft, 1948–1952*. Wuppertal, 1981.

Baumgart, Egon. *Investitionen und ERP Finanzierung*. Berlin, 1961.

Booms, Hans, ed., *Die Kabinettsprotokolle der Bundesregierung*. Boppard, 1988.

Borchard, Knut, and Christoph Buchheim. "Die Wirkung der Marshall Plan Hilfe in Schlüsselbereichen der deutschen Wirtschaft." *Vierteljahrshefte für Zeitgeschichte* 35, no. 3 (1987): 317–47.

Buchheim, Christoph. "Das Londoner Schuldenabkommen." In *Westdeutschland 1945–1955: Unterwerfung, Kontrolle, Integration*, edited by Ludolf Herbst, 219–29. Munich, 1986.

Dickhaus, Monika. *Die Bundesbank im westeuropäischen Wiederaufbau*. Munich, 1996.

Federal Minister for the Marshall Plan, ed. *Twelfth, Final Report of the German Federal Government on the Progress of the Marshall Plan*. Bonn, 1953.

Gall, Lothar. *Der Bankier Herman Josef Abs*. Munich, 2004.

Giersch, Herbert, Karl-Heinz Paque, and Holger Schmieding. *The Fading Miracle: Four Decades of Market Economy in Germany*. Cambridge, 1994.

Glossner, Christian L. *The Making of the German Post-War Economy: Political Communication and Public Reception of the Social Market Economy after World War Two*. London, 2010.

Grünbacher, Armin. "Cold War Economics: The Use of Marshall Plan Counterpart Funds in Germany 1948–1960." *Central European History* 45 no. 4 (2012): 697–716.

———. *The Making of German Democracy: West Germany during the Adenauer Era, 1945–1965*. Manchester, 2010.

———. *Reconstruction and Cold War in Germany: The Kreditanstalt für Wiederaufbau 1948–1961*. Aldershot, 2004.

Hardach, Gerd. *Der Marshall Plan: Auslandshilfe und Wiederaufbau in Westdeutschland 1948–1952*. Munich, 1994.

Holtfrerich, Carl-Ludwig. "Monetary Policy under Fixed Exchange Rates." In *Fifty Years of the Deutsche Mark: Central Bank and Currency in Germany since 1948*, edited by Deutsche Bundesbank, 307–401. Oxford, 1999.

Institut für Zeitgeschichte und Deutscher Bundestag, eds. *Wörtliche Berichte und Drucksachen des Wirtschaftsrates des Vereinigten Wirtschaftsgebietes 1947–1949*. Munich, 1977.

Schwarz, Hans-Peter, ed. *Die Wiederherstelllung des deutschen Kredits: Das Londoner Schuldenabkommen*. Stuttgart, 1982.

Shonfield, Andrew. *Modern Capitalism: The Changing Balance of Public and Private Power.* London, 1965.
Smith, Eric Owen. *The German Economy.* London, 1994.
Tooze, Adam. "Reassessing the Moral Economy of Post-War Reconstruction: The Terms of the West German Settlement in 1952." *Past and Present* 210, no. 6 (2011): 47–70.

CHAPTER SEVENTEEN

Between Memorialization and Monetary Revaluation
The 1990 Currency Union as a Site of Post-Unification Memory Work

URSULA M. DALINGHAUS

Endings and Beginnings

November ninth, 2009 marked the twenty-year anniversary of the fall of the Berlin Wall. Unquestionably a joyous event, it was nonetheless a metonymic marker of the end of German division and beginning of new democratic freedoms for Eastern Germans. But what was, and is, the nature of that freedom? This question remains open even today especially due to the uneven experiences of monetary and economic unification. The festivities, staged facing west, symbolized and reinforced (whether intended or not) the prevalent framing of "the rush toward unity" as primarily about Eastern German desires to tap into the locus of value, signified most viscerally by the West German mark, the metonym for West German success and prosperity.

This festive event represented one version of the "fall of the wall." Many in Leipzig emphasized a different perception: in 1989 the motivating force for change came from East Germany. In this view, 9 November was a night in which East Germans acted while West Germans observed. Something fundamentally democratic in the form of grassroots activities had occurred in this otherwise "unfree" state.[1] One former dissident remarked: "West Germans have never quite gotten over the fact that the events of '89 took them by surprise, and that they could only claim the role of observer to this historical event."[2] In the days and months before 9 November, ordinary people overcame their fear and openly challenged state claims by going to the streets, and as one explained, "these were the best days of my life. And then came the money (the

D-Mark.")."³ The fall of the Berlin Wall changed the dynamics of what had until then largely been a call for economic, political, and cultural reforms. Change now became folded into a story of inevitable reunification with the Federal Republic of Germany (FRG).

While the anniversary was focused on commemorating political unity and democratic opening, cost/benefit analysis quickly appeared. Just as the fall of the wall festivities were underway, a report by the new transportation minister appeared under the headline, *Ramsauer will Aufbau West* (Ramsauer calls for development for the West). The article used the term generally applied to the ongoing transfer of federal funds to support the still structurally weak new *Länder*.⁴ Since 2009, a growing number of Western Germans have linked the EUR 1.3 trillion transfers to East German regions as causing economic decline in the "old" West German federal states.⁵ This argument restaged economic debates that emerged as early as the first opening of the wall in November 1989 about who would bear the costs of an anticipated reunification, and on what terms. The currency union of 1990 utterly changed the terms of debate and formal structures through which East Germans would be included and inserted in the post-unification German state.⁶ Thus, another form of collective remembering was also at work on this anniversary in the ritual of measuring, assessing, and weighing the financial costs and economic progress of German unity.

In this essay, I argue that one crucial form of post-unification memorialization work that is not treated as such is that of taking stock (*Bilanz ziehen*) at several chronological and sociocultural points involving lived experience and historical production.⁷ One of the key staging grounds for this commemorative accounting is in the public and political domains of collective debate that include media reports, talk shows, documentaries, and political education forums.⁸ Ossis and Wessis alike continue to calculate and contest the balance sheet of German unity.⁹ These forms of remembering and debate are substantially intertwined with private and institutional forms of evaluating the financial progress and outcomes of German unity. Rather than relegate these calculative debates to the domain of technical quibbles over economic "facts,"¹⁰ I argue instead that what may appear to be "purely economic disagreements" about monetary investments in the East are in fact substantial forms of negotiating memory about the process of German unity.¹¹ In so doing, I challenge and expose the "politics of distinction" between economic fact and historical memory.¹² As John Gillis writes, "Commemorative activity is by definition social and political, for it involves the coordination of individual and group memories, whose results may appear consensual when they are in fact the product of processes of intense contest, struggle, and in some instances, annihilation."¹³

Measuring the economic progress of unity through metaphorical and literal forms of balancing accounts—economic and social—animate the commemorative and historical structure of official and scholarly readings of the entire unification process. By exploring how enduring questions of socio-monetary value infuse commemorative forms of evaluating, narrating, and remembering the price, cost, and ambiguities of monetary value set into motion by the 1990 currency union, this essay contributes to a body of work on the politics of nostalgia, materiality, and consumption in the former German Democratic Republic (GDR).[14] Because the GDR is a contested object of historical memory, which parts (if any) should be retained or remediated is always open to question and to polarizing disagreements. Efforts to account for and reckon with notions of material equivalence in evaluating the progress of "catching up" economically cannot be understood separately from this larger context. The 1990 currency union remains a meaningful index of this process of "catching up," which in turn constitutes an ongoing litmus test of inner unity and relatedness in Germany.

Tracing the 1990 Currency Union in Retrospect

The insights presented here are based on ethnographic and interview research I conducted in Frankfurt, Leipzig, and Berlin from 2007 to 2010 on the social meanings and practices surrounding currency union projects in the context of central bank-led efforts to communicate monetary policy histories and goals to the public.[15] I interacted with West and East German respondents of different generations and socioeconomic backgrounds, including some who participated directly in the currency changeover and transitional process from 1990 onward. Through a variety of grassroots and political-education institutions and events primarily in Leipzig,[16] I recruited twenty-five participants (men and women between the ages of thirty-five and seventy-five) for extended economic life history interviews (three to four hours). Print and electronic media, including televised and local political forums and panel discussions among diverse experts and historical actors, formed a basis for generating points of critical reflection with my respondents on the impact of monetary and economic policies since 1989. However, only through multiple and long-term interactions with some respondents did a greater understanding of the embodied experience of these changes over time develop.

Eastern Germans experienced the 1990 currency union as both a "generous" inclusion and form of economic shock therapy. The existing scholarship on German unification offers ways to understand these transformations.[17] However, less attention has been devoted to understanding the ongoing significance for people of these changes over a longer time. In particular, East German iterations of socialist and post-unification economic transformation have been marginalized and the narrative space appropriated by Western concerns.[18]

Most Eastern German respondents found it difficult to discuss the currency union because its negative effects were so bound up with positive feelings about the D-Mark. In this sense, remembering monetary aspects of unification differed from, but was intertwined with, the commemorative politics around East German material culture and objects analyzed in studies of *Ostalgie*.[19] An explicitly East German critical stance is neither coherent nor uniform, nor is it entirely separate from critiques that crosscut any East/West divide, such as in anti-communist or anti-economic forms of resistance. However, critical reflection on the meanings and outcomes of the 1990 currency and economic union remain subject to, and reinforce asymmetries of power and Western hegemony that have characterized this process from the outset. They also signal the unequal power relations that have shaped how the events of 1989–90 have been inscribed and sanctioned in national histories and commemorative celebrations that by their very nature excise the messy and processual incoherence of histories experienced on the ground.[20] By sharing stories and experiences of the 1990 currency union, respondents indexed how changes in the monetary order of a society have deep reverberations long after the event.[21]

Monetary Revaluation and Its Messy Remainders

On 1 July 1990, the German currency union, and the D-Mark, became a reality for East Germany.[22] Nonetheless, East Germany remained a separate, sovereign nation. The currency union predated political unification, which occurred some months later. Perhaps the most iconic image capturing this event was video footage of a group of East Germans clutching a 100-D-Mark bill in their outstretched hands and singing "Hallelujah D-Mark." Only months earlier, in one of the many Monday demonstrations that took place after the fall of the Berlin Wall, one banner bore the now famous phrase: "If the D-Mark does not come to us, we will go to it."[23] Another banner shows the desired rate of equal exchange, 1:1. The final decision about the rates of exchange developed within the context of contentious debates among politicians and the Bundesbank; not everything was converted at the 1:1 rate. Arcane details about the calculation of the money supply or the nominal values eligible for the 1:1 conversion were crucially important, logistically, materially, and symbolically in the politics of unifying the long divided states through the establishment of a currency union.

Because East Germans who fled to the West were automatically accorded the rights of German citizens before reunification, those words "we will come to it" have acquired the force of a causal explanation in almost every account of these events since 1990, popular and scholarly.[24] Many West Germans argue that this step was the only way to dam a catastrophic "flood" out of the East.

These same visceral fears have also provided a powerful explanatory framework for making sense of policy decisions at the time.[25] Critically, this interpretation has allowed West Germans to claim ever since that "we were just giving them what they demanded." Occluded in this dominant framing is the simultaneous and ongoing redistribution of wealth and property from East to West.[26] Critical analysts and expert participants attribute the disappearance of this counter-narrative to the spectacular "offer" made by Helmut Kohl in offering the West German mark to the East German people.

Revisiting discussions and arguments that animated different actors in 1989–90 to argue for a 1:1 exchange rate for the introduction of the D-Mark reveals the shared ontological assumption about monetary value in both capitalist and socialist German states: a national money expresses not only an economic value but also one's social value. Precisely because of the economic gap in value between West and East German economies, East Germans argued for their equal status with West Germans as a material commitment to bridge this gap in the near future. East German demonstrators demonstrated under banners like "Wir sind nicht nur die Hälfte wert! 1:1" ("We are not only worth half!"), or "Wir sind nicht die Nigger der Bundis.... M:DM = 1:1" ("We are not the West Germans' niggers"),[27] that expressed a strong sense of what should constitute shared values and an awareness of potential unequal power relations as the result of a nominally disproportionate ratio of monetary value.[28] This process was messy and turbulent not because political and economic realities were mutually incompatible and utterly opposed but because the tensions and pragmatic problems posed by the rush of events brought the entanglement of the economic and the political into stark relief.[29]

Just as the introduction of separate currencies in 1948 effectively divided the two states, so, too, was currency unification the point for negotiating the terms of coming together again. The decision of both West and East German political leaders for a "joining" (*Beitritt*) rather than a unification left little room to initiate policies that might have brought change in both directions. Technically, German unification proceeded through a *Beitritt* or "accession" to the FRG. In fact, East Germany did not unify with the FRG. Rather, East Germany was first reorganized into the five new *Länder* (states), each of which was subsequently added to the FRG. A number of experts, authors, former dissidents, and citizens in both East and West argue that here was a missed chance to unify along more equitable terms by shaping new and collectively agreed upon political arrangements for a unified Germany.[30] Fear of a bankrupt and disintegrating East German economy and the (presumed) impatience of East Germans for unification required a quick answer, many policy makers believed. These "imperatives" pressured West and East German political actors alike to find a speedy solution that effectively ended any search for a third way. Instead, the post-1989 transformation processes meant an almost complete transfer of West German bureaucratic, political, and economic structures and institutions, including the transfer of Western elites to the former East.

Not only did 1 July 1990 mark the arrival of the D-Mark as the official currency of the GDR, it also was the beginning of the end of familiar (and suddenly disdained) East German products as stores opened with shelves full of West German goods, in one sense mimicking the origin story of the West German post-World War II *Wirtschaftswunder* or "economic miracle."[31] In hindsight, many respondents expressed remorse for having participated in what they later recognized as the destruction of their own market in their desire to buy only West German brands during those early days. But the fall in prices of GDR goods and uncertainties about the economic future of industry was in fact fueled by the evolving policy decisions and technical arrangements that were preparing the way for currency union.

Although the prevailing assumption is that East German desires for the D-Mark caused them to fail to recognize the economic challenges that would come with unification, many examples show that this narrative also needs to be problematized. Not all East Germans shared the optimism about the beneficial effects of the D-Mark, even in those early days. Whether from their experiences in visiting relatives in the West or from reflecting on the nature of the relationship between an economic base and a money-price complex, many East Germans were already skeptical that East German industry could withstand such a conversion. More importantly, through experiences of crossing the border into the West and receiving the DM 100 "welcome money" (*Begrüßungsgeld*), respondents became painfully aware of a new and heightened sense of poverty relative to Western Germans.[32]

Western interlocutors familiar with, as well as participants in, these processes of policy implementation and evaluation emphasize instead the topsy-turvy reality created by the currency union's 1:1 ratio of value—where suddenly an East German Trabant automobile cost the equivalent in D-Marks as a Volkswagen-Golf. One former employee of the privatization trust (*Treuhand*) described how his account book was filled with "red numbers" that signified an almost daily decline in value. "You can't sell things for ten times their value," he groaned, recalling his frustration at the absurdity of it all. In a context when the East German market was opened up to market capitalism and competition in the West while simultaneously closed off from existing socialist markets, he, like many others, was forced to make impossible decisions about the viability of socialist enterprises. Also deeply critical of the currency union and its modalities, he shrugged in frustration saying that as a result, "our hands were tied."

The economic consequences accompanying these conversions of value unfolded over a long period of time and remain unsettled even today. The speed and scale of these decisions were unprecedented; they occurred within the space of a few months. Equally abrupt and rapid was the privatization—

some might say the fire sale—of the East German economy in its entirety within four years. By many accounts, only 6 percent of the wealth and property liquidated or created ended up in East German hands; West German capital was the biggest winner. A relative silence surrounds many aspects of this highly complex process both before and after privatization by the trust agency (*Treuhandanstalt*) set up to mediate the reorganization and privatization of the "People's property."[33] Yet because the *Treuhand* ended its work with a balance sheet in the red of over DM 2 billion, the precise value of the East German economy remains undetermined. At the center of these different narratives is the question of how to account for these monetary and economic ruptures and who—or what—is to blame.

Edgar Most, the former vice president of the East German State Bank, and one of few East German bankers who went on to a successful career at a West German bank, argues that the distinction between the conversion at the micro-level (personal savings, debts) and the macro-economic levels (*Gesamtvolkswirtschaftlich*) is important. Most believes that the conversion at the macro-level could have been treated differently but was not.[34] He described how there were multiple currency systems, each with their own rate of exchange and mechanisms of evaluation. Each of these should have been figured separately in determining the rates of exchange. By converting the debts and liabilities of socialist enterprises at the rate of 2:1, the opening D-Mark balances of firms on the day of the currency union meant that enterprises were already burdened with debts, making them unprofitable on paper at the stroke of the clock hand. According to Most, the attempt to determine the market value of the East German Combine (*Kombinate*) and East German industry as a whole and not the conversion of private savings,[35] bankrupted East German industry almost literally overnight.[36] Overvaluing the currency, in effect, devalued assets while exponentially increasing liabilities. The currency union required that the ownership of assets and liabilities be converted and redistributed in capitalist market terms. Credits and debts that once circulated between the state and the people in the socialist planned economy were converted into capitalist market debts that now burdened the balances of socialist firms and communal property.[37]

While many of my respondents in Leipzig would agree with Most's assessment of the *Treuhand* and the problems stemming from currency conversion, they remain critical of the ways in which both West German officials and former SED (*Sozialistische Einheitspartei Deutschlands*, Socialist Unity Party) functionaries impeded equitable privatizations. In the words of one economist and activist, "Where was Edgar Most twenty years ago? Why speak out now, and not earlier when it could have made a difference?" The fault lines not only run between East and West, but also split East Germans, who quite often held contradictory views on the continued importance of the East/West distinction itself, whether as a marker of personal and professional biographies or an accounting tool for evaluating the integration process.

Many other Western interlocutors emphasized instead East German chants for the D-Mark and the "floods" of people coming, leaving the East for West Germany. They felt the real problem of monetary valuation in this story was the temporality of events and the "impatience" of Eastern Germans, who because they were considered citizens in the FRG, could "make demands." Narratives of "impatient Easterners" were widely shared and invoked by many of my Eastern interlocutors, too—whether as inward looking reflections on one's own stance at the time or as a commentary on the actions and sentiments of others. As a prominent Leipzig historian and former dissident described it, "East Germans had an uncanny greed for West German money. Of course, you can't hold that against them," he added apologetically. "They had been denied access for decades and differential access to West German D-Marks in the GDR contributed to inequality there." He described how after the currency union Eastern products were cleared away: "People stood in front of the shop windows then and applauded. How much greater was the disappointment when people recognized that access to western money was not enough."

The full extent and significance of how the 1990 currency union abruptly revalued the East German economy is undetermined. In spite of all its "deficiencies," the East German productive industry and state assets embodied forty years of collective labor on the part of East German workers. Thus, the negative monetary value affixed to this legacy constitutes an open wound in unified Germany.

Disproportionate Experiences of Transformation

In day-to-day life, German unification brought few changes to the lives of most West Germans. For East Germans, however, every aspect of society changed overnight. One woman recalled: "What do I remember? Back then everything was new. Back then it was impossible to make any real judgment about it. I knew what money was worth in the GDR, how much everything cost; rent, bread, and the everyday things one needed had stable prices that seldom changed. But then everything was suddenly different. Not just prices, but everything: work, professional qualifications, insurance—money was only part of it."

New laws, bureaucracies, financial, and work relationships presented a steep learning curve. Experiences of money mapped unevenly onto the old geographical and historical boundaries. Many felt that by virtue of having lived in both systems that they could stand back and look reflexively at money matters. Still, most of my eastern respondents grew to share the dominant economic sensibilities of those in the West about the enduring problems that the rush toward unity entailed. While many expressed a sense of pride about all the obstacles they overcame in this process of transformation, these accomplishments have surprisingly little social capital in the dominant discourses of a unified Germany. Worse, the high price of German unification has left many West Germans with the feeling that their taxes finance new streets and modern infrastructure in the East, while at home things are falling apart.

Respondents in Leipzig willingly agreed that West German taxpayers had been asked to make great sacrifices. What upset them, however, was the lack of awareness in the West that Easterners, too, paid a price. All German employees pay the solidarity tax (5.5 percent on earned income), although surveys and my interviews indicated that most West Germans were unaware of this. Even when this fact is known, the general conviction expressed privately and in public discourse remains that it is primarily Western wealth being funneled to the East with no return.

High unemployment and the resulting diminution of the tax base, as well as low-productivity measured in terms of industrial output, have meant that money flowing East is not exclusively viewed in terms of financial equalization. Rather, Westerners tend to view these payments as siphoning off the wealth of the West to keep the Eastern ship afloat. If indeed Westerners disproportionately sacrifice tax money, Easterners disproportionately bear the weight of structural adjustment. These adjustments come not in the now familiar guise of austerity measures eroding a social safety net but rather in the unsettling of all aspects of life through the abrupt and wholesale adoption of foreign infrastructures, bureaucracies, and monetary sensibilities.

Even though the 1990 currency union messily but officially settled the accounts of the vanished GDR state, the value difference of West and East German currencies endured as a reference point in the politics of financial equalization schemes. More than twenty years after unification, East German labor, as reflected in wages and retirement points, was still "worth less" than labor in the old states of the FRG. Political elites, economic experts, as well as ordinary citizens have framed the gap in wealth and productivity as one that must be closed in order to complete German unity. Simultaneously experts and policy makers have argued that inequality between regions naturally resulted from uneven capitalist development.

In the early 1990s, national conceptions of the monetary and economic union envisioned the establishment of equivalent living standards, but the meanings of equalization have shifted over the years with greater emphasis being placed on the chance or opportunity for the same quality of life. Equalization could and sometimes did imply "becoming the same" or assimilating to the Western status quo. However, for analysts and critics alike, expressions of longing to live like those in the West are often conflated with the expectation that former structures and practices be abandoned entirely. For Easterners who wish for a more nuanced understanding of this process of coming together, this conflation reinforces the sense that East Germans brought nothing of real economic value to the new arrangement. It also leaves unquestioned the assumption that forty years of differences needed to be effaced as rapidly as possible.

Lower wages in the East have not led to more investment and less unemployment in the East compared with the West, as prevailing theories would suggest. Estimates in 2010 projected that it would take another twenty years or more for wages to converge, signaling the enduring importance of equalization as an anticipated end point of unity. With the introduction of a national minimum wage in 2014, the East/West designation has been dropped for the first time since 1990, even while the gap in real wages will remain for some time, according to most estimates. Arguments about these gaps between West and East German livelihoods cannot be dismissed as a mere mental hangover from the past given the salience of these differences in symbolic and material terms. These forms of debate trace back to the questions of value difference that have animated the ratios of conversion that index both equivalence and difference. Arguments about the relationship between money and labor productivity, between earned pension funds and work biographies, can therefore be viewed as ongoing problems of German unification and the paradoxical indexing of value equivalence and difference the currency union marked in time.

Whether in public commentaries or private conversations between family members, colleagues, or acquaintances, Western perceptions that it is "real" money (D-Marks, now Euros!) that pays East Germans' pension benefits to which East Germans did not contribute (or only contributed valueless money) resurrect the East/West divide.[38] Ironically, both West and East Germans share the conviction about the "realness" of the D-Mark, even if many East Germans emphasize that their pensions are nevertheless the product of a lifetime of labor in the GDR. One could argue that socialist money (the East German Mark, "Ost Mark") became more real after the fact as a unit of account that signified a different but relative value vis-à-vis the D-Mark that should be accounted for in determining the costs of economic unification. Yet despite various efforts to arrive at a proper balance of accounts, the sentiment about who has paid and sacrificed the most has altered little. On his guided tours of the key stations of the peaceful revolution in Leipzig, one elderly former engineer turned volunteer replies to Western tourists' queries and commentaries about the costs of unification by reminding them the Cold War could have ended differently: "If there had been a war in 1989, you would have lost your wealth. With the peaceful unification, we not only saved your lives, but also your savings. That is something you should not forget."

Material claims always stand behind people's relationship to a currency, even one deemed worthless. The economic costs of German unification get tangled up in the qualitative differences ascribed to East and West German currencies and the calculations of gain, loss, and misunderstandings they represent. Different valuations of wages, pensions, and debts are the traces of these monetary conversions. As moral forms, these divergences continue to mark East and West German difference.[39]

Memorialization as Deflection

To return to the space of official commemoration, I turn now to the anniversary of the social, economic, and monetary union between East and West Germany as it was commemorated in the summer of 2010. While it was less spectacular than the festivities of 2009, it was no less significant. Unlike in past years, key figures from West and East spoke publicly about their role in the process, about their feelings at the time, and about their retrospective analyses. The process of assessing and remembering the progress and process of German unity was expressed in a proliferation of literal and figurative accountings—taking stock—that index the paradoxical ratios of value marked by the 1990 currency union. In formally memorializing the 1990 currency union in 2010, the impulse to account was often deflected, focusing instead on questions of accountability. This is because by Western experts' own accounts, the 1990 monetary revaluation contributed to an economic depression in the East, "seen normally only in times of war," and which arguably led to new forms of dispossession and inequality. Arriving at a representative balance of payments was therefore enmeshed in the politics of who (or what) should be held accountable.

During one panel discussion in Berlin, Thilo Sarrazin, then a Bundesbank board member, and the economist Karl-Heinz Paqué were among the expert guests. Sarrazin worked in the Finance Ministry in 1989 and was a key contributor to policy recommendations, including calculation of conversion modalities for the currency union. Paqué's newly published book on the economics of unification contained in its title the term, *Die Bilanz* (balance of accounts).[40] Ursula Weidenfeld, a Western German economic journalist who in 1990 was writing a dissertation on the introduction of the market economy in West Germany, and an Eastern German entrepreneur who regained ownership of a family canning business, completed the panel of expert guests. Although including "Eastern perspectives," the consensus and direction of debate nonetheless reinforced a longstanding narrative about the modalities of economic unification as without alternative.[41] This narrative reiterated the dominant and apologetic narrative of the German monetary, economic, and social union as a process without an economic model,[42] and in this case, the economists Sarrazin and Paqué even celebrated how the successful handling at the time went against all of the economists' textbook theories. In contrast, Weidenfeld felt that one should have paid more attention to the economic warnings since most of these did in fact come true. However, even if the policy decisions of 1990 have been consistently presented in scholarly and policy accounts alike as lacking a model, the structural economic problems of the new *Länder* would still appear within the context of other, well-accepted models of economic development despite the extraordinary character of the situation.

For Thilo Sarrazin, the very mobility of East Germans posed the greatest problem, with the debate conjuring once again the "floods" of East Germans moving to the West as a persistent counter-argument to critical reflection on the currency union.[43] Because East Germans would necessarily have earned less in the East, they would have exercised their right as German citizens to flee to the Western *Länder* where they would then collect unemployment benefits, what is today called "welfare tourism."[44] Ironically, many East Germans have been forced to leave or commute long distances since 1990 in order to obtain work not to avoid it. Few East Germans imagined lives *without* work.[45]

Before the offer was made to move to the D-Mark as the single currency, agency was seen as resting with the East German masses that demanded not only the West German currency but the 1:1 ratio of exchange. After the implementation of the currency deal, agency shifted to the workings of the market and the parameters of value the currency union fixed in place. Thus, the narrative of 1990 is simultaneously one of exception and one of inevitability. Both narratives work in tandem to disguise the dispossession and politics of devaluation the currency revaluation enabled.

By framing structural economic weaknesses as accruing from a bankrupt system and the pressures of the East German populace "demanding" the D-Mark, other forms of critique that point to failed post-unification investment strategies or transfer of wealth and property from East to West are deflected. Moral responsibility is relocated to the collective actions of East Germans. Or, the structural problems in Western regions, like the deindustrialized Ruhr area, are invoked to resituate the debate in terms of changing market forces, erasing the specificity of the monetary union's financial conundrums. It is also important to note that at the time of this anniversary, Sarrazin and other economic experts responsible for the economic and monetary policies in 1990 were responding to the emergent state insolvency in Greece, and for the first time, journalists and other intellectuals raised the comparison to monetary policies in 1990.[46] However, experts now took pains to argue that the problems of monetary fracture and economic instability that monetary integration produced in 1990 bore little relation to or significance for contemporary projects of economic integration like the euro, which, on this 2010 anniversary was unexpectedly in crisis. Thus, while the ratio of 1:1 in 1990 was concerned with preventing East German "pauperism," it also needed to be marked as exceptional in relation to non-German others.[47]

The pragmatic problems in 1990 of determining the monetary and economic value of the GDR—that indeed there never was a D-Mark balance of what it all was worth—have made visible the entanglements of political and economic power in the commemorative account-keeping of currency union projects. Because the dilemmas associated with the rapid revaluation of the currency union were deemed faulty even by Western terms, the events of 1990 placed the monetary phenomenon of relative exchange rate values and the consequences of their volatility on the terrain of "working through the past" (*Vergangenheitsbewältigung*) of German division and reunification, as well as the project of building the European Union.[48]

Herr Most, who had appeared at various panel discussions commemorating the fall of the wall and could hold his own with the Western experts because of his wit and detailed inside knowledge, told me in a 2009 interview that he felt frustrated at how the direction of debate always swings toward the equation of the GDR with Hitler's Germany. In a more recent discussion about the relationship between justice, equalization, and the past, the question was raised about whether the state in fact owed it to each individual to settle the balance or compensate for the "damage" of German division. In this dialogue, economic decline is seen as the outcome of Hitler's war and the GDR dictatorship, with economic damage and inequality glossed as the rubble and debris of war.[49] But, on the other side of the equation of the currency union, as it was commemorated in 2010, empirical and political analyses account for the damages not as "economic conquest" but the outcome of market forces to which the 1990 currency union was a destructive yet benevolent and ultimately pragmatic response.[50]

All of these efforts can be seen as participating in the commemorative anxieties around reinscribing the 1990 currency union within its "proper" memorial form. To put it in today's context of the fractured euro zone, these efforts to settle the account of the 1990 currency union are enmeshed within historical anxieties about and efforts to call forth a "European Germany" rather than a German Europe.[51] In other words, "taking stock" makes visible the forms and practices of negotiating value in 1990—and beyond—that do not sit well within the nationally desired narratives of political unity, of the legacy of German division, and of Germany's redemption through Europeanization. Thus, attention to how a monetary event is continually enfolded within the commemorative structures of German unity makes visible money's politics.

Conclusion

This essay has repositioned different kinds of memory work taking place around the 1990 currency union, with its rearranging of social and monetary value, in order to reflect on the afterlives of this financial event in peoples' lives over time and its incorporation into the politics of memorialization. By tracking ethnographically and historically the forms through which monetary "events" are reworked over time and commemorated in post-unification practices of balancing accounts (monetary and otherwise), it is possible to consider how a temporally situated moment of monetary revaluation may become a purposive site of both remembering and forgetting and a commemorative act in its own right. In the shadow of yet another unifying project around money—the shift to the euro—one with its own emergent fault lines, the salient point to notice here is the narrative power of money to perpetually account for the messy remainders of this coming together.

Ursula M. Dalinghaus has been a Postdoctoral Scholar at the Institute for Money, Technology, and Financial Inclusion at the University of California, Irvine since 2015. She completed her PhD in Anthropology at the University of Minnesota, Twin Cities, specializing in economic anthropology and ethnographic approaches to money, currency unions, and central banks. Her publications include, "A Question of Value(s): Money, Currency Unions and the Re-Making of Post-Unification Identities," in *Deutschland seit 1990: Perspektiven auf die Vereinigungsgesellschaft*. Thomas Großbölting and Christoph Lorke, eds. (Stuttgart, Franz Steiner Verlag, 2017). She is currently working on a new project that examines German-Greek responses to the euro crisis.

Notes

1. See Kerry Kathleen Riley, *Everyday Subversion: From Joking to Revolting in the German Democratic Republic* (East Lansing, MI, 2008).
2. Identities of respondents have been anonymized except where a respondent has given permission to identify them by name.
3. Throughout this essay I refer to the West German mark (deutsche Mark, abbreviated DM and D-Mark) by its most iconic term, "D-Mark," a term in many respects synonymous with the commemorative structure described here. The official designation of the East German Mark was *Mark der DDR* and colloquially, *Ostmark*. The pejorative term often used for East German coins was *Alu-chips* (aluminum chips).
4. ARD Tagesschau, 9. November 2009.
5. This was the figure cited in 2009.
6. The 1990 currency union refers to the German monetary, economic, and social union between the FRG and GDR. Here I highlight the monetary dimension while

subsuming the formal economic and social aspects within the rubric of money (and monetary policy) as also cultural.
7. I am grateful for Mary Lindemann's editing expertise and to an anonymous reviewer for valuable provocations. Erika Briesacher generously read multiple versions. Bill Maurer, Taylor Nelms, Elizabeth Reddy, and Mrinalini Tankha also gave helpful feedback early on. Deepest thanks to Karen Ho. This essay is dedicated to the memory of Daphne Berdahl.
8. The negative media coverage about the GDR is important here—see Hanna Behrend, "Inglorious German Unification," in *German Unification: The Destruction of an Economy*, ed. Hanna Behrend (London, 1995) and her later discussion in "Viewpoints on German partition and reunification," *Social Semiotics* 21, no. 1 (2011): 61–63; Dominic Boyer, *Spirit and System: Media, Intellectuals, and the Dialectic in Modern German Culture* (Chicago, 2005). Here, I leave the critique of the media to one side except to note that it, too, enables recomposition and unsettling of old debates about the price, cost, and value of unification.
9. "Ossi" is a colloquial term for East German, with "Wessi" designating its Western counterpart. Importantly, "Ossi" connoted a new Eastern German subjectivity within the post-unification context. See Daphne Berdahl's essays on Ostalgie and consumption in Matti Bunzl, ed., *On the Social Life of Postsocialism: Memory, Consumption, Germany* (Bloomington, IN, 2010).
10. As Timothy Mitchell argues, the notion of a totality called "economy" must itself be historicized. "Fixing the Economy," *Cultural Studies* 12, no. 1 (1998): 82–101. Likewise Mary Poovey historicizes the modern notion of the "fact" and calls attention to accounting's origins in rhetoric. *A History of the Modern Fact: Problems of Knowledge in the Sciences of Wealth and Society* (Chicago, 1998). See also Martha Lampland, "False Numbers as Formalizing Practices," *Social Studies of Science* 40, no. 3 (2010): 377–404.
11. Other forms of commemorative activity in building the nation have been analyzed extensively in a variety of disciplines—see especially John R. Gillis, ed., *Commemorations: The Politics of National Identity* (Princeton, NJ, 1994). Economic events are not typically analyzed as objects of commemoration. The significance of the German hyperinflation of the 1920s for national and institutional identity building has been analyzed, but not in relation to collective commemorative acts. See Bernd Widdig, *Culture and Inflation in Weimar Germany* (Berkeley, CA, 2001); Carlo Tognato, *Central Bank Independence: Cultural Codes and Symbolic Performance* (New York, 2012).
12. Daphne Berdahl, "(N)ostalgie for the Present: Memory, Longing, and East German Things," in Bunzl, *On the Social Life of Postsocialism*. Berdahl understands nostalgia for GDR products as forms of active commemoration, thus challenging the distinction between "mere" nostalgia and sanctioned commemorative practices (48–49).
13. John R. Gillis, "Introduction. Memory and Identity: The History of a Relationship," in *Commemorations: The Politics of National Identity*, ed. John R. Gillis (Princeton, NJ, 1994), 5.
14. See Berdahl, "(N)ostalgie for the Present"; Jonathan Bach, "Consuming Communism. Material Cultures of Nostalgia in Former East Germany," in *Anthropology and Nostalgia*, ed. Olivia Angé and David Berliner (New York, 2014); Elizabeth Ten Dyke, *Dresden: Paradoxes of Memory in History* (London, 2001).
15. Research was supported through a National Science Foundation Doctoral Dissertation Improvement Grant and a Doctoral Dissertation Fellowship from the University

of Minnesota, Twin Cities. I am thankful to all the research participants who have generously contributed their time and expertise to this study.
16. Some interviews were also conducted in Berlin.
17. See Daphne Berdahl, *Where the World Ended: Re-Unification and Identity in the German Borderland*, (Berkeley, CA, 1999); Charles S. Maier, *Dissolution: The Crisis of Communism and the End of East Germany* (Princeton, NJ, 1997); Jonathan R. Zatlin, *The Currency of Socialism: Money and Political Culture in East Germany* (Washington, DC, 2007).
18. Benjamin Robinson, *The Skin of the System: On Germany's Socialist Modernity* (Stanford, CA, 2009).
19. See note above for GDR-specific examples. On the social practice of commemoration, see the definitive texts by Paul Connerton, *How Societies Remember* (Cambridge, 1989); Paul Connerton, *How Modernity Forgets* (Cambridge, 2009).
20. Cf. Michel Rolph-Trouillot's analysis of Columbus commemorations across time and space, in *Silencing the Past: Power and the Production of History* (Boston, 1995), 141–56.
21. I initially assumed that the 1990 currency union would provide historical background to my primary focus on the euro. In the process of conducting interviews and triangulating political, technical, and discursive themes with archival and specialist materials, however, I recognized how the 1990 currency union figured centrally in the memory work of research participants and historical actors.
22. While there are different estimates of the value of the East German mark relative to the D-Mark, the internal GDR accounting value was approximately 4.4:1, the black-market rate fluctuated between E 8:W 1 in November 1989 to 20:1 thereafter. The modalities of the currency union on 1 July 1990 established a virtual conversion of bank accounts, which required cash savings be deposited in banks before the conversion date. Ost Marks were converted according to the following values: 1:1 up to 4,000 for people of 14–59 years, 2,000 for children younger than 14, and 6,000 for seniors over 59. Savings above these amounts were converted at a rate of 2:1. Wages, pensions, and similar obligations were exchanged at the rate of 1:1 with debts and liabilities calculated at the rate of 2:1. See Maier, *Dissolution*, 242–43.
23. Importantly, this slogan appeared after, not before, Helmut Kohl and close advisors proposed plans (behind closed doors) for a currency union with the GDR. See Dieter Grosser, *Das Wagnis der Währungs-, Wirtschafts- und Sozialunion: Politische Zwänge im Konflikt mit ökonomischen Regeln* (Stuttgart, 1998).
24. An analysis of this pairing of currency union and mobility will be examined further in my book manuscript (in progress).
25. See Thilo Sarrazin's remarks, Podiumsdiskussion, "1:1?" 20 Jahre Währungs-, Wirtschafts-, und Sozialunion (discussed below). June 24, 2010, Bundesstiftung Aufarbeitung. A report of the event in German can be accessed here: http://www.friedlicherevolution.de/index.php?id=karte0&tx_comarevolution_pi10%5Bcontribid%5D=264
26. Attention to the technical and legal aspects of this process are necessary to conceptualize this claim, which is given weight through a variety of studies, from those published by the Bundesbank and Western economists, to "subaltern" empirical studies. For the latter, see Ulrich Busch, *Am Tropf: Die Ostdeutsche Transfergesellschaft* (Berlin, 2002).

27. Photograph by Martin Naumann in Martin Naumann, *Wende-Tage-Buch: Ein Tagebuch von der Wende bis zur Einheit* (Leipzig, 2008), 124–25.
28. Cf. Jonathan R. Zatlin, "Hard Marks and Soft Revolutionaries: The Economics of Entitlement and the Debate over German Unification, November 9, 1989–March 18, 1990," *German Politics and Society*, no. 33 (1994): 57–84.
29. See Jonathan Zatlin's insightful analysis of the monetary politics of German unification, the role of the Bundesbank, and the policy implications for the European monetary union. Jonathan R. Zatlin, "Rethinking Unification: German Monetary Union and European Integration," in *German Unification: Expectations and Outcomes*, ed. Peter C. Caldwell and Robert R. Shandley (New York, 2011), 61–98.
30. See especially Ulrich K. Preuss, "Political Institutions and German Unification," in *German Unification: Expectations and Outcomes*, 137–51.
31. See also Elizabeth Ten Dyke's example, p. 255, of how types of coffee marked anniversaries of historic shifts in the GDR, in "Tulips in December: Space, Time and Consumption before and after the End of German Socialism," *German History* 19, no. 2 (2001): 253–76.
32. Beginning with the closing of the wall in 1961, the West German state instituted the practice of providing visitor's money (*Begrüßungsgeld*), in literal terms "Welcome Money" for East Germans visiting the FRG. After November 1990, the West German government in an agreement with the GDR made a one-time DM 100 grant to all East German citizens visiting the West, which could be collected at West German banks. See Zatlin, "Rethinking Unification."
33. The *Treuhand*, proposed in early 1990 by members of a New Forum working group in the GDR, aimed to protect GDR citizens' claims on shared ownership of the planned economy and enable alternative property forms in an eventual unification with the West. In a series of legal revisions, its mandate was altered, ultimately placing the *Treuhand* under the ministry of finance after unification. Because it was not subject to the usual forms of legal oversight and transparency, the *Treuhand's* politics of valuation in discharging assets has continued to polarize scholarly and popular debate. See also Wolfgang Seibel, *Verwaltete Illusionen: Die Privatisierung der DDR-Wirtschaft durch die Treuhandanstalt und ihre Nachfolger 1990–2000* (Frankfurt, 2005).
34. Edgar Most (2009) personal interview; see also Edgar Most with Katrin Rohnstock and Frank Nussbücker, *Fünfzig Jahre im Auftrag des Kapitals: Gibt es einen dritten Weg?* (Berlin, 2009).
35. As Charles S. Maier, *Dissolution: The Crisis of Communism and the End of East Germany* (Princeton, NJ, 1997), and others have argued, the discrepancy between the new higher wages and productivity ended up being the nail in the coffin of East German industry, as few factories could afford to pay the new wages. This problem connects to theories about how the relative value of a national currency represents "the economy" as a whole. It also shows money's non-neutrality, contrary to conventional economic thinking. In other words, a change in money and/or its value impacts existing economic arrangements and outputs.
36. See Edgar Most, personal interview; see also Sarrazin, who admits that relatively speaking, East and West Germany had a comparable cost of living (*Binnenwert*) in 1989, Podiumsdiskussion, "1:1?" 20 Jahre Währungs-, Wirtschafts-, und Sozialunion, June 24, 2010, Bundesstiftung Aufarbeitung.
37. See Jonathan R. Zatlin, *The Currency of Socialism: Money and Political Culture in East Germany* (Washington, DC, 2007), 346.

38. This perception was especially prevalent in short interviews I conducted with visitors to the *Geldmuseum der deutschen Bundesbank* (visitor's center of the German Central Bank), which was my key field site in Frankfurt am Main.
39. On monetary equivalence as a moral form, see Bill Maurer, *Mutual Life, Limited: Islamic Banking, Alternative Currencies, Lateral Reason* (Princeton, NJ, 2005).
40. Karl-Heinz Paqué, *Die Bilanz: Eine Wirtschaftliche Analyse der Deutschen Einheit* (Munich, 2009).
41. Sarrazin was asked to step down from his position as Bundesbank board member in 2010 after controversy erupted over his arguments about the negative impact of Muslim immigration to Germany in *Deutschland Schafft Sich Ab: Wie wir unser Land aufs Spiel setzen* (Berlin, 2010).
42. This is the dominant narrative presented in *Treuhand* official reports and publications.
43. Podiumsdiskussion, "1:1?" 20 Jahre Währungs-, Wirtschafts-, und Sozialunion, June 24, 2010, Bundesstiftung Aufarbeitung.
44. Podiumsdiskussion, ibid.
45. As a number of anthropological studies on German unification have shown, see especially Berdahl, *Where the World Ended: Re-Unification and Identity in the German Borderland*; John Borneman, *Belonging in the Two Berlins: Kin, State, Nation* (Cambridge, 1992); Dominic Boyer, *Spirit and System*; Birgit Müller, *Disenchantment with Market Economics: East Germans and Western Capitalism* (New York, 2007).
46. Podiumsdiskussion, "1:1?" 20 Jahre Währungs-, Wirtschafts-, und Sozialunion, June 24, 2010, Bundesstiftung Aufarbeitung. "Without a model" is a signature trope of financial retrospectives of the currency union and economic reorganization. See also efforts to argue that German economic integration and European economic integration should not be compared. Deutschlandfunk interview with former Bundesbank President Hans Tietmeyer, "Es gab überhaupt kein Modell. Es war ein völlig neuer Vorgang"; see also "Ein alternativloser Vorgang," http://www.dradio.de/aktuell/1214943/ interviews with Hans Tietmeyer; Thilo Sarrazin.
47. Cf. Juliane Edler, "The Wages of Germanness: Working-Class Recomposition and (Racialized) National Identity After Unification," *Debatte: Journal of Contemporary Central and Eastern Europe* 18, no. 3 (2010): 313–39.
48. See Chris Shore, *Building Europe: The Cultural Politics of European Integration* (London, 2000).
49. "Gespräch zwischen Bernhard Vogel und Arnold Vaatz," 212–13; Michael Borchard, Thomas Schrapel, and Bernhard Vogel, eds., *Was ist Gerechtigkeit? Befunde im Vereinten Deutschland* (Vienna, 2012).
50. Cf. Wolfgang Seibel, "The Quest for Freedom and Stability: Political Choices and the Economic Transformation of East Germany 1989–1991," in *German Unification: Expectations and Outcomes*, ed. Peter C. Caldwell and Robert R. Shandley (New York, 2011), 114–15.
51. Cf. Ulrich Beck, *German Europe*, trans. Rodney Livingstone (Cambridge, 2012).

Bibliography

Angé, Oliva, and David Berliner, eds. *Anthropology and Nostalgia*. New York, 2014.
Bach, Jonathan, "Consuming Communism. Material Cultures of Nostalgia in Former East Germany." In *Anthropology and Nostalgia*, edited by Olivia Angé and David Berliner, 123–38. New York, 2014.
Beck, Ulrich. *German Europe*. Translated by Rodney Livingstone. Cambridge, 2012.
Berdahl, Daphne, "(N)Ostalgie for the Present: Memory, Longing, and East German Things." In *On the Social Life of Postsocialism: Memory, Consumption, Germany*, edited by Matti Bunzl, 45–59. Bloomington, IN, 2010.
———. *Where the World Ended: Re-Unification and Identity in the German Borderland*, Berkeley, CA, 1999.
Behrend, Hanna, "Viewpoints on German partition and reunification." *Social Semiotics* 21, no. 1 (2011), 55–65.
———, ed. *German Unification: The Destruction of an Economy*. London, 1995.
Borchard, Michael, Thomas Schrapel, and Bernhard Vogel, eds. *Was ist Gerechtigkeit? Befunde im Vereinten Deutschland*. Vienna, 2012.
Borneman, John. *Belonging in the Two Berlins: Kin, State, Nation*. Cambridge, 1992.
Boyer, Dominic. *Spririt and System: Media, Intellectuals, and the Dialectic in Modern German Culture*. Chicago, 2005.
Bunzl, Matti, ed. *On the Social Life of Postsocialism. Memory, Consumption, Germany*. Bloomington, IN, 2010.
Busch, Ulrich. *Am Tropf: Die Ostdeutsche Transfergesellschaft*. Berlin, 2002.
Caldwell, Peter C., and Robert R. Schandley, eds. *German Unification: Expectations and Outcomes*. New York, 2011.
Connerton, Paul. *How Modernity Forgets*. Cambridge, 2009.
———. *How Societies Remember*. Cambridge, 1989.
Edler, Juliane. "The Wages of Germanness: Working-Class Recomposition and (Racialized) National Identity After Unification." *Debatte: Journal of Contemporary Central and Eastern Europe* 18, no. 3 (2010), 313–39.
Gillis, John R. "Introduction. Memory and Identity: The History of a Relationship." In *Commemorations: The Politics of National Identity*, edited by John R. Gillis, 3–26. Princeton, NJ, 1994.
———, ed. *Commemorations: The Politics of National Identity*. Princeton, NJ, 1994.
Grosser, Dieter. *Das Wagnis der Währungs-, Wirtschafts- und Sozialunion. Politische Zwänge im Konflikt mit ökonomischen Regeln*. Stuttgart, 1998.
Maier, Charles S. *Dissolution: The Crisis of Communism and the End of East Germany*. Princeton, 1997.
Lampland, Martha. "False Numbers as Formalizing Practices," *Social Studies of Science* 40, no. 3 (2010), 377–404.
Maurer, Bill. *Mutual Life, Limited: Islamic Banking, Alternative Currencies, Lateral Reason*. Princeton, NJ, 2005.
Mitchell, Timothy. "Fixing the Economy." *Cultural Studies* 12, no. 1 (1998), 82–101.

Most, Edgar, Katrin Rohnstock, and Frank Nussbücker. *Fünfzig Jahre im Auftrag des Kapitals: Gibt es einen dritten Weg?* Berlin, 2009.

Müller, Birgit. *Disenchantment with Market Economics: East Germans and Western Capitalism.* New York, 2007.

Naumann, Martin. *Wende-Tage-Buch: Ein Tagebuch von der Wende bis zur Einheit.* Leipzig, 2008.

Paqué, Karl-Heinz. *Die Bilanz: Eine Wirtschaftliche Analyse der Deutschen Einheit.* Munich, 2009.

Poovey, Mary. *A History of the Modern Fact: Problems of Knowledge in the Sciences of Wealth and Society.* Chicago, 1998.

Preuss, Ulrich K. "Political Institutions and German Unification." In *German Unification: Expectations and Outcomes,* edited by Peter C. Caldwell and Robert R. Shandley, 137–51. New York, 2011.

Riley, Kerry Kathleen. *Everyday Subversion: From Joking to Revolting in the German Democratic Republic.* East Lansing, MI, 2008.

Robinson, Benjamin. *The Skin of the System: On Germany's Socialist Modernity.* Stanford, CA, 2009.

Rolph-Trouillot, Michel. *Silencing the Past: Power and the Production of History.* Boston, 1995.

Sarrazin, Thilo. *Deutschland Schafft Sich Ab: Wie wir unser Land aufs Spiel setzen.* Berlin, 2010.

Seibel, Wolfgang. "The Quest for Freedom and Stability: Political Choices and the Economic Transformation of East Germany 1989–1991." In *German Unification: Expectations and Outcomes,* edited by Peter C. Caldwell and Robert R. Shandley, 99–119. New York, 2011.

———. *Verwaltete Illusionen: Die Privatisierung der DDR-Wirtschaft durch die Treuhandanstalt und ihre Nachfolger 1990–2000.* Frankfurt, 2005.

Shore, Chris. *Building Europe: The Cultural Politics of European Integration.* London, 2000.

Ten Dyke, Elizabeth. *Dresden: Paradoxes of Memory in History.* London, 2001.

———. "Tulips in December: Space, Time and Consumption before and after the End of German Socialism." *German History* 19, no. 2 (2001), 253–76.

Tognato, Carlo. *Central Bank Independence: Cultural Codes and Symbolic Performance.* New York, 2012.

Widdig, Bernd. *Culture and Inflation in Weimar Germany.* Berkeley, CA, 2001.

Zatlin, Jonathan R. "Rethinking Unification: German Monetary Union and European Integration." In *German Unification: Expectations and Outcomes,* edited by Peter C. Caldwell and Robert R. Shandley, 61–98. New York, 2011.

———. *The Currency of Socialism: Money and Political Culture in East Germany.* Washington, DC, 2007.

———. "Hard Marks and Soft Revolutionaries: The Economics of Entitlement and the Debate over German Unification, November 9, 1989–March 18, 1990." *German Politics and Society,* no. 33 (1994), 57–84.

AFTERWORD

Simmel's Berlin and Money as Social Consensus

MICHAEL J. SAUTER

This collection of essays comprises a striking example of the power of Georg Simmel's historical-critical approach to money as it is outlined in his *Philosophie des Geldes*.[1] Like Simmel's great work, the essays in this collection extend across time and delve into many topics, ranging from seventeenth-century Saxon mines to the twenty-first-century cultivation of memory.[2] Moreover, again like Simmel's work, these essays are attentive to money's historically tectonic power. I mean this in two ways. First, they demonstrate how money can reframe existing disciplinary approaches in a way that enriches both the resulting whole and the individual parts. For Simmel, the disciplines were philosophy, sociology, and economics, with each mode of analysis reinforcing the other. Nevertheless, as these essays show, contemporary anthropological and cultural approaches can be thrown into the mix to great effect.[3] Second, as a group, the essays offer an important perspective on the ways that money has undergirded the formation of social consensus. Whether one looks to eighteenth-century Hamburg or twentieth-century Weimar, money was discussed continually, as people debated who should have it and what its possession should mean.[4] This emphasis on contestation highlights Simmel's greatest insight: money's use signifies not only a form of assent, but also the belief that this assent is binding on others.

Simmel (1858–1918) was the first to notice that money had become, in its ubiquity, a site of social debate. Put another way, by pursuing money he hit upon a central problem of modernity; there existed ideas and processes that everyone could identify, but no one could see. Money, therefore, increasingly implicated people in what appeared to be a limitless pool of anonymity. The power of his approach is obvious throughout *Philosophie des Geldes*, especially in how it comingles broad theoretical propositions, grand historical sweep, and quotidian details. Simmel used money, in short, to reproduce in schematic form what was becoming a more intensely modern world.⁵ Although his formidable tome has yet to attract the readership that it deserves, the completion of the definitive German edition in 1989 and the publication of multiple translations has fostered a sustained interest among not only sociologists but also practitioners in other academic disciplines, including all of the scholars whose work appears in this volume.⁶

As an historian, I see Simmel's great work as having made two major contributions. First, by pursuing money into every corner, *Die Philosophie des Geldes* underscored how any pervasive social practice can, simultaneously, bind society together and atomize it. More specifically, Simmel outlined the possibility of a historical narrative that maintains its coherence even as it insists on chronicling the tensions and tiffs of daily life. Second, Simmel's work illuminates the relationship between practice and the formation of consent, broadly understood. That is, the concentration on money allows historians to highlight both the historically constructed nature of systems of exchange, which formed a major theme in Simmel's work, and to underscore how money's use has continually generated new social and moral claims. Money's omnipresent status as a repository of value indicates, thus, the functioning of a larger system of values that is continually debated and contested—and as German history teaches us, when money loses its value, a society can lose contact with its values.

The benefits of concentrating on how society's values were intertwined with the value of its money are displayed throughout this book's chapters, which range from the early modern period up through the modern one. Given Simmel's concentration on the modern world, it will be particularly instructive to consider, briefly, the first eight chapters, which cover the period before 1850. A quick overview reveals that money bound together a bewildering variety of beliefs and practices. Dillinger's contribution on magic (Chapter 1) and Keller's on alchemy (Chapter 2) demonstrate how even the metaphysical realm was "monetized," in so far as otherworldly "value" became fixed in this world via gold. Spalding and Hatje's works (Chapters 3 and 8, respectively) take us into money's different roles in early modern Hamburg. The former reveals how families were bound together through money's distribution, and the latter how the mercantile city's growing wealth bred attempts to alleviate poverty, i.e. to address inequalities in distribution. Consistent especially with Hatje's main point are Wakefield, Rosenhaft, and Marschke's contributions (Chapters 4–6), all of which highlight an unexpected early modern sophistication in the understanding of money's valences. Among other things, early modern Germans saw money as a foundation for innovation, as a potential source of moral education and as a means of imposing social discipline. Finally, Frey's work in Chapter 7 makes a particularly arresting point: people of humble means understood money as something that one accumulated, in order to survive difficult economic times. Put another way, the humble saw their daily lives as being subject to a true money economy (i.e. in the modern sense) only when times of economic crisis arrived. Thus, from a historian's perspective, although money in general is still around, the values that it has incorporated have changed profoundly over time.

At this point, I would like to shift my perspective forward and to fold Simmel's critical apparatus into an historical reading of *Philosophie des Geldes* itself. In other words, I propose to treat Simmel's own history—that is, what he experienced directly—as an important aspect of the *Philosophie des Geldes*'s apparatus. Writ large, Simmel's great work emerged from a cocktail of three powerful traditions that dominated the German intellectual scene in the second half of the nineteenth century. These were German idealism, which reached back into the eighteenth century; the still emerging European tradition of sociology, which boasted the likes of Émile Durkheim and Max Weber; and the rise of German economic analysis, which included not only Marxist criticism but also the Prussian historical school of economics, whose dominant figure was Gustav Schmoller. A mere glance at Simmel's work indicates how heavily he was influenced by all three currents, as the text includes many references to German philosophy—especially to the enlightened thinker Immanuel Kant—and also applies analytical tools that were developed by sociologists and economists of Simmel's era. With reference to economics, it is particularly important to note that Simmel was Schmoller's student while at the University of Berlin. And Schmoller's insistence on the value of detail-oriented, inductive research is apparent in *Philosophie des Geldes*'s innovative oscillation between the elaboration of theory, to which German academic culture was no stranger, and concrete analysis of practice.

This broad-brush intellectual backdrop helps us to understand the richness of Simmel's thought, but it does not situate him sufficiently as an individual. In order to do the latter, we must put Simmel into the history of his hometown, Berlin. Mack Walker has emphasized the significance for German history of what he called hometowns, the small to medium-sized cities in which many Germans lived—and continue to live.[7] Simmel's daily experience was, however, quite different from the developments that Walker chronicled, as his hometown was confronting a period of rapid transformation. Born in 1858 in what was, at the time, Prussia's dingy capital city, Simmel followed a traditional path. He studied at a local *Gymnasium* before heading to the University of Berlin, where in 1881 he completed his doctorate, and where he would remain as a teacher until 1914, the year when a richly deserved professorship lured him to Strasbourg.[8] This personal timeline frames the massive changes that accompanied Simmel's intellectual development. Returning to the economic realm, let us consider how the formation of the city's industrial base and accompanying labor pool changed Simmel's Berlin. The famous Borsig train works opened in the city in 1837, while the Siemens-Halske factory followed ten years later, and the industrial behemoth known as AEG (the *Allgemeine Elektrizitäts-Gesellschaft*) began operations in 1883, albeit under a different name. Concomitantly, with the production of new factory jobs came waves of migration, as foreigners—both German and non-German—flowed into Berlin in search of work. What had been a stodgy court town only a few decades before Simmel's birth rapidly became both a foundry for new wealth and home to host of new arrivals.

Berlin's increasing affluence and growing population was rapidly inscribed on the city's face—for better and worse. The S-Bahn, whose stations and elevated tracks still dominate many of Berlin's neighborhoods, began construction in the 1870s, while construction on the city's estimable U-Bahn started in 1896. The rise of public transportation arose in concert with Berlin's somber *Mietskasernen*, whose massive edifices housed not only incoming workers, but also the city's growing *Mittelstand*, which was settling comfortably into an economic niche that the city's industrial growth had made possible. At a higher social level, in 1876 the Kurfürstendamm initiated its transformation from a thoroughfare into Berlin's answer to Paris's Champs-Élysées, growing rapidly into not only a representative urban space but also an axis of the conspicuous consumption that would soon characterize life in Berlin. Indeed, the *Kaiser-Wilhelm-Gedächtniskirche*, another of the city's signature structures that was completed in 1891 on a plot that sits along the Ku'damm, is visible from the Tautzienstrasse's *Kaufhaus des Westens* (best known as *Ka-De-We*), which opened its doors in 1907 as an altogether different kind of temple.

Meanwhile, Berlin's city center was transforming in ways that marked a significant departure from its stuffy recent past. The respectable parish church that dated back to Frederick II was demolished in 1893 to make way for the architectural error known as the Berlin Cathedral. And barely a kilometer away is the *Museumsinsel*, or Museum Island, on which four important museums were constructed between 1830 and 1904, and through which Berlin cemented its recently acquired status as a *European* cultural capital. Of course, all of the construction on this island—not to mention the acquisition of new items for the collection—required wealth, and this was being produced in ever-greater quantities. The tremendous extent of this wealth was, in turn, memorialized in Imperial Germany's most iconic structure, the drab lump of stone known as the *Reichstag*, which was completed in 1894 and became the physical seat of the German people's all-too-limited legislative power. The *Reichstag*'s completion provides, in many ways, a particularly fitting moment against which to understand Simmel's thought. His interest in money as a foundation for social consensus, as opposed to democratic institutions, hovers between his hometown's cramped political culture and its remarkable ability to craft new public spaces.[9]

Concomitant to Berlin's domestic hustle and bustle was, of course, its burgeoning significance, both within Germany and across the world. In 1871, in the wake of the victory over Imperial France, Prussia's capital city became the capital of the new German Empire, with the king garnering a promotion to emperor. And with these political watersheds behind it, Berlin entered an exclusive club, becoming a true *Weltstadt*, as issues of global significance were regularly decided in the now-imperial capital. It was, for instance, in Berlin in 1878 that the political borders of Eastern Europe were redrawn by a conference of diplomatic heavyweights that included Otto von Bismarck and Benjamin Disraeli, and whose collective machinations set in motion the forces that produced World War I. And in 1884, Berlin hosted another international conference that carved up Africa, inaugurating the rank predation that became dubbed the "Scramble for Africa." It is, thus, no accident that Simmel was in tune with European history's most prominent currents; he lived in a place where daily life intersected with surging global issues.

Yet, even this sketch of Berlin's imperial glory does not complete the picture of Simmel's little, global world. In order to add the final touches to my portrait, I turn to Hans Simmel, Georg's son, who described his father's early years in Berlin, thus:

> My father, Georg Simmel, was born on March 1st 1858 in the house that formed the northwestern side of the intersection between Leipziger- and Friedrichstrasse. At that time, still to the west of the old city center, these streets would become, later, the [city's] most representative and important commercial streets. One could not, as it were, have been any more a Berlin native, than to have been born at the corner of Leipziger- and Friedrichstrasse.[10]

Georg Simmel was, therefore, not merely from Berlin, but was an archetypical *Berliner*—and this particular characterization was inextricable from the city's recent growth and prosperity. I am not breaking new ground in associating Simmel's thought with the chaotic bundle of energy that was Berlin in its imperial age. I would suggest, however, that we may understand the connection between this restless city and Simmel's own thought by listening for its urban echoes in *Philosophie des Geldes* itself.

Along these interpretive lines, consider Simmel's discussion of systems of exchange, which appears in the first chapter, "Value and Money."[11] Here, Simmel wrote:

> Every interaction has to be regarded as an exchange: every conversation, every affection (even if it is rejected), every game, every glance at another person. The difference that seems to exist, that in interaction a person offers what he does

not possess whereas in exchange he offers only what he does possess, cannot be sustained. For in the first place, it is always personal energy, the surrender of personal substance, that is involved in interaction; and conversely, exchange is not conducted for the sake of the object that the other person possesses, but to gratify one's personal feelings which he does not possess.[12]

If we juxtapose Simmel's heavily theoretical approach to exchange with his son's picayune recollections, we can begin to pinpoint a *location* for the father's genius. First, we can embed Simmel's thought in the city's own geography. One reason why Hans Simmel could describe the corner of Leipzigerstrasse and Friedrichstrasse as defining the trueborn Berliner is the manner in which this site was embedded in Berlin's urban space. The corner where Georg Simmel was born is about a fifteen-minute walk to Potsdamerplatz, the commercial center into which teeming masses were crowding, with impressive results. As Peter Fritzsche has highlighted, on 1 October 1900, researchers counted 146,146 people walking through Potsdamerplatz in a sixteen-hour period. Nine years earlier, following the same method, only 87,266 people had been counted.[13] Simmel's association of money and exchange with multiple conversations and stolen glances, which I cited above, can be easily understood as a reflection of Potsdamerplatz's vitality.

Second, Hans Simmel's recollections situate his father not only geographically, but also socially within Berlin's urban landscape. Georg Simmel's father was a relatively prosperous entrepreneur; he had founded a successful chocolate factory. Although the financial resources that the son inherited from the father were hardly great, they, along with the financial help from an uncle, allowed Simmel to move within a respectable social circle, whose values naturally reflected that peculiar fin de siècle mix of cosmopolitanism and Victorianism.[14] As an example, I turn to Georg Simmel's discussion of prostitution.[15] A rigorous thinker, Simmel extended his theory of money even into his era's darkest corners, embedding prostitution directly within the expanding and developing system of exchange. This was quite forward thinking, for the time, especially when we consider that, since September 2014, Germany has included prostitution in its official GDP figures.[16] Of course, having emerged from respectable circles, Simmel could not resist a bit of moral commentary. He wrote:

> This is the basis for the fact that the terrible degradation that is inherent in prostitution is most clearly expressed by its money equivalent. It certainly signifies the nadir of human dignity if a woman surrenders her most intimate and most personal quality, which should be offered only on the basis of a genuine personal impulse and also only with equal personal devotion on the part of the male—in so far as this might have a different importance for the man compared with the woman—for a totally impersonal, purely extraneous and objective compensa-

tion. We experience here the fullest and most distressing incongruity between giving and taking. More accurately, we can say that the degradation of prostitution lies in the fact that it so degrades a woman's most personal possession, one that is dependent upon the greatest reserve, that the most neutral value devoid of all personal qualities is considered to be an appropriate equivalent.[17]

Simmel's approach to money may have had broad theoretical implications. He, however, continued to reflect the values of his social class, which resided, as it were, at the intersection of Leipzigerstrasse and Friedrichstrasse.

My concentration on Simmel's physical location within Berlin also highlights a strange lacuna in both Simmel's own work and the literature that has sprung from it. For all the talk about money and value within both Simmel's text itself and the excellent contemporary work on his thought, there is almost no discussion of the actual currency that Simmel used.[18] Here, it will be profitable to return our imaginations to the house where Simmel was born, since a fifteen-minute walk in the direction opposite (roughly) to Potsdamerplatz lies Jägerstrasse 34–38, which in Simmel's lifetime was the address of the *Reichsbank*. This institution, which was founded on 1 January 1876, moved into its impressive edifice on Jägerstrasse two years later, when Simmel would have been twenty years old. (The building was destroyed in World War II.) It also issued the *Goldmark*, the currency that passed through every Berliner's hands, not to mention that of most imperial German citizens.[19] Before its value was destroyed by the financial shenanigans that came with the Reich's dubious means of financing World War I, the *Goldmark* was considered solid and reliable, i.e., it maintained its value. Although I cannot enter into a detailed discussion of the matter, it seems worthwhile to relate Simmel's views on money's recent expansion to the *Goldmark*'s growing reputation. The *Reichsbank*'s rise to preeminence was a slow process, as Germany's previous system of multiple reserve banks, the so-called *Notenbanken*, did not disappear until 1914. In this sense, Simmel's views on the expansion of monetary relations may well have had some connection to the *Reichsbank*'s growing prestige and power as an institution.

The *Reichsbank*'s position within German financial history leads me back to the issue of money and consent. Simmel's manner of weaving money and the practices that accompanied it into a broader social tapestry affords us, as the editors of this volume suggest in their introduction, a particularly sharp view into not only politics of the past but also the debates of today. With the respect to the past, the essays in this volume that pertain to German history after World War I paint a stark picture of a state and society that proved incapable of regaining the monetary stability that had characterized the *Goldmark*'s reign.[20] None of this is new, of course, as the torment caused by worthless money has long been a staple of contemporary literature on German history.

If we seek to understand this history, however, with respect to the sometimes-turbulent debates about the European Monetary Union's continuing difficulties, we would do well to take into account Simmel's association of money's daily use with the formation of consent.

In pursuit of this point I turn, here, to more recent history, that is, the period since the end of World War II. As this collection's penultimate essay explains, the West German Deutsche Mark enjoys, among many Germans, but especially those who experienced the immediate postwar period, an almost sacred reputation as the foundation of Germany's prosperity.[21] Although not entirely accurate, the memory of sound-money-fueled growth and stability remains pervasive and, as a result, permeates every aspect of contemporary discussions about European finance. And it is here, amid contemporary German outrage toward the now-serial Greek bailouts, that I note democracy's conspicuous absence from the German government's decision to adopt the euro. The German people were never asked whether to dump their beloved Deutsche Mark, ostensibly because the German constitution had no provision for referenda. Of course, this was a rather convenient constraint for a political elite that was fully aware of the negative response that would have greeted any request to consider such a change. Moreover, if we take into account that the Greek government has admitted that the budgetary numbers it presented in its application for admission to the euro were fudged—to say the least—we can begin to understand the intensity of the flames of rage that the daily rag known as the *Bild Zeitung*, in its customary counterproductive way, has insisted on fanning.[22]

In this respect, *Philosophie des Geldes* serves as not only a critical analytical tool but also a poignant cautionary tale. Hans Simmel, like so many others, suffered in the wake of the Weimar era's monetary chaos, as the subsequent Nazi regime turned a loyal German into an enemy. The grandson of a German Jew who had converted to Catholicism and the son of a *Berliner* who had been raised a Lutheran, Hans Simmel lost his livelihood to the Nazis and, eventually, fled his homeland. *Philosophie des Geldes* casts in particularly stark terms the dangers that lurk behind the betrayal of a monetary consensus. Moreover, through its analysis Simmel's work helps us to understand the massive social effects of irresponsible fiscal policies. The average person's use of money and his or her concomitant accumulation of value in money leave every aspect of daily life vulnerable to high-level errors in judgment. In such circumstances, rants about money are as predictable as they can be ugly. More importantly, wise political leaders will not treat such outbursts as something other than inconvenient speech to be marginalized, but as a warning sign that they are undermining core social values. And if a return to Simmel's *Philosophie des Geldes* helps to diffuse that lesson throughout our contemporary political culture, then the work's true value will prove to be incalculable.

Michael J. Sauter is Profesor-Investigador in the División de Historia at the Centro de Investigación y Docencia Económicas (CIDE) in Mexico City. He is the author of *Visions of the Enlightenment: The Edict on Religion of 1788 and the Politics of the Public Sphere in Eighteenth-Century Prussia* (2009). His next book, *The Spatial Reformation: Spatial Sense and the Early Modern Global Imagination, 1350–1850*, is under contract at the University of Pennsylvania Press.

Notes

1. Two versions of this work appeared, with the latter one being slightly expanded: Georg Simmel, *Philosophie des Geldes* (Leipzig, 1900); Georg Simmel, *Philosophie des Geldes*, 2. verm. Aufl. ed. (Leipzig, 1907).
2. See the contributions to this volume by Andre Wakefield and Ursula Dalinghaus.
3. See, for example, the contributions to this volume by Benjamin Marschke and Michael Hughes.
4. See the work included in this volume by Almut Spalding and Erica Briesacher.
5. See the chapter written by Elizabeth Goodstein.
6. Georg Simmel, *Philosophie Des Geldes*, Georg Simmel Gesamtausgabe (Frankfurt, 1989). The main English translation is now in its third edition. Georg Simmel, *The Philosophy of Money*, trans. David Frisby and Tom Bottomore, 3rd ed. (London, 2004).
7. Mack Walker, *German Home Towns: Community, State, and General Estate, 1648–1871* (Ithaca, NY, 1971).
8. Harry Liebersohn, *Fate and Utopia in German Sociology, 1870–1923: Studies in Contemporary German Social Thought* (Cambridge, MA, 1988), 126–27.
9. Political consensus can be built on many foundations. See Margaret L. Anderson, *Practicing Democracy: Elections and Political Culture in Imperial Germany* (Princeton, NJ, 2000).
10. First published in Hannes Böhringer and Karlfried Gründer, *Ästhetik und Soziologie um die Jahrhundertwende: Georg Simmel, Studien zur Literatur und Philosophie des neunzehnten Jahrhunderts* (Frankfurt, 1976), 247–48 (Author's translation).
11. I have used the more accessible English translation, in order to make referring to Simmel's text easier. Simmel, *The Philosophy of Money*, 56–128.
12. Ibid., 83.
13. Peter Fritzsche, *Reading Berlin 1900* (Cambridge, MA, 1996), 63.
14. Simmel, *The Philosophy of Money*, 519.
15. Ibid., 378–82.
16. Rolf Wenkel, *German GDP Swells on Sex, Drug and Weapons* (Deutsche Welle, 2014).
17. Simmel, *The Philosophy of Money*, 379.
18. Some examples: David Frisby, *Georg Simmel*, rev. ed. (London, 2002); Liebersohn, *Fate and Utopia in German Sociology*; Gianfranco Poggi, *Money and the Modern Mind: George Simmel's Philosophy of Money* (Berkeley, CA, 1993); Patrick Watier, *Georg Simmel: la sociologie et l'expérience du Monde Moderne* (Paris, 1986); Claudius Härpfer, *Georg Simmel und die Entstehung der Soziologie in Deutschland: Eine netzwerksoziologische Studie* (Wiesbaden, 2014).
19. Simmel mentions the *Reichsbank* twice and the Goldmark not at all. Simmel, *The Philosophy of Money*, 137, 194.

20. See the work in this volume by Briesacher, Hughes, and Larkin.
21. See Grünbacher's contribution to this volume.
22. "Griechenland Erschwindelte Euro-Beitritt," *Frankfurter Allgemeine Zeitung*, 16 November 2004; Tony Barber, "Greece Condemned for Falsifying Data," *The Financial Times*, 12 January 2010.

Bibliography

Anderson, Margaret L. *Practicing Democracy: Elections and Political Culture in Imperial Germany*. Princeton, NJ, 2000.
Barber, Tony. "Greece Condemned for Falsifying Data." *The Financial Times*, 12 January 2010.
Böhringer, Hannes, and Karlfried Gründer. *Ästhetik und Soziologie um die Jahrhundertwende: Georg Simmel, Studien zur Literatur und Philosophie des neunzehnten Jahrhunderts*. Frankfurt, 1976.
Frisby, David. *Georg Simmel*. rev. ed. London, 2002.
Fritzsche, Peter. *Reading Berlin 1900*. Cambridge, MA, 1996.
"Griechenland Erschwindelte Euro-Beitritt." *Frankfurter Allgemeine Zeitung*, 16 November 2004.
Härpfer, Claudius. *Georg Simmel und die Entstehung der Soziologie in Deutschland: Eine netzwerksoziologische Studie*. Wiesbaden, 2014.
Liebersohn, Harry. *Fate and Utopia in German Sociology, 1870–1923: Studies in Contemporary German Social Thought*. Cambridge, MA, 1988.
Poggi, Gianfranco. *Money and the Modern Mind: George Simmel's Philosophy of Money*. Berkeley, CA, 1993.
Simmel, Georg. *Philosophie des Geldes*. Leipzig, 1900.
———. *Philosophie des Geldes*. Georg Simmel Gesamtausgabe. Frankfurt, 1989.
———. *Philosophie des Geldes*. 2. verm. Aufl. ed. Leipzig, 1907.
———. *The Philosophy of Money*. Translated by David Frisby and Tom Bottomore. 3rd ed. London, 2004.
Walker, Mack. *German Home Towns: Community, State, and General Estate, 1648–1871*. Ithaca, NY, 1971.
Watier, Patrick. *Georg Simmel: la sociologie et l'expérience du Monde Moderne*. Paris, 1986.
Wenkel, Rolf. *German GDP Swells on Sex, Drugs and Weapons*. Deutsche Welle, 2014.

INDEX

A
Abs, Hermann Josef, 272, 278
Actien. See under stocks
Actionnaires, 85
alchemy, 26–35
alienation, 174–76
Amthor, Christoph Heinrich, 31
Aristotelianism, 31
artisans, 122, 126–31
assignats, 140
August the Strong (August II of Saxony and Poland), 60, 102

B
balance of payments crisis (post-WWII), 273, 275–77
bankers, 141–42, 144, 148
Banking Act 1934 (*Reichsgesetz über das Kreditwesen*), 236
bankruptcy, 141–42, 164
banks, *Bank deutscher Länder (BdL)*; 269–70, 277; Hamburg, 140; private, 237; savings, 228, 234–44, 272, 289, 292
baptismal gifts, 49–51
baroque, gardens, 105; opulence, 110; representation crisis, 96–98, 100
barter, 251, 254, 258
barter marts, 258–59
Barth, Christian Gottlob, 157–59, 161–65
Becher, Johann Joachim, 26, 31–32, 64–65
Beneke, Ferdinand, 5, 137–48
Bergstaat. See under mining
Berlin, 306–7
Berlin wall, 283–84
Besold, Christopher, 30–35

bills of exchange, 74, 140–43, 148
black market, 250–60, 269, 271. See also cigarettes; markets
Blumhardt, Johann Christoph, 159
bookkeeping ("Italian"), 34, 45, 53
Bornitz, Jacob, 28–30
Bourdieu, Pierre, 205, 209
Brandenburg Africa Company, 83
bubbles, financial effects (1720s), 5, 74–78, 81, 83, 85, 88–89; Louisiana, 76, 78, 80–82, 84, 88–89; Mississippi, 74–84, 89–90; South Sea, 74–77, 81, 88; Venusiana, 84–88
Bundesverband der deutschen Industrie (BDI, Federation of German Industry), 276–78
Bürgertum, 138–39, 145, 147
Büsch, Johann Georg, 139–42, 148–49
butt-collecting, 250–51, 254–58. See also cigarettes

C
cameralism, 35, 58–59, 64–67, 79–80, 83
capital, cultural, 63–64, 148–49; market, 278; shortage of, 276; social, 49, 148–49; symbolic, 46, 50
capitalism, denunciation of, 225; Marx on, 174–79, 181–83
cash, 47, 50, 121–29
Charles XII (Sweden), 97–98
cigarette economy, 258–60
cigarettes, American brands, 251–54; and black market, 252–54; as currency substitute, 250–53; as economy, 258–60
Clay, Lucius D., 253, 259
coal; mining, 60, 274–75; shortages of, 269–70, 272–73, 275–76

collecting, cultural aspects of, 203–4, 209; and politics, 210–11. *See also* Notgeld
commerce, 4, 27–28, 32, 34, 58, 90, 129, 140
communism, 174, 179, 182
Communist Manifesto, 177
consumer goods, 220, 235, 239–40, 258, 260, 269–71, 273, 275
consumerism, 5, 97, 122, 126–28, 131, 139, 156, 166, 196, 210, 240; and monetary institutions, 174; suppression by NSDAP, 243
consumer revolution, 96
consumption, conspicuous, 5, 96–99, 105, 110, 137, 144–45
cosmopolitanism, 80, 142, 145
cost-cutting, at court of Frederick William I, 98–99, 102, 109
credit, 5, 45, 74, 88–89, 131, 139, 149, 178, 180, 205, 237–39, 269–70, 274–77; among *gebildete Stände*, 146–48; paper, 88; social and cultural factors, 141
creditors, 141, 146; in Weimar Republic, 219–29
currency, conversion, 268, 270, 286, 288–89, 292–93; devaluation, 204–5; reform (post-WWII), 268, 270, 273, 289; union (1990) 7, 283–96

D

debtors, 45–47, 74–75, 141; in Weimar Republic, 219–22, 224–28
debts, 45–47, 74–75, 128–30, 141, 289, 293
Delius, Christoph Traugott, 66
demons, 11, 17–21
Deutsche Mark, 251–52, 259–60, 268–71
donation economy, 234, 244
dragon (*Drache*), 10, 15–21
Durchhalten (persistence) 124–25, 129, 131
Dutch East India Company, 80, 83, 90

E

Economic Cooperation Administration (ECA), 274

"Economic Miracle," 7, 260, 277, 288; myth of, 268–71
emergency money. *See under* Notgeld
Engels, Friedrich, 4, 173–74, 177
English East India Company, 90
Erhard, Ludwig, 268, 270, 273
Europäische Fama, 76–79, 81, 100, 104–5
European Monetary Union, 310
European Payment Union, 275
European Recovery Plan (ERP), 270–73
euro zone, 219, 295

F

family. *See under* Beneke, Ferdinand; kinship; Reimarus family
fashion, 96–97, 99–100, 104, 107, 109
Feder, Gottfried, 237
Federal Republic of Germany, 268–78
Festival of Saturn, 60
Finxius, Peter, 31
Francke, August Hermann, 102
Frederick I/III (Prussia), 98
Frederick William I (Prussia), 96–110; building projects, 105–8
free market. *See under* markets
French West India Company, 75, 78, 83
friendship, 137–49
financial crisis, of 1720s, 75–76, 90; of 1799, 141. *See also* bubbles
Frick, Wilhelm, 237
Fugger, Jacob, 4
Funk, Walther, 237, 243
Fürstenau, Johann Hermann, 31–34

G

gebildete Stände (educated middle classes), 139, 145–49
Geldmännchen (money manikin/figurine), 10–15, 18
Geldumlauf. *See under* money, circulation of
General Poor Relief (Hamburg), 137–38, 147
George II (England), 104
German Democratic Republic, 283–96
global economy, 3–4, 76, 81, 83, 89–90, 126
goldmakers, 26, 31

Index ∻ 315

Goldmark, 309
Greek insolvency, 1, 294, 310

H
Harz Mountains, 62–63, 67. See also mining
Haushaltung (household management), 28, 124–25, 129, 131
Hausväterliteratur, 27–28, 33
Hegel, Georg Wilhelm Friedrich, 174, 193, 198. See also Marx, Karl; Young Hegelians
Hess, Moses, 174–75
history of science, 27–28, 35
Hofacker, Ludwig, 157
Hoffmann, Christian Gottfried, 77
Hoffmann, Gottfried August, 33–35
Hohenthal, Peter Freiherr von, 34
Holländisches Viertel (Dutch Quarter) 105, 108
homeownership, 235, 239
hometownsmen, 121–22, 130
Hörnigk, Wilhelm von, 65
hyperinflation. See under inflation
Hypothekengläubiger und Sparer Verband (HGSSV), 225, 227

I
imperialism (*ersatz*), 83
inflation, 125, 127, 177, 204–7, 210, 212, 222–23; hyperinflation (1920s), 212–13, 219–23, 228; and interest rates, 147–48; price of sixteenth century, 62; post-1934, 238; post-WWII, 268–70; and WWI, 220
inheritance (partible), 122–24
interest, 46–47, 147–48, 178, 222, 272, 276, 278
inventories (probate), 122–24, 126–28
Investitionshilfe Gesetz (1952), 275–76, 278

J
joint-stock companies, 74, 82, 89. See also stocks
Journal des Luxus und der Moden, 157
Justi, Johann von, 64–66
just price, 143

K
Kant, Immanuel, 140
Kapff, Sixt Carl, 157, 160–61, 164–65
Das Kapital, 173–77, 181
Keller, Arnold, 208
kinship, 43–45, 50–52. See also Reimarus family
Kippensammlung. See under butt-collecting
Kombinate, 289
Korean War, 275–78
Kraft durch Freude. See under Strength through Joy
Kreditanstalt für Wiederaufbau (KfW), 271–76, 278. See also reconstruction (post-WWII)
Kunstkammer, 29

L
labor theory of value, 174–75, 179, 181–83
Langendyk, Pieter, 83–84
Lather, Hermann, 29–31, 33
Law, John, 74–80, 85, 89–90
life history interviews, 285–86, 291
loans, 47, 49, 51, 122, 128–31, 141–42, 145, 147–48, 270, 273–74, 276, 278
Löhneyß, Georg Engelhard, 64–65
London Debt Agreement, 277–78
Lousiana. See under bubbles
luciferous arts, 26
lucriferous arts, 26–28, 35
luxury, 5, 29, 96–110, 140, 156–66; criticism of, 156–57, 159–63; debates about, 6, 109–10, 158–59; and eschatology, 165; and pauperism, 163–65; and revolutions of 1848, 160; rejection of, 99, 110. See also Pietism

M
McNarney, Joseph T., 251, 253
magic, 10–21, 28
Mandeville, Bernard, 156
Manufactures House (Vienna), 65
markets, 28, 30, 129, 143, 175, 177, 180–81, 183, 221, 223–24; capital, 272–73, 276–78; free, 220, 225, 228, 272; financial, 237. See also black market; cigarettes

Marperger, Paul Joseph, 74, 78–80
Marshall Plan, 268–72, 274–75, 277–78
Marx, Karl, 4–6; on money, 173–83
masculinity, 97
memory, 204, 210, 283–85, 296
mercantile society, 139–42
mercantilism, 58–59
merchants, 43, 45, 58, 76, 140–47
Mercurius, 79
militarization, of Prussia, 98–99
Mill, James, 174, 176–77, 182
Mill, John Stuart, 173, 177–78, 182
mining, 32, 60, 62–67. See also coal, mining
Mississippi. See under bubbles
monetarization, 131, 305, 309
money; of account, 140; attitudes toward; 122, 220; circulation (velocity) of, 139–40, 148, 176; in communist society, 181–82; contingent nature of, 260; and culture, 2, 190, 193–95, 203–5; and honor, 148; and magical beliefs, 10; and meaning, 187; as means of exchange, 179–80, 193; as metaphor, 191; and morality, 3, 219–28; and national identity, 205–7, 226; and natural world, 4; paper, 76, 221–22, 226–27; philosophy of, 188–89, 196–97; political nature of, 1–3; and precious metals, 179; reevaluation of, 285–90; as "second blood," 29; social debate on, 303; and spirits, 10; symbolic nature of, 2, 125, 129–30, 144, 197; as synecdoche, 191–92, 194, 196–97; and trust, 125; and values, 189, 195, 197, 304. See also cash; currency; dragon; Geldmännchen; Hegel, Georg Friedrich Wilhelm; Marx, Karl; Simmel, Georg
moral economy, 219
Mun, Thomas, 58–59

N
National Savings Day, 236
neoliberalism, 268, 277
Notgeld, 203–4; collecting, 205–13; as cultural construct, 207, 214; exhibitions of, 204, 207, 209, 213–14; and identity, 203–5, 207, 209, 214; and nationalism, 210; *Serienscheine* (series notes), 203–4, 206–8, 210, 212, 215

O
Oberbergamt, 60
occupation (post-WWII), 251, 257–58, 268–69, 277. See also OMGUS
oeconomia, 26–35
Office of the Military Government of the United States (OMGUS), 252–53, 258–59
Ore Mountains, 61–63, 67. See also mining
Ostend Company (Austrian East India Company), 89–90

P
Patriotic Society (Hamburg), 137, 144, 146
People's Welfare Organization (NSDAP), 234–35
Peter I (the Great, of Russia), 97–98
Pietism, 5, 110, 156–66
Philosophy of Money (Philosophie des Geldes). See under Simmel, Georg
Potsdam, 105–8
privatization trust (in GDR), 288–89
profit, 21, 26, 29–30, 32, 34–35, 124, 140, 143–44, 148, 269–70, 309
profiteering. See under speculation

Q
Quincampoix, play, 84; street, 75

R
rationing, 220, 223, 269, 276
Recession of 1857, 173, 177–78, 180, 183
reconstruction (post-WWII), 268–77, 287
regalian rights, 64–66
Reichsbank, 203, 236, 268, 309–10
Reichsmark (RM), 234, 240
Reimarus family, 43–52; account books of, 44–46; Elise, 45, 49–51; Hermann Samuel, 43; Johann Christian, 46–48; Margareta Dorothea, 47–48; Maria Sophia, 47–48
Rentenmark, 222
reparations, 221, 254

reunification. *See under* unification (German, 1990)
Revolutions of 1848, 160, 164
Ricardo, David, 174, 176–77, 180, 182

S
Sarrazin, Thilo, 293–94
saving, 228, 237–54. *See also* banks, savings
Say, Jean-Baptiste, 174, 176, 182
Schacht, Hjalmar, 236
Schemnitz mines (Carpathians), 62–64
Schreber, Daniel Gottfried, 65
Schroeder, Wilhelm von, 31–32, 65
Schupp, Johann Balthasar, 30–32
Seckendorff, Veit Ludwig von, 31, 33, 65
SED (*Sozialistische Einheitsparteik Deutschlands*). *See under* Socialist Unity Party
sentimentalism (literary), 143, 147
Serienscheine. *See under* Notgeld
Sieveking, Georg Heinrich, 140, 144–46
Siewers, Ehrfried, 209–10
silver coinage (silver *Thaler*), 59–67
Simmel, Georg, 4, 6, 186–87; influence of Berlin on, 306–9; money as "synecdoche of synecdoches," 187; phenomenological approach, 190; philosophical modernism, 189–92; philosophical relativism, 187–89; *Philosophy of Money*, 186–99, 303–11; on prostitution, 308
Smith, Adam, 47, 58–59, 65, 140, 174–77, 180, 182
Socialist Unity Party (SED), 289
Sonnenfels, Joseph von, 64
South Sea Company. *See under* bubbles
Sparkassen. *See under* banks, savings
speculation, 79–81, 140–41, 144, 164, 219–28, 269
spirits, 10–13, 16–17, 19–20. *See also* money, and magical beliefs; treasure hunting
stock exchange (Hamburg), 141
stocks (*Actien*), 74, 79, 85, 89, 164; venusianen, 84–88. *See also* bubbles
Strength Through Joy, 239, 243
stub-collecting. *See under* butt-collecting

T
Tabakskollegium, 100
taste, 97, 105, 109, 145, 204
Thirty Years War, 28, 31, 62
tobacco, 250–55; home-grown, 254–55; shortages, 250–52, smuggling, 259–60. *See also* cigarettes; black market; barter market
treasure hunting, 10–12, 19–20. *See also* money, and magical beliefs; dragon; *Geldmännchen*
Treuhand. *See under* privatization trust (in GDR)

U
unemployment, 205, 238, 242, 269, 291–92, 294
unification (German, 1990), 284, 286–93

V
Vayhinger, Ernst Jacob, 121–31
Venusiana, *See under* bubbles
Volksgemeinschaft, 235, 237, 241, 243–44
Völter, Johann Ludwig, 157–59, 161–63

W
"War Savings Day" (1940), 243
wealth (patrician), 43–52, 139–42
Weimar Germany, 203–14, 219–28
welfare tourism, 294
Wichern, Johann Hinrich, 160
Wiederaufbau. *See under* reconstruction
wigs, 99–100, 102, 104, 109
witches, 11–21. *See also* money, and magical beliefs
Wirtschaftswunder. *See under* "Economic Miracle"

Y
Young Hegelians, 174–76

Z
Zenner, Gottfried, 77, 81–83, 89–90
Zincke, Georg Heinrich, 65

www.ingramcontent.com/pod-product-compliance
Lightning Source LLC
Chambersburg PA
CBHW072144100526
44589CB00015B/2087